Contents

VERB CONJUGATIONS 121

BARRON'S

1001 PITFALLS IN
English Grammar

Third Edition

Ruth Parlé Craig
Chairperson, Department of Foreign Languages
Santa Rosa Junior College

Vincent F. Hopper
Formerly, Professor of English
New York University

Barron's Educational Series, Inc.
New York / London / Toronto / Sydney

All inquiries should be addressed to:
Barron's Educational Series, Inc.
250 Wireless Boulevard
Hauppauge, New York 11788

Library of Congress Catalog Card No. 86-14177

International Standard Book No. 0-8120-3719-7

Library of Congress Cataloging in Publication Data

Craig, Ruth Parlé.
   1001 pitfalls in English grammar.

   Rev. ed. of: 1001 pitfalls in English grammar, spelling and usage.
c1970.
   Includes index.   1. English language — Errors of usage.
2. English language — Verb.   I. Craig, Ruth Parlé.   II. Hopper,
Vincent Foster, 1906 –   . 1001 pitfalls in English grammar, spelling
and usage.   III. Title.   IV. Title: One thousand one pitfalls in
English grammar.   V. Title: One thousand and one pitfalls in
English grammar.
PE1460.H63   1986   428'.2   86-14177
ISBN 0-8120-3719-7

PRINTED IN THE UNITED STATES OF AMERICA

012   800   98765

Preface

In the Preface to the second edition of this work, the late Vincent F. Hopper stated, "This book has been prepared to give both native-born and foreign students a sense of security in their mastery of the English language."

For this newly revised and expanded edition, I have maintained this original aim with the specific purpose of clarifying patterns in American English and of indicating detailed solutions for the "pitfalls," or trouble spots, of English grammar. The book is divided into four major sections: Parts of Speech; The Sentence and its Parts; Special Aids and Other Concerns; and lastly, Conjugations of 120 Irregular Verbs in Alphabetical Order. Rules of English grammar and common pitfalls have been highlighted throughout the text to help you find the information you need, faster and with greater ease.

This edition further aims to help you to understand, by explanation and by example, what is behind grammatical terminology, as such. Even in the correct usage of a language, it is the "little things" that count. To lead you to the comprehension and resolution of your difficulties, this book also discusses those "little" — but all important — things which, when not observed, can betray you badly in letters, reports, in all your writing, and, most importantly, in all your speech.

My very sincere and warm thanks to my husband, Wilson Craig, for his genuinely helpful professional suggestions and judgments in the preparation of this edition, as well as for his patience and general assistance in "getting it off the ground."

Ruth Parlé Craig
Santa Rosa Junior College
Santa Rosa, California

PARTS OF SPEECH

1 ■ Adjectives and Adverbs

ADJECTIVES

Adjectives are descriptive words like *sweet, big, ripe, tender.* Adjectives modify (describe) nouns or pronouns: *sweet* Sue.

Adjectives are said to limit the meaning of the words they describe, and they usually do in the sense that the word *woman* applies to all females while the addition of an adjective like *beautiful* limits the noun *woman* by excluding all the women who are not beautiful.

Predicate Adjectives

RULE

Adjectives usually precede the words they describe: *deep* river; *fine, strong* man. However, to make statements or sentences out of these phrases, place the adjectives in the predicate, following a *linking verb* (*see* Transitive and Intransitive verbs).

The river is *deep.*	(Adjective modifies *river.*)
The man is *fine* and *strong.*	(Adjectives modify *man.*)
He is *fine* and *strong.*	(Adjectives modify *He.*)

PITFALL

Linking verbs, especially the verbs of sense (taste, look, smell, etc.) are often followed by an adjective.

This peach tastes so *sweet.*

Since *feel* is a linking verb, correct usage requires the adjective *bad* and the adjective *well*, which has three meanings: *to be in good health, to be satisfactory, to appear well-dressed.*

I feel *bad*, but he feels *well.*

She feels *well* in that suit.

All is *well* that ends well.

Articles

The most commonly used adjectives are the **articles**, *the*, *a*, and *an*.

The is the **definite article**. It calls attention to a specific person, place, or thing: *the* boy, *the* city, *the* typewriter.

A and *an* are known as **indefinite articles** because they refer to any single member of the class specified by whatever noun they modify; *a* tree, *an* apple.

Use *a* before words beginning with a consonant sound: *a* cat, *a* train.

Use *an* before words beginning with a vowel sound: *an* artist, *an* apple, *an* honor.

NOTE: It is the sound, not the letter, which determines whether *a* or *an* should be used: *a* uniform, *an* L-shaped room, *an* 80-year-old man.

Demonstrative Adjectives

Demonstrative adjectives are *this* (singular) and *these* (plural) for persons or objects which are near and *that* (singular) and *those* (plural) for persons or objects that are far. They precede the noun.

I like *this* book better than *that* book on the table.

Do you like *these* books which I am holding?

I prefer *those* books on the shelf.

Possessive Adjectives

Possessive adjectives are *my, our, your, his, her, its,* and *their.* They indicate ownership. They precede a noun and do not indicate number.

My sister is younger than *her* husband.

Their children are older than *your* children.

Our trees are not so tall as *his* trees.

That new car? What do you think of *its* color?

Comparison of Adjectives

Positive	Comparative	Superlative

Most one-syllable adjectives add the suffix *er* for the comparative form and *est* for the superlative form.

sweet	sweeter	sweetest
rich	richer	richest

One-syllable adjectives ending in *e* add *r* for the comparative form and *st* for the superlative form.

late	later	latest
free	freer	freest

Two-syllable adjectives ending in *e* — if the accent is on the first syllable — add *r* for the comparative form and *st* for the superlative form.

little	littler	littlest
gentle	gentler	gentlest

Two-syllable adjectives ending in *y* preceded by a consonant change the *y* to *i* before adding *er* or *est*.

pretty	prettier	prettiest
handy	handier	handiest

2

Most other adjectives of two or more syllables form the comparative and superlative by the use of the auxiliary adverbs *more* and *most*.

sedate	more sedate	most sedate
beautiful	more beautiful	most beautiful

PITFALL

Avoid using *more* or *most* together with the suffix *er* or *est*.

a better book   (NOT: a more better book)
the happiest man   (NOT: the most happiest man)

ADVERBS

Adverbs are descriptive words which modify verbs, adjectives, or other adverbs: *sweetly, beautifully, softly, tenderly*.

She sang *sweetly*. (how she sang)	Adverb: *sweetly*.
This is a *very* sweet dessert. (how sweet)	Adverb: *very*.
The children sang *very* sweetly. (how sweetly)	Adverb: *very*.

Adverbs usually describe how, why, when, where, or to what extent.

Yesterday (when)
at school (where)
he worked *ambitiously* (how)
for many hours (to what extent)
to boost his grades (why)

RULE

Adverbs are frequently formed from adjectives by adding *ly* to the adjective.

---

beautiful	*beautifully*
quick	*quickly*

PITFALL

Remember that many adjectives also end in *ly* (*lovely, elderly, daily, early*).

RULE

Most adverbs form the comparative and superlative by the use of the auxiliaries *more* and *most*.

---

more quickly
most quickly

WORDS SERVING BOTH FUNCTIONS

A few words like *fast, slow, early, late, well, long, hard* function as either adverbs or adjectives depending on what they modify.

Adjective	Adverb
a *fast* train (modifies *train*)	He ran *fast*. (modifies *ran*)
a *slow* watch (modifies *watch*)	Go *slow*. (modifies *go*)
an *early* bird (modifies *bird*)	She came *early*. (modifies *came*)
the *late* student (modifies *student*)	They slept *late*. (modifies *slept*)
a *well* child (modifies *child*)	She played *well*. (modifies *played*)
a *long* novel (modifies *novel*)	He waited *long*. (modifies *waited*)
a *hard* chair (modifies *chair*)	He works *hard*. (modifies *works*)

COMPARISON OF TWO, OR MORE THAN TWO

The **comparative degree** of adjectives and adverbs is used when comparing two things. The **superlative degree** is used when comparing more than two things.

This book is *better* than that one.

Of the three books, I like this one the *best*.

RULE

Include the word *other* or *else* when comparing one person or thing with a group of which the person or thing is a part.

He was taller than any *other* boy in his class.

Jeanne is a better dancer than anyone *else* in her ballet class.

RULE

When comparing amounts, use *less* and *least*.

There is *less* wood in this pile than in that one.

Let's use the *least* electricity possible.

RULE

When comparing items in a group, use *fewer* and *fewest*.

Fewer stores remained open in the evenings this year than last.

Of the three shopping centers, this one has the *fewest* stores.

PITFALL

When using a comparison within a comparison, be sure to include all parts of each comparison.

He is now *as* tall *as*, if not *taller than*, his uncle Wilson.

IRREGULAR COMPARATIVE FORMS OF ADJECTIVES AND ADVERBS

	Comparative Degree	Superlative Degree
bad(ly)	worse	worst
ill	worse	worst
good	better	best
many, much	more	most
well	better	best
little	less	least

2 ■ Conjunctions

Coordinating Conjunctions

Coordinating conjunctions join words, phrases, and clauses of equal value. The coordinating conjunctions are: *and, but, or, nor, for, whereas, yet, so.*

and	He likes bread and butter.
	She bought a black-and-white dress.
	He did it quickly and well.
	Over the fence and into the woods went the ball.
	They sang and danced all night.
	The crowds were inside and outside the church.
	Drinking too much and eating too little was bad for him.
	Mary prepared the salad, and Jane made the cake.
but	(As a preposition it means *except.*)
	He did it quickly but well.
	They did not sing but danced all night.
	The crowds were not inside but outside the church.
	Drinking too much but eating too little was bad for him.
	Mary prepared the salad, but Jane made the cake.
for	They decided to leave, for they could see that a storm was coming.
nor	He didn't mind leaving the party, nor would anyone miss him.
or	Do you want tea or coffee?
	I want a red or a green dress.
	Do it immediately or not at all.
	Put it on the table or on the counter.
	They sang or danced all night long.
	They were either inside or outside the church.
	Eating too much or drinking too much was bad for him.
	Get dressed quickly, or I won't wait for you.
so	The driver explained the reason for the delay, so everybody was willing to wait patiently.
whereas	(formal usage)
	Whereas the council has deliberated this matter for several weeks, be it resolved that no sensible action can be taken.

6

yet	She was a pretty, yet not very attractive girl.
	He did it quickly, yet well.
	He heard the clock strike, yet did not pay attention to the time.
	Speaking with apparent frankness, yet concealing his inner thoughts, he swayed the crowd.
	He cried for help, yet nobody paid any attention to him.

Correlative Conjunctions

Correlative conjunctions are pairs of words used to join sentence elements of equal importance.

as	The tree was as tall as the house.
...as	He did it as well as he could.
so (after a negative) **...as**	He was not so tall as his sister. He was not so happy as he pretended to be.
not only ...but also	He played not only jazz but also classical music. He not only worked hard, but he also played hard.
both ...and	Both the men and the women took part in the sports. He was both older and wiser as a result of long experience.
either ...or	Either John or Fred is at home. Either John or his sisters are at home. Either his sisters or John is at home. We can either walk or ride to the picnic.
neither ...nor	Neither John nor Fred is at home. Neither John nor his sisters are at home. Neither his sisters nor John is at home. We can neither walk nor ride to the picnic.

RULE

When the parts of a compound subject are joined by *either...or* or *neither...nor*, the verb agrees with the part of the compound subject nearest to it.

CORRECT:	Either the whole engine or some of its *parts are* defective.
CORRECT:	Neither the students nor the *teacher agrees to the new ruling.*

7

PITFALL   V. I.

AN IMPOSSIBLE SITUATION: SINGULAR AND PLURAL ANTECEDENTS JOINED BY *or* OR *nor.*

When there are two possible antecedents, one of which is singular and the other plural, English offers no grammatical solution.

> EXAMPLE: Either the *boy* or his *parents* have lost *his? their?* mind.

The only escape from such a problem is to recast the sentence.

> SOLUTION: Either the *boy* has lost *his* mind, or his *parents* are out of *their* wits.

Subordinating Conjunctions

Subordinating conjunctions join sentence elements of unequal rank. They are the following: *as, after, although, because, before, how, in order that, than, if, since, that, though, unless, until, when, where, while.* Subordinating conjunctions are most frequently used to join dependent clauses to independent clauses.

He whistled *while* he worked.

Most of the subordinating conjunctions frequently introduce participial phrases.

He read the paper *while* eating his breakfast.
Although driven to the wall, he kept calm.

PITFALL

The word *after* usually requires a participial phrase in the present perfect form.

> WRONG: *After cleaning* the house, she took a nap.
> CORRECT: *After* having cleaned the house, she took a nap.

RULE

When indicating a causal relationship, the conjunctions *because, since,* and *as* are preferable in that order. *Since* is weaker than *because,* for it also refers to time (*She has been unhappy since she left the city*). *As* is the weakest because it refers to both time and comparison (*He tackled each problem as he came to it. He played as hard as he worked*).

> CORRECT: *She has been unhappy because she left the city* (cause).
> CORRECT: *He tackled each problem as he came to it* (time).

PITFALL

A few words like *after* function both as prepositions and conjunctions.

He came *after* me. (preposition)
He came *after* I did. (conjunction)

PITFALL

The conjunctions *as* and *than* are sometimes confused with prepositions because they frequently introduce elliptical clauses (clauses where words are omitted because the meaning is clear without them).

> He worked as rapidly *as* I (worked).
> I worked more rapidly *than* he (worked).
> She disliked him as much *as* (she disliked) me.
> The rain soaked him more *than* (it soaked) me.

PITFALL

The relative pronouns *(who, which, that)* frequently act as subordinating conjunctions.

> John, *who* was ill, recovered.
> He did not know *which* of the girls he liked best.
> The cake *that* she made was good.

Conjunctive Adverbs

A few adverbs, like *also, consequently, furthermore, however, moreover, nevertheless, then, therefore,* function with the effect of conjunctions because they refer to the subject matter of the preceding sentence. They are not actually conjunctions because they may not be used to join sentence elements of either equal or unequal value.

> He was sick. *Consequently,* he did not go to work.
> It costs more than it's worth. *Furthermore,* I don't need it.
> He was not poor. He was glad, *however,* to inherit the money.
> He was tired from lack of sleep. *Moreover,* he had a bad cold.
> She hated the town. *Nevertheless,* she was willing to live there.

3 ■ Interjections

The word *interjection* means *thrown in*. Interjections are words which either stand alone or are thrown into a sentence without becoming a part of the grammatical structure of the sentence. They are such words as *yes, no, oh, goodbye, hello,* or sometimes phrases like *oh my, ouch, help.*

RULE

Since interjections are not intrinsic parts of sentence structure, they either stand alone followed by an exclamation mark or are separated from the remainder of the sentence by commas.

Hello! How are you? or *Hello,* how are you?
No! Please! Don't say it!
Yes, I'll come with you.
Oh, you can't mean that!
I was resigned, *unfortunately,* to my situation.

4 ■ Nouns

A **noun** is a word used to name a person, place, thing, idea, or action. A word before which *the* can be used is at that moment a noun: *the man, the city, the toy, the happiness, the running* (as in: *The running* that he does every morning would tire me for a week!).

PLURALS OF NOUNS

> **RULE**
>
> Most nouns form their plurals by adding *s* to the singular. Nouns ending in *s, sh, ch, x,* or *z* add *es* to the singular.

Singular	Plural
son	sons
house	houses
boss	bosses
gas	gases
dish	dishes
church	churches
tax	taxes
waltz	waltzes

> **RULE**
>
> Nouns ending in *f* or *fe* change the *f* to *v* and add *es.*

Singular	Plural
half	halves
wife	wives
shelf	shelves
scarf	scarves

Other nouns keep the *f* and add *s*.

roof	roofs
gulf	gulfs
chief	chiefs

RULE

Nouns ending in *y* preceded by a consonant change the *y* to *i* and add *es*.

Singular	**Plural**
penny	pennies
laboratory	laboratories
country	countries

Nouns ending in *y* preceded by a vowel keep the *y* and add *s*.

day	days
boy	boys
key	keys

RULE

The following nouns ending in *o* add *es* when forming their plurals.

Singular	**Plural**
buffalo	buffaloes
calico	calicoes
cargo	cargoes
desperado	desperadoes
domino	dominoes
embargo	embargoes
hero	heroes
mosquito	mosquitoes
potato	potatoes
tomato	tomatoes

RULE

Compound nouns written as one word add *s* or *es* to make their plurals.

Singular	**Plural**
cupful	cupfuls
leftover	leftovers

Compound nouns consisting of a noun plus a modifier pluralize the modified word, NOT the modifier.

Singular	Plural
notary public	notaries public
brother-in-law	brothers-in-law
runner-up	runners-up

RULE

Letters, signs, and words as countable items add an apostrophe plus *s*.

Singular	Plural
one c	two c's
one *but*	three *but's*
in 1980	in the 1980's

NOUNS WITH IRREGULAR PLURALS

Singular	Plural
addendum	addenda
alumna	alumnae
alumnus	alumni
analysis	analyses
antithesis	antitheses
appendix	appendices
axis	axes
bacterium	bacteria
basis	bases
beef	beeves
cannon	cannon
cherub	cherubim
child	children
curriculum	curricula
datum	data
deer	deer
die	dice
drive-in	drive-ins
dynamo	dynamos
elf	elves
ellipsis	ellipses

Singular	Plural
emphasis	emphases
fish	fish (*fishes*—different kinds)
focus	foci
foot	feet
fungus	fungi
goose	geese
half	halves
hoof	hooves
hypothesis	hypotheses
knife	knives
leaf	leaves
life	lives
loaf	loaves
louse	lice
man	men
maximum	maxima
metamorphosis	metamorphoses
minimum	minima
mouse	mice
oasis	oases
ourself	ourselves
ox	oxen
parenthesis	parentheses
phenomenon	phenomena
piano	pianos
radio	radios
self	selves
seraph	seraphim
sheaf	sheaves
sheep	sheep
stand-by	stand-bys
swine	swine
synopsis	synopses
synthesis	syntheses
terminus	termini
thesis	theses
thief	thieves
tie-up	tie-ups
tooth	teeth
two-year-old	two-year-olds
vertebra	vertebrae
virtuoso	virtuosi
yourself	yourselves
wife	wives
wolf	wolves
woman	women

POSSESSIVE CASE OF NOUNS

> **RULE**
>
> The **possessive case** of nouns, meaning *belonging to*, is usually formed by adding the apostrophe and *s* to words which do not end with an *s* or *z* sound and by adding only the apostrophe to words which end with an *s* or *z* sound.

the boy's room   the children's school
the boys' room   Dickens' novels

PITFALL

In singular one-syllable nouns ending in the *s* or *z* sound, it is customary to add the apostrophe and *s* and to pronounce the possessive as if it ended in *es: the boss's hat.*

To be certain about the correct placing of the apostrophe, remember that the apostrophe always means the idea of belonging to whatever immediately precedes it:

the boy's suit	belonging to the boy
the boys' room	belonging to the boys
the boss's office	belonging to the boss
the bosses' office	belonging to the bosses
the women's department	belonging to the women

When possession is shared by two or more nouns, this fact is indicated by using the possessive case for the last noun in the series: *John, Fred, and Edward's canoe.* They all own the same canoe. If each one separately owns a canoe, each name is placed in the possessive case: *John's, Fred's, and Edward's canoes.* Notice also: *Wilson's and my car, secretary-treasurer's report,* and *mother-in-law's smile.*

PITFALL

Inanimate objects are not capable of possession. The relationship meaning *a part of* is indicated by the use of the preposition *of:*

the wall of the castle NOT *the castle's wall*

EXCEPTIONS: Objects which are personified, such as ships and airplanes, may use the possessive case: *the ship's compass, the plane's gyroscope.* Idiomatic usage also allows the possessive case for time and money: *a day's work, a dollar's worth, three years' time.* In such instances be careful in placing the apostrophe to observe whether the noun is singular or plural: *a month's vacation, two months' vacation.*

5 ■ Prepositions

Prepositions are connecting words used to show the relationship of one word to another. The word *preposition* means *placed before*. It is so named because it is usually placed before a noun or a pronoun or a noun phrase or clause.

The river is *at* the edge *of* town.
He acted *like* a friend *of* the family.

RULE

A preposition takes an object (a noun or a pronoun). Therefore, if that object is a pronoun, the pronoun must be in the objective case:

To whom are you speaking?

PITFALL

When pronouns are used as compound objects of a preposition, assure correct usage by this test: Have each pronoun stand *alone* with the preposition, e.g.:

for you and him (for him)
with him and her (with her)
between you and me (between us)
to her and me (to me)

RULE

Prepositional phrases at the beginning of a sentence are usually followed by a comma.

On the other hand, you may be right after all.

about	There were fences about the estate.
	He inquired about my health.
	I must be about my business.
above	The birds flew above the house.
	Look at the sentence above the last one.
	He was above suspicion.
across	They rowed across the river.
after	After the storm, the sun shone brightly.
	The son was after his father's money.
	In rank a captain is after a general.
against	He leaned against the wall.
	The enemy is always against us.
	The teacher is against talking in class.
	He is saving his money against a rainy day.
	He charged twenty dollars against the customer's account.
ahead of	The fastest car was ahead of the others.
	He was ahead of his brother in school because he was more intelligent.
along	They drove along the road while others rowed along the shore.
along with	The boy went along with his parents.
	Along with my loose change, I have $41.53.
	I am willing to go along with you in your beliefs.
among	Among her friends, she is also very shy.
(used with more than two items)	Among the five guests was a man from Kauai.
around	He ran around the farm.
	The baseball player ran around the bases.
	Twenty-four and twenty-six are around twenty-five.
as	He went to the masquerade dressed as a king.
	The boy was as tall as his father.
	He was not so tall as his uncle.
at	The store was at the corner of Vine Street and First Avenue
	His sister was away at college.
	At nine o'clock he had breakfast.
	He usually read at night.
	The audience applauded at the entrance of the star.
	Do it at your own convenience.
	The oranges are priced at sixty cents a dozen.
	The prisoner was at the mercy of the jailer.
	During vacations I find myself at leisure.
	He gave the command to fire at will.
away from	He swam away from the boat.
	You are far away from the answer.
	He stayed away from home.

in back of	The fire house was in back of the city center.
	When he changed his plans, we did not know what was in back of his mind.
before	He put the cart before the horse.
	He got out of bed before sunrise.
	Page 40 comes before page 50.
	Job asked to come before the presence of God.
behind	The caboose was behind all the other cars on the train.
	He was behind his brother in finishing the job.
	The books were hidden behind the fence.
below	The cellar was below the first floor.
	The temperature dropped below twenty degrees.
	He thought that laughter was below his dignity.
	His performance was below his ability.
beneath	They put rafters beneath the roof.
	Cheating on examinations was beneath him.
	They lived beneath the rule of a dictator.
beside	He sat beside her on the bench.
between (used for two items)	On a piano the black keys are between the white keys.
	The bus ran between New York and San Francisco.
	He divided the money between his two sons.
	He felt as if he were between the frying pan and the fire.
	Between you and me [confidentially] I think we're in trouble.
	The audience went out for refreshments between the acts.
but (meaning *except*)	Nobody was left but me.
	All but one were able to get on the bus.
by	He passed by the bank on his way home.
	He was assisted by his friends.
	He was paid by the week, but he paid his rent by the month.
	Coal is sold by the ton.
	He talked to me by telephone.
	He is not a carpenter by choice; he would rather be an electrician.
down	It was easy to run down the hill.
	He played down the scale from f to c.
down from	He dropped down from the roof to the ground.
down to	After paying for lunch, he was down to his last nickel.
except	Everybody sang except John.
	He saw everyone except me.
for	He took aspirin for his headache.
	She would do anything for a friend.
	This is a perfect location for a store.
	He is hoping for a prize.
	He has a talent for painting.
	I voted for him in the last election.
	I paid too much money for my shoes.
	He failed for many reasons.

	He was bedridden for seven months.
	I would not cross the ocean for anything.
	Father bought a new suit for me.
	The son was named for his father.
	As for me, I would rather not say what I think.
from	He jumped from the boat.
	They took my money from me.
	John drove from Washington to New York.
	He was a good man from birth to death.
	I can tell a good play from a bad one.
	His unusual knowledge came from intensive studying.
in front of	I stood in front of the theater.
in	He lived in a hotel in Washington where he was in the army.
	Let us cut the apple in half.
	America was discovered in 1492.
	I hope to be ready in a few minutes.
	In fact, it may take me longer
	The boat was twenty feet in length.
	In my opinion, the enemy will soon be defeated.
	He read the book in German.
	She delighted in the sunshine of a warm spring day.
	He spoke in opposition to the views of the majority.
	He owned property in addition to his home.
	His writing was in connection with his job.
	Put the milk in the refrigerator.
inside	Inside the house, the temperature was warm.
into	He walked into the store.
	I shall look into the matter.
	Put the carrots into the stew now.
	He tried to change lead into gold.
like	She looks like her sister.
	It looks like rain.
	It would be like him to do it.
	He ate like a horse.
of	That is the tower of Pisa.
	He was the owner of the yacht.
	Of necessity, he lived where he did.
	Give me a glass of water.
	He lived in the village of Ilion.
	He was a man of many talents.
	He got tired of working very quickly.
	Nothing good was said of him after he left.
	There have been very few thunderstorms of late.
off	Take the books off the table, please.
	The theater was off Broadway.
on	Put the bread on the counter.
	He piled one box on the other.

They had a house on the Mississippi River.
He owned a watch on a chain.
He set sail on the twentieth of May.
I will let you have it on your assurance that it will be returned.
On my word I will not be late.
The detective was on my track.
He went on record in stating his belief in capital punishment.
He was working on a new book.
He was writing a book on witchcraft.

out	He ran out the door.
out of	He was out of money
	The elevator was out of order.
out with	He had a falling out with his father over money matters.
outside	Put the garbage outside the house.
	Being unpopular, he was always outside the group.
over	The plane flew over the city.
	The boss has power over his employees.
	Put a blanket over you when you go to bea.
	He jumped over the fence.
	They drove over the fields.
	The river rose over its banks.
	The students went home over the holidays.
	We laughed over his description of his embarrassment.
	He talked to me over the telephone
	The dress costs over fifty dollars.
	Nuclear physics is over my head.
past	It is past ten o'clock.
	He drove past the restaurant without stopping.
	He has become so ill that he is past hope.
since	He has not been here since last week.
through	He threw a ball through a window.
	He read through the entire newspaper.
	He aged gracefully through the years.
	He succeeded through the help of his father.
throughout	He was happy throughout his entire life.
till	We will wait till next week.
(used only with	Wait till tomorrow.
verb *to wait*)	
to	He traveled to the fair.
	To his sorrow, he found out that his house had fallen down.
	The final bill came to fifty dollars.
	He owed duty to his family.
	They stood back to back.
	This is the key to the car.
	It is twenty minutes to five.
	Let us drink to his health.
	To my knowledge, she has not left the city.

	The race is not always to the swift.

The race is not always to the swift.
Two is to four as four is to eight.

toward Toward the city, the fog was thick.
He walked slowly toward me.

under The sheet was under the blanket.
He built a house under the cliff.
He took her under his guidance.
You will find definitions under *U* in the dictionary.
He fought under General Clark.
She insisted that her age was under forty.
He felt nothing because he was under an anesthetic.
Under the terms of the contract, you must complete the job quickly

underneath You will find paper underneath the book.
She kept the brushes underneath the sink.

until I won't leave until six o'clock.

up We walked slowly up the hill.
They sailed their boat up the river.
The beauty parlor is up the street.
She kept her diary up to date.

upon He stacked the books upon the table.

with I shall go to the store with you.
He reached the airport with twenty minutes to spare.
In the military service, he is with the Navy.
He looked with sorrow on his wasted life.
She swept the floor with a broom.
He was sick with influenza.
He was believed to be a person with sound principles.
I hate to part with my money.
I am angry with you because of your neglect

within He resided within the city limits.
He always drove within the speed limits.
He was within his right in doing so.

without He went without food for two days
I left the house without my coat.

6 ■ Pronouns

A **pronoun** is a word used in place of one or more nouns or pronouns.

TYPES OF PRONOUNS

Personal Pronouns

The **personal pronouns** are distinguished by *person, case,* and *number.* To begin, note the designations of person:

1. First Person (the person speaking or writing)

2. Second Person (the person addressed)

3. Third Person (the person, place, or thing spoken or written about); singular pronouns are also distinguished by gender

PERSON	CASE	NUMBER				
		Singular				**Plural**
FIRST	Nominative (Subjective) Possessive Objective	I (my), mine me				we (our), ours us
SECOND	Nominative (Subjective) Possessive Objective	you (your), yours you				you (your), yours you
		Masc.	**Fem.**	**Neuter**		
THIRD	Nominative (Subjective) Possessive Objective	he his him	she (her), hers her	it its it		they (their), theirs them

Though traditionally classified as pronouns in English, the words *my, our, your, his, her, its, their* are correctly known as *possessive pronominal adjectives.* Adjectives modify nouns: my book, big book, thick book, our book, the book. Pronouns *stand for* a noun and therefore cannot modify it. "Mine is a good book." "Ours is good, too."

DETERMINING CORRECT CASE FOR PRONOUNS

Nominative Case

1. The subject of a verb should be in the nominative case.

I, we, you, he, she, it, they fell down.
We students want a change of policy.

2. Put a predicate pronoun (following any finite form of the verb *to be*) in the nominative case.

They suspected that the masquerader was *I, you, he, she.*
They suspected that the masqueraders were *we, you, they.*

3. Put the appositive of a subject in the nominative case.

The clergy, *we* of the cloth, are dedicated people.

Objective Case

1. The object of a verb should be in the objective case.

A bolt of lightning struck *me, him, her, it, us, you, them.*

2. Put the object of a participle in the objective case.

She spent her whole life hating *me, him, her, it, us, you, them.*

3. Put the object of an infinitive in the objective case.

He tried very hard to understand *me, him, her, it, us, you, them.*

4. Put the subject of an infinitive in the objective case.

They asked *me* to do it.
They trained *him* to be a doctor.

5. The object of a preposition should be in the objective case.

He aimed the rifle at *me, him, her, it, us, you, them.*

Relative Pronouns

The **relative pronouns,** *who, whom, whose, which* and *that,* are used to relate a dependent clause of a sentence to a word or an idea in the independent clause.

The man *who* is standing over there is my husband.
The tools *which he used* were rusty.
The girl *whose* book you borrowed would like you to return it.

The pronoun *who* is used to refer to persons; *which* refers to things; *that* refers to both persons and things. For references to persons it is preferable to use the pronoun *who* rather than *that*.

Like the personal pronouns, *who* takes different forms depending on its case.

Case	Singular and Plural
Nominative (Subjective)	who
Possessive	whose
Objective	whom

WHO OR WHOM?

The principles for determining the case for all pronouns are the same for *who* (nominative case) and *whom* (objective case).

SUBJECT OF A VERB: *Who* is going to the party? (subject of *is*)
My friend, *who* is a doctor, is very clever. (subject of *is*)

PITFALL

Be cautious when *who* is separated from its verb.

WRONG: The writer *whom* you told me won the Nobel Prize, etc.

CORRECT: The writer *who* you told me won the Nobel Prize was one I had never heard of. (*who* is subject of *won; you told me* is a parenthetical expression)

OBJECT OF A VERB: *Whom* have they invited? (object of *invited*)
My friend, *whom* you know, is a doctor. (object of *know*)

OBJECT OF A PREPOSITION: The man from *whom* I got it is honest (object of *from*)
To *whom* it may concern: (object of *to*)
Whom did you give it to? (object of *to*)

PITFALL

The case of a relative pronoun is determined by its use in the clause in which it appears. The case is not affected by any word *outside the clause:*
There was no question about *who was* the winner.
Give the book to *whoever needs* it.
BUT words *outside the clause* will conform to their own required usage:
Give the book *to him who needs* it most.
Guard liberty *for us citizens who know* how to act with responsibility.

Interrogative Pronouns

The **interrogative pronouns,** *who, whom, whose, which, what,* are used to ask a question. Their antecedents (words to which they refer) are the answers to the questions.

Who is the chairman?	Answer: John (the antecedent).
What is he carrying?	Answer: a suitcase (the antecedent).

Who as an interrogative pronoun is distinguished by case.

NOMINATIVE	*Who* is coming to dinner?
(SUBJECTIVE):	*Which* is better?
	What would you like?
POSSESSIVE:	*Whose* gloves are these?
OBJECTIVE:	*Whom* were you talking to? (object of preposition *to*)
	Whom did you see in the car? (direct object of the verb *see*)

Demonstrative Pronouns

The **demonstrative pronouns** are used to point out people, places, or things without naming them. The antecedent of a demonstrative pronoun is whoever or whatever is being pointed out.

I like *this*.   *Those* are good to eat.

Singular	Plural
this	these
that	those

Intensive and Reflexive Pronouns

Singular	Plural
myself	ourselves
yourself	yourselves
himself, herself, itself	themselves

Intensive Usage: I *myself* will do it.   He *himself* was the culprit.
Reflexive Usage: I hurt *myself*.   They fooled *themselves*.

PITFALL

Do not use a reflexive or intensive pronoun in place of a simple personal pronoun.

WRONG:	He is going with Wilson and *myself*.
CORRECT:	He is going with Wilson and *me*.

WRONG:	Wilson and *myself* are going there.
CORRECT:	Wilson and *I* are going there.

Indefinite Pronouns

The **indefinite pronouns** are so named because their antecedents are vague or unknown. They are such words as *each, all, either, neither, any, anyone, both, everyone, everybody, everything, somebody, nobody, none, few, many, much, more, some, someone, somebody,* etc.

PRONOUNS AND ELLIPTICAL CLAUSES

In **elliptical clauses** introduced by *as* or *than,* part of the clause is omitted because it would be repetitious. To determine the case of the pronoun, supply the omitted words (in parentheses below) in your mind.

He doesn't work as hard as *I (do).*
Nobody in the class is taller than *he* (is).
He likes me better than (he likes) *him.*
He praised me as much as (he praised) *her.*

COMPOUND PRONOUN AGREEMENTS

RULE

    In a **compound subject,** all pronouns must be subject pronouns (nominative case).

He and I will do the job together.
Wilson and I went to France last summer.
We students like this book very much.
Which movie *did his mother and he see?*

RULE

    In a compound object, all pronouns must be object pronouns.

He *took Marie and me* to the show last night.
Please *take him and her* with you
Do you want us men to help?

RULE

    In a compound object of a preposition, all pronouns must be object pronouns.

There seems to be a misunderstanding *between you and him.*
He gave it *to her and me* for our birthdays.
Women like *Anne and her* are very much respected.

TROUBLE SPOTS IN PRONOUN - ANTECEDENT AGREEMENT

RULE

A referent must agree with its noun or pronoun antecedent in person, number, and gender. The antecedent is the noun or pronoun to which the referent refers.

PITFALL: SINGULAR MASCULINE AGREEMENT FOLLOWING INDEFINITE SINGULAR ANTECEDENTS

Indefinite singular pronouns like *each, everyone, everybody, anyone, anybody, nobody, no one, someone, either, neither* are treated for convenience as masculine unless the situation is such (as in a woman's college) that the reference is clearly feminine or unless (as it might be for *each* or *either* or *neither*) the reference is neuter.

CORRECT: Everybody in the country is naturally concerned for *his* welfare.

CORRECT: Nobody in the Girl Scouts shirks *her* duty.

CORRECT: Either of the plans should be considered on *its* merits.

PITFALL: PLURAL AGREEMENT FOLLOWING TWO OR MORE SINGULAR ANTECEDENTS JOINED BY *and*

When the pronoun refers to more than one person, place, or thing, it must be a plural pronoun.

CORRECT: He and she ate *their* dinner quickly.

CORRECT: The church and the school had a playground which *they* shared in common.

PITFALL: SINGULAR AGREEMENT AFTER TWO OR MORE SINGULAR ANTECEDENTS JOINED BY *or* OR *nor*

When the pronoun refers to only one of two or more from which a selection is to be made, the pronoun is singular.

CORRECT: Either Jack or Paul is bound to forget *his* appointment.

CORRECT: Neither the train nor the bus can be expected to keep *its* schedule.

PITFALL: SINGULAR AGREEMENT AFTER COLLECTIVE NOUNS THE SENSE OF WHICH IS SINGULAR

Many nouns like *army, class, committee, group,* refer to more than one person, place, or thing. When such a group is considered as a single unit, as is usual, pronouns referring to the unit should be singular, neuter in gender.

CORRECT:	The class elected *its* officers at the end of the term.
CORRECT:	An army marches on *its* stomach.

Only when a group is thought of as made up of many individuals should a plural pronoun be used.

CORRECT.	The members of the glee club sang *their* parts perfectly.

PITFALL. FEMININE AGREEMENT FOR SOME NEUTER ANTECEDENTS Traditionally, a few inanimate and actually sexless things are referred to as feminine: ships, airplanes, nations, colleges. Neuter pronouns are correct when referring to such antecedents, but the use of feminine pronouns is not infrequent in such instances.

CORRECT:	The ship sailed Friday on *its* last voyage.
CORRECT:	The ship sailed Friday on *her* last voyage.

PITFALL: AN IMPOSSIBLE SITUATION: SINGULAR AND PLURAL ANTECEDENTS JOINED BY *or* OR *nor*

When there are two possible antecedents, one of which is singular and the other plural, English offers no grammatical solution.

EXAMPLE:	Either the *boy* or his *parents* have lost *his? their?* mind.

The only escape from such a dilemma is to recast the sentence.

SOLUTION:	Either the *boy* has lost *his* mind or his *parents* are out of *their* wits.

PROBLEMS IN REFERENCE OF PRONOUNS

Since a pronoun has no meaning without an antecedent, it is important that the antecedent of every pronoun be clearly stated and unmistakable. Apart from such obvious idiomatic usage as *"It* is raining" or *"It* is two o'clock," or the deliberate indefiniteness of *"They* say . . ." or the lazy vagueness of "Why don't *they* repair this sidewalk?" or a conversational situation where the antecedent is obvious ("It won't start."), the exact antecedent of every pronoun must be made clear.

PITFALL: AVOID AMBIGUOUS REFERENCE Be sure that a pronoun cannot be taken to refer to more than one possible antecedent.

AMBIGUOUS:	My mother told the secretary that *she* had made a mistake.

QUESTION:	Who made a mistake? *She* could refer to *mother* or *secretary.*
SOLUTION:	My mother reprimanded the secretary for making a mistake.
SOLUTION:	My mother said to the secretary, "You have made a mistake."

PITFALL: AVOID REMOTE REFERENCE

Be sure that a pronoun is reasonably close to its antecedent.

REMOTE:	The curtain rose on *Carmen* which is a very popular opera with lively music, a colorful cast of characters, and a large chorus. *It* is made of a heavy brocade.
PROBLEM:	The *it* is so far from its antecedent *curtain* that the reader is put to unnecessary effort in clarifying the meaning of the pronoun.
SOLUTION:	The *curtain, which* is made of a heavy brocade, rose . .

PITFALL: AVOID INDEFINITE REFERENCE

Be sure that a pronoun has a definite antecedent instead of a vague idea.

VAGUE:	He played golf all morning and tennis all afternoon *which* was probably bad for his health.
SOLUTION:	He played golf all morning and tennis all afternoon. So much exertion was bad for his health.
VAGUE:	They asked me to join them at six o'clock in the morning, but *this* is something I can't stand.
SOLUTION:	They asked me to join them at six o'clock in the morning, but early rising is something I can't stand.

PITFALL: AVOID REFERENCE TO A NOUN IN THE POSSESSIVE CASE

However clear such reference may be, usage of this kind constitutes slovenly English.

EXAMPLE:	Goethe's *Faust* has been called the epic of modern man. *He* was particularly fitted to write such an epic because of his extraordinarily broad experiences.
SOLUTION:	Goethe's *Faust* has been called the epic of modern man. *Goethe* was particularly . . .

7 ■ Verbs

CORRECT VERB USAGE

Verbs *are* the asserting words. Without a verb it *is* usually impossible to make a sentence. On the other hand, a sentence *can be made* of one word if it *is* a verb: *Go. Eat. Wait.* These *are* one-word sentences. All the italicized words above are verbs.

An assertion can involve action (*Write* me a letter.) or a state of being (I *feel* sick.), or it can be nothing more than a device for making a statement (Gold *is* valuable.) or asking a question (*Are* you happy?).

But since action or state of being or even a statement involves time—past, present, future—verbs have tenses to indicate the time. A very few verbs like *ought* do not have a complete sequence of tenses and are therefore known as defective verbs.

Principal Parts of Verbs

The essential forms of a verb are known as its principal parts:

Infinitive:	to go OR go
Present Tense:	go
Past Tense:	went
Present Participle:	going
Past Participle:	gone

Number and Person Related to Verbs

Number

Most English verbs have very easy conjugations because for nearly all verbs the forms for number (singular and plural) are the same. For example:

Singular: I sing   Plural: We sing

Person

Person alludes to the subject of the verb.

First person is the person speaking or writing:

Singular: I   Plural: we

Second person is the person spoken or written to:

Singular: you   Plural: you

Third person is anybody or anything else:

Singular: he, she, it   Plural: they

street   streets

beauty   beauties

PITFALL

In nearly all verbs the only change of form occurs in the third person singular of the present and present perfect tenses and in the first person of the future and future perfect tenses. For example:

PRESENT TENSE: I, you, we, they *go* BUT he, she, it *goes*.

PRESENT PERFECT TENSE: I, you, we, they *have gone* BUT he, she, it *has gone*.

PITFALL

FUTURE TENSE: I, you, he, she, it, we, they *will go* BUT *shall I, shall we go?*

FUTURE PERFECT TENSE
(no change):   I, you, he, she, it, we, they *will have gone*

PAST TENSE
(no change):   I, you, he, she, it, we, they *went.*

PAST PERFECT TENSE
(no change):   I, you, he, she, it, we, they *had gone.*

EXCEPTION: An important exception is the verb *to be* which has several different forms. (See Irregular Verb Conjugations: *to be.*)

Mood of Verbs

Differences in the intention of the speaker or writer are shown by mood.

INDICATIVE MOOD

The indicative mood is used to make a statement or ask a question. Conjugations of English verbs are usually in the indicative mood·

The old man *walked* slowly down the street

Why *do* you *eat* so rapidly?

IMPERATIVE MOOD

The **imperative mood** of English verbs is identical with the infinitive (without the *to*): *be, work, eat, run.*

It is used for commands, requests, or directions:

COMMAND: *Sit* down and *eat* your supper.

REQUEST: Please *be* on time, and *bring* your lunch.

DIRECTION: *Fold* the paper vertically and *put* your name at the top.

SUBJUNCTIVE MOOD

The **subjunctive mood** is less used in modern English than in other languages possessing the subjunctive.

The following usages are listed in order of frequency of occurrence from most frequent to least frequent:

1. *To express a wish or to describe a condition contrary to fact*, the verb form is the same as in the indicative mood except for the verb *to be* where the form *were* is used for all persons.

WISH:	I wish I *were* as healthy as I used to be.
CONDITION CONTRARY	If she *were* younger, we could give her the job.
TO FACT:	If I *were* you, I would do that anyway.

2. *A second use of the subjunctive occurs in a dependent clause after a verb that expresses determination or a command, a request, or a suggestion.* In this usage the subjunctive form is the same as the imperative.

DETERMINATION:	I insist that he *meet* me at the bank.
COMMAND:	The general commanded that all troops *be* in dress uniform.
	They require that he *pay* the fee.
REQUEST:	I request that I *be allowed* to leave after the wedding. (passive voice)
SUGGESTION:	We suggest that she *go* first.

3. The same form of the subjunctive is used in *formal parliamentary procedure to introduce a motion or resolution.*

I move that this resolution *be* adopted: *"Be it resolved that the Senate go on record as endorsing Article Seven of the Constitution."*

Transitive and Intransitive Verbs

The distinction between **transitive** and **intransitive verbs** is useful principally for the grammatical purpose of determining the case of a pronoun which follows a verb. Is it correct to say "It is I" or "It is me"? The answer is *I* because *is* is an intransitive verb. Transitive verbs are followed by the objective case (*me*); intransitive verbs are followed by the nominative case (*I*).

When a verb indicates a motion or a passing over from one person or thing to another, it is called *transitive:* He *hit* the ball. She *ate* her dinner. Usually, something is being done to something or somebody.

Many verbs are both transitive and intransitive, depending on the meaning of the sentence in which they are used. "He *is* still *breathing*" means that he is alive. "He *is breathing* the fresh air of the seashore" implies that he is having a fine vacation. The first *is breathing* is intransitive; the action is self-contained. The second *is breathing* is a transitive verb because the sense of the verb requires the object *air.*

A simple test for a transitive verb is to find out if the sentence can be reversed by being stated in the passive voice, since only transitive verbs have a passive voice:

ACTIVE VOICE: He is breathing the air.

PASSIVE VOICE: The air is being breathed by him.

If the object of the verb *(air)* cannot be made the subject and the subject expressed in a "by-phrase" *(by him)*, the verb is not transitive.

An intransitive verb makes an assertion without requiring any object.

The bell *rings*.

The church *stands* on the top of a little hill.

The books *are* on the desk.

Linking verbs

This distinction is important grammatically only for one small class of intransitive verbs known as linking verbs. (They join a subject to a noun, pronoun, or adjective in the predicate.) *To be* is the most frequently used linking verb. Pronouns following linking verbs should be in the nominative case.

It is *I, we, you, he, she, it, they.* (subject)

Adjectives, not adverbs, follow linking verbs in the predicate.

He is *tall, good, bad, weak, sick, strong.*

Besides *to be*, the most frequently used linking verbs are *become, seem, smell, look, grow, feel, sound, get, taste, appear.*

The food smells bad. (not *badly*)

The orchestra sounded *good.* (not *well*)

I feel *well.* (*Well* is here an adjective meaning "not sick.")

I feel *good.* (in good spirits)

PITFALL

WRONG: I feel *badly.*

CORRECT: I feel bad. (*Bad* is here an adjective meaning "sick" as in "I have a bad *(sick)* feeling.")

RULE

The subject and object of an infinitive—even the infinitive *to be*—are always in the objective case.

At the masquerade they all believed *him* to be *me.*

Voice of Verbs

Transitive verbs—and only transitive verbs—depend on voice to indicate whether the emphasis in a sentence should be placed on the doer or the receiver of the action stated by the verb.

ACTIVE VOICE emphasizes the doer.

Andrew plays the piano.

The sentence implies that one of Andrew's talents is piano playing since *Andrew* is the subject of the transitive verb *plays* in the active voice. *Piano* is the object of the verb.

PASSIVE VOICE   emphasizes the receiver of the action.

The piano is played by Andrew.

This sentence implies that someone has asked who uses the piano which is part of the furniture of a room. Therefore *piano* is the subject of the sentence. But the piano isn't doing anything; something is being done *to* it. Therefore the passive form *is played* of the transitive verb *play* is followed by the prepositional phrase *by Andrew* to explain the use of the piano.

The passive voice is necessary on occasions where the doer is unknown or where it is preferable that he remain anonymous.

The wine was spilled on the floor.

It is mostly used when the doer is of no importance or when his identity is already known, or on occasions where the performer of the action is obvious.

The programs were distributed during the concert.

The Eiffel Tower was built in 1889.

The job will be completed in two weeks.

RULE

The active voice is preferred over the passive voice whenever possible in order to assure a lively or forceful quality to the style of speaking or writing. The passive is more formal and more impersonal than desirable in modern American-English.

WEAK: The flowers were cut by the children.
STRONG: The children cut the flowers.

TENSES OF VERBS

THE PRESENT TENSE

RULE

Use the present tense to indicate that something is so at the moment of speaking or writing.

He *is* sorry.   That *looks* like an expensive dress.

RULE

Use the present tense to describe something that is true regardless of time.

Justice *is* important.   Bees *sting.*

RULE

To make the verb *negative* or *interrogative* or *emphatic,* use *do, does.*

The children *do not* play well together.
He *does not* like to sing.
Do you read to the children every night?
Doesn't the mail leave later on Saturdays?
I *do work* hard, believe me!
She *does understand* you, no doubt about it!

The present tense is frequently used to refer to artistic productions which exist in the present even though they were created in the past and to make statements about artists (in the sense that they continue to live because of their works). Sim larly, synopses of plots are usually given in the present tense.

In *Romeo and Juliet,* Shakespeare's verse *has* a lyric quality.
Verdi *is* one of the greatest composers of all time.
At the beginning of *The Divine Comedy,* Dante *is* lost in a forest.
The hero *attempts* to climb a nearby hill.

RULE

Use the *progressive* form of the present tense to indicate a continuing action or situation. The *progressive* form of a verb consists of a conjugated form of the verb *to be* followed by the present participle of the principal verb (___ *ing):*

The clock *is striking.*   The organ *is playing.*   The people *are listening.*
When the progressive form is not used for such continuing events, a dramatic effect is produced.
The clock *strikes,* the organ *plays,* the people *listen.*

THE FUTURE TENSE

RULE

Use the future tense to indicate an event predicated to occur in the future. In informal conversation, most people use only the auxiliary verb *will* for all persons or else use contractions.

35

I (we) will do it.   I'll do it.   We'll do it.
You will do it.   You'll do it.
He (she, it, they) will do it.   He'll, she'll, they'll do it.

RULE

For questions, use *shall* in the first person and *will* in the second and third.

Shall I (we) write?
Will you write?
Will he (she, it, they) write?

RULE

To indicate intensity, implying a promise or determination, use *will* in the first person and *shall* in the second and third.

I (we) *will* succeed.
You *shall* succeed.
He (she, it, they) *shall* succeed.

RULE

In expressions of implied future or immediate future, use the present tense.

When he goes to New York next year, he will see the U.N. building.
As soon as she arrives at the airport, she will telephone us.
I am going to San Francisco tomorrow.
They are leaving next week.

The immediate future is often implied by the use of the present progressive form of *to go* before the infinitive.

I am going to speak to them about it.
He is going to take a trip to Hawaii.
What are you going to do tomorrow?

A future intention in the past is often implied by the use of the past progressive form of *to go* before the infinitive.

I was going to do it, but I did not have the time.
They were going to take a trip to Hawaii.

CONDITIONAL TENSE

RULE

Use the **conditional tense** (*would*) to indicate an event predicted to occur in future time depending on a condition which has been expressed or implied (an *if* clause).

We *would like* to visit Washington, D.C., if we had the time or money.
What *would you like* to see? (if you went there)
First, I *would go* to the Washington Monument, and then I'd visit the Lincoln Memorial. (If I went to Washington, D.C., if I had the time or money, etc.)

The conditional tense indicator *would* is also used often to replace the past tense to indicate that the event in the past was continued or was repeated over a period of time.

When he was a child, he *would walk* to school (walked, used to walk) every day.
He *would* often *take* his dog, too. (took, used to take)

THE PAST TENSE

RULE

Use the past tense to refer to something that occurred at a definite time in the past.

He *opened* a bank account two years ago.

RULE

Use the auxiliary *did* for negations and questions.

It *did not take* him long to write that letter.
What *did you say* to him?
Why *didn't they do* their work?
Did you see her?

RULE

Use the progressive form of the past tense to indicate that the event in the past continued over a period of time.

When he w⁓⁓ ⁓even years old, he *was learning* to write.

RULE

Use the intensive form of the past tense to secure emphasis.

It took a long time, but he *did learn* to write.

THE PRESENT PERFECT TENSE

RULE

Use the present perfect tense to describe an event which began at some time in the past and which has just been completed.

I *have finished* my homework.
Have you *seen* her recently?

RULE

To emphasize the recency of the action, use the idiomatic structure: *have just.*

I *have just* finished my homework. (a moment ago)
I *have just* seen her. (an hour ago or most recently)

RULE

Use the present perfect tense to describe an event which began at some time in the past but which is continuing into the present.

How long *have* you *been* here?
I *have been* here for seven months.
He *has been working* there since last year.

RULE

Use the progressive form of the present perfect tense to indicate a continuing action which has just been completed.

I *have been looking* all over for you.
I *have been shopping* for groceries.

> RULE
>
> Use the present perfect tense when the emphasis is on the fact that something that occurred once or several times in the past is considered from a present point of view.

"I *have been* in London" gives no indication of when the event occurred or even how many times it occurred except that it happened in the past. The emphasis is on the fact that at the present time a trip to London is a part of the speaker's or writer's experience.

THE PAST PERFECT TENSE

> RULE
>
> Use the past perfect tense to refer to an event which ended prior to some definite time in the past.

She *had finished* her work before she went to bed.

Since the past perfect tense implies a past event before another past event, it is usually accompanied by another verb in the past tense (*went* in the example above) though not necessarily in the same sentence.

He *caught* a bad cold.   He *had been* out in the rain all day.

> RULE
>
> Use the progressive form of the past perfect tense to indicate a continuing action.

He *had been waiting* a long time when the train came.

THE FUTURE PERFECT TENSE

> RULE
>
> Use the future perfect tense to indicate that something will be completed before some definite time in the future.

The use of *shall* and *will* in forming the future perfect tense is the same as in the future tense.

By the time she gets married, she *will have learned* to cook.

RULE

Use the progressive form of the future perfect tense to indicate a continuing action.

When we reach the top of the mountain, we *will have been climbing* for more than seven hours.

CONDITIONAL PERFECT TENSE

RULE

Use the conditional perfect tense to indicate that something would be completed before some future time depending on a condition which has been expressed or implied (an *if* clause).

What *would* you *have done* if the money had not arrived in time?
I *would have stayed* home (if the money had not arrived).
I *would have asked* you to lend me some (if the money had not arrived).

SEQUENCES WITH *IF*

RULE

If clauses always balance in either direction with the main clause on which they are dependent:

If I *went* early, he *would go*, too.
He *would go*, too, if I *went* early.
If I *had gone* early, he *would have gone*, too.
He *would have gone*, too, if I *had gone* early.

RULE

When a past participle with auxiliary appears in the *if* clause, a past participle with auxiliary must appear in the main clause as well

---

I would have *seen* her if she had *been* there early.
If we had *known* this, we would have *done* better.

Therefore a system of balances:

If I go there tomorrow, I *will buy* the books for you.	(present tense *if* clause with future)
If you *have* already *done* your homework, you *will have earned* a good grade for yourself.	(present perfect *if* clause with future perfect)
If I *went* there with you I *would see* much more.	(past tense *if* clause with conditional)
I *would have done* better *if* I *had been* there in the morning.	(conditional perfect balancing with past perfect *if* clause)

VERBALS

Verbals are words which are derived from verbs but which function as other parts of speech. Unlike finite verbs, they do not have tense, nor are they limited by person and number. They serve as nouns or adjectives, and they may have objects or modifiers.

Infinitives

Present Infinitive:	*to be, to go*
Perfect Infinitive:	*to have been, to have gone*
Progressive Forms:	*to be going, to have been going*

The *to* is sometimes omitted because of idiomatic usage: *Let him go. (Ask him to go.)*

Infinitives usually function as nouns, serving the concept of *the action of.* In the sentence *to die is common*, the infinitive *to die* could be replaced by the noun *death.*

To sing beautifully was her ambition.

(*The action of singing* was her ambition; *beautifully* modifies *to sing; to sing* is the subject of *was*.)

He loved *to eat* candy.

(*The action of eating* is the object of *loved; candy* is the object of *to eat.*)

The Gerund

A **gerund** is a present participle that functions as a noun. It is the name of an action or state of being. It serves the concept of *the action of.* Like the infinitive it may have modifiers and complements.

He enjoyed *driving* the car.	(the action of driving)
Heavy *drinking* was his only bad habit.	(the action of drinking)
Being sensible was difficult for him.	(the action of being)
She enjoyed *cooking* on her new stove.	(the action of cooking)

PITFALL

The gerund requires a possessive rather than a direct object form of a pronoun.
He does not like *my writing* to you about his accident. (my action of writing)
They object to *our doing* it today. (our action of doing)

INCORRECT: I am concerned about *him seeing* the show.
CORRECT: I am concerned about *his seeing* the show. (his action of seeing)

Participles as Adjectives

In all their forms (present, present perfect, past, and past perfect passive), participles can function as adjectives with or without objects or modifiers.

The *sinking* ship.   The *rising* sun. (modify *ship* and *sun*)
Having lost his notebook, he failed the test. (modifies *he*)
The lobsters, *flown* in from the ocean, were delicious. (modifies *lobsters*)
Having been drenched by the rain, he caught a cold. (modifies *he*)

RULE

When a modifying participial phrase initiates a sentence, the subject of that phrase *must* follow immediately (after the comma).

INCORRECT: Arriving at the stadium late, the game had
                    already started. (The game did not arrive late.)
CORRECT: Arriving at the stadium late, he found that the
                    game had already started. (*He* arrived late. *He* is
                    the subject of both actions: *arriving* and *found*.)

THE SENTENCE AND ITS PARTS

A **sentence** is a group of words that makes sense. It says something definite. It must contain a verb because the verb is the asserting word. It ends with a period (.), a question mark (?), or an exclamation mark (!). A sentence can be made of only one word if that word is a verb: *Go!* On the other hand, many words even if they are related to each other cannot form a sentence without a verb: *all the friends of my family in their best clothes and on their best behavior.* What *about* all the friends of my family, etc., etc.?

8 ■ The Elements of a Sentence

THE SUBJECT

The **subject** is what is being talked or written about. The **simple subject** is the basic word, usually a noun or a pronoun. The **complete subject** is the simple subject together with any modifiers it may have.

> *She* is sick.
> *The clever student* completed the test before all the others.
> *The test* was long.

In the sentence above, *student* is the simple subject; *the clever student* is the complete subject. In the following sentence *dispute* is the simple subject; the complete subject is italicized:

> A *lengthy dispute about wages and hours of employment* led to a strike.

In an *interrogative sentence*, the subject is the person, place, idea, or thing about whom or which the question is being asked.

> Is *my book* lying on the table?

If in doubt, you can usually find the subject of such a sentence by answering the question: *My book* is lying on the table.
When talking directly to another person or persons (*you*), the subject is frequently omitted because it is understood.

> (You) Come to the table. Dinner is getting cold.

A **compound subject** contains two or more subjects joined by coordinating or correlative conjunctions.

The boys and *the girls* played nicely together.
Dogs, cats, goats, and *mules* were all over the street.
Neither *an apartment in the city* nor *a house in the country* could serve to keep him happy.

THE PREDICATE

Everything in a sentence besides the complete subject is the **predicate.** It says whatever there is to be said about the subject. In an interrogative sentence it asks the question.

The house *was falling apart because nobody lived in it any longer.*
Why is the house *falling apart?*

The **simple predicate** is the principal verb of the sentence (*was falling*). All the other words except the complete subject constitute the complete predicate.

PITFALL

Do not write a "sentence" without a finite verb (a verb that is complete).

WRONG:	All the little children miserable and poor and hungry.
CORRECT:	All the little children *were* miserable and poor and hungry.

PITFALL

Do not omit any part of a finite verb.

WRONG:	All the little children singing and dancing in the garden.
CORRECT:	All the little children *were* singing and dancing in the garden.

A **compound predicate** contains two or more predicates joined by coordinating or correlative conjunctions.

He *eats* and *drinks* heartily every day.
My friends either *go to Europe on their vacations* or *stay at home in their air-conditioned apartments.*

PITFALL

Do not separate one part of a compound predicate from the sentence in which it belongs.

WRONG:	The weary clerk finally completed the tally of all his accounts. And then went home for a good meal and a long night's sleep.
CORRECT:	The weary clerk finally completed the tally of all his accounts and then went home for a good meal and a long night's sleep.

There, Here, and *It* may indicate that the subject will follow the verb: "There are many books in our library."

PHRASES

A **phrase** is a group of related words that function in sentences as single parts of speech. It does not have a subject and a predicate.

Prepositional Phrase

A **prepositional phrase** contains a preposition, the object of the preposition, and often modifiers of the object. The whole phrase functions as an adjective or an adverb.

> The man *in the blue suit* worked *at the bank.*

In this sentence, *in the blue suit* is an adjective phrase modifying *man; at the bank* is an adverbial phrase modifying *worked*

> **PITFALL**
>
> Do not mistake a prepositional phrase for a complete sentence.
> | | |
> |---|---|
> | WRONG: | Over the hills and dales and mountains and valleys. |
> | CORRECT: | He roamed over the hills and dales and mountains and valleys. |

Participial Phrase

A **participial phrase** contains a participle and either a complement or one or more modifiers or both.

> *Happily singing an old familiar song,* he wandered down the country road.

This is a **present participial phrase** used as an adjective to modify *he. Singing* is the present participle. *Happily* is an adverb modifying *singing.* The remainder of the phrase is the complement of *singing.*

> *Driven into a corner by the dog,* the cat hissed defiance.

This is a **past participial phrase** used as an adjective to modify *cat. Driven* is the past participle. *Into the corner* and *by the dog* are prepositional phrases modifying *driven.*

Infinitive Phrase

An **infinitive phrase** contains an infinitive and possible modifiers or an object or both. It functions as a *noun,* an *adjective,* or an *adverb.*

> *To live a good life* was his only ambition.

Functioning as a noun, this phrase is the subject of the verb *was*. *To live* is the infinitive. *Life* is the object of the infinitive. *A* and *good* are adjectives modifying *life*.

She had a lifetime ambition *to live in style*.

This is an adjective phrase modifying *ambition* (describing her ambition). *In style* is an adverbial prepositional phrase modifying the infinitive.

It was much too cold *to go outdoors*.

This is an adverbial phrase modifying the adjective *cold*. *Outdoors* is an adverb modifying the infinitive.

> **PITFALL**
>
> Do not consider an infinitive phrase to be a complete sentence.
>
> WRONG: To visit every famous museum, castle, and cathedral in the entire world.
>
> CORRECT: To visit every famous museum, castle, and cathedral in the entire world *is my ambition*.

Note: Unlike other verbals, an infinitive **may** have a subject, as well as complements and modifiers:

They asked *me to visit* them next week.
(*me* is the subject of the infinitive *to visit*)

Do you want *them to mail* the birth announcements?
(*them* is the subject of the infinitive *to mail*)

When an infinitive has a subject, the structure is called an **infinitive clause.**

Verb Phrase

A **verb phrase** is any group of verbal units that functions as a single verb.

I *can do* it.   You *should be* happily *married*.

Gerund Phrase

A **gerund phrase** is introduced by a gerund and acts as a noun.

Flying a kite is easy at the seashore.

Flying is the gerund. *Kite* is its object. The phrase is the subject of the sentence.

CLAUSES

A **clause** is a group of words containing a subject and a predicate. It is not a sentence only because it is part of a sentence and so is not complete in itself.

Independent Clause

An **independent clause** (sometimes called a *main clause*) is one that could stand by itself and be written as a sentence; such a sentence is called a *simple sentence*.

> SIMPLE: *I am always late to dinner.*
> INDEPENDENT CLAUSE: *I am always late to dinner* because the bus is so slow.

Dependent Clause

A **dependent** (or *subordinate*) **clause** cannot stand alone because it depends on something else in the complete sentence.

> I am always late to dinner *because the bus is so slow.*

PITFALL

Do not write a dependent clause without a complete independent clause in the same sentence.

> WRONG: No point in doing anything if nothing could be done about it.
> CORRECT: *There was* no point in doing anything if nothing could be done about it.

Since they depend on something else in the sentence, dependent clauses function as *nouns, adjectives,* or *adverbs*.

NOUN CLAUSES

He hoped *that he would pass the course.* (object of verb *hoped*)
Why he did it was not clear to anybody. (subject of verb *was*)

ADJECTIVE CLAUSES

The money *that I lost* was quickly replaced. (modifies noun *money*)
I admire a person *who knows his way around.* (modifies noun *person*)

ADVERBIAL CLAUSES

He was pleased *that he could master the problem.* (modifies adjective *pleased*)
She cried *when he went away.* (modifies verb *cried*)

They work better *than we do.* (modifies adverb *better*)

9 ■ Types of Sentences

Simple Sentence

A **simple sentence** is the same as an independent clause standing alone. It actually contains no clauses:

> They all enjoyed their trip to Canada.

Complex Sentence

A **complex sentence** is composed of one independent clause and one or more dependent clauses. The dependent clauses are italicized in the following complex sentences:

> The opera, *which was written by Wagner,* didn't end until midnight.
> *While I was waiting for the train,* an old man *who reminded me of my grand-father* entertained me with stories of people *who had lived in the neighborhood years ago.*

Compound Sentence

A **compound sentence** contains two or more independent clauses and no dependent clauses. Numbers in parentheses indicate the beginnings of the clauses in the following sentences:

> (1) The flowers were blooming, (2) the birds were singing, (3) and spring was in the air.
> (1) There is one important rule in this factory: (2) haste makes waste.
> (1) Lord Gladstone rose to speak; (2) the house listened attentively.

PITFALL

Do not combine two sentences into one by attempting to make a single word do double duty.

WRONG:	It is difficult to explain what he came for he was extremely bewildered about everything.
CORRECT:	It is difficult to explain what he came for. For he was extremely bewildered about everything.

Compound-Complex Sentence

A **compound-complex sentence** contains two or more independent clauses and one or more dependent clauses. In the following sentences, the dependent clauses are italicized:

Men *who are wise* are often mistaken, and fools are sometimes right.

The captain, *who was standing on the bridge,* thought he saw a shape looming ahead in the fog, but it turned out to be only an illusion *which fooled his tired eyes.*

10 ▪ Obtaining Agreement of Subject and Verb

RULE

A singular subject requires a singular form of the verb.
A plural subject requires a plural form of the verb.

PITFALL: Singular Pronouns

Even when the sense of the subject seems to be plural, the following pronouns are singular: *each, every, everybody, anybody, anyone, nobody, no one, someone, either, neither, one.*

CORRECT: Everybody *is coming* to the party.
Neither of the two sisters *is* really attractive.
One of the men *is* already here.

PITFALL: Singular-Plural Pronouns

With *some, most,* and *none,* a singular verb is used when the sense is a single quantity. Use a plural verb when a number of individual units seem to be implied.

CORRECT: Most of the sugar *is* stored in the warehouse.
Most of the apples *are* rotten.
None of the cereal *has* been eaten.
None of the guests *are* going to stay all night.

PITFALL: Compound Subjects

When the parts of a compound subject are joined by *and,* the verb must be plural because at least two subjects are involved.

CORRECT: The house and the barn *are* for sale.
CORRECT: The captain and his men *are* ready to set sail.
CORRECT: The men and their captain *are* ready to set sail.

50

PITFALL: Compound Subjects

When the parts of a compound subject are joined by *either . . . or* or *neither . . . nor,* the verb agrees with the part of the compound subject which is nearest to it.

CORRECT: Either the whole engine or some of its parts *are* defective.

CORRECT: Neither the students nor the instructor *agrees* with the principal.

RULE: Singular-Plural Nouns as Subjects

Some nouns like *committee, crew, jury, club* are sometimes singular and sometimes plural in meaning. As a general principle, use a singular verb if the form of the noun is singular. Use a singular verb if all the members of the named group are acting as a unit. If they are being thought of as individuals, it is usually less awkward to substitute another noun.

CORRECT: The club *meets* every Friday.

CORRECT· The *members of the jury* find themselves in disagreement.

CORRECT: The *jurors* find themselves in disagreement.

PITFALL: Subjects Separated From or Following Verbs

Use special care when the subject does not immediately precede the verb. Be sure the verb agrees with the subject wherever it appears in the sentence.

WRONG: The *house* which is surrounded by junkyards and filling stations *are* going to be sold.

CORRECT: The *house* which is surrounded by junkyards and filling stations *is* going to be sold.

WRONG: The *leader* together with his twenty followers *are* approaching the town.

CORRECT: The *leader* together with his twenty followers *is* approaching the town.

WRONG: How many coats, shoes, and dresses *do she* own?

CORRECT: How many coats, shoes, and dresses *does she* own?

WRONG: There *is* too many *cars* in the city streets.

CORRECT: There *are* too many *cars* in the city streets.

NOTE: *There* is called an expletive. It is not to be confused with the subject although it usually immediately precedes the verb. When a sentence is introduced by *there*, the verb nearly always precedes the subject and agrees with it.

There *are cars* in the street.

PITFALL: Number and Predicate Nominative

On rare occasions, the subject of a sentence and the predicate nominative may not agree in number. Nevertheless, the verb must agree with the subject in number.

CORRECT: Our greatest *asset is* the many loyal customers who buy regularly from us.

CORRECT: Our many loyal *customers are* our greatest asset.

11 ■ Clarity in Sentence Construction

A good sentence is a tightly constructed sentence where the meaning is unmistakably clear.

RULE

To avoid flabby sentences, keep all modifiers close to the words they modify, and be sure that no modifier is left without a definite word to modify or describe.

PITFALL: Dangling Phrases

Such phrases are called *dangling* because they are connected to nothing. The writer knows what they refer to and the reader can usually guess, but the reader will know that he is reading the work of an inept writer.

DANGLING:	Driving through the rain, the street lights were scarcely visible.
AMUSED READER:	Were the street lights driving a car or a bus?
TIGHTENED·	Driving through the rain, I could hardly see the street lights.
DANGLING:	To learn how to care for pets, hamsters are ideal to begin with.
AMUSED READER:	I didn't know that hamsters had pets.
TIGHTENED:	To learn how to care for pets, children should begin with hamsters.

PITFALL: Ambiguous Modifiers

Avoid placing modifiers in such a position in a sentence that they may apply to either a preceding or following word.

AMBIGUOUS·	We decided *in the morning* to pack the car and take a long trip.

QUESTION:	Was the decision made in the morning or is the packing planned for the morning?
SOLUTION:	In the morning, we decided to pack the car and take a long trip.
SOLUTION:	We decided to pack the car in the morning and take a long trip.

PITFALL: Remote Modifiers

Remote modifiers are those which are so far removed from the word or words they describe that meaning becomes unclear.

REMOTE:	He said that he was willing to sign the contract *yesterday.*
COMMENT:	Clear if *yesterday* is meant to apply to the signing of the contract but misleading if the intended meaning was that he made the remark *yesterday.*
TIGHTENED:	He said yesterday that he was willing to sign the contract.

REMOTE:	He took two aspirin tablets to cure his headache which made him feel much better.
COMMENT:	If his headache made him feel much better, why did he want to cure it?
TIGHTENED:	To cure his headache, he took two aspirin tablets which made him feel much better.

PITFALL: One Word For Two

Don't make a single word do double duty in a sentence.

DOUBLE DUTY:	The famous mathematician was baffled *for* a minute the problem seemed insoluble.
CLARIFIED:	The famous mathematician was baffled *for* a minute, *for* the problem seemed insoluble.

PITFALL: Meaningless Repetition

If a connecting word has already been used, don't repeat it even though it seems to come naturally.

REPEATED:	He had so many friends that there were scores of people *to* whom he thought he could appeal *to* for advice.
CORRECTION:	He had so many friends that there were scores of people *to* whom he thought he could appeal for advice.

PITFALL: Mixed Verb Tenses

Don't mix verb tenses without reason. Keep all verbs in the same tense in relating a sequence of events.

MIXED TENSES: John *ran* to the store, *bought* a bag of oranges, and *walked* slowly home. The grocer *noticed* that he *had* a Canadian nickel in his till and *wonders* if he *had gotten* it from John.

CORRECTION: *wonders* should be *wondered*.

COMMENT: *had gotten* is past perfect tense because the event occurred before he wondered.

PITFALL: Mixed Clause Structure

Don't combine clauses that make a statement with clauses that ask a question.

MIXED CLAUSES: They asked me (declarative) would I run for councilman (interrogative).

CORRECTED: They asked me if I would run for councilman.

PITFALL: Omission of *other*

Do not omit *other* after *than* when comparing two members of the same class.

OMITTED: She was taller than any girl in her club.

QUESTION: Taller even than herself? She was a member of the club.

CORRECTED: She was taller than any *other* girl in her club.

PITFALL: Inconsistent Comparisons

Even though the meaning is understandable, do not compare things which are not really comparable.

INCONSISTENT: The motor in the Elixir Vacuum Cleaner is more powerful than any other cleaner.

QUESTION: A motor is more powerful than a cleaner?

SOLUTION: The motor in the Elixir Vacuum Cleaner is more powerful than *that of* any other cleaner.

PITFALL: Comparative for Two; Superlative for Three or More

Do not use the comparative form to compare more than two; do not use the superlative form to compare fewer than three.

INCORRECT
COMPARATIVE: He is the *oldest* of the two brothers.

CORRECT
COMPARATIVE: He is the *older* of the two brothers.

INCORRECT
SUPERLATIVE: She is the *older* of the three sisters.

CORRECT
SUPERLATIVE: She is the *oldest* of the three sisters.

PITFALL: Omission of Necessary Articles or Possessive Pronouns

When two or more terms are in parallel construction and refer to separate people or things, be sure to supply an article or appropriate possessive pronoun for each of the terms.

OMITTED ARTICLE: He bought a brown and gray coat.

COMMENT: This is correct if the same coat was brown and gray.

SUPPLIED ARTICLE: He bought a brown and *a* gray coat.

OMITTED PRONOUN: She always consulted her maid and accountant about her income tax.

COMMENT: This is correct if the maid was her accountant.

SUPPLIED PRONOUN: She always consulted her maid and *her* accountant about her income tax.

PITFALL: Omission of Necessary Prepositions

Usually it is sufficient to use a single preposition to connect two parallel words to the object of the preposition, but occasionally because of idiomatic prepositional usage, the same preposition is not suitable to both of the parallel words.

CORRECT: She spoke about her love and admiration *for* her father.

COMMENT: *Love for her father* and *admiration for her father* are both correct.

INCOMPLETE: She spoke of her confidence and love *for* her father.

COMMENT: The idiom is *confidence in,* not *confidence for.*

COMPLETE: She spoke of her confidence *in* and love *for* her father.

PITFALL: Omission of Part of a Verb Phrase

When two parts of a compound verb are in different tenses, be sure that each tense is completely expressed.

INCOMPLETE: The food at the party will probably be good because it always has.

COMPLETE: The food at the party will probably be good because it always has *been.*

INCOMPLETE: Many of our clients have and probably will be unable to pay their bills.

COMPLETE: Many of our clients have *been* and probably will be unable to pay their bills.

PITFALL: Omission of *that* after Certain Verbs

When verbs like *saying, thinking, hoping, feeling, wishing* introduce a dependent noun clause as object of the verb, the dependent clause should be introduced by *that*.

OMITTED:	She thought her husband was not good enough for her.
CORRECTED:	She thought *that* her husband was not good enough for her.
OMITTED:	He believed his friend would not desert him.
CORRECTED:	He believed *that* his friend would not desert him.

12 ■ Sentence Word Order

NORMAL WORD ORDER IN ENGLISH

In English many words like adjectives and adverbs have only one form. Nouns have only singular and plural forms. Only verbs and most pronouns have anything like the several forms of a single word that occur in Latin and ancient Greek. For this reason, the position of a word in a sentence frequently determines its meaning in relation to the entire sentence. In "Home is a nice place," the word *home* is the subject because it precedes the verb. In "He bought a new home," the word *home* is the object of the verb *bought* because it follows the verb. In "He went home," the same word is an adverb telling where he went because it follows the intransitive verb *went*.

RULE

Normal sentence word order in English is subject—verb—complement.

John ate *dinner.*	(object of verb *ate*)
John is *boss.*	(predicate noun)
John is *sick.*	(predicate adjective)

PITFALL

The expletives *here* and *there* usually precede the verb which is followed by the subject.

Here is your *hat.*   (subject in italics)
There are *dozens* of roses in the garden.   (subject in italics)

Order of Direct and Indirect Objects

1. Direct objects usually precede indirect objects.

We gave the check to him.

2. If only the indirect object is a pronoun, it may precede the direct object noun(s) but without the word *to.*

We gave him the check.

3. If both the direct and indirect objects are pronouns, then direct precedes indirect.

We gave it to him.

Modifiers

RULE

Modifiers are placed as close as possible to the words they modify. Adjectives usually precede the words they modify.

---

the *tall* building   the *sick old* man

Example of a declarative sentence with modifiers:
The strong smell of gas which pervaded all the rooms of the house quickly drove the guests at the party out into the street.

RULE

Adjective phrases or clauses usually follow the words they modify.

The man *in the dark suit*   (adjective phrase)
The woman *who was in the grocery store*   (adjective clause)

RULE

Adverbs usually follow the verbs they modify.

She ran *rapidly*.   (adverb)
She ran *into the house*.   (adverbial phrase)
She ran *when she saw her mother coming*.   (adverbial clause)

PITFALL: Single Adverbs

Single adverbs of one, two, or three syllables often precede the verbs they modify.
They *rapidly* took advantage of the situation.
Single adverbs are usually inserted after the first element of a verb phrase.
They *will* really *have* trouble.   (verb phrase in italics)
He *has* certainly *been trying* hard.   (verb phrase in italics)

Single adverbs modifying adjectives or other adverbs precede the words they modify.

His uncle was *very* rich.   (modifies adjective *rich*)
The train was *extraordinarily* fast.   (modifies adjective *fast*)
He finished his work *more* quickly than the others.   (modifies adverb *quickly*)

PITFALL: Dependent Phrases and Clauses

For variety of sentence structure, or for emphasis, dependent phrases and clauses frequently precede the subject.

In the late afternoon, Father usually took a nap.   (dependent phrase)
When they discovered their mistake, the workmen tried to correct it.   (dependent clause)

Exclamations

RULE

How as an exclamation requires an adjective or an adverb immediately following it. Note the word order: How—adjective or adverb—declarative sentence.

How beautiful the weather is here in Hawaii!
How well he plays the guitar!

RULE

What a as an exclamation is immediately followed by a noun or an adjective. *What a* is always singular.

What a beautiful day! What a day!

The plural form of *What a* is *What*, followed immediately by a noun or an adjective.

What beautiful clouds! What clouds!

Negative

No and *not* are the usual words to express negation.

He has *no* money left. (*no* before noun)
We will *not* go there tomorrow. (*not* before verb)

RULE

With all verbs *except* certain modal auxiliaries (e.g., *can, must, have, be,* etc.), the negative of the present and past tenses is expressed by using a form of the verb *to do* as an auxiliary for the verb being negated.

I *do not want* to go there now.
She *did not see* Mary at the airport.

The verb *to do* is not used with modal auxiliaries.

I *will not be* here next week.
Campuss, the cat, *was not running* from the dog.
We *must not do* that.
Felix *can't* (cannot) *go* out tonight.
They *have not done* what is expected of them.

RULE

In informal usage, the contraction *n't* is more frequently used than *not* with modal auxiliaries: *to be, can, to do, to have, must,* etc.

Contraction	Negative	Example
aren't	are not	They *aren't* able to come.
can't	cannot	They *can't* come.
couldn't	could not	He *couldn't* care less about his future.
didn't	did not	He *didn't* want to join the club.
doesn't	does not	He *doesn't* want to join the club.
don't	do not	They *don't* want to join the club.
hasn't	has not	He *hasn't* any money.
hadn't	had not	He *hadn't* enough time to pack before the train came.
haven't	have not	We *haven't* anything in the house for dessert.
isn't	is not	He *isn't* interested in her.
mustn't	must not	They *mustn't* think that we avoided them.
shan't (rare)	shall not	He *shan't* get any of my money.
shouldn't	should not	He *shouldn't* expect the impossible.
wasn't	was not	She *wasn't* able to complete her assignment.

weren't	were not	They *weren't* expecting him to come.
wouldn't	would not	He insisted that he *wouldn't* do the job.
won't	will not	She *won't* come even if you beg her to be agreeable.

Questions

INTERROGATIVE WORD ORDER

RULE

The subject is usually placed after the first word of a verb phrase.

PRESENT TENSE:	Is the train coming?
	Is Paul coming to dinner?
	Does he know the way?
	Have you any money?
	May I borrow your eraser?
	Which book does she want?
	What do they have for breakfast?
FUTURE TENSE:	Will Paul come to dinner?
	Whose book will you borrow?
	What will they have for breakfast?
PAST TENSE:	Was Paul eating his dinner?
	Was the train on time?
	Did he know the way?
	Whom did you see there?
	What did they have for breakfast?
PRESENT PERFECT TENSE:	Has Paul eaten his dinner?
	Have I finished the assignment?
	Has he been working regularly?
PAST PERFECT TENSE:	Had he eaten his dinner?
	Had I finished the assignment?
	Had he been working regularly?
FUTURE PERFECT TENSE:	Will he have eaten his dinner?
	Will I have finished the assignment?
	Will he have been working regularly?

OTHER INTERROGATIVE FORMS

A statement may end by asking negatively for listener's or reader's agreement.

They have all gone to the movies, *haven't they*?
The window was closed, *wasn't it*?
He did know what to do, *didn't he*?

You would do that, *wouldn't you?*
She is coming to see us, *isn't she?*
I am expected there at seven o'clock, *am I not?*

A declarative sentence used as a question is so indicated by a rising voice intonation pattern in speaking or by a question mark in writing.

You believe that I am not telling the truth?
He is arriving tonight?
The plane is on time?

SPECIAL AIDS AND OTHER CONCERNS

13 ■ Abbreviations

A.B.	Bachelor of Arts
A.C.	alternating current
A.D.	at the birth of Christ
AK	Alaska
AL	Alabama
A.M.	before noon
Apr.	April
AR	Arkansas
Ass'n.	association
Ass't.	assistant
Aug.	August
Ave.	avenue
AZ	Arizona
b.	born
B.C.	before Christ
Blvd.	boulevard
B.S.	Bachelor of Science
c., ca.	about
CA	California
Capt.	Captain
cf.	compare
ch.	chapter, chapters
Co.	company
CO	Colorado
Col.	Colonel
conj.	conjunction
Corp.	Corporation
CT	Connecticut
d.	died
D.C.	District of Columbia, direct current
D.D.	Doctor of Divinity

D.D.S.	Doctor of Dental Surgery
DE	Delaware
Dec.	December
Dem.	Democrat
dep't.	department
doz.	dozen
Dr.	Doctor, Drive
D.S.	Doctor of Science
E.	East
ed.	editor, edition, edited by
Ed.D.	Doctor of Education
e.g.	for example
esp.	especially
Esq.	Esquire
et al.	and others, and elsewhere
etc.	and so forth
ex.	example
f.	and the following page
F.	Fahrenheit
Feb.	February
ff.	and the following pages
fig.	figure
fl.	flourished
FL	Florida
Fri.	Friday
ft.	foot, feet
GA.	Georgia
Gen.	General
G.O.P.	Grand Old Party (Republican)
Gov.	Governor
gov't.	government
GU	Guam

HI	Hawaii	ME	Maine
Hon.	Honorable	M.E.	Mechanical Engineer
h.p.	horsepower	Messrs.	plural of *Mr.*
hr.	hour	mg.	milligram
hrs.	hours	mgr.	manager
		MI	Michigan
I.	Island	MN	Minnesota
IA	Iowa	MO	Missouri
ibid.	the same	Mon.	Monday
ID	Idaho	M.P.	Military Police, Member of
idem.	the same		Parliament
i.e.	that is	m.p.h.	miles per hour
IL	Illinois	Mr.	mister
IN	Indiana	Mrs.	missus
in.	inch	ms.	manuscript
Inc.	Incorporated	Ms.	miss or missus
I.Q.	Intelligence Quotient	MS	Mississippi
		M.S.	Master of Science
Jan.	January	mss.	manuscripts
Jr.	Junior	mt.	mountain
Jul.	July	MT	Montana
Jun.	June	n.	noun
		N.	North
kg.	kilogram	N.B.	Note well
km.	kilometer	NC	North Carolina
KS	Kansas	n.d.	no date
KY	Kentucky	ND	North Dakota
		NE	Nebraska
l.	line	NE	Northeast
LA.	Louisiana	NH	New Hampshire
lat.	latitude	NJ	New Jersey
lb.	pound	NM	New Mexico
lbs.	pounds	No.	number
ll.	lines	Nov.	November
LL.D.	Doctor of Laws	NV	Nevada
log.	logarithm	NW	Northwest
long.	longitude	N.Y.	New York
Lt.	Lieutenant		
ltd.	limited	Oct.	October
		OH	Ohio
m.	meter, married	OK	Oklahoma
MA	Massachusetts	O.K.	all right
M.A.	Master of Arts	OR	Oregon
Mar.	March	oz.	ounce
MD	Maryland	p.	page
M.D.	Medical Doctor	PA	Pennsylvania
mdse.	merchandise	par.	paragraph

pd.	paid	**St.**	Street, Saint
Ph.D.	Doctor of Philosophy	**Ste.**	Saint (feminine)
pkg.	package	**Sun.**	Sunday
pl.	plural	**SW**	Southwest
P.M.	after noon	**syn.**	synonym
pp.	pages		
PR	Puerto Rico	**Thurs.**	Thursday
prep.	preposition	**TN**	Tennessee
pron.	pronoun	**tr.**	translated by
P.S.	postscript	**Tues.**	Tuesday
pseud.	pseudonym	**TV**	television
pt.	part	**TX**	Texas
pub.	published by		
Pvt.	Private	**U.S.**	United States
		U.S.A.	United States of America
q.v.	which see	**UT**	Utah
R.C.	Roman Catholic	**v.**	verb, verse
reg.	registered	**VA**	Virginia
Rev.	Reverend	**VI**	Virgin Islands
RI	Rhode Island	**viz.**	namely
R.N.	Registered Nurse	**vol.**	volume
R.S.V.P.	Please reply.	**vs.**	opposite
		VT	Vermont
S.	South		
Sat.	Saturday	**W.**	West
SC	South Carolina	**WA**	Washington
SD	South Dakota	**Wed.**	Wednesday
SE	Southeast	**WI**	Wisconsin
Sept.	September	**Wm.**	William
Sgt.	Sergeant	**WV**	West Virginia
sing.	singular	**WY**	Wyoming
sp.	spelling		
sq.	square	**yd.**	yard
Sr.	Senior		

14 ■ Contractions

A **contraction** is a word made up of two words combined into one by omitting one or more letters. Contractions are used in conversation and in informal writing.

RULE

Contractions should be confined to forms consisting of subject pronouns joined with a verb or to forms consisting of a verb with the negative.

Contraction	Meaning	Contraction	Meaning
aren't	are not	shan't	shall not (rare)
can't	cannot	she'd	she would
couldn't	could not	she'll	she will
didn't	did not	she's	she is, she has
doesn't	does not	shouldn't	should not
don't	do not	they'd	they would
hadn't	had not	they'll	they will
hasn't	has not	they're	they are
haven't	have not	they've	they have
he'd	he would	wasn't	was not
he'll	he will	we'd	we would
he's	he is, he has	we'll	we will
I'd	I would	we're	we are
I'll	I shall, I will	weren't	were not
I'm	I am	we've	we have
isn't	is not	won't	will not
it's	it is	wouldn't	would not
I've	I have	you'd	you would
mightn't	might not	you'll	you will
mustn't	must not	you're·	you are
		you've	you have

67

PITFALL

Do not use contractions with nouns. Use only subject pronouns, *not* nouns, with contractions.

INCORRECT:	Bob's going now.
CORRECT:	Bob is going now.
INCORRECT:	The student's listening.
CORRECT:	The student is listening.
INCORRECT:	What'll he write?
CORRECT:	What will he write?

15 ■ Glossary of Troublesome Words and Phrases

a, an
: Use *a* before words beginning with a consonant sound: *a book, a unique ring.* Use *an* before words beginning with a vowel sound: *an apple, an urchin.*

accept, except
: *Accept* means to *receive:* "Please *accept* my offer." The verb *except* means to *leave out* or *omit:* "Will you *except* the last provision of the contract?"

adverse, averse
: *Adverse* means *opposing: adverse circumstances. Averse* means *opposed to:* "He was *averse* to my proposal." *Adverse* usually relates to actions or things. *Averse* usually applies to people (who have an aversion).

advert, avert
: *Advert* means *refer:* "The speaker *adverted* to an earlier talk he had given." *Avert* means *ward off:* "He narrowly *averted* a bad fall."

advice, advise
: *Advice* is a noun meaning *recommendation concerning an action* or *decision:* "Few people will take my *advice* when I give it to them." *Advise* is a verb: "I *advise* you to take fewer courses next year."

affect, effect
: *Affect* means *to influence:* "His attitude in class *affected* his grade." *Affect* is never used as a noun except in psychological terminology. *Effect* as a noun means *result:* "The *effect* of the explosion was disastrous." *Effect* as a verb means *to accomplish:* "The new machinery *effected* a decided improvement in the product."

aggravate
: Do not use *aggravate* to mean *irritate. Aggravate* means *to make a bad situation worse:* "I was *irritated* by his behavior when he came in; I became really *aggravated* with him after he slammed the door when he went out."

aggravation
: *Aggravation* means *an act or circumstance that increases the gravity or seriousness of a situation:* "His job was difficult enough without the unexpected *aggravation* of overtime work."

69

agree to, with	Good usage suggests that we *agree to an idea or to a proposal,* etc., and that *we agree with a person:* "I agree *with him* and *to his suggestion.*"
almost, most	*Almost* means *nearly:* "He was *almost* ready when we called for him." "*Almost* every girl in the class had long hair." *Most* as an adjective or adverb means *in the greatest degree:* "A *most* difficult problem was presented." "*Most* people prefer sunny climates." *Most* as a noun means *the largest number* or *the greatest quantity:* "The food will be given to those who need it the *most.*" *Most* must not precede an indefinite pronoun, e.g. Incorrect: "*Most everybody* wants that job." Correct: "*Almost* everybody..."
all ready, already	*All ready* (two words) is used in such sentences as "They are *all ready* to go,*" meaning *all of them* are ready. *Already* is an adverb meaning *previously:* "We ran to catch the train, but it had *already* left."
alright	Illiterate for *all right.* Do not confuse the spelling with words like *almost, already, altogether.*
altogether, all together	*All together* (two words) is used in such sentences as "They were *all together* in the same room," meaning *all of them* were together. *Altogether* is an adverb meaning *completely:* "You are *altogether* wrong in your assumption."
allusion illusion	*Allusion* means *reference:* "He made an *allusion* to last week's meeting." *Illusion* is *an unreality:* "That a pair of railroad tracks seem to meet in the distance is an optical *illusion.*"
alternative, choice	*Alternative* means *a choice in a situation where a choice must be made:* "If you can't take the test tomorrow, your only *alternative* is to receive a zero."
alumnus, alumna alumni alumnae	An *alumnus* is *a male graduate. Alumni* is the plural. An *alumna* is *a female graduate. Alumnae* is the plural. *Alumni* is used for male and female combined.
among, between	*Between* is used in connection with two persons or things: "He divided the money *between* his two children." *Among* is used for more than two: "He divided the money *among* his three children." EXCEPTIONS: If more than two are involved in a united situation, *between* is used: "*Between* the four of us, we raised a thousand dollars." If a comparison or an opposition is involved, *between* is used: "There was great rivalry *between* the three colleges. It was difficult to choose *between* them."
amount, number	*Amount* refers to *bulk* or *quantity: amount* of sugar, grain, flour, money. *Number* refers to *objects which are thought of as indi-*

vidual units: number of oranges, children, diamonds. Notice that most words following *amount* are singular (*coal, butter, water*) and that most words following *number* are plural (*apples, bottles, glasses*).

any one, anyone	*Any one* means *any single person* or *thing of a group:* "*Any one* of the students in the class was capable of passing the course." *Anyone* is an indefinite pronoun meaning *anybody:* "*Anyone* can tell that you are not so stupid as you pretend."
appraise, apprise	*Appraise* means *to make an estimate:* "Will you *appraise* the value of this ring?" *Apprise* means *inform* (usually in a formal sense): "He was *apprised* by registered mail that his lease would not be renewed."
apt, liable, likely	*Apt* refers to *a habitual disposition:* "Having a good brain, he is *apt* to get good grades." *Likely* merely *expresses probability:* "It is *likely* to rain." *Liable* implies *the probability of something unfortunate:* "The firm is *liable* to fail."
as . . . as, so . . . as	*As . . . as* is used for affirmative comparisons. "He was *as* tall *as* his father." *So . . . as* is used for negative comparisons: "She was not *so* tall *as* her mother."
as, like, as if	When used as a preposition, *like* should never introduce a clause (NOT *like I was saying*). When introducing a clause, *as* is used (*as I was saying*) even if some of the words of the clause are implied: "He did it as well *as* I [did]. "They acted *as if* they were guilty."
beside, besides	*Beside* means *by the side of:* "Ask him to sit *beside* me." *Besides* means *in addition:* "She was an expert secretary. *Besides*, she had a wonderful disposition."
bring, take, fetch, carry	*Bring* refers *to action toward the writer* or *speaker:* "*Bring* the book to me." *Take* refers *to action away from the writer* or *speaker:* "*Take* this bottle back to the store."*Fetch* means *to go and get something and bring it back.* "If you throw the stick into the lake, the dog will *fetch* it." However, *get* is usually substituted for *fetch*. *Carry* means *to convey from one place to another regardless of direction:* "We need a suitcase to *carry* all our clothes."
can, may	*Can* implies *ability:* "*Can* you (are you able to) lift that heavy box?" *May* denotes *permission:* "*May* I (Have I permission to) swim in your pool?"
claim, assert	*Claim* refers *to a justified demand* or *legal right:* "I *claim* this piece of property." "I *claim* the prize." It should not be used when only an assertion is intended: "He *asserted* (not *claimed*) that his demands were reasonable."

71

compare to, compare with	*Compare to* is used *to indicate a definite resemblance:* "He compared the railroad *to* a highway." *Compare with* is used *to indicate an examination of similarities and dissimilarities:* "He compared the middle ages *with* modern times."
complement, compliment	*Complement* as a verb means *complete:* "He needed a typewriter to *complement* his office equipment." As a noun *complement* means *whatever is needed for completion:* "I am sending you fifty books as a *complement* to your law library." It can also mean whatever is needed to complete an operation: "The officers and crew are the *complement* of a ship." *Compliment* is a noun meaning *an expression of admiration:* "He paid her the *compliment* of saying that she had exquisite taste in clothes."
common, mutual	*Common* means *shared by two or more people* or *things:* "The classmates had a *common* admiration for their school." "All the houses in the development had a big recreation area in *common*." *Mutual* means *reciprocal:* "The classmates had a *mutual* admiration for each other."
consul, council, counsel	A *consul* is *a government agent who lives in a foreign country* to protect the interests of the citizens of his own country: "When I lost my passport, I went immediately to the *consul*." *Council* is a *group* of individuals who act in an advisory capacity or who meet for the purposes of discussion or decision-making: "The mayor met with the *council*." "They called a *council* to make plans for the future." *Counsel* as a noun means *advice*, or, in legal parlance, a lawyer or lawyers: "He sought my *counsel*." "He retained *counsel* to represent him at the trial." As a verb *counsel* means *advise:* "I would *counsel* you to accept his offer."
councilor, counselor	A *councilor* is *a member of a council*. A *counselor* is an *adviser*. The term is also used to denote a leader, guardian, or supervisor of children or young people as at a summer camp.
contemptuous, contemptible	*Contemptuous* means *showing contempt:* "My teacher was contemptuous of my performance." *Contemptible* means *deserving of contempt:* "His rude behavior at the wedding was *contemptible*."
continual, continuous	*Continual* means *constantly with interruptions:* "She smoked *continually*." *Continuous* means *without interruptions:* "The water flows *continuously* over Niagara Falls."
credible, creditable, credulous	*Credible* means *believable:* "His story was entirely *credible*." *Creditable* means *meritorious, praiseworthy*—but *not outstanding:* "His performance was *creditable*, but I wouldn't pay admission to hear him again." *Credulous* means *ready to believe:* "Being a *credulous* person, he believed everything he read."

different from	*Different from* is the correct idiom, NOT *different than.*
differ from, differ with	*Differ from* applies to differences between one person or thing and another or others: "My car *differs from* his because it is a newer model." *Differ with* means *to have a difference in opinion:* "I *differ with* him in his views about government."
dominate, domineer	*Dominate* means *to rule over:* "He *dominated* the audience with his oratory." *Domineer* means *to rule tyrannically:* "One of his daughters *domineered* over the entire family."
don't	*Don't* is the contraction of *do not: I don't, you don't, we don't, they don't.* Do not confuse it with *doesn't,* the contraction of *does not: He doesn't, she doesn't, it doesn't.*
dual, duel	*Dual* means *double:* "Since he was born in England of American parents, he could lay claim to *dual* citizenship." A *duel* is a combat between two men: "He challenged his enemy to a *duel* with pistols."
due to	*Due to* acts grammatically as an adjective. It usually follows a form of the verb *to be,* and must therefore modify a specific noun or pronoun: "The flood was *due to* the rapid spring thaw." If there is no specific noun or pronoun for *due* to modify, use the phrase *because of:* "He was late *because of* an accident." Or rephrase the sentence: "His *lateness* [noun] was *due to* an accident."
elicit, illicit	*Elicit* means *to draw* or *bring forth:* "After hours of questioning, they *elicited* the truth from him." *Illicit* is an adjective meaning *not permitted* or *illegal:* "Traffic in drugs is *illicit.*"
emigrant, immigrant, migrant	A *migrant* is *a member of a mass movement of people from one region to another.* A migrant who leaves a country or place of residence is called an *emigrant;* one who comes in is an *immigrant.*
fewer, less	*Fewer* is used in connection with people or with objects which are thought of as individual units: *fewer oranges, fewer children, fewer books, fewer dollars. Less* is used in connection with the concept of bulk: *less money, less coal, less weight, less grain.* Notice that most words following *fewer* are plural (*oranges, books, dollars*); most words following *less* are singular (*money, coal, weight*).
flaunt, flout	*Flaunt* means *to display in an ostentatious fashion:* "He *flaunted* his learning before his friends." *Flout* means *to treat with contempt:* "They *flouted* the law by parking in front of a hydrant."
forcible, forceful	*Forcible* means *effected by force,* no matter how much or how little force is used: "Since the key wouldn't fit, they made a *forcible* entry into the house by breaking a window." *Forceful* means full of force: "He was a very *forceful* speaker."

former, latter	*Former* and *latter* are used to designate one of two persons or things: "Of the two possibilities, I prefer the *former* to the *latter*." If more than two persons or things are involved, *first* or *first named* and *last* or *last named* are used: "He had a choice of yellow, rose, pink, and brown. He preferred the *first* and *last* to the others."
formerly, formally	*Formerly* means *at an earlier time:* "He is a rich man, but he was *formerly* poor." *Formally* means done *in a very correct manner:* "He was *formally* inducted into the lodge."
farther, further	*Farther* means *more distant:* "One town is *farther* from here than the other one." *Further* means to a *greater degree:* "Let me consider your advice *further*."
had ought	*Ought* is known as a defective verb because it has only one form and cannot be used with an auxiliary: "They *ought* (NOT *had ought*) to have told her."
hanged, hung	*Hanged* is used in connection with executions: "He was condemned to be *hanged* by the neck until dead." *Hung* is the past tense of *hang* and denotes any other kind of suspension: "The pictures were *hung* on the wall."
hardly	Like *barely* and *scarcely*, *hardly* should not be used with a negative. "He was *hardly* (*barely*, *scarcely*) able to do it." (NOT *not hardly, barely, scarcely*.)
healthful, healthy	*Healthful* means *health-giving:* a *healthful* climate. *Healthy* means *in a state of health:* "She was a *healthy* young girl."
imply, infer	*Imply* means *to throw out a hint or suggestion:* "She *implied* by her manner that she was unhappy." *Infer* means *to take in a hint or suggestion:* "I *inferred* from her manner that she was unhappy."
in, into	*In* means *within; into* means *from the outside to the inside:* "The paper is *in* the drawer." "I threw the trash *into* the wastebasket."
indict, indite	*Indict* means *to make a formal charge of an offense as a means of bringing a suspect to trial:* "He was *indicted* for evasion of income tax." *Indite* means to compose a formal or literary work: "Robert Frost *indited* many poems about New England."
ingenious, ingenuous	*Ingenious* means *possessing unusual powers of invention* when applied to a person and showing the result of clever inventiveness when applied to a thing: "The *ingenious* inventor perfected a most *ingenious* mechanical toy." *Ingenuity* is the noun. *Ingenuous* means *naïve* or *unsophisticated:* "He was so *ingenuous* that he believed everything he read."

isle, aisle	*Isle* is a poetic term for *island:* "Byron wrote about the *isles* of Greece." *Aisle,* with identical pronunciation (ile) means a *narrow passage between seats, trees, etc.* "He walked down the *aisle* of the theater to his seat."
its, it's	*Its* (no apostrophe) is the possessive case of *it:* "The pig suckled *its* young." Note that *its* has the same function as *his,* therefore no apostrophe is used. *It's* is the contraction of *it is:* "*It's* too late to go to church."
kind, sort, type, variety	Since these words are singular in number, they should never be prefaced by plural modifiers: *This kind of people* (NOT *these* kind of people).
kind of, sort of, type of, variety of	Never place an article after these expressions: *This kind of pistol* (NOT this kind of *a* pistol).
lay, lie	*Lay, laid, laid* are the principal parts of the transitive verb which means *to put down:* "I shall *lay* the rug." "I *laid* the rug." "I have *laid* the rug." "I am *laying* the rug." *Lie, lay, lain* are the principal parts of the intransitive verb (it cannot take an object) which means *to recline* or *repose:* "She will *lie* in the hammock." "She *lay* in the hammock yesterday." "She has *lain* there all afternoon." "She *is lying* in the hammock."
lead, led	When pronounced alike, the noun *lead* is the metal; *led* is the past tense and past participle of the verb *to lead* (pronounced *leed*).
learn, teach	*Learn* means *to acquire information* or *knowledge:* "I *learned* my lesson." *Teach* means *to impart information* or *knowledge:* "I intend to *teach* him as much as he *taught* me."
liable	See *apt.*
like	See *as.*
likely	See *apt.*
loose, lose	*Loose* is an adjective meaning *not completely attached:* "The screw is *loose.*" *Lose* is a verb meaning *to be deprived of:* "I *lost* a lot of money at the race track, and I don't intend to *lose* any more."
majority, plurality	In voting, *majority* means *the number of votes constituting more than half of the total number cast:* "Since fifty-one of the one hundred members voted for Jane, she won by a *majority.*" *Plurality* is used when there are *three or more candidates.* It means *the excess of votes received by the leading candidate* over those

75

received by the next most popular candidate: "The results of the ballot are as follows: Smith, 254; Jones, 250; Marshall, 243; Edwards, 23. Therefore, Smith won by a *plurality* of 4. *Plurality* is also used to mean *the largest number of votes received by a single candidate:* "In the results listed above, Smith received a *plurality* but not a *majority*."

militate, mitigate	*Militate* (connected with *military*) means *to have a strong influence for or against,* usually against: "His grouchy manner *militated* against his success as a salesman." *Mitigate* means *to lessen:* "The cold compress on his leg *mitigated* the pain."
miner, minor	A *miner* is *one who extracts minerals from the earth.* When used as a noun a *minor* means *one who is under age.* As an adjective *minor* means *unimportant.* "Since he was a *minor,* the judge let him off with a *minor* penalty."
moral, morale	*Moral* is an adjective meaning *pertaining to the accepted customs of a society* with reference to right or wrong: "I know that he didn't steal my book because he is a very *moral* young man." *Morality* is the noun. *Morale* means a *state of well being:* "The *morale* of the employees was very good."
myself	*Myself* (like *yourself, himself, herself, itself, yourselves, themselves*) is an intensive and reflexive pronoun. It should be used only to refer to another word or to emphasize another word in the sentence: "*I myself* will do it." "*I* hurt *myself.*" "They sent for John and *me*" (NOT *myself*). "John *himself* did it, not Joe!"
officially, officiously	*Officially* means *with authority:* "I have not yet *officially* notified the firm of my resignation." *Officiously* means *intruding one's services* unnecessarily or without being wanted: "He announced *officiously* that he would take charge of the program."
personal, personnel	*Personal* is an adjective meaning *pertaining to an individual:* "The watch was his *personal* property." *Personnel* is a noun meaning the *group of people employed in an organization:* "The *personnel* manager is in charge of the welfare of the *personnel* of the firm."
plain, plane	*Plain* is an adjective meaning *simple* or *unadorned:* "Carl Sandburg loved the *plain* people." *Plain* is also a noun meaning *flat country. Plane* is a noun meaning *a flat surface.* It is also a tool used to make a flat surface smooth. It is also an accepted abbreviation for *airplane.* "When he went by *plane* to the great *plain* between the mountains, he took several *planes* with him along with his other carpenter's tools."
plurality	See *majority.*

76

practicable, practical	*Practicable* means *capable of being put into practice:* "He found a *practicable* way of depositing money without going to the bank." *Practical* means *useful* or *related to actual experience* as opposed to *theoretical:* "The *practical* nurse knew several *practical* methods to stop the flow of blood."
principal, principle	*Principal* is usually an adjective meaning *main: principal* cities, *principal* people. It has become a noun in a few usages where the noun it formerly modified is understood. "He was the *principal* (teacher) of the school." "I withdrew the *principal* (amount) and interest from my savings account." "He acted as the *principal* (person) rather than as an agent." The noun *principle* means a *basic law* or *doctrine:* "The country was founded on the *principle* that all men are created free and equal."
quiet, quite	*Quiet* means *free from noise:* "*Quiet* must be preserved in the library." *Quite* means either *fully* or *to a considerable extent,* depending on the sense of the sentence: "By the time the doctor arrived, the mother was *quite* upset because she thought her child was *quite* ill."
reason is because	The words *reason is* (*was*, etc.) should be followed by a statement of the reason: "The *reason* for his failure *was* illness." "The *reason* for the strict rules *is* to enforce discipline." Similar statements can be made by using *because:* "He failed *because* of illness." "The rules are strict *because* it is necessary to enforce discipline." *Reason* and *because* convey the same sense. It is illogical to use both words to indicate the same meaning. NOTE: When the statement of the reason is expressed in a clause, that clause should be introduced by *that*, NOT *because:* "The reason for his delay is *that* he missed the plane connection."
recommend, refer	*Recommend* means *to present as worthy of confidence:* "Do you know any doctor you could *recommend* to me?" *Refer* means *to direct attention to:* "Can you *refer* me to a good doctor?"
rise, raise	*Rise* means *to ascend* or *go up. Raise* means *to cause something or somebody to move upward, to lift something or somebody.* "The sun *rose* at 5:40 this morning." "The cost-of-living index *has risen* steadily." "She carefully *raised* the lid of the box." "For permission to leave the class, he always *raises* his hand before he *rises* from his seat."
same	Do not use *same* as a pronoun: "I have your order for the books and will send them (NOT will send *same*)."
sit, set	*Sit* means *to take or be in an upright sitting position:* "He always *sat* quietly in the big chair." "Will you please *sit* (*down*) over here?" *Set* means *to place or put something:* "She *set* the table

neatly." "They *set* their books on their desks." Specialized meanings of the verb *set* are these: "They *set out* before dawn," "The sun *sets* earlier in winter," and "The cement *has not set* (congealed) yet."

so, so that, therefore

So becomes *so that* to introduce a clause showing purpose: "He opened the windows wide *so that* we could enjoy the cool air." *So* becomes *therefore* (meaning *for that reason*) before a clause showing result: "*So* is an overworked word: *therefore*, avoid it whenever possible."

stationary, stationery

Stationary is an adjective meaning *fixed* or *attached:* "The benches are *stationary* because they are fastened to the floor." *Stationery* is *writing paper used in correspondence:* "He bought a box of *stationery* at the *stationery* store so that he could write to his friends." Notice that the *er* in *stationery* corresponds to the *er* in *paper*.

terse, trite

Terse means *concise:* "Francis Bacon wrote in a very *terse* style." *Trite* means *hackneyed, worn out from overuse:* "As different as night and day is a *trite* expression."

than, then

Than is a conjunction, usually to express comparisons: "She was wealthier *than* her sister." *Then* is an adverb denoting time, past or future: "She remembered her youth because her sister was richer *then*. But *then* she herself fell heir to a fortune."

their, there, they're

Be careful to distinguish the spelling of the possessive case of the adjective *their* (*their* books) from the spelling of the adverb and expletive *there*. "I got *there* before I knew it." "*There* are forty oranges in the crate." *They're* is a contraction of *they are:* "*They're* good friends of mine!"

to, too, two

To is a preposition meaning *direction toward:* "Take this package *to* the store." It is used to make the infinitive when combined with the root of a verb: *to eat, to sing*. *Too* is an adverb meaning *more than enough:* "He was *too* tired to eat." *Too* may mean *also:* "I like ice cream, *too*." *Two* is the number 2.

unique

Unique means *the only one of its kind:* "His was a *unique* personality." It cannot logically be used in a comparative or superlative form. Something may be more or most odd, rare, unusual, peculiar, remarkable, etc., but NOT more or most *unique*.

verbal, oral, aural

Verbal means *pertaining to words; oral* means *pertaining to spoken words:* "She nodded assent, but gave no *verbal* confirmation, either written or *oral*." *Aural* means *receiving through the ear:* "Babies learn *aurally* rather than visually."

waist, waste	*Waist* is *the middle section of the body* or *an upper garment:* "He wore a belt around his *waist*." "She bought a beautifully embroidered *waist*." As a verb *waste* means *to squander;* as a noun it means *that which is squandered or useless:* "He *wasted* his money." "Reading that stupid novel was a *waste* of time."
when, where, that	Do not use *when* or *where* as a substitute for a noun which usually follows a form of the verb *to be:* "Spring is *the season* for blossom festivals" (NOT "Spring is when there are festivals.") "The language laboratory is *the place* where students practice orally" (NOT "The language laboratory is where students practice orally.") Do not use *where* in place of *that* in a clause: "I read in the paper *that* a new manager was appointed" (NOT "I read in the paper where a new manager was appointed.")
who's, whose	*Who's* is the contraction for *who is* and *who has:* "I don't know *who's* coming." "*Who's* taken my matches?" *Whose* is the possessive form of *who:* "We knew the family *whose* house was robbed." Notice the relationship of *whose* with *his;* therefore, no apostrophe: *whose house, his house.*
woman, women	Just as the plural of *man* is *men,* so the plural of *woman* is *women.*
your, you're	*Your* is the possessive case of *you:* "I have read *your* notes." "*You're* is the contraction of *you are:* "*You're* sure to be there on time if you leave now." "*You're* welcome." Notice that possessive adjectives do not use the apostrophe (e.g., *your* notes, her notes, its notes, etc.).

16 ■ Idiomatic Usage

Every language has its own idioms. An idiom usually consists of a group of words which is either meaningless or absurd if the words are understood to mean what they usually do. For example, *catch* is a simple and common word in such sentences as "He will catch a fish" and "He will catch the ball." However, in English it is commonplace to say, "He will catch the train," meaning that he will be at the station in time to board the train before it leaves. Similarly, a common English idiom for suffering from a common winter ailment is "to catch cold." People are not being proud of their abilities when they say, "I caught a bad cold." Actually, the cold caught them.

The list of common idioms below is arranged alphabetically according to the key word in the idiom. The usual meaning of the key word can be found in any dictionary. Only the idiomatic meanings are described in this section.

IDIOMS

ABOUT

> The store is *about* five miles from here.   (approximately)
> I was *about to invite* you to the party.   (on the verge of inviting)
> It is *about* time you decided to pay back what you owe me.   (certainly)
> What are you thinking *about?*   (of)
> Nellie asked *about you* when I saw her yesterday.   (concerning you)

AFRAID

> My sister would like to join us, but *I'm afraid* she has another engagement.
> (I regret that it is likely that)

AFTER

> Who will *look after* the dog while we are on vacation?   (take care of)
> John won't be able to join us *after all.*   (in spite of previous expectation)

BACK

> The mayor *backed* my brother for councilman.   (supported)
> The councilman had the mayor's *backing.*   (support)
> The tree stood *in back of* the house.   (behind)

BALL

> Stop loafing and *get on the ball.*   (become efficient)
> The noisy young people were having *a ball.*   (a good time)
> After losing his money, John found himself *behind the 8-ball.*   (in serious trouble)

BLUE

The departure of her friend left Mary feeling *blue*. (depressed, melancholy)

BUCK

It is foolish to try to *buck* an established system. (battle against)

He always tries to *pass the buck*. (to blame someone else)

BRIGHT

All *bright* young people should go to college. (intelligent)

CAR

The entire family went for a long ride in the *car*. (automobile)

CATCH

Take off your wet shoes and socks before you *catch cold*. (become ill from a cold)

They were late in leaving the house, but they *caught* the train. (arrived in time to board it before it left)

I *caught* his eye from across the room. (got his attention)

CHISEL

The dishonest storekeeper tried to *chisel* the customer. (cheat)

The storekeeper had the reputation of being a *chiseler*. (cheater)

COME

Father *came to grief* when he invested in a new speculative stock. (suffered misfortune)

The skeptical employee finally *came to believe* in the business. (acquired faith)

The dogmatic professor got *his come-uppance* when he was proved to be entirely wrong. (what he deserved)

Yellow tomatoes are *hard to come by*. (difficult to find)

COOL

Only a few of the people *kept cool* during the panic. (remained unexcited)

After his friend's apology, John *cooled down*. (lost his anger)

The labor arbitrator ordered *a cooling-off period*. (time to think calmly)

Cool off with a glass of cold beer. (lower body temperature)

He was very *cool* toward her. (aloof, impersonal)

DEAD

They were startled by the sound of sirens in the *dead* of night. (darkest hours)

I should have taken Fred's advice; he was *dead* right. (entirely)

The bus came to a *dead* stop at the railroad crossing. (complete)

DESERT

The judge gave the convicted criminal his *just deserts*. (justified punishment)

DISH

Mother asked me to *dish up* the peas. (serve from a bowl or pot)

DO

How *do you do?*   (greeting upon introductions)
Will you please *do up* my package?   (wrap)
The soldiers *did away with* their prisoner.   (killed)
Numbers *have to do* with arithmetic.   (are connected)
Thank you. That *will do.*   (is enough, is satisfactory)
I have eaten so much that I *can do without* dessert.   (am willing to omit)
That steak is really *well done.*   (thoroughly cooked)
The job was *well done* by the efficient clerk.   (excellently completed)
Most missionaries are *do-gooders* at heart.   (determined to help others)

DOWN

Fearing the dark, my mother hoped to arrive by *sundown.*   (dusk)
Amy went *downtown* to buy some new clothes.   (business section or southern part of a town or city)
I made a *down* payment on the car and will pay the rest in installments. (first, initial)
I paid $500 *down* and will pay $10 a week for three years.   (as a first payment)
Poor man, he is *down and out!*   (without friends)
It is warmer *down south* and colder *up north.*   (*down* is south on map and *up* is north)

DRIVE

After taking lessons, she learned to *drive* our car.   (operate)
The entire family has gone out for *a drive.*   (an automobile ride)
I don't understand what you are *driving at.*   (trying to convey)
The vigorous young woman had lots of *drive.*   (energy and determination)

DROP

Drop in (by) to see me some day.   (make a casual visit)
The dull-eyed boy was a *high school drop-out.*   (left school before graduating)

EYE

The detective *eyed* the shopper suspiciously.   (scrutinized)
The pretty girl *gave me the eye.*   (flirted with me)
My shrewd friend *has his eyes open.*   (isn't easily fooled)
My little daughter was *all eyes* when she saw her birthday presents. (amazed and delighted)
My father and I hardly ever *see eye to eye.*   (agree)
That decaying old building is certainly *an eyesore.*   (ugly)
The plane flew into the *eye* of the hurricane.   (center)

FACE

Let him *face up to* his mistakes.   (admit)
If he does, he will have to *face the music.*   (be responsible for past errors)
Your explanation puts a new *face* on the matter.   (interpretation of)
Most pompous people are apt to be *two-faced.*   (hypocritical)

FALL

John and Mary *fell in love.* (became enamored of each other)

The baby will soon *fall* asleep. (be)

FIRE

The employee was *fired* because of his inefficiency. (dismissed)

FIX

The automobile mechanic *fixed* our car. (repaired)

I was really in a *fix* when I lost my job. (difficult predicament)

FOOT

John was so naive that he was always *putting his foot in it.* (making embarrassing blunders)

Our wealthy friend offered to *foot* the bill at the hotel. (pay)

GET

The patient is feeling better and will soon *get* well. (become)

There are so many clouds that it is *getting* dark. (becoming)

Please try to *get along* with what you have. (manage)

The two children *get along* well. (are agreeable together)

Instead of talking so much, let's *get on with it.* (make progress)

The cheated customer *got even with* the salesman by calling the police. (received justice from)

Not knowing that he was being observed, the student expected to *get away with* his cheating. (evade discovery of)

GIVE

After several useless attempts, they *gave up.* (stopped trying)

During the earthquake a corner of the building *gave way.* (broke off)

She always *gives in* to his arguments. (yields)

GO

Tomorrow I *am going to* finish my work. (shall, will)

My energetic wife is always *on the go.* (active)

The mediator of the dispute acted as a *go-between.* (intermediary)

I believe the baby is *going to sleep.* (will soon be asleep)

It *goes without saying* that winters are cold in the north. (is self-evident)

The new fall styles are *all the go.* (popular)

The manufacturing company is a *going* concern (thriving)

If you were only older, I could *go for* you. (fall in love with)

The job may be difficult, but let's *have a go at* it. (attempt)

We tried to finish the job, but it was *no go.* (unsuccessful)

HARD

The feeble old man was *hard of hearing.* (partially deaf)

The planning expert was a *hard-headed* man. (obstinate)

The boss was too *hard-hearted* to raise my salary. (unsympathetic)

Being paid so little, I was always *hard up.* (poor)

HAVE

The construction workers *have to* be careful.   (must)
The *haves and* the *have-nots* have been studied by sociologists.   (rich and poor)

HEART

Agnes *learned* the entire poem *by heart.*   (memorized)
When his friend deserted him, he *took it to heart.*   (was deeply troubled)
Mother couldn't resist a beggar, because she was *all heart.*   (emotionally generous)

HIGH

After several cocktails, our guests became quite *high.*   (intoxicated)
The professor *was* very *high handed* in assigning grades.   (did as he pleased)
Emerson was a *high-minded* American author.   (idealistic)
It is *high time* for all of us to go to bed.   (latest reasonable time)
His experiences in the war left him very *high strung.*   (nervous and hypersensitive)
The *highbrows* usually scorn the ordinary lowbrow people.   (intellectuals)
After having been awarded the Nobel prize, he became very *high hat.* (snobbish)
I'll meet you at the station at *high noon.*   (on the dot of 12 noon)

HOLD

The lecturer *held forth* on the subject for nearly an hour.   (orated)
How long can the enemy *hold out?*   (endure)
The bandits *held up* the train.   (stopped and robbed)

JUST

He is a *just* judge.   (honest, fair)
They arrived *just* a minute ago.   (only)
She *has just finished* the book.   (has finished in the immediate present)
We *had just left* the house when the telephone rang.   (had left in the immediate past)

KNOW

Max was *in the know about* his sister's plans.   (acquainted with)
After forty years in his firm, he had a lot of *know-how.*   (expert knowledge)

LOOK

She gave him an angry *look.*   (stare)
The boys like her because of her *good looks.*   (attractive appearance)
That is another way of saying that she is *good-looking.*   (pleasant to look at)
Please *look after* my dog while I am away.   (take care of)
Please *take a look at my oil.*   (verify the level on the oil gauge)
It *looks like rain.*   (appears as if rain is imminent)

LONG

The people at the beach basked in the sunshine *all day long.*   (the entire day)
Did he live *long?*   (a long time)

MAKE

The shy young man was too timid to *try to make love* to her.   (attempt sexual advances)

After their lover's quarrel, they kissed and *made up*.   (were reconciled)

If we don't really have a good time, let's *make believe* it was fun.   (pretend)

This hammer isn't really satisfactory, but I'll try to *make do* with it.   (serve my purpose)

The salesman *made good* on the defective merchandise he sold us.   (corrected the defect either by refunding money or substituting a satisfactory product)

They *made it known* that they wanted to sell their house.   (revealed the information)

Let us eat, drink, and *make merry*.   (have a good time)

After having finished college, he had to *make* his *way* in the world.   (succeed)

The three men who robbed the bank *made off with* nearly a million dollars.   (ran away with)

She *made up to* the professor, hoping that she would pass the course.   (flattered)

MOUTH

He was so nervous at the meeting that he *mouthed his words*.   (talked indistinctly)

I didn't read it in the newspaper; I heard it *by word of mouth*.   (orally)

My brother was really *down in the mouth* after his house was robbed.   (depressed)

OUT

The new book on outer space has just *come out*.   (been published)

Mary and Jane quarreled a week ago; they are still *on the outs*.   (unfriendly)

I never believe what he says because he is an *out-and-out* liar.   (complete)

Your outrageous demands are *out of the question*.   (impossible to fulfill)

The Chinese have been growing rice since *time out of mind*.   (extremely remote past)

PASS

His grandfather *passed away* six months ago.   (died)

One of the guests became so drunk that he *passed out*.   (lost consciousness)

The counterfeiter tried to *pass* one of his bills at the bank.   (have it accepted)

It *came to pass* that there was a new prophet in Israel.   (happened)

The clever actor *passed himself off as* a doctor.   (convinced the public that he was)

Things will come to a *pretty pass* if we don't act immediately.   (critical situation)

PRETTY

After several months of practice, he became *pretty* good at golf.   (quite)

Considering the short time he studied, he learned the lesson *pretty* well.   (quite)

After her wealthy husband died, she found herself *sitting pretty.* (in an affluent position)

PUT

James was very much *put out* when the bank refused to give him a loan. (annoyed)

I can't believe you; you must be *putting me on.* (deceiving me)

It is so late now that we will have to *put up with* this miserable hotel. (tolerate)

"*Put up or shut up,*" said my partner when I argued about my share of the business. (Produce or be quiet.)

RED

The young man *saw red* when he was evicted from his room. (became very angry)

There is too much *red tape* involved in registering for this course. (tiresome details)

The thief was caught *red handed* as he exited from the bank. (with the evidence)

He threw a *red herring* into the case by pretending deafness. (misleading clue)

REST

Rest assured that I will do everything I can to help you. (Be)

RUN

When my father became ill, I had to *run* the establishment. (manage)

I believe that we will succeed *in the long run.* (over an extended period of time)

Our competitor is not exactly thriving, but he is still *in the running.* (competitive)

The splinter in the chair caused a *run* in Mary's stocking. (long vertical tear)

Don't you dare *run down* my achievement. (deprecate)

He *ran up* a big bill at the hotel. (accumulated)

The old building on the corner is in a *run-down* condition. (deteriorating)

The gambler decided to give his friend a *run* for his money. (contest)

SET

Early in the morning, they *set off* for the country. (departed)

The angry heirs had a real *set-to* about dividing the estate. (dispute)

Each month he *set aside* part of his salary for his daughter's education. (saved)

SHARP

The millionaire was very *sharp* in running his business. (shrewd, clever)

With your new suit, you are really looking *sharp.* (well-groomed)

SHORT

I'll pay you tomorrow when I won't be so *short* of funds. (lacking in)

The business operation was *short-handed* during vacation periods. (deficient in number of employees)

He left the main road and took a *short cut* to his house.   (shorter way)
It never pays to be *shortsighted.*   (remiss in foreseeing the future)
He was very *short* with her.   (said very little; was curt)

SHUT

"*Shut up,*" said the angry boy to his barking dog.   ("Be quiet"; said in a rude manner)

SMALL

I hate to go to the store with nothing but *small change* in my pocket.   (pennies, nickels, dimes)
Bothered by his many worries, he stayed awake during the *small hours* of the night.   (1, 2, 3 A.M.)
That was very *small* of him.   (petty, cheap)

STAND

In spite of strong opposition, he took a firm *stand* on the matter.   (position)
He left the room because he couldn't *stand* the noise.   (endure)
Don't stand on ceremony; take off your jackets.   (be informal)
Throughout the entire trial, the attorney *stood up for* his client. (supported)
He asserted his rights and *stood up to* the boss.   (was firm in his attitude toward)
The snow was so heavy that everything came to a *standstill.*   (complete stop)
The *standing* committee gave its annual report.   (permanent)

STICK

Our best plan to avoid trouble is for all of us to *stick* together.   (stay)
Let's *stick to the point!*   (remain on the subject)

TAKE

I expect to *take a train* to Boston.   (go on a train)
It doesn't seem sensible to *take* the time to pack.   (use)
The strange dog *took to* me right away.   (liked)
Both of the children *take after* their mother.   (resemble)
I am so tired of this job that I think I'll *take off* for a day.   (leave)
I can't *take* him seriously when he talks so wildly.   (consider)
It *took* four hours for me to do this.   (required)
How much time does it *take?*   (require)

TIE

At 8 to 8, the score was *tied.* It was a *tie* score.   (even)
The busy executive was *tied up* at the office.   (too busy to leave)
The ballplayer was *fit to be tied* when the umpire ruled against him. (extremely angry)

TIME

It isn't a perfect job, but it will do for the *time being*.   (present)
If the plane isn't *on time*, we will have to wait.   (punctual in arriving)
Once upon a time, there was a fairy princess.   (in the remote past)
I hope I can finish *in time*.   (on schedule)

EXPRESSIONS OF TIME

8:30	Eight-thirty, half-past eight
9:15	Nine-fifteen, a quarter after (past) nine
10:45	Ten-forty-five, a quarter to eleven
2:50	Two-fifty, ten of (to) three
4:20	Four-twenty, twenty minutes past four, twenty after four

TRY

The tailor asked me to *try on* the suit.   (put it on for fitting and appearance)
I met so many difficult customers that I had a *trying* day.   (nerve-wracking)
The actor *tried out* for the part of Hamlet.   (auditioned for)

TURN

He did me a *good turn* by mowing the lawn when I was away.   (favor)
The old car *turned out* to be in good condition.   (was actually)
I *turned over* my account to another bank.   (transferred)
Our whole success in this undertaking *turns* on his ability.   (depends)
Appearing so suddenly, you gave me quite a *turn*.   (fright)

USE

I *used to enjoy* drinking milk, but now I prefer coffee.   (formerly enjoyed)
The new stove is very difficult to *get used to*.   (become adjusted to)
His first car was a *used* car   (second-hand, not new)

WEATHER

It is raining, snowing, hailing, thundering and lightning, fair, warm, dry, humid, etc.
It *looks like* rain, snow, etc.   (appears likely that it will rain, etc.)
It has been a rainy, snowy, etc. day.

17 ■ Numbers

CARDINAL AND ORDINAL NUMBERS

Numerals	Cardinal Numbers	Ordinal Numbers
1	one	first
2	two	second
3	three	third
4	four	fourth
5	five	fifth
6	six	sixth
7	seven	seventh
8	eight	eighth
9	nine	ninth
10	ten	tenth
11	eleven	eleventh
12	twelve	twelfth
13	thirteen	thirteenth
14	fourteen	fourteenth
15	fifteen	fifteenth
16	sixteen	sixteenth
17	seventeen	seventeenth
18	eighteen	eighteenth
19	nineteen	nineteenth
20	twenty	twentieth
21	twenty-one	twenty-first
30	thirty	thirtieth
40	forty	fortieth
50	fifty	fiftieth
60	sixty	sixtieth
70	seventy	seventieth
80	eighty	eightieth
90	ninety	ninetieth
100	one hundred	one hundredth
1000	one thousand	one thousandth
1001	one thousand one	one thousand and first
1,000,000	one million	one millionth
1,000,000,000	one billion (U.S.)	one billionth (U.S.)

Note: *Million* and *billion* are nouns and are followed by *of* before the item measured: three millions *of* dollars.

WORD ELEMENTS MEANING NUMBER

Word Element	Meaning	Examples
uni	one	unit, universe, unicycle
du, bi, di	two	duet, bicycle, disect
tri	three	tricycle, tri-semester
quadr, quart	four	quadrangle, quartet
quint, penta	five	quintuplet, pentagon
ses, sext, hexa	six	sestet, sextet, hexagon
sept	seven	septennial, septuple
oct	eight	octagon, octet
non, nov	nine	nonagenarian, November
deca	ten	decade, decasyllable

USAGES WITH NUMBERS

RULE

Spell out numbers of one or two words.

---

fifty cents
fifty-one
nine hundred

RULE

Use numerals for numbers of more than two words.

1981
$453.21
4,500,000

PITFALL

Do not begin a sentence with a numeral; spell out the number:
Nine hundred ninety-nine cases out of a thousand were approved.

RULE

Hyphenate all two-word numbers from twenty-one to ninety-nine.
Hyphenate fractions (except *one half*) only if they serve as adjectives.

---

one-third cup
one half quart

RULE

Write out cardinal numbers like fourth, thirty-first, etc., rather than use numerals with letter endings (4th, 31st, etc.).

This is my *fourth* visit.

PITFALL

Street numbers may be written with letters or numbers:
    She lives at 825 N. *2nd* Street.
    She lives at 825 N. *Second* Street.

18 ■ Prefixes and Suffixes

SOME COMMON PREFIXES

For convenience in pronunciation, prefix spellings are sometimes slightly altered.

Prefix	Meaning	Examples
a	not	amoral, atypical, anomalous
ab	away from	abduct, abstain, absent
ad	to	adapt, adhere, adroit
anti	against	antitoxin, antithesis
bi	two	biennial, bi-weekly, bicycle
circum	around	circumnavigate, circumscribe, circumvent
co, com, con	with, together with	combine, coeditor, coincide, concede

Note: *n* becomes *m* before *b* and *p*: combine, impossible

contra	against	contrary, contradict, controversy
de	down, away from	debase, deflate, depose
dis	not, off, away	distrust, dissociate, disinterested
ex	out, from, former	expel, exit, exhume ex-wife, ex-convict, ex-president
extra	outside	extracurricular, extraterritorial, extraordinary
for	away, off, from	forget, forswear
fore	before, previous	forefathers, foresee
hyper	excessive, over	hypercritical, hypertension
hypo	under, beneath	hypothesis
in, im	in, not	induct, invert, implicit, intend, insane, improper, inarticulate, incapable

Note: *n* becomes *m* before *b* and *p*: imbecile, impossible

inter	between, among	interstate, international, intervene
intra	within	intrastate, intramural, introvert
mal	bad	malevolent, malediction, malefactor
mis	wrong	mistake, miscalculation, misadventure
omni	all	omnipotent, omniscient, omniverous
post	after	postpone, postgraduate, postoperative

pre	before	predate, preface, premarital
pro	before, for	program, promote
re	again, back	remake, restate, reimburse
retro	back, backward	retroactive, retro-rockets, retrospect
sub	under	subway, substandard, subordinate
super	over	superintendent, superstructure, supervise
syn, sym	together	synthetic, symphony, sympathy
trans	across	transfer, transmit, transom, transport
un	not	unnatural, uncivilized, unobtrusive

SOME COMMON SUFFIXES

Noun Suffixes:

Suffix	Meaning	Examples
ance, ence, ancy, ency	act of, state of, condition of	attendance, precedence, hesitancy, presidency
ation, ition	action, state, result	expedition, hesitation
dom	state or condition of	wisdom, kingdom
er, or, ar, eer, ist	one who	painter, governor, bursar, profiteer, segregationist
ess	one who (feminine)	actress, mistress
hood	state of	manhood, nationhood, falsehood
ism	doctrine or practice of	totalitarianism, mannerism
ment	state, quality, act of	wonderment, treatment, payment
ness	state of	fullness, shyness, sickness
th	act, state, quality	warmth, width

Adjective Suffixes:

Suffix	Meaning	Examples
able, ible	capable of	eatable, visible
ant, ent	like	hesitant, independent
ate	having, showing	desolate, separate
en	made of, like	wooden, ashen
ful	full of	hopeful, meaningful
ish, y, ic, ac, al	like, pertaining to	childish, sandy, demonic, cardiac, practical
less	without	careless, comfortless
ly	like, in the nature of	friendly, kindly
ory, ary	relating	sensory, funerary
ous, ose	full of, like	cancerous, verbose
ward	in the direction of	upward, homeward

Verb Suffixes:

Suffix	Meaning	Examples
en	to become, cause to be	strengthen, deepen
ate	form, become	animate, donate, cooperate
fy	make, cause to have	fortify, rarify, pacify

19 ■ Punctuation and Capitalization

CAPITALIZATION

RULE

The first word of a sentence is always capitalized.

RULE

The pronoun *I* is always capitalized.

John and *I* are good friends.

RULE

Proper nouns (names) are always capitalized.

The individual name or title of any person, place, or thing is a proper noun. A good dictionary indicates proper nouns by capitalizing them. Some examples of proper nouns are: *James Madison High School, The Pine Tree Tavern, Hamilton College, Florida, Elm Street, Crescent City, New York State, French, France, Mary Roberts Rinehart, Second Avenue, Mr. Smith, Judge Black, Asia, Spanish, The White House, Mount St. Helens, San Francisco Bay.* Notice that words like *school* and *city* are capitalized when they are part of the title. So are honorary or distinguishing titles (whether abbreviated or not) when placed before names: *Miss Halpern, Mrs. Smith, Doctor Johnson, Dr. Johnson, Capt. Darcy, Professor Edwards, Prof. Edwards.* Capitalize abbreviations *Sr.* and *Jr.* when they follow a name: *Richard Thomas, Jr.*

> **RULE**
>
> Abbreviations of titles, usually placed after a name, are capitalized.

John Larkin, M.D., Frank Loeser, Jr., James Donovan, Ph.D.

> **RULE**
>
> Titles of books, plays, poems, essays, newspapers, etc., are capitalized.

The first word of the title is always capitalized and all other words except the articles (*a, an, the*) and short prepositions and conjunctions (like *and, but, in, of*). The last word of the title is always capitalized: *Mourning Becomes Electra, The Mill on the Floss, A Rose for Emily, For Whom the Bell Tolls.*

> **RULE**
>
> The names of geographical regions are capitalized: the *Southwest*, the *South*.

> **PITFALL**
>
> Such geographical words are not capitalized when they merely indicate direction: "He went *west*." BUT "He settled in the *West*."

> **RULE**
>
> Days of the week, months of the year, holidays are capitalized: *Monday, Tuesday, January, February, Easter, Lincoln's Birthday.*

> **PITFALL**
>
> Names of the seasons are not capitalized unless personified: *spring, autumn, fall, winter.*
> I saw *Spring* laying her mantle on the meadow.

> **RULE**
>
> Do not capitalize a common noun unless it is part of a name:

Angel Island is one of the many islands in San Francisco Bay.

Common nouns are capitalized when they become proper nouns (a name used to identify a *specific* person, place, or thing). For example, *history* is a common noun. But *History of the United States* or *History 201* might be names of academic courses. *Mother* is a common noun in a phrase like *my mother*. But in the sentence *I will ask Mother*, the absence of the identifying word *my* makes *Mother* the identification or name of one specific person. In similar identifications like *Uncle John* or *President Smith*, the nouns *uncle* and *president* become proper nouns because they are part of the identifications of specific people.

In American English, names lose their capitalization when they become common nouns for an item or action: *kleenex* (for any paper handkerchief), *boycott* (a procedure originated by a man named Boycott).

RULE

The first word of a line of verse is usually capitalized.

RULE

The opening word or words used for the salutation of a letter are capitalized: *Gentlemen: Dear Madam: Dear Sir: My dear Mrs. Smith: Dear Fred, Dear Mr. Strong,*.

The opening word of the complimentary close of a letter is capitalized: *Sincerely, Sincerely yours, Yours very truly, Cordially yours,*.

CORRECT COMMA USAGE

MAXIM: *When in doubt, leave it out.* This well-known maxim makes relatively good sense because most uncertain punctuators annoy their readers by scattering commas at random through their writings.

A BETTER MAXIM: *Master the few definite principles of correct comma usage.*

COMMAS TO SEPARATE PARTS OF A SERIES

When the parts of a series are not joined by a connecting word like *and* or *or*, commas separate the parts of the series.

She was tall, young, beautiful.

The last term of any series is usually preceded by the conjunction *and* or *or*. The conjunction may take the place of a comma, but since it is not unusual for an *and* or an *or* to occur within one element of the series, careful writers place a comma before the final *and* or *or* to indicate the termination of the series.

A SERIES OF WORDS:	This bus goes to Trenton, Baltimore, and Washington.
A SERIES OF PHRASES:	They ran into the house, through the livingroom, and up to his room.
A SERIES OF VERBS:	He combed his hair, put on a clean shirt, and went to the party.
A SERIES OF CLAUSES:	The food was good, the service was excellent, and the dinner-music was enchanting.
A SERIES OF ADJECTIVES:	It was a big, ugly, unfriendly dog.
A SERIES WITH *and*'s:	For breakfast he had orange juice, ham and eggs, toast and butter, and coffee.
A SERIES WITH *or*'s:	When he invested his money, he had choices of buying common or preferred stock, safe or speculative stock, or corporate or municipal bonds.

PITFALL

Frequently a single adjective modifying a noun is so much a part of the identification that the adjective and noun are thought of as a single word: *oak tree, dress shirt, straw hat*. Whenever such combinations are thought of as units, no comma is required to separate a preceding adjective: *tall oak tree, dirty dress shirt, old straw hat*. Similarly, when an adjective is used only for identification, it is felt to be part of the noun: She wore her old *red dress*. If the intention is to emphasize the color of the dress instead of identifying it, a comma is used: *her old, red dress*.

COMMA TO SEPARATE THE CLAUSES OF A COMPOUND SENTENCE

In a compound sentence all clauses joined by a coordinating conjunction are separated by a comma immediately preceding the conjunction (*and, but, or, nor, for, yet, so, whereas*).

COMPOUND SENTENCE:	My father was born and raised on a large farm in New England, and I learned a great deal about rural life from him.

| COMPOUND SENTENCE: | I have been studying French for the last seven years, so I am sure that I shall feel at home in Paris. |
| SHORT CLAUSES: | He wrote to me, and I answered his letter. |

PITFALL

The conjunctions *and, but, or, nor, for, yet, so, whereas* are preceded by a comma only when followed by a subject and a verb.

He wrote to me and answered all my questions. (No comma before *and* because the subject *he* is omitted before *answered*.)

He wrote to me, and he answered all my questions. (Comma before *and* because *and* is followed by a subject and a verb.)

PITFALL

Do not mistake a compound predicate for a compound sentence. A compound predicate does not require a comma because its subject is understood, even though it is not expressed.

INCORRECT:	The doctor spent the entire day driving about town, and was able to visit nearly all his patients.
CORRECT:	The doctor spent the entire day driving about town and was able to visit nearly all his patients.
CORRECT:	The doctor spent the entire day driving about town, and he was able to visit nearly all his patients. (compound sentence)

PITFALL

Place a comma before, not after, the coordinating conjunction in a compound sentence.

| INCORRECT: | The architects drew excellent plans for the building but, the builder was unwilling to follow them. |
| CORRECT: | The architects drew excellent plans for the building, but the builder was unwilling to follow them. |

PITFALL

Don't separate two sentences or two independent clauses by using a comma.

INCORRECT:	The robins came early that spring, the weather was unusually warm.
CORRECT:	The robins came early that spring. The weather was unusually warm.
CORRECT:	The robins came early that spring; the weather was unusually warm.

COMMA TO SEPARATE AN INTERJECTION OR TERM OF DIRECT ADDRESS

> **RULE**
>
> When a word or phrase is clearly not a part of the structure of a sentence, separate it from the sentence by a comma; separate it by two commas if the word or phrase falls in the middle of the sentence.

INTERJECTION:	*Hello,* I didn't expect to see you.
INTERJECTION:	*Oh no,* you can't expect me to do that!
INTERJECTION:	He's going to be late again, *darn it!*
DIRECT ADDRESS:	*John,* come over here at once!
DIRECT ADDRESS:	That vegetable soup, *Mother,* is delicious!

COMMA TO SET OFF A SENTENCE MODIFIER

Instead of modifying a single word, a sentence modifier modifies the whole sentence in which it occurs because it usually refers the sense of the entire sentence to something preceding that sentence.

Kinds of Sentence Modifiers

1. Common sentence modifiers are *however, moreover, therefore, nevertheless, furthermore, in addition, on the other hand, on the contrary.*

He made no effort to take care of his health. *Nevertheless,* he was never sick.

She cooked all the meals, kept the house clean, and raised four children. *In addition,* she was a member of three clubs.

Banks observe a shorter business day than almost any other kind of commercial operation. Bankers, *on the other hand,* often work longer hours than other business men.

2. Another kind of sentence modifier is the absolute phrase, made up of a noun or pronoun and a participle. The absolute phrase is not needed to form a complete sentence.

ABSOLUTE PHRASE:	*The sun having risen,* we set forth on our journey.
ABSOLUTE PHRASE:	It seemed entirely reasonable, *things being what they were,* to expect a disastrous outcome of the affair.

COMMA AFTER A LONG PHRASE OR CLAUSE PRECEDING THE SUBJECT

> **RULE**
>
> Since the subject of a sentence is usually expected at the beginning, a comma should be placed at the end of any phrase or clause consisting of more than four words before the subject. (The comma will assist the reader in determining the subject.)

LONG PHRASE: *After a long afternoon of tedious debate,* the meeting was adjourned.

LONG CLAUSE: *When I think of all the things I might have done,* I feel very discouraged.

COMMAS TO INDICATE INTERRUPTIONS OF NORMAL WORD ORDER

When unexpected or interrupted word order occurs, commas are very helpful to the reader.

UNEXPECTED: Our neighbor, loved and respected by all, went to his rest.

COMMENT: Adjectives (*loved, respected*) usually precede the word they modify.

INTERRUPTION: The price of eggs, *ninety cents a dozen,* was exorbitant.

INTERRUPTION: He was lazy and shiftless and, *to put it bluntly,* untrustworthy.

PITFALL

Don't interrupt a natural flow of thought with a comma, e.g.: unnatural separation of a subject from its verb or a verb from its object.

INCORRECT: The many hours of painstaking effort that he spent in completing his dissertation, were rewarded when his thesis was praised by all the members of the department.

CORRECT: The many hours of painstaking effort that he spent in completing his dissertation were rewarded when his thesis was praised by all the members of the department.

INCORRECT: He said, that he was anxious to see me.

CORRECT: He said that he was anxious to see me.

COMMAS TO SET OFF NONRESTRICTIVE ELEMENTS

Any word, phrase, or clause that is not essential to the meaning of a sentence is called *nonrestrictive*. Such elements may be highly informative, but the fact that they are not essential is indicated by setting them off with commas.

RESTRICTIVE: Fielding's novel *Tom Jones* was made into a motion picture.

COMMENT: Fielding wrote more than one novel. *Tom Jones* is essential to the meaning.

NONRESTRICTIVE: Dante's epic, *The Divine Comedy*, is an undisputed masterpiece.

COMMENT: Dante wrote only one epic. Supplying its name is useful but not essential.

RESTRICTIVE: The people *who came by train* missed the first race.

COMMENT: No commas because *who came by train* is essential to the meaning. (Only the train people missed the race.)

NONRESTRICTIVE: The people, *who came by train*, enjoyed their vacations at the summer resort. (They merely happened to have come by train.)

NOTE: By using commas, the writer makes clear whether the word, phrase, or clause in question is intended to be restrictive or not. The preceding sentence implies that everybody came by train. The information is added, but it is not essential. If some people came by other means of transportation and only the people who came by train enjoyed their vacations, the commas should not be used.

COMMAS TO EMPHASIZE CONTRASTS

If one part of the meaning of a sentence is in contrast to the other, a comma emphasizes the contrast.

CONTRAST: She was beautifully, yet inexpensively dressed.

CONTRAST: The singing was noisy, not melodious.

COMMAS TO PREVENT MISREADING

Occasionally, a comma is used when none of the above principles is involved but when it is helpful to avoid possible confusion on the part of the reader.

MOMENTARY POSSIBLE CONFUSION: "Whatever is, is right."

COMMENT: If Pope had omitted the comma from this famous quotation, the reader might have been momentarily troubled by the repetition of *is*.

MOMENTARY CONFUSION: During the winter nights become longer.

INSTANTLY CLARIFIED: During the winter, nights become longer.

CONVENTIONAL COMMA USAGES

There are a few comma usages which have been established by convention. These are entirely arbitrary.

1. After the salutation of an informal letter:
   Dear John, Dear Mr. Smith, Dear Mrs. Jones,

2. After the complimentary close of a letter:
   Yours truly, Sincerely, With love,

3. Separating dates of the month from the year:
   July 16, 1948

4. Separating parts of an address:
   Mrs. Andrew Clark, 142 South Street, New Lebanon, Indiana, 10765

5. Separating numbered or lettered divisions or subdivisions:
   Book VII, Canto 42, Stanza 17; Section B, 4, d

6. Separating distinguishing titles from names:
   John J. Darcy, Jr.   Jacob Elson, M.D.

7. Separating thousands in large figures:
   7,639,420

8. Placed before and after introductory words and abbreviations such as i.e., e.g.:
   Some colleges are coeducational, for example, Cornell. Some books need to be digested, i.e., they must be read slowly and thoughtfully.

TERMINAL PUNCTUATION MARKS
The Period

RULE

If a sentence is not a question or an exclamation, it should always be terminated by a period.

There are forty students in the room. (statement)
I asked if she was ready. (indirect question)
Please write to me. (request or command)

RULE

Even when a sentence is not involved, the period is used for terminal purposes.

Hello. I am delighted to see you.
Yes. I'll be there at eight.

Other Uses for Periods

1. In an enumerated list:
    1. The Manager
    2. The Foremen
    3. The Workers

2. The period is used to terminate most abbreviations: *Mr.*, *Mrs.*, *Rev.*, *U.S.A.*, *i.e.*, *etc.*

3. Three spaced periods are used to indicate the omission of one or more words or sentences in a quotation:
    "In the beginning God created . . . the earth."

4. When the omission occurs after the end of a sentence, the three spaced periods are added after the period which terminates the sentence.
    "The Lord is my shepherd. . . . Surely, goodness and mercy . . ."

The Question Mark

The question mark is used to terminate a direct question:
    Where are you going? Why? You are? May I come with you?
The question mark enclosed in parentheses is used to indicate uncertainty or doubt.
    He was born in 1914 (?) and died in 1967.

The Exclamation Mark

The exclamation mark is used to emphasize a strong expression of feeling.
    Never! I will never sign that document!
    Don't you dare take the car without my permission!

THE SEMICOLON AND THE COLON
The Semicolon

RULE

The semicolon is used to separate the clauses in a compound sentence when they are not joined by a coordinating conjunction.

The judge instructed the jury; the jurors listened patiently.
The professor was an expert in his subject; nevertheless, he was a dull lecturer.

She bought a rib roast of beef, ten lamb chops, and a pound of liver at the butcher shop; potatoes, apples, and oranges at the grocery store; and tooth paste and hand lotion at the drug store.

The Colon

The following members of the committee were present: James Anderson, Mary Montgomery, Nelson Danforth, John Winters, and Francis Dunn.
The most important rules of this organization are these:
1. Attendance is required at two-thirds of the regular meetings.
2. Dues must be paid during the first month of every year.
3. All members must be willing to serve on committees.

Other Uses for Colons

1. The colon is used after the salutation of a business letter: *Gentlemen:*   *Dear Sirs:*   *My dear Mr. Holstead:*

2. The colon is used to divide subdivisions from major divisions when indicating the time of day (7:25) or when making references to Biblical passages (Genesis 12:2).

THE DASH, THE HYPHEN, AND THE APOSTROPHE
The Dash

The dash indicates a sudden, and usually unexpected, break in the anticipated sequence of thought. Since most typewriters do not have a dash on the keyboard, two connected hyphens are used (- -) with a space before and after the hyphens.

I believed that my country—but why should I have believed it?—was always right.

Other Uses for Dashes

1. The dash can be used to indicate a suspension or breaking off of thought.

> I always wanted to—. But it's too late now to want anything.

2. The dash sometimes separates parenthetical material from the main body of a sentence.

> His hopeless condition—it seemed hopeless at the time—caused his wife intolerable anguish.

3. The dash is useful to indicate that a remark at the end of a sentence has been inserted as an afterthought, sometimes with ironic effect.

> The president of the firm was a man of absolute integrity—or so it seemed to the stockholders before the firm collapsed.

4. In dialogue the dash can be used to indicate hesitant or halting speech.

> "I wish—I wish—I wish," he said haltingly, as he held his end of the wishbone, "I wish for a vacation in Europe."

The Hyphen

Uses for Hyphens

1. The hyphen is used to make a compound word out of two or more words which are to be thought of as a single unit.

> The 1986-87 academic year
> The Princeton-Yale game
> A blue-green dress
> He played a better-than-average game.

2. The hyphen is used where a word must be broken (hyphenated) at the end of a line because there is not enough space to write, type, or print all of it. Words must not be divided arbitrarily; they may be hyphenated only between syllables. Syllables are the parts of a word which are pronounced as units. When in doubt about correct hyphenation, consult a good dictionary. When possible avoid hyphenating proper names.

> Samuel Johnson, who was an outstanding liter-
> ary figure of the eighteenth century in Eng-
> land, was known as the great lexicographer.
> He compiled the first real English dictionary.

3. The hyphen is sometimes required to eliminate misreading when a prefix ends with the same letter as the initial letter of the word to which it is added.

> re-estimate   co-ownership   de-escalate

4. The hyphen is used in compound numbers from twenty-one to ninety-nine.

5. The hyphen is used to separate dates of birth and death: James Finch (1714-1778); scores of games: Princeton-Dartmouth, 78-67; and similar opposing or terminal relationships: Nearly everything goes in pairs: sun-moon, day-night, man-woman, winter-summer.

The Apostrophe

Uses for Apostrophes

1. The apostrophe is used to indicate the possessive case of a noun. Add the apostrophe and *s* to words which do not end with an *s* or *z* sound. Add only the apostrophe to words which end with an *s* or *z* sound:

the boy's room	*the children's school*
the boys' room	*Dickens' novels*

EXCEPTION: In singular one-syllable nouns ending in the *s* or *z* sound, it is customary to add the apostrophe and *s* and to pronounce the possessive as if it ended in *es: the boss's hat.*

2. The apostrophe is used to indicate missing letters in a contraction:

He's ready to join us. (He is)
Martha *can't* be with us. (cannot)

3. The apostrophe is used to form plurals of letters, figures, or symbols for which there is no conventional plural:

I counted seven 8's, twenty m's, and four *'s on the page.

PARENTHESES AND BRACKETS

Parentheses ( ) and brackets [ ] are both used to exclude extraneous or interrupting material from a sentence or from a paragraph.

Parentheses

Parentheses are used to enclose anything that interrupts the sense of what is being written.

I was born in 1906. (That was the year of the San Francisco earthquake.)
I met my future wife (my first date, incidentally) at a high school dance.
The dam was built (1) to provide water for irrigation, (2) to prevent flooding, and (3) to provide power for the generation of electricity.
His seventh novel, *The Errant Wife* (1836), was a failure.

Brackets

Brackets are used only to enclose additions by an editor of any kind of quoted material.

"The composer [Brahms] was frequently entertained by the nobility."
"Jonathan Swift [1667-1745] lived during the War of the Spanish Succession."

QUOTATIONS AND QUOTATION MARKS

QUOTATION MARKS TO INDICATE TITLES

Quotation marks should enclose titles of short pieces such as essays, articles in magazines, chapters in books, short stories, one-act plays, short musical compositions, short poems, etc.

"The Afternoon of a Faun" (short musical composition)
"The Piece of String" (short story)
"Ode to the West Wind" (short poem)

NOTE: Titles of lengthier works are placed in italics, indicated by underlining in typed or handwritten material: Shakespeare's *Macbeth*.

DIRECT QUOTATIONS

The exact words of a quotation, spoken or written, should be placed in quotation marks. A paraphrase of what someone spoke or wrote (indirect quotation) does not require, and should not be indicated by, quotation marks.

DIRECT: She said, "I am not going to wait for my husband."

INDIRECT: She said that she wasn't going to wait for her husband.

DIRECT: Dickens introduces his novel *David Copperfield* by saying, "Whether I shall turn out to be the hero of my own life, or whether that station will be held by anybody else, these pages must show."

INDIRECT: Dickens introduces his novel *David Copperfield* by saying that the pages which follow will show whether he will be the hero of his own life, or whether that position will be held by somebody else.

PUNCTUATION OF DIALOGUE

When a dialogue between two or more persons is set down (usually in a story or novel), a new paragraph is used for each new speaker. Descriptive or other matter relevant to the speaker is placed in the same paragraph as the quotation. When only two speakers are involved, the alternation of paragraphs makes it unnecessary to identify the speaker every time and so permits the dialogue to proceed more rapidly and without interruption.

"Herbert," said I, after a short silence, in a hurried way, "can you see me best by the light of the window, or the light of the fire?"

"By the firelight," answered Herbert, coming close again.

"Look at me."

"I do look at you, my dear boy."

"Touch me."

"I do touch you, my dear boy."

"You are not afraid that I am in any fever, or that my head is much disordered by the accident of last night?"

"N-no, my dear boy," said Herbert, after taking time to examine me. "You are rather excited, but you are quite yourself."

—Charles Dickens, *Great Expectations*

In the reporting of speech or dialogue, reference to the speaker (*I said, he answered*) is separated from the quotation by a comma. Two commas are required if the reference to the speaker is inserted within the quotation.

"Let me know where I can reach you," I said.
"I'm not at all sure," she replied, "that I want you to reach me."
I answered abruptly, "Then don't bother."

The comma is omitted if a question mark or an exclamation mark is required where the comma would ordinarily be placed.

"Why can't you finish your dinner?" I asked.
"I refuse to see anybody!" he shouted.

If the quotation consists of more than one sentence, only one sentence is joined by a comma to the reference to the speaker.

"I have come home after a long journey," he said. "I want to rest."

QUOTATIONS OTHER THAN DIALOGUE

> RULE
>
> When quoting printed or written subject-matter, reproduce the punctuation and capitalization of what is quoted exactly as it originally appeared.

Benjamin Franklin believed that "A penny saved is a penny earned."
The author expressed "a sinking feeling about our domestic problems."

> RULE
>
> If the quotation is longer than one paragraph, no end-quotation marks are placed at the conclusion of the first paragraph. All succeeding paragraphs are prefaced by quotation marks, but only the final paragraph is concluded with end-quotation marks.

In describing Don Quixote, Cervantes offers many illustrations of the fact that the Don is usually so preoccupied with his own dream that he pays no attention to reality. Here is a brief example:

"While Don Quixote was singing a ballad about the noble Marquis of Mantua, a neighbor from his own village happened to come along. Amazed at the appearance of Don Quixote and wondering about the sadness of his song, he asked what was the matter with him.

"Don Quixote was firmly persuaded that this was the Marquis of Mantua so his only answer was to go on singing his ballad.

"The neighbor was amazed at such nonsense, and taking off Don Quixote's helmet, he recognized him as Señor Don Quixada which had been his real name when he was still possessed of his senses."

RULE

Long quotations (five lines or more) from writings are not usually enclosed in quotation marks. They are indicated as quotations by being indented at both right and left sides. Smaller typeface is customary for printed matter and single spacing for typescript, with indentions on both sides.

Charles Dickens' *Child's History of England* is written in a very simple and vivid style. As a way of delineating the character of Oliver Cromwell, Dickens describes Cromwell's leadership of the Irish campaign.

> Oliver had been appointed by the Parliament to command the army in Ireland, where he took a terrible vengeance for the sanguinary rebellion, and made tremendous havoc, particularly in the siege of Drogheda, where no quarter was given, and where he found at least a thousand of the inhabitants shut up together in the great church, every one of whom was killed by his soldiers, usually known as Oliver's Ironsides. There were numbers of friars and priests among them; and Oliver gruffly wrote home in his dispatch that these were "knocked on the head" like the rest.

QUOTATIONS WITHIN QUOTATIONS

Single quotation marks are used to set off a quotation within another quotation.

"Have you read Poe's 'Ulalume' lately?" I asked.

At the trial the star witness testified, "On the night of the murder I distinctly heard Mrs. Knox say, 'I would give anything to get him out of the way.' "

QUOTATION MARKS RELATED TO OTHER PUNCTUATION

RULE

Without regard to logic, periods and commas are always placed inside quotation marks; colons and semicolons are always placed outside quotation marks.

"They insisted that I go with them," she said. "So I did."

There are four characters in the Brome "Abraham and Isaac": God, the angel, Abraham, and Isaac.

He glanced rapidly through Frost's "Mending Wall"; he was in a hurry to finish his assignment.

PITFALL

Other punctuation marks are placed where they logically belong: inside the quotation marks if they punctuate the quotation, outside if they punctuate the entire sentence of which the quotation is a part.

What is the theme of Longfellow's "Excelsior"?

She inquired, "Is this the road to Denver?"

Don't let me catch you reading "The Love Song of Alfred Prufrock"!

As he fell off the dock, the child screamed, "Help!"

20 ■ Spelling

DICTIONARY AND SPELLING ASSISTANCE

Sounds and spelling in English are frequently at variance with each other. Only the following sounds are dependable in English spelling. They are almost invariably represented by the corresponding letters of the alphabet.

B	bat	SH	shut
D	dog	T	toy
L	love	TH	think *or* then
P	push	V, F	vat; fat

The following sounds are listed in alphabetical order, followed by suggestions of what letters may represent these sounds in English (and, consequently, how you may look up words in the dictionary that are apparently not spelled as they should be).

When looking for a word, if you do not find it spelled phonetically:

1. sound it out carefully,
2. then consult the following list of sounds, and
3. check the corresponding letters in your dictionary.

VOWEL SOUNDS

Sound	As In	May Be Represented By	Illustration
A	wake	A	able
		AE	Aegean Sea
		AI	aid
		E	crepe
		EI	eight
A	fat	A	atom
AH	start	A	art
		O	octave
AW	straw	AW	awful
		AU	auto
		O	office
		OU	ought

Sound	As In	May Be Represented By	Illustration
E	he	E	emotion
		EA	each
		EE	eel
		EI	either
		EY	money
		I	unique
		IE	mien
		Y	carry
E	wet	E	edify
		AE	aesthetic, aerial
		AI	said
		EA	dead
I	white	I	idea
		IE	pie
		AI	aisle
		AY	aye
		EI	height
		Y	fly
I	hid	I	if
		A	stoppage
		Y	myth
O	slow	O	obey
		OA	oak
		OW	low
OI	boil	OI	ointment
		OY	boy
OW	plow	OW	owl
		OU	out
OO	mood	OO	ooze
		EW	news
		U	astute
		UI	fruit
OO	foot	OO	took
		OU	would
U	mute	U	unity
		EAU	beauty
		EU	eulogy
		EW	ewe
UH	but	U	until
		A	above
		E	her
		O	oven
		OU	rough

CONSONANT SOUNDS

Sound	As In	May Be Represented By	Illustration
CH	child	CH	chill
		TCH	stretch
F	after	F	far
		GH	tough, cough
		PH	philosophy, telephone
G	drag	G	game
		GH	ghost
GS	legs	X (before vowel)	exist
H	hoot	H	house
		WH	who
J	reject	J	jet
		G	gentle (usually before *E*)
		G	giant (usually before *I*)
		G	gyroscope (sometimes before *Y*)
		DG	pledge
K	kitten	K	key
		C	cat, cot, cut, clip (usually before *a*, *o*, *u*, or consonants)
		CH	chorus, echo
KS	ducks	X (before consonant)	expert
M	moon	M	mad
		MN	condemn
N	noon	N	now
		GN	gnome
		KN	know
		PN	pneumatic
R	art	R	reach
		WR	write
S	sing	S	sun
		SC	science
		ST	fasten
		C	cease, city (usually before *e*, *i*, and *y*)
		PS	psalm
SF	glassful	SPH	sphere
SH	wish	SH	shirt
		SS (before *ion*)	mission
		T (before *ion*)	fiction

Sound	As In	May Be Represented By	Illustration
SK	flask	SK	skirt
		SC	scandal
		SCH	school
		SQ	squirrel
SW	sweet	SW	swim
		SU	suede
W	wind	W	waste
		WH	white
		O	one
X (KS)	expert	X (before consonant)	wax
Y	you	Y	yet
		U	unit
		EU	eulogy
		EW	ewe
Z	ooze	Z	zip
		S	cosy
		X	xylophone
ZH		Z	seizure
		S	division

SOME SPELLING PRINCIPLES
Doubling the Final Consonant Before Adding Suffixes

RULE

Words of one syllable ending in a single consonant preceded by a single vowel double the final consonant before adding a suffix beginning with a vowel.

hop plus *ed*:	*hopped*
bat plus *er*:	*batter*
spin plus *ing*:	*spinning*

RULE

Words of more than one syllable which are accented on the final syllable and which end in a single consonant preceded by a single vowel double the final consonant before adding a suffix beginning with a vowel.

occur plus *ed*:	*occurred*
admit plus *ing*:	*admitting*

PITFALL

Do not double the final consonant if the sound of the preceding vowel is that of the alphabet sound.

to dine in the *dining* room.
to have *dinner* in the *dining* room.

Changing the Final *Y* to *I* Before Adding Suffixes

RULE

Words ending in *Y* preceded by a consonant change the *Y* to *I* before adding suffixes.

salary	*salaries*
marry	*married*
fancy	*fanciful*
merry	*merriment*
lonely	*loneliness*

PITFALL

The *Y* is retained when adding the suffix *ING* or if the word is one syllable.

carry	*carrying*
dry	*drying*

Dropping the Final *E* Before Adding Suffixes

RULE

The final *E* is dropped when adding suffixes which begin with a vowel.

white plus *er*:	*whiter*
choice plus *est*:	*choicest*
move plus *ing*:	*moving*
love plus *able*:	*lovable*

PITFALL

Words ending in double *E* (*EE*) never drop the final *EE*.

    agree   *agreeing*

Words ending in E preceded by *C* or *G* do not drop the final *E* unless the suffix begins with an *I* or a *Y*.

grace	*graceful*
engage	*engagement*
price	*pricing*
ice	*icy*
mortgage	*mortgaging*

EXCEPTIONS: *judge, judgment; acknowledge, acknowledgment*

SPELLING RULES

The spelling of English words is so inconsistent that there are only *two important rules*. The first applies to a considerable number of common words and should be mastered.

RULE 1

When diphthongs *ei* or *ie* have the single sound of *EE*, the rule is:

I before E
Except after C
Or when sounded like A
As in *neighbor* and *weigh*.

After C	Not After C
deceive	chief
receive	yield
conceit	piece
ceiling	believe

There are a few exceptions even to this rule, but the exceptions can be learned by memorizing a silly question:

Did *either* or *neither financier seize* a *weird species* of *leisure?*

PITFALL

The following frequently used *ei* and *ie* words do not have the sound of *EE*, but they are exceptions to the rule. Special attention should be given to the spelling of the following words:

foreign	*friend*
eight	*science*
height	*conscience*

RULE 2

To maintain the alphabet sound of a vowel, the single consonant that follows the vowel must in turn be followed by a vowel which can be either silent or expressed.

hike	but *hit*
cape	but *cap*
cope	but *cop*
cute	but *cut*
meter	but *met*

RULE

To maintain the non-alphabet sound of the vowel, double the consonant before adding a vowel.

cap	but *capped*
stop	but *stopping*
cut	but *cutting*
pet	but *petting*
din	but *dinner*

318 WORDS FREQUENTLY MISSPELLED

abbreviation	agreeable	apologize
absence	aisle	appearance
acceptable	all right	appreciate
accidentally	alley	arguing
accommodate	already	arrangement
accompanied	altar	arrive
account	altogether	article
accustom	always	ashamed
achieve	amateur	assignment
acknowledge	among	association
acquaintance	amount	athlete
across	analysis	attendance
address	analyze	author
advertisement	annihilate	awful
advice	annual	awkward
advise	anonymous	beginning
aerial	answer	behavior
against	anxious	believe

benefited
brake
break
breathe
bruise
business
calendar
campaign
candidate
capital
captain
carrying
catastrophe
cemetery
characteristic
clothes
coarse
college
color
committed
compel
complexion
conceivable
conference
conscience
conscientious
conscious
consistent
continuous
convenience
cordially
correspondence
counsel
courageous
course
courteous
criticize
cupboard
dealt
decide
defense
definite
dependent
descendant
descent
describe
desert

desirable
despair
dessert
develop
dictionary
different
difficult
dining
disappear
disappoint
disastrous
discipline
discuss
disease
dissatisfied
divide
divine
division
doubt
earnest
economical
ecstasy
efficient
eighteen
eighth
embarrass
eminent
emphasize
envelope
environment
equipped
especially
exaggerate
exceed
excellent
exercise
exhaust
existence
expense
extraordinary
familiar
fascinate
fatigue
February
feminine
fiery
finally

financial
foreign
foresee
forty
fourth
genius
government
grammar
guarantee
guard
handle
headache
height
heroes
hindrance
hoping
horizon
hospital
humorous
hypocrisy
imaginary
immediate
independence
indispensable
inevitable
influence
initial
interest
irrelevant
irresistible
judgment
knowledge
laboratory
later
latter
leisure
license
lightning
likelihood
likely
loneliness
luncheon
luxurious
maintenance
maneuver
manual
marriage

mathematics	potatoes	stationary
medicine	practice	stationery
mention	precede	stopped
miniature	preference	strategy
mischievous	preferred	strength
misspell	prejudice	stretch
mortgage	prevalent	studying
movable	previously	subtle
murmur	principal	succeed
naturally	principle	sufficient
necessary	privilege	superintendent
neighborhood	probably	supersede
niece	procedure	surprise
ninety	proceed	sympathy
ninth	professor	temperament
noticeable	pursue	temperature
occasionally	questionnaire	therefore
occur	quiet	thorough
occurrence	quite	though
omitted	realize	thought
opinion	receive	through
opportunity	recognize	tomorrow
optimism	recommend	traffic
pageant	referred	tragedy
pamphlet	relief	transferred
parallel	religious	tremendous
parliament	repetition	truly
particular	restaurant	twelfth
pastime	rhythm	unforgettable
peaceable	salary	vacuum
perceive	schedule	vengeance
perhaps	secretary	vicinity
permanent	seize	villain
permissible	sensitive	wealth
perseverance	separate	weather
persuade	sergeant	Wednesday
piece	shepherd	weird
playwright	shining	whether
pleasant	similar	wiry
poison	sincerely	woman
possess	souvenir	women

NOTE: Only one English word ends in -*sede: supersede.* Only three words end in -*ceed: exceed, proceed, succeed.* All other verbs with that sound end in -*cede: concede, precede, recede.*

VERB CONJUGATIONS

21 ■ Some Basics

SPELLING IRREGULARITIES OF SOME REGULAR VERBS

RULE

Regular verbs ending in a consonant (push, cook, float):
• form the present participle by adding *ing* (pushing, cooking, floating).
• form the past tense and past participle by adding *ed* (pushed, cooked, floated).

PITFALL

Regular verbs ending in a single consonant preceded by a single vowel (drop, grip):
• double the final consonant before adding *ing* or *ed* (dropping, dropped, gripping, gripped).

RULE

Regular verbs ending in a vowel (veto):
• form the present participle by adding *ing* (vetoing).
• form the past tense and past participle by adding *ed* (vetoed).

PITFALL

Regular verbs ending in *e* preceded by a single consonant (make, smoke):
• form the present participle by dropping the *e* before adding *ing* (making, smoking)
• form the past tense and past participle by adding only *d* (raked, smoked).

Regular verbs ending in *y* preceded by a consonant (try, hurry):
• change the *y* to *i* before adding *ed* (tried, hurried)
• change the *y* to *i* for third person singular (tries, hurries).

PRINCIPAL AUXILIARY VERBS

Pronoun	Pres. Tense	Past Tense
I, you, he, she, it, we, they	can	could
I, you, we, they	do	did
he, she, it	does	did
I, you, we, they	have	had
he, she, it	has	had
I, you, he, she, it, we, they	may	might
I, you, he, she, it, we, they	must	had to
I, you, he, she, it, we, they	should	should have,
	ought	ought to
		have
I, we	shall (future)	shall have
I, you, he, she, it, we, they	will (future)	will have
I, you, he, she, it, we, they	would	would have

(See *to be* for full conjugation of that verb as an auxiliary, as well as a linking verb.)

TYPICAL VERB USAGES
(with *to forget* as Model)

The verb *to forget* demonstrates the many shades of meaning made possible by the different voices, moods, and tenses of English verbs.

NOTE: For a summary of uses of the progressive forms, see the end of this model.

INDICATIVE MOOD

Active Voice

Present: I *forget* nearly everything I learn.
Present Progressive: She *is* always *forgetting* to bring her notebook.
Present Intensive: You certainly *do forget* a great deal.
Future: You *will* probably *forget* me before long.
Future (Promise): I *will* never *forget* you.
Future (Command): The observers of this crime *shall forget* what they have seen, or they will live to regret it.
Conditional: I *would forget* that if I were you.
Past: John *forgot* to lock the door.
Past Progressive: The children *were* always *forgetting* to drink their milk.
Past Intensive: They really *did forget* to drink their milk.
Present Perfect: The old man *has forgotten* his childhood.
Past Perfect: I *had forgotten* that I promised to meet you.
Future Perfect: When winter comes, I *will have forgotten* our summer vacation.
Conditional Perfect: I *would have forgotten* it if you had not reminded me.

Present: *If* I *forget* to meet you, go without me.
Past: *If* they *forgot* their tickets, they weren't able to hear the concert.
Future: *If* I *should forget* to leave a key, go to my neighbor's house.

PASSIVE VOICE OF INDICATIVE

Present: Telephone numbers *are* easily *forgotten.*
Present Progressive: I *am being forgotten* by all my friends.
Present Intensive: Your directions really *do get forgotten* easily.
Future: The words of the song *will be forgotten* very quickly.
Future (Promise): I will so live that I *will* not *be forgotten.*
Future (Command): Your bad habits *shall be forgotten!*
Conditional: They *would be forgotten* before the end of the week.
Past: The novel *was forgotten* by most people.
Past Progressive: The lessons *were being forgotten* almost as quickly as they were learned.
Past Intensive: You *did* not *get forgotten* after all.
Present Perfect: All the old times *have been forgotten.*
Past Perfect: They *had been forgotten* long ago.
Future Perfect: When you have reached my age, your youth *will have been forgotten.*
Conditional Perfect: If you had not reminded us, the books *would have been forgotten.*

PASSIVE VOICE OF SUBJUNCTIVE

Present: *If* his words *be forgotten,* he will have spoken in vain.
Past: *If* you *were forgotten,* it was through no fault of mine.
Future: *If* the lesson *should be forgotten,* it can be easily learned again.

USES OF PROGRESSIVE FORMS
(with *to forget* as Model)

The *progressive form* of a verb consists of the use of any tense of the verb *to be* with the present participle (-*ing*) of any following verb, in order to indicate the progression or continuity of an action, actively or passively.

I am always saying that. (I continue to say that.)
We were always doing that. (We continued to do that.)

123

They will often be doing that. (They will often continue to do that.)
It was being sold at the market. (It was continuing to be sold at the market.)

Active Voice

Present Progressive: I *am* always *forgetting* to bring my keys.
Future Progressive: By this time tomorrow, I *will be forgetting* them again.
Conditional Progressive: I *would* always *be forgetting* them if I did not need them for my car.
Past Progressive: We *were* always *forgetting* to lock the door to the storage room.
Present Perfect Progressive: Each day the old man *has been forgetting* more and more.
Past Perfect Progressive: They *had been forgetting* so often to take care of the mail that the boss had to fire them.
Future Perfect Progressive: If you forget this again, you *will have been forgetting* this every day for the last three weeks!
Conditional Perfect Progressive: I *would have always been forgetting* to do that job if the boss hadn't reminded me of it every single day!

Passive Voice

Present Progressive: He *is being forgotten* by all his friends.
Past Progressive: The tunes *were being forgotten* as fast as they were being sung.

22 ■ Conjugation of a Regular Verb With *to push* as Model

to push (active voice)   *Principal Parts:* push, pushing, pushed, pushed

---

Infinitive: to push, push   *Present Participle:* pushing
Perfect Infinitive: to have pushed   *Past Participle:* pushed

INDICATIVE MOOD

Pres.	I push	we push
	you push	you push
	he (she, it) pushes	they push
Pres.	I am pushing	we are pushing
Prog.	you are pushing	you are pushing
	he (she, it) is pushing	they are pushing
Pres.	I do push	we do push
Int.	you do push	you do push
	he (she, it) does push	they do push
Fut.	I shall push	we shall push
	you will push	you will push
	he (she, it) will push	they will push
Cond.	I would push	we would push
	you would push	you would push
	he (she, it) would push	they would push
Past	I pushed	we pushed
	you pushed	you pushed
	he (she, it) pushed	they pushed
Past	I was pushing	we were pushing
Prog.	you were pushing	you were pushing
	he (she, it) was pushing	they were pushing
Past	I did push	we did push
Int.	you did push	you did push
	he (she, it) did push	they did push
Pres.	I have pushed	we have pushed
Perf.	you have pushed	you have pushed
	he (she, it) has pushed	they have pushed
Past	I had pushed	we had pushed
Perf.	you had pushed	you had pushed
	he (she, it) had pushed	they had pushed
Fut.	I shall have pushed	we shall have pushed
Perf.	you will have pushed	you will have pushed
	he (she, it) will have pushed	they will have pushed
Cond.	I would have pushed	we would have pushed
Perf.	you would have pushed	you would have pushed
	he (she, it) would have pushed	they would have pushed

IMPERATIVE MOOD

push   push

SUBJUNCTIVE MOOD

Pres.	if I push	if we push
	if you push	if you push
	if he (she, it) push	if they push
Past	if I pushed	if we pushed
	if you pushed	if you pushed
	if he (she, it) pushed	if they pushed
Fut.	if I should push	if we should push
	if you should push	if you should push
	if he (she, it) should push	if they should push

126

(passive voice)

Infinitive: to be pushed, be pushed   *Present Participle:* being pushed
Perfect Infinitive: to have been pushed   *Past Participle:* been pushed

INDICATIVE MOOD

Pres.	I am pushed	we are pushed
	you are pushed	you are pushed
	he (she, it) is pushed	they are pushed
Pres.	I am being pushed	we are being pushed
Prog.	you are being pushed	you are being pushed
	he (she, it) is being pushed	they are being pushed
Pres.	I do get pushed	we do get pushed
Int.	you do get pushed	you do get pushed
	he (she, it) does get pushed	they do get pushed
Fut.	I shall be pushed	we shall be pushed
	you will be pushed	you will be pushed
	he (she, it) will be pushed	they will be pushed
Cond.	I would be pushed	we would be pushed
	you would be pushed	you would be pushed
	he (she, it) would be pushed	they would be pushed
Past	I was pushed	we were pushed
	you were pushed	you were pushed
	he (she, it) was pushed	they were pushed
Past	I was being pushed	we were being pushed
Prog.	you were being pushed	you were being pushed
	he (she, it) was being pushed	they were being pushed
Past	I did get pushed	we did get pushed
Int.	you did get pushed	you did get pushed
	he (she, it) did get pushed	they did get pushed
Pres.	I have been pushed	we have been pushed
Perf.	you have been pushed	you have been pushed
	he (she, it) has been pushed	they have been pushed
Past	I had been pushed	we had been pushed
Perf.	you had been pushed	you had been pushed
	he (she, it) had been pushed	they had been pushed
Fut.	I shall have been pushed	we shall have been pushed
Perf.	you will have been pushed	you will have been pushed
	he (she, it) will have been pushed	they will have been pushed
Cond.	I would have been pushed	we would have been pushed
Perf.	you would have been pushed	you would have been pushed
	he (she, it) would have been pushed	they would have been pushed

IMPERATIVE MOOD
be pushed

SUBJUNCTIVE MOOD

Pres.	if I be pushed	if we be pushed
	if you be pushed	if you be pushed
	if he (she, it) be pushed	if they be pushed
Past	if I were pushed	if we were pushed
	if you were pushed	if you were pushed
	if he (she, it) were pushed	if they were pushed
Fut.	if I should be pushed	if we should be pushed
	if you should be pushed	if you should be pushed
	if he (she, it) should be pushed	if they should be pushed

23 ■ Conjugation of 120 Irregular Verbs In Alphabetical Order

to arise (active voice only)   *Principal Parts:* arise, arising, arose, arisen

---

(intransitive verb)

Infinitive: to arise   *Present Participle:* arising
Perfect Infinitive: to have arisen   *Past Participle:* arisen

INDICATIVE MOOD

Pres.	I arise	we arise
	you arise	you arise
	he (she, it) arises	they arise
Pres.	I am arising	we are arising
Prog.	you are arising	you are arising
	he (she, it) is arising	they are arising
Pres.	I do arise	we do arise
Int.	you do arise	you do arise
	he (she, it) does arise	they do arise
Fut.	I shall arise	we shall arise
	you will arise	you will arise
	he (she, it) will arise	they will arise
Cond.	I would arise	we would arise
	you would arise	you would arise
	he (she, it) would arise	they would arise
Past	I arose	we arose
	you arose	you arose
	he (she, it) arose	they arose
Past	I was arising	we were arising
Prog.	you were arising	you were arising
	he (she, it) was arising	they were arising
Past	I did arise	we did arise
Int.	you did arise	you did arise
	he (she, it) did arise	they did arise
Pres.	I have arisen	we have arisen
Perf.	you have arisen	you have arisen
	he (she, it) has arisen	they have arisen
Past	I had arisen	we had arisen
Perf.	you had arisen	you had arisen
	he (she, it) had arisen	they had arisen
Fut.	I shall have arisen	we shall have arisen
Perf.	you will have arisen	you will have arisen
	he (she, it) will have arisen	they will have arisen
Cond.	I would have arisen	we would have arisen
Perf.	You would have arisen	you would have arisen
	he (she, it) would have arisen	they would have arisen

IMPERATIVE MOOD
arise

SUBJUNCTIVE MOOD

Pres.	if I arise	if we arise
	if you arise	if you arise
	if he (she, it) arise	if they arise
Past	if I arose	if we arose
	if you arose	if you arose
	if he (she, it) arose	if they arose
Fut.	if I should arise	if we should arise
	if you should arise	if you should arise
	if he (she, it) should arise	if they should arise

to awake (active voice) *Principal Parts:* awake, awaking, awoke (awaked), awaked (awakened)

Infinitive: to awake   *Present Participle:* awaking
Perfect Infinitive: to have awakened   *Past Participle:* awaked, awakened

INDICATIVE MOOD

Pres.	I awake	we awake
	you awake	you awake
	he (she, it) awakes	they awake
Pres.	I am awaking	we are awaking
Prog.	you are awaking	you are awaking
	he (she, it) is awaking	they are awaking
Pres.	I do awake	we do awake
Int.	you do awake	you do awake
	he (she, it) does awake	they do awake
Fut.	I shall awake	we shall awake
	you will awake	you will awake
	he (she, it) will awake	they will awake
Cond.	I would awake	we would awake
	you would awake	you would awake
	he (she, it) would awake	they would áwake
Past	I awoke, awaked	we awoke, awaked
	you awoke, awaked	you awoke, awaked
	he (she, it) awoke, awaked	they awoke, awaked
Past	I was awaking	we were awaking
Prog.	you were awaking	you were awaking
	he (she, it) was awaking	they were awaking
Past	I did awake	we did awake
Int.	you did awake	you did awake
	he (she, it) did awake	they did awake
Pres.	I have awaked, awakened	we have awaked, awakened
Perf.	you have awaked, awakened	you have awaked, awakened
	he (she, it) has awaked, awakened	they have awaked, awakened
Fut.	I shall have awakened	we shall have awakened
Perf.	you will have awakened	you will have awakened
	he (she, it) will have awakened	they will have awakened
Cond.	I would have awakened	we would have awakened
Perf.	you would have awakened	you would have awakened
	he (she, it) would have awakened	they would have awakened

IMPERATIVE MOOD
awake

SUBJUNCTIVE MOOD

Pres.	if I awake	if we awake
	if you awake	if you awake
	if he (she, it) awake	if they awake
Past	if I awoke	if we awoke
	if you awoke	if you awoke
	if he (she, it) awoke	if they awoke
Fut.	if I should awake	if we should awake
	if you should awake	if you should awake
	if he (she, it) should awake	if they should awake

130

Infinitive: to be awakened   *Present Participle:* being awakened
Perfect Infinitive: to have been awakened *Past Participle:* been awakened

INDICATIVE MOOD

Pres. I am awakened you are awakened he (she, it) is awakened	we are awakened you are awakened they are awakened
Pres. I am being awakened *Prog.* you are being awakened he (she, it) is being awakened	we are being awakened you are being awakened they are being awakened
Pres. I do get awakened *Int.* you do get awakened he (she, it) does get awakened	we do get awakened you do get awakened they do get awakened
Fut. I shall be awakened you will be awakened he (she, it) will be awakened	we shall be awakened you will be awakened they will be awakened
Cond. I would be awakened you would be awakened he (she, it) would be awakened	we would be awakened you would be awakened they would be awakened
Past I was awakened you were awakened he (she, it) was awakened	we were awakened you were awakened they were awakened
Past I was being awakened *Prog.* you were being awakened he (she, it) was being awakened	we were being awakened you were being awakened they were being awakened
Past I did get awakened *Int.* you did get awakened he (she, it) did get awakened	we did get awakened you did get awakened they did get awakened
Pres. I have been awakened *Perf.* you have been awakened he (she, it) has been awakened	we have been awakened you have been awakened they have been awakened
Past I had been awakened *Perf.* you had been awakened he (she, it) had been awakened	we had been awakened you had been awakened they had been awakened
Fut. I shall have been awakened *Perf.* you will have been awakened he (she, it) will have been awakened	we shall have been awakened you will have been awakened they will have been awakened
Cond. I would have been awakened *Perf.* you would have been awakened he (she, it) would have been awakened	we would have been awakened you would have been awakened they would have been awakened

IMPERATIVE MOOD
be awakened

SUBJUNCTIVE MOOD

Pres. if I be awakened if you be awakened if he (she, it) be awakened	if we be awakened if you be awakened if they be awakened
Past if I were awakened if you were awakened if he (she, it) were awakened	if we were awakened if you were awakened if they were awakened
Fut. if I should be awakened if you should be awakened if he (she, it) should be awakened	if we should be awakened if you should be awakened if they should be awakened

Infinitive: to be, be
Perfect Infinitive: to have been

Present Participle: being
Past Participle: been

INDICATIVE MOOD

Pres.
I am
you are
he (she, it) is

we are
you are
they are

Pres.
Prog.
I am being
you are being
he (she, it) is being

we are being
you are being
they are being

Fut.
I shall be
you will be
he (she, it) will be

we shall be
you will be
they will be

Cond.
I would be
you would be
he (she, it) would be

we would be
you would be
they would be

Past
I was
you were
he (she, it) was

we were
you were
they were

Past
Prog.
I was being
you were being
he (she, it) was being

we were being
you were being
they were being

Pres.
Perf.
I have been
you have been
he (she, it) has been

we have been
you have been
they have been

Past
Perf.
I had been
you had been
he (she, it) had been

we had been
you had been
they had been

Fut.
Perf.
I shall have been
you will have been
he (she, it) will have been

we shall have been
you will have been
they will have been

Cond.
Perf.
I would have been
you would have been
he (she, it) would have been

we would have been
you would have been
they would have been

IMPERATIVE MOOD
be

SUBJUNCTIVE MOOD

Pres.
if I be
if you be
if he (she, it) be

if we be
if you be
if they be

Past
if I were, were being
if you were, were being
if he (she, it) were, were being

if we were, were being
if you were, were being
if they were, were being

Fut.
if I should be
if you should be
if he (she, it) should be

if we should be
if you should be
if they should be

Common Uses of *To Be*

The basic meaning of *to be* is *to exist,* as in Hamlet's well-known soliloquy "To be or not to be: that is the question."

The principal use of *to be* is to make an assertion. An observation like "cold ice" becomes an assertion by adding the appropriate form of the verb *to be:* Ice *is* cold.

To be is called a linking verb because it joins many kinds of sentence elements: nouns as in "Mr. Price *is* the mayor," nouns and predicate adjectives as in "The girl *was* beautiful," infinitives and predicate adjectives as in "To err *is* human," expletives and phrases as in "There *would be* many more people in the hall tonight if it *were* not raining," etc.

To be is also used to create the progressive forms of other verbs: "The water *is flowing,*" as well as the passive voice: "I *was beaten.*"

to bear (active voice)   *Principal Parts:* bear, bearing, bore, borne

---

Infinitive: to bear   *Present Participle:* bearing
Perfect Infinitive: to have borne   *Past Participle:* borne

INDICATIVE MOOD

Pres.	I bear	we bear
	you bear	you bear
	he (she, it) bears	they bear
Pres.	I am bearing	we are bearing
Prog.	you are bearing	you are bearing
	he (she, it) is bearing	they are bearing
Pres.	I do bear	we do bear
Int.	you do bear	you do bear
	he (she, it) does bear	they do bear
Fut.	I shall bear	we shall bear
	you will bear	you will bear
	he (she, it) will bear	they will bear
Cond.	I would bear	we would bear
	you would bear	you would bear
	he (she, it) would bear	they would bear
Past	I bore	we bore
	you bore	you bore
	he (she, it) bore	they bore
Past	I was bearing	we were bearing
Prog.	you were bearing	you were bearing
	he (she, it) was bearing	they were bearing
Past	I did bear	we did bear
Int.	you did bear	you did bear
	he (she, it) did bear	they did bear
Pres.	I have borne	we have borne
Perf.	you have borne	you have borne
	he (she, it) has borne	they have borne
Past	I had borne	we had borne
Perf.	you had borne	you had borne
	he (she, it) had borne	they had borne
Fut.	I shall have borne	we shall have borne
Perf.	you will have borne	you will have borne
	he (she, it) will have borne	they will have borne
Cond.	I would have borne	we would have borne
Perf.	you would have borne	you would have borne
	he (she, it) would have borne	they would have borne

IMPERATIVE MOOD
bear

SUBJUNCTIVE MOOD

Pres.	if I bear	if we bear
	if you bear	if you bear
	if he (she, it) bear	if they bear
Past	if I bore	if we bore
	if you bore	if you bore
	if he (she, it) bore	if they bore
Fut.	if I should bear	if we should bear
	if you should bear	if you should bear
	if he (she, it) should bear	if they should bear

(passive voice)

Infinitive: to be borne, to be born
Perfect Infinitive: to have been borne, to have been born
Present Participle: being borne, being born
Past Participle: been borne, been born

INDICATIVE MOOD

Pres. I am borne, born you are borne, born he (she, it) is borne, born	we are borne, born you are borne, born they are borne, born

Pres. I am being borne, born
Prog. you are being borne, born
    he (she, it) is being borne, born

we are being borne, born
you are being borne, born
they are being borne, born

Pres. I do get borne, born
Int. you do get borne, born
    he (she, it) does get borne, born

we do get borne, born
you do get borne, born
they do get borne, born

Fut. I shall be borne, born
    you will be borne, born
    he (she, it) will be borne, born

we shall be borne, born
you will be borne, born
they will be borne, born

Cond. I would be borne, born
    you would be borne, born
    he (she, it) would be borne, born

we would be borne, born
you would be borne, born
they would be borne, born

Past I was borne, born
    you were borne, born
    he (she, it) was borne, born

we were borne, born
you were borne, born
they were borne, born

Past I was being borne, born
Prog. you were being borne, born
    he (she, it) was being borne, born

we were being borne, born
you were being borne, born
they were being borne, born

Past I did get borne, born
Int. you did get borne, born
    he (she, it) did get borne, born

we did get borne, born
you did get borne, born
they did get borne, born

Pres. I have been borne, born
Perf. you have been borne, born
    he (she, it) has been borne, born

we have been borne, born
you have been borne, born
they have been borne, born

Past I had been borne, born
Perf. you had been borne, born
    he (she, it) had been borne, born

we had been borne, born
you had been borne, born
they had been borne, born

Fut. I shall have been borne, born
Perf. you will have been borne, born
    he (she, it) will have been borne,
    born

we shall have been borne, born
you will have been borne, born
they will have been borne, born

Cond. I would have been borne, born
Perf. you would have been borne, born
    he (she, it) would have been borne, born

we would have been borne, born
you would have been borne, born
they would have been borne, born

IMPERATIVE MOOD

be borne, be born

SUBJUNCTIVE MOOD

Pres. if I be borne, born
    if you be borne, born
    if he (she, it) be borne, born

if we be borne, born
if you be borne, born
if they be borne, born

Past. if I were borne, born
    if you were borne, born
    if he (she, it) were borne, born

if we were borne, born
if you were borne, born
if they were borne, born

Fut. if I should be borne, born
    if you should be borne, born
    if he (she, it) should be borne,
    born

if we should be borne, born
if you should be borne, born
if they should be borne, born

135

to beat (active voice)   *Principal Parts:* beat, beating, beat, beaten

Infinitive: to beat   *Present Participle:* beating
Perfect Infinitive: to have beaten   *Past Participle:* beaten

INDICATIVE MOOD

Pres.	I beat	we beat
	you beat	you beat
	he (she, it) beats	they beat
Pres.	I am beating	we are beating
Prog.	you are beating	you are beating
	he (she, it) is beating	they are beating
Pres.	I do beat	we do beat
Int.	you do beat	you do beat
	he (she, it) does beat	they do beat
Fut.	I shall beat	we shall beat
	you will beat	you will beat
	he (she, it) will beat	they will beat
Cond.	I would beat	we would beat
	you would beat	you would beat
	he (she, it) would beat	they would beat
Past	I beat	we beat
	you beat	you beat
	he (she, it) beat	they beat
Past	I was beating	we were beating
Prog.	you were beating	you were beating
	he (she, it) was beating	they were beating
Past	I did beat	we did beat
Int.	you did beat	you did beat
	he (she, it) did beat	they did beat
Pres.	I have beaten	we have beaten
Perf.	you have beaten	you have beaten
	he (she, it) has beaten	they have beaten
Past	I had beaten	we had beaten
Perf.	you had beaten	you had beaten
	he (she, it) had beaten	they had beaten
Fut.	I shall have beaten	we shall have beaten
Perf.	you will have beaten	you will have beaten
	he (she, it) will have beaten	they will have beaten
Cond.	I would have beaten	we would have beaten
Perf.	you would have beaten	you would have beaten
	he (she, it) would have beaten	they would have beaten

IMPERATIVE MOOD
beat

SUBJUNCTIVE MOOD

Pres.	if I beat	if we beat
	if you beat	if you beat
	if he (she, it) beat	if they beat
Past	if I beat	if we beat
	if you beat	if you beat
	if he (she, it) beat	if they beat
Fut.	if I should beat	if we should beat
	if you should beat	if you should beat
	if he (she, it) should beat	if they should beat

136

Infinitive: to be beaten   *Present Participle:* being beaten
Perfect Infinitive: to have been beaten   *Past Participle:* been beaten

INDICATIVE MOOD

Pres.
I am beaten
you are beaten
he (she, it) is beaten

we are beaten
you are beaten
they are beaten

Pres. Prog.
I am being beaten
you are being beaten
he (she, it) is being beaten

we are being beaten
you are being beaten
they are being beaten

Pres. Int.
I do get beaten
you do get beaten
he (she, it) does get beaten

we do get beaten
you do get beaten
they do get beaten

Fut.
I shall be beaten
you will be beaten
he (she, it) will be beaten

we shall be beaten
you will be beaten
they will be beaten

Cond.
I would be beaten
you would be beaten
he (she, it) would be beaten

we would be beaten
you would be beaten
they would be beaten

Past
I was beaten
you were beaten
he (she, it) was beaten

we were beaten
you were beaten
they were beaten

Past Prog.
I was being beaten
you were being beaten
he (she, it) was being beaten

we were being beaten
you were being beaten
they were being beaten

Past Int.
I did get beaten
you did get beaten
he (she, it) did get beaten

we did get beaten
you did get beaten
they did get geaten

Pres. Perf.
I have been beaten
you have been beaten
he (she, it) has been beaten

we have been beaten
you have been beaten
they have been beaten

Past Perf.
I had been beaten
you had been beaten
he (she, it) had been beaten

we had been beaten
you had been beaten
they had been beaten

Fut. Perf.
I shall have been beaten
you will have been beaten
he (she, it) will have been beaten

we shall have been beaten
you will have been beaten
they will have been beaten

Cond. Perf.
I would have been beaten
you would have been beaten
he (she, it) would have been beaten

we would have been beaten
you would have been beaten
they would have been beaten

IMPERATIVE MOOD
be beaten

SUBJUNCTIVE MOOD

Pres.
if I be beaten
if you be beaten
if he (she, it) be beaten

if we be beaten
if you be beaten
if they be beaten

Past
if I were beaten
if you were beaten
if he (she, it) were beaten

if we were beaten
if you were beaten
if they were beaten

Fut.
if I should be beaten
if you should be beaten
if he (she, it) should be beaten

if we should be beaten
if you should be beaten
if they should be beaten

to begin (active voice)   *Principal Parts:* begin, beginning, began, begun

Infinitive: to begin   *Present Participle:* beginning
Perfect Infinitive: to have begun   *Past Participle:* begun

INDICATIVE MOOD

Pres.	I begin	we begin
	you begin	you begin
	he (she, it) begins	they begin
Pres.	I am beginning	we are beginning
Prog.	you are beginning	you are beginning
	he (she, it) is beginning	they are beginning
Pres.	I do begin	we do begin
Int.	you do begin	you do begin
	he (she, it) does begin	they do begin
Fut.	I shall begin	we shall begin
	you will begin	you will begin
	he (she, it) will begin	they will begin
Cond.	I would begin	we would begin
	you would begin	you would begin
	he (she, it) would begin	they would begin
Past	I began	we began
	you began	you began
	he (she, it) began	they began
Past	I was beginning	we were beginning
Prog.	you were beginning	you were beginning
	he (she, it) was beginning	they were beginning
Past	I did begin	we did begin
Int.	you did begin	you did begin
	he (she, it) did begin	they did begin
Pres.	I have begun	we have begun
Perf.	you have begun	you have begun
	he (she, it) has begun	they have begun
Past	I had begun	we had begun
Perf.	you had begun	you had begun
	he (she, it) had begun	they had begun
Fut.	I shall have begun	we shall have begun
Perf.	you will have begun	you will have begun
	he (she, it) will have begun	they will have begun
Cond.	I would have begun	we would have begun
Perf.	you would have begun	you would have begun
	he (she, it) would have begun	they would have begun

IMPERATIVE MOOD
begin

SUBJUNCTIVE MOOD

Pres.	if I begin	if we begin
	if you begin	if you begin
	if he (she, it) begin	if they begin
Past	if I began	if we began
	if you began	if you began
	if he (she, it) began	if they began
Fut.	if I should begin	if we should begin
	if you should begin	if you should begin
	if he (she, it) should begin	if they should begin

(passive voice)

Infinitive: to be begun   *Present Participle:* being begun
Perfect Infinitive: to have been begun   *Past Participle:* been begun

INDICATIVE MOOD

Pres.	I am begun	we are begun
	you are begun	you are begun
	he (she, it) is begun	they are begun
Pres.	I am being begun	we are being begun
Prog.	you are being begun	you are being begun
	he (she, it) is being begun	they are being begun
Pres.	I do get begun	we do get begun
Int.	you do get begun	you do get begun
	he (she, it) does get begun	they do get begun
Fut.	I shall be begun	we shall be begun
	you will be begun	you will be begun
	he (she, it) will be begun	they will be begun
Cond.	I would be begun	we would be begun
	you would be begun	you would be begun
	he (she, it) would be begun	they would be begun
Past	I was begun	we were begun
	you were begun	you were begun
	he (she, it) was begun	they were begun
Past	I was being begun	we were being begun
Prog.	you were being begun	you were being begun
	he (she, it) was being begun	they were being begun
Past	I did get begun	we did get begun
Int.	you did get begun	you did get begun
	he (she, it) did get begun	they did get begun
Pres.	I have been begun	we have been begun
Perf.	you have been begun	you have been begun
	he (she, it) has been begun	they have been begun
Past	I had been begun	we had been begun
Perf.	you had been begun	you had been begun
	he (she, it) had been begun	they had been begun
Fut.	I shall have been begun	we shall have been begun
Perf.	you will have been begun	you will have been begun
	he (she, it) will have been begun	they will have been begun
Cond	I would have been begun	we would have been begun
Perf.	you would have been begun	you would have been begun
	he (she, it) would have been begun	they would have been begun

IMPERATIVE MOOD
be begun

SUBJUNCTIVE MOOD

Pres.	if I be begun	if we be begun
	if you be begun	if you be begun
	if he (she, it) be begun	if they be begun
Past	if I were begun	if we were begun
	if you were begun	if you were begun
	if he (she, it) were begun	if they were begun
Fut.	if I should be begun	if we should be begun
	if you should be begun	if you should be begun
	if he (she, it) should be begun	if they should be begun

to bend (active voice)   *Principal Parts:* bend, bending, bent, bent

Infinitive: to bend   *Present Participle:* bending
Perfect Infinitive: to have bent   *Past Participle:* bent

INDICATIVE MOOD

Pres.	I bend	we bend
	you bend	you bend
	he (she, it) bends	they bend
Pres.	I am bending	we are bending
Prog.	you are bending	you are bending
	he (she, it) is bending	they are bending
Pres.	I do bend	we do bend
Int.	you do bend	you do bend
	he (she, it) does bend	they do bend
Fut.	I shall bend	we shall bend
	you will bend	you will bend
	he (she, it) will bend	they will bend
Cond.	I would bend	we would bend
	you would bend	you would bend
	he (she, it) would bend	they would bend
Past	I bent	we bent
	you bent	you bent
	he (she, it) bent	they bent
Past	I was bending	we were bending
Prog.	you were bending	you were bending
	he (she, it) was bending	they were bending
Past	I did bend	we did bend
Int.	you did bend	you did bend
	he (she, it) did bend	they did bend
Pres.	I have bent	we have bent
Perf.	you have bent	you have bent
	he (she, it) has bent	they have bent
Past	I had bent	we had bent
Perf.	you had bent	you had bent
	he (she, it) had bent	they had bent
Fut.	I shall have bent	we shall have bent
Perf.	you will have bent	you will have bent
	he (she, it) will have bent	they will have bent
Cond.	I would have bent	we would have bent
Perf.	you would have bent	you would have bent
	he (she, it) would have bent	they would have bent

IMPERATIVE MOOD
bend

SUBJUNCTIVE MOOD

Pres.	if I bend	if we bend
	if you bend	if you bend
	if he (she, it) bend	if they bend
Past	if I bent	if we bent
	if you bent	if you bent
	if he (she, it) bent	if they bent
Fut.	if I should bend	if we should bend
	if you should bend	if you should bend
	if he (she, it) should bend	if they should bend

Infinitive: to be bent
Perfect Infinitive: to have been bent

Present Participle: being bent
Past Participle: been bent

INDICATIVE MOOD

Pres.	I am bent	we are bent
	you are bent	you are bent
	he (she, it) is bent	they are bent
Pres.	I am being bent	we are being bent
Prog.	you are being bent	you are being bent
	he (she, it) is being bent	they are being bent
Pres.	I do get bent	we do get bent
Int.	you do get bent	you do get bent
	he (she, it) does get bent	they do get bent
Fut.	I shall be bent	we shall be bent
	you will be bent	you will be bent
	he (she, it) will be bent	they will be bent
Cond.	I would be bent	we would be bent
	you would be bent	you would be bent
	he (she, it) would be bent	they would be bent
Past	I was bent	we were bent
	you were bent	you were bent
	he (she, it) was bent	they were bent
Past	I was being bent	we were being bent
Prog.	you were being bent	you were being bent
	he (she, it) was being bent	they were being bent
Past	I did get bent	we did get bent
Int.	you did get bent	you did get bent
	he (she, it) did get bent	they did get bent
Pres.	I have been bent	we have been bent
Perf.	you have been bent	you have been bent
	he (she, it) has been bent	they have been bent
Past	I had been bent	we had been bent
Perf.	you had been bent	you had been bent
	he (she, it) had been bent	they had been bent
Fut.	I shall have been bent	we shall have been bent
Perf.	you will have been bent	you will have been bent
	he (she, it) will have been bent	they will have been bent
Cond.	I would have been bent	we would have been bent
Perf.	you would have been bent	you would have been bent
	he (she, it) would have been bent	they would have been bent

IMPERATIVE MOOD
be bent

SUBJUNCTIVE MOOD

Pres.	if I be bent	if we be bent
	if you be bent	if you be bent
	if he (she, it) be bent	if they be bent
Past	if I were bent	if we were bent
	if you were bent	if you were bent
	if he (she, it) were bent	if they were bent
Fut.	if I should be bent	if we should be bent
	if you should be bent	if you should be bent
	if he (she, it) should be bent	if they should be bent

to bid (active voice)   *Principal Parts:* bid, bidding, bid, bid
                                              (as at an auction)

Infinitive: to bid   *Present Participle:* bidding
Perfect Infinitive: to have bid   *Past Participle:* bid

INDICATIVE MOOD

Pres.	I bid	we bid
	you bid	you bid
	he (she, it) bids	they bid
Pres.	I am bidding	we are bidding
Prog.	you are bidding	you are bidding
	he (she, it) is bidding	they are bidding
Pres.	I do bid	we do bid
Int.	you do bid	you do bid
	he (she, it) does bid	they do bid
Fut.	I shall bid	we shall bid
	you will bid	you will bid
	he (she, it) will bid	they will bid
Cond.	I would bid	we would bid
	you would bid	you would bid
	he (she, it) would bid	they would bid
Past	I bid	we bid
	you bid	you bid
	he (she, it) bid	they bid
Past	I was bidding	we were bidding
Prog.	you were bidding	you were bidding
	he (she, it) was bidding	they were bidding
Past	I did bid	we did bid
Int.	you did bid	you did bid
	he (she, it) did bid	they did bid
Pres.	I have bid	we have bid
Perf.	you have bid	you have bid
	he (she, it) has bid	they have bid
Past	I had bid	we had bid
Perf.	you had bid	you had bid
	he (she, it) had bid	they had bid
Fut.	I shall have bid	we shall have bid
Perf.	you will have bid	you will have bid
	he (she, it) will have bid	they will have bid
Cond.	I would have bid	we would have bid
Perf.	you would have bid	you would have bid
	he (she, it) would have bid	they would have bid

IMPERATIVE MOOD
bid

SUBJUNCTIVE MOOD

Pres.	if I bid	if we bid
	if you bid	if you bid
	if he (she, it) bid	if they bid
Past	if I bid	if we bid
	if you bid	if you bid
	if he (she, it) bid	if they bid
Fut.	if I should bid	if we should bid
	if you should bid	if you should bid
	if he (she, it) should bid	if they should bid

Infinitive: to be bid   *Present Participle:* being bid
Perfect Infinitive: to have been bid   *Past Participle:* been bid

INDICATIVE MOOD

Pres. I am bid
you are bid
he (she, it) is bid

we are bid
you are bid
they are bid

Pres.
Prog. I am being bid
you are being bid
he (she, it) is being bid

we are being bid
you are being bid
they are being bid

Pres.
Int. I do get bid
you do get bid
he (she, it) does get bid

we do get bid
you do get bid
they do get bid

Fut. I shall be bid
you will be bid
he (she, it) will be bid

we shall be bid
you will be bid
they will be bid

Cond. I would be bid
you would be bid
he (she, it) would be bid

we would be bid
you would be bid
they would be bid

Past I was bid
you were bid
he (she, it) was bid

we were bid
you were bid
they were bid

Past
Prog. I was being bid
you were being bid
he (she, it) was being bid

we were being bid
you were being bid
they were being bid

Past
Int. I did get bid
you did get bid
he (she, it) did get bid

we did get bid
you did get bid
they did get bid

Pres.
Perf. I have been bid
you have been bid
he (she, it) has been bid

we have been bid
you have been bid
they have been bid

Past
Perf. I had been bid
you had been bid
he (she, it) had been bid

we had been bid
you had been bid
they had been bid

Fut.
Perf. I shall have been bid
you will have been bid
he (she, it) will have been bid

we shall have been bid
you will have been bid
they will have been bid

Cond.
Perf. I would have been bid
you would have been bid
he (she, it) would have been bid

we would have been bid
you would have been bid
they would have been bid

IMPERATIVE MOOD
be bid

SUBJUNCTIVE MOOD

Pres. if I be bid
if you be bid
if he (she, it) be bid

if we be bid
if you be bid
if they be bid

Past if I were bid
if you were bid
if he (she, it) were bid

if we were bid
if you were bid
if they were bid

Fut. if I should be bid
if you should be bid
if he (she, it) should be bid

if we should be bid
if you should be bid
if they should be bid

to bind (active voice)   *Principal Parts:* bind, binding, bound, bound

Infinitive: to bind
Perfect Infinitive: to have bound

Present Participle: binding
Past Participle: bound

INDICATIVE MOOD

Pres.	I bind	we bind
	you bind	you bind
	he (she, it) binds	they bind
Pres.	I am binding	we are binding
Prog.	you are binding	you are binding
	he (she, it) is binding	they are binding
Pres.	I do bind	we do bind
Int.	you do bind	you do bind
	he (she, it) does bind	they do bind
Fut.	I shall bind	we shall bind
	you will bind	you will bind
	he (she, it) will bind	they will bind
Cond.	I would bind	we would bind
	you would bind	you would bind
	he (she, it) would bind	they would bind
Past	I bound	we bound
	you bound	you bound
	he (she, it) bound	they bound
Past	I was binding	we were binding
Prog.	you were binding	you were binding
	he (she, it) was binding	they were binding
Past	I did bind	we did bind
Int.	you did bind	you did bind
	he (she, it) did bind	they did bind
Pres.	I have bound	we have bound
Perf.	you have bound	you have bound
	he (she, it) has bound	they have bound
Past	I had bound	we had bound
Perf.	you had bound	you had bound
	he (she, it) had bound	they had bound
Fut.	I shall have bound	we shall have bound
Perf.	you will have bound	you will have bound
	he (she, it) will have bound	they will have bound
Cond.	I would have bound	we would have bound
Perf.	you would have bound	you would have bound
	he (she, it) would have bound	they would have bound

IMPERATIVE MOOD
bind

SUBJUNCTIVE MOOD

Pres.	if I bind	if we bind
	if you bind	if you bind
	if he (she, it) bind	if they bind
Past	if I bound	if we bound
	if you bound	if you bound
	if he (she, it) bound	if they bound
Fut.	if I should bind	if we should bind
	if you should bind	if you should bind
	if he (she, it) should bind	if they should bind

Infinitive: to be bound   *Present Participle:* being bound
Perfect Infinitive: to have been bound   *Past Participle:* been bound

INDICATIVE MOOD

Pres. I am bound	we are bound
you are bound	you are bound
he (she, it) is bound	they are bound
Pres. I am being bound	we are being bound
Prog. you are being bound	you are being bound
he (she, it) is being bound	they are being bound
Pres. I do get bound	we do get bound
Int. you do get bound	you do get bound
he (she, it) does get bound	they do get bound
Fut. I shall be bound	we shall be bound
you will be bound	you will be bound
he (she, it) will be bound	they will be bound
Cond. I would be bound	we would be bound
you would be bound	you would be bound
he (she, it) would be bound	they would be bound
Past I was bound	we were bound
you were bound	you were bound
he (she, it) was bound	they were bound
Past I was being bound	we were being bound
Prog. you were being bound	you were being bound
he (she, it) was being bound	they were being bound
Past I did get bound	we did get bound
Int. you did get bound	you did get bound
he (she, it) did get bound	they did get bound
Pres. I have been bound	we have been bound
Perf. you have been bound	you have been bound
he (she, it) has been bound	they have been bound
Past I had been bound	we had been bound
Perf. you had been bound	you had been bound
he (she, it) had been bound	they had been bound
Fut. I shall have been bound	we shall have been bound
Perf. you will have been bound	you will have been bound
he (she, it) will have been bound	they will have been bound
Cond. I would have been bound	we would have been bound
Perf. you would have been bound	you would have been bound
he (she, it) would have been bound	they would have been bound

IMPERATIVE MOOD
be bound

SUBJUNCTIVE MOOD

Pres. if I be bound	if we be bound
if you be bound	if you be bound
if he (she, it) be bound	if they be bound
Past if I were bound	if we were bound
if you were bound	if you were bound
if he (she, it) were bound	if they were bound
Fut. if I should be bound	if we should be bound
if you should be bound	if you should be bound
if he (she, it) should be bound	if they should be bound

to bite (active voice)   *Principal Parts:* bite, biting, bit, bitten (bit)

Infinitive: to bite
Perfect Infinitive: to have bitten, bit

Present Participle: biting
Past Participle: bitten, bit

INDICATIVE MOOD

Pres.	I bite	we bite
	you bite	you bite
	he (she, it) bites	they bite
Pres.	I am biting	we are biting
Prog.	you are biting	you are biting
	he (she, it) is biting	they are biting
Pres.	I do bite	we do bite
Int.	you do bite	you do bite
	he (she, it) does bite	they do bite
Fut.	I shall bite	we shall bite
	you will bite	you will bite
	he (she. it) will bite	they will bite
Cond.	I would bite	we would bite
	you would bite	you would bite
	he (she, it) would bite	they would bite
Past	I bit	we bit
	you bit	you bit
	he (she, it) bit	they bit
Past	I was biting	we were biting
Prog.	you were biting	you were biting
	he (she, it) was biting	they were biting
Past	I did bite	we did bite
Int.	you did bite	you did bite
	he (she, it) did bite	they did bite
Pres.	I have bitten, bit	we have bitten, bit
Perf.	you have bitten, bit	you have bitten, bit
	he (she, it) has bitten, bit	they have bitten, bit
Past	I had bitten, bit	we had bitten, bit
Perf.	you had bitten, bit	you had bitten, bit
	he (she, it) had bitten, bit	they had bitten, bit
Fut.	I shall have bitten, bit	we shall have bitten, bit
Perf.	you will have bitten, bit	you will have bitten, bit
	he (she, it) will have bitten, bit	they will have bitten, bit
Cond.	I would have bitten, bit	we would have bitten, bit
Perf.	you would have bitten, bit	you would have bitten, bit
	he (she, it) would have bitten, bit	they would have bitten, bit

IMPERATIVE MOOD
bite

SUBJUNCTIVE MOOD

Pres.	if I bite	if we bite
	if you bite	if you bite
	if he (she, it) bite	if they bite
Past	if I bit	if we bit
	if you bit	if you bit
	if he (she, it) bit	if they bit
Fut.	if I should bite	if we should bite
	if you should bite	if you should bite
	if he (she, it) should bite	if they should bite

146

Infinitive: to be bitten   *Present Participle:* being bitten (bit)
Perfect Infinitive: to have been bitten (bit)   *Past Participle:* been bitten (bit)

INDICATIVE MOOD

Pres.	I am bitten	we are bitten
	you are bitten	you are bitten
	he (she, it) is bitten	they are bitten
Pres.	I am being bitten	we are being bitten
Prog.	you are being bitten	you are being bitten
	he (she, it) is being bitten	they are being bitten
Pres.	I do get bitten	we do get bitten
Int.	you do get bitten	you do get bitten
	he (she, it) does get bitten	they do get bitten
Fut.	I shall be bitten	we shall be bitten
	you will be bitten	you will be bitten
	he (she, it) will be bitten	they will be bitten
Cond.	I would be bitten	we would be bitten
	you would be bitten	you would be bitten
	he (she, it) would be bitten	they would be bitten
Past	I was bitten	we were bitten
	you were bitten	you were bitten
	he (she, it) was bitten	they were bitten
Past	I was being bitten	we were being bitten
Prog.	you were being bitten	you were being bitten
	he (she, it) was being bitten	they were being bitten
Past	I did get bitten	we did get bitten
Int.	you did get bitten	you did get bitten
	he (she, it) did get bitten	they did get bitten
Pres.	I have been bitten	we have been bitten
Perf.	you have been bitten	you have been bitten
	he (she, it) has been bitten	they have been bitten
Past	I had been bitten	we had been bitten
Perf.	you had been bitten	you had been bitten
	he (she, it) had been bitten	they had been bitten
Fut.	I shall have been bitten	we shall have bitten
Perf.	you will have been bitten	you will have been bitten
	he (she, it) will have been bitten	they will have been bitten
Cond.	I would have been bitten	we would have been bitten
Perf.	you would have been bitten	you would have been bitten
	he (she, it) would have been bitten	they would have been bitten

IMPERATIVE MOOD
be bitten

SUBJUNCTIVE MOOD

Pres.	if I be bitten	if we be bitten
	if you be bitten	if you be bitten
	if he (she, it) be bitten	if they be bitten
Past	if I were bitten	if we were bitten
	if you were bitten	if you were bitten
	if he (she, it) were bitten	if they were bitten
Fut.	if I should be bitten	if we should be bitten
	if you should be bitten	if you should be bitten
	if he (she, it) should be bitten	if they should be bitten

to blow (active voice) *Principal Parts:* blow, blowing, blew, blown

Infinitive: to blow
Perfect Infinitive: to have blown

Present Participle: blowing
Past Participle: blown

INDICATIVE MOOD

Pres.	I blow	we blow
	you blow	you blow
	he (she, it) blows	they blow
Pres.	I am blowing	we are blowing
Prog.	you are blowing	you are blowing
	he (she, it) is blowing	they are blowing
Pres.	I do blow	we do blow
Int.	you do blow	you do blow
	he (she, it) does blow	they do blow
Fut.	I shall blow	we shall blow
	you will blow	you will blow
	he (she, it) will blow	they will blow
Cond.	I would blow	we would blow
	you would blow	you would blow
	he (she, it) would blow	they would blow
Past	I blew	we blew
	you blew	you blew
	he (she, it) blew	they blew
Past	I was blowing	we were blowing
Prog.	you were blowing	you were blowing
	he (she, it) was blowing	they were blowing
Past	I did blow	we did blow
Int.	you did blow	you did blow
	he (she, it) did blow	they did blow
Pres.	I have blown	we have blown
Perf.	you have blown	you have blown
	he (she, it) has blown	they have blown
Past	I had blown	we had blown
Perf.	you had blown	you had blown
	he (she, it) had blown	they had blown
Fut.	I shall have blown	we shall have blown
Perf.	you will have blown	you will have blown
	he (she, it) will have blown	they will have blown
Cond.	I would have blown	we would have blown
Perf.	you would have blown	you would have blown
	he (she, it) would have blown	they would have blown

IMPERATIVE MOOD
blow

SUBJUNCTIVE MOOD

Pres.	if I blow	if we blow
	if you blow	if you blow
	if he (she, it) blow	if they blow
Past	if I blew	if we blew
	if you blew	if you blew
	if he (she, it) blew	if they blew
Fut.	if I should blow	if we should blow
	if you should blow	if you should blow
	if he (she, it) should blow	if they should blow

148

(passive voice)

Infinitive: to be blown
Perfect Infinitive: to have been blown

Present Participle: being blown
Past Participle: been blown

INDICATIVE MOOD

Pres. I am blown you are blown he (she, it) is blown	we are blown you are blown they are blown
Pres. Prog. I am being blown you are being blown he (she, it) is being blown	we are being blown you are being blown they are being blown
Pres. Int. I do get blown you do get blown he (she, it) does get blown	we do get blown you do get blown they do get blown
Fut. I shall be blown you will be blown he (she, it) will be blown	we shall be blown you will be blown they will be blown
Cond. I would be blown you would be blown he (she, it) would be blown	we would be blown you would be blown they would be blown
Past I was blown you were blown he (she, it) was blown	we were blown you were blown they were blown
Past Prog. I was being blown you were being blown he (she, it) was being blown	we were being blown you were being blown they were being blown
Past Int. I did get blown you did get blown he (she, it) did get blown	we did get blown you did get blown they did get blown
Pres. Perf. I have been blown you have been blown he (she, it) has been blown	we have been blown you have been blown they have been blown
Past Perf. I had been blown you had been blown he (she, it) had been blown	we had been blown you had been blown they had been blown
Fut. Perf. I shall have been blown you will have been blown he (she, it) will have been blown	we shall have been blown you will have been blown they will have been blown
Cond. Perf. I would have been blown you would have been blown he (she, it) would have been blown	we would have been blown you would have been blown they would have been blown

IMPERATIVE MOOD
be blown

SUBJUNCTIVE MOOD

Pres. if I be blown if you be blown if he (she, it) be blown	if we be blown if you be blown if they be blown
Past if I were blown if you were blown if he (she, it) were blown	if we were blown if you were blown if they were blown
Fut. if I should be blown if you should be blown if he (she, it) should be blown	if we should be blown if you should be blown if they should be blown

to break (active voice)   *Principal Parts:* break, breaking, broke, broken

---

Infinitive: to break
Perfect Infinitive: to have broken

Present Participle: breaking
Past Participle: broken

INDICATIVE MOOD

Pres.	I break	we break
	you break	you break
	he (she, it) breaks	they break
Pres.	I am breaking	we are breaking
Prog.	you are breaking	you are breaking
	he (she, it) is breaking	they are breaking
Pres.	I do break	we do break
Int.	you do break	you do break
	he (she, it) does break	they do break
Fut.	I shall break	we shall break
	you will break	you will break
	he (she, it) will break	they will break
Cond.	I would break	we would break
	you would break	you would break
	he (she, it) would break	they would break
Past	I broke	we broke
	you broke	you broke
	he (she, it) broke	they broke
Past	I was breaking	we were breaking
Prog.	you were breaking	you were breaking
	he (she, it) was breaking	they were breaking
Past	I did break	we did break
Int.	you did break	you did break
	he (she, it) did break	they did break
Pres.	I have broken	we have broken
Perf.	you have broken	you have broken
	he (she, it) has broken	they have broken
Past	I had broken	we had broken
Perf.	you had broken	you had broken
	he (she, it) had broken	they had broken
Fut.	I shall have broken	we shall have broken
Perf.	you will have broken	you will have broken
	he (she, it) will have broken	they will have broken
Cond.	I would have broken	we would have broken
Perf.	you would have broken	you would have broken
	he (she, it) would have broken	they would have broken

IMPERATIVE MOOD
break

SUBJUNCTIVE MOOD

Pres.	if I break	if we break
	if you break	if you break
	if he (she, it) break	if they break
Past	if I broke	if we broke
	if you broke	if you broke
	if he (she, it) broke	if they broke
Fut.	if I should break	if we should break
	if you should break	if you should break
	if he (she, it) should break	if they should break

Infinitive: to be broken
Perfect Infinitive: to have been broken

Present Participle: being broken
Past Participle: been broken

INDICATIVE MOOD

Pres. I am broken
you are broken
he (she, it) is broken

we are broken
you are broken
they are broken

Pres.
Prog. I am being broken
you are being broken
he (she, it) is being broken

we are being broken
you are being broken
they are being broken

Pres.
Int. I do get broken
you do get broken
he (she, it) does get broken

we do get broken
you do get broken
they do get broken

Fut. I shall be broken
you will be broken
he (she, it) will be broken

we shall be broken
you will be broken
they will be broken

Cond. I would be broken
you would be broken
he (she, it) would be broken

we would be broken
you would be broken
they would be broken

Past I was broken
you were broken
he (she, it) was broken

we were broken
you were broken
they were broken

Past
Prog. I was being broken
you were being broken
he (she, it) was being broken

we were being broken
you were being broken
they were being broken

Past
Int. I did get broken
you did get broken
he (she, it) did get broken

we did get broken
you did get broken
they did get broken

Pres.
Perf. I have been broken
you have been broken
he (she, it) has been broken

we have been broken
you have been broken
they have been broken

Past
Perf. I had been broken
you had been broken
he (she, it) had been broken

we had been broken
you had been broken
they had been broken

Fut.
Perf. I shall have been broken
you will have been broken
he (she, it) will have been broken

we shall have been broken
you will have been broken
they will have been broken

Cond.
Perf. I would have been broken
you would have been broken
he (she, it) would have been broken

we would have been broken
you would have been broken
they would have been broken

IMPERATIVE MOOD
be broken

SUBJUNCTIVE MOOD

Pres. if I be broken
if you be broken
if he (she, it) be broken

if we be broken
if you be broken
if they be broken

Past if I were broken
if you were broken
if he (she, it) were broken

if we were broken
if you were broken
if they were broken

Fut. if I should be broken
if you should be broken
if he (she, it) should be broken

if we should be broken
if you should be broken
if they should be broken

to bring (active voice) *Principal Parts:* bring, bringing, brought, brought

Infinitive: to bring
Perfect Infinitive: to have brought

Present Participle: bringing
Past Participle: brought

INDICATIVE MOOD

Pres.	I bring	we bring
	you bring	you bring
	he (she, it) brings	they bring
Pres.	I am bringing	we are bringing
Prog.	you are bringing	you are bringing
	he (she, it) is bringing	they are bringing
Pres.	I do bring	we do bring
Int.	you do bring	you do bring
	he (she, it) does bring	they do bring
Fut.	I shall bring	we shall bring
	you will bring	you will bring
	he (she, it) will bring	they will bring
Cond.	I would bring	we would bring
	you would bring	you would bring
	he (she, it) would bring	they would bring
Past	I brought	we brought
	you brought	you brought
	he (she, it) brought	they brought
Past	I was bringing	we were bringing
Prog.	you were bringing	you were bringing
	he (she, it) was bringing	they were bringing
Past	I did bring	we did bring
Int.	you did bring	you did bring
	he (she, it) did bring	they did bring
Pres.	I have brought	we have brought
Perf.	you have brought	you have brought
	he (she, it) has brought	they have brought
Past	I had brought	we had brought
Perf.	you had brought	you had brought
	he (she, it) had brought	they had brought
Fut.	I shall have brought	we shall have brought
Perf.	you will have brought	you will have brought
	he (she, it) will have brought	they will have brought
Cond.	I would have brought	we would have brought
Perf.	you would have brought	you would have brought
	he (she, it) would have brought	they would have brought

IMPERATIVE MOOD
bring

SUBJUNCTIVE MOOD

Pres.	if I bring	if we bring
	if you bring	if you bring
	if he (she, it) bring	if they bring
Past	if I brought	if we brought
	if you brought	if you brought
	if he (she, it) brought	if they brought
Fut.	if I should bring	if we should bring
	if you should bring	if you should bring
	if he (she, it) should bring	if they should bring

Infinitive: to be brought   *Present Participle:* being brought
Perfect Infinitive: to have been brought   *Past Participle:* been brought

INDICATIVE MOOD

Pres.	I am brought	we are brought
	you are brought	you are brought
	he (she, it) is brought	they are brought
Pres.	I am being brought	we are being brought
Prog.	you are being brought	you are being brought
	he (she, it) is being brought	they are being brought
Pres.	I do get brought	we do get brought
Int.	you do get brought	you do get brought
	he (she, it) does get brought	they do get brought
Fut.	I shall be brought	we shall be brought
	you will be brought	you will be brought
	he (she, it) will be brought	they will be brought
Cond.	I would be brought	we would be brought
	you would be brought	you would be brought
	he (she, it) would be brought	they would be brought
Past	I was brought	we were brought
	you were brought	you were brought
	he (she, it) was brought	they were brought
Past	I was being brought	we were being brought
Prog.	you were being brought	you were being brought
	he (she, it) was being brought	they were being brought
Past	I did get brought	we did get brought
Int.	you did get brought	you did get brought
	he (she, it) did get brought	they did get brought
Pres.	I have been brought	we have been brought
Perf.	you have been brought	you have been brought
	he (she, it) has been brought	they have been brought
Past	I had been brought	we had been brought
Perf.	you had been brought	you had been brought
	he (she, it) had been brought	they had been brought
Fut.	I shall have been brought	we shall have been brought
Perf.	you will have been brought	you will have been brought
	he (she, it) will have been brought	they will have been brought
Cond.	I would have been brought	we would have been brought
Perf.	you would have been brought	you would have been brought
	he (she, it) would have been brought	they would have been brought

IMPERATIVE MOOD
be brought

SUBJUNCTIVE MOOD

Pres.	if I be brought	if we be brought
	if you be brought	if you be brought
	if he (she, it) be brought	if they be brought
Past	if I were brought	if we were brought
	if you were brought	if you were brought
	if he (she, it) were brought	if they were brought
Fut.	if I should be brought	if we should be brought
	if you should be brought	if you should be brought
	if he (she, it) should be brought	if they should be brought

to broadcast (active voice) *Principal Parts:* broadcast, broadcasting, broadcast (broadcasted) broadcast (broadcasted)

Infinitive: to broadcast
Perfect Infinitive: to have broadcast

Present Participle: broadcasting
Past Participle: broadcast

INDICATIVE MOOD

Pres.	I broadcast	we broadcast
	you broadcast	you broadcast
	he (she, it) broadcasts	they broadcast
Pres.	I am broadcasting	we are broadcasting
Prog.	you are broadcasting	you are broadcasting
	he (she, it) is broadcasting	they are broadcasting
Pres.	I do broadcast	we do broadcast
Int.	you do broadcast	you do broadcast
	he (she, it) does broadcast	they do broadcast
Fut.	I shall broadcast	we shall broadcast
	you will broadcast	you will broadcast
	he (she, it) will broadcast	they will broadcast
Cond.	I would broadcast	we would broadcast
	you would broadcast	you would broadcast
	he (she, it) would broadcast	they would broadcast
Past	I broadcast(ed)	we broadcast(ed)
	you broadcast(ed)	you broadcast(ed)
	he (she, it) broadcast(ed)	they broadcast(ed)
Past	I was broadcasting	we were broadcasting
Prog.	you were broadcasting	you were broadcasting
	he (she, it) was broadcasting	they were broadcasting
Past	I did broadcast	we did broadcast
Int.	you did broadcast	you did broadcast
	he (she, it) did broadcast	they did broadcast
Pres.	I have broadcast(ed)	we have broadcast(ed)
Perf.	you have broadcast(ed)	you have broadcast(ed)
	he (she, it) has broadcast(ed)	they have broadcast(ed)
Past	I had broadcast(ed)	we had broadcast(ed)
Perf.	you had broadcast(ed)	you had broadcast(ed)
	he (she, it) had broadcast(ed)	they had broadcast(ed)
Fut.	I shall have broadcast(ed)	we shall have broadcast(ed)
Perf.	you will have broadcast(ed)	you will have broadcast(ed)
	he (she, it) will have broad-cast(ed)	they will have broadcast(ed)
Cond.	I would have broadcast(ed)	we would have broadcast(ed)
Perf.	you would have broadcast(ed)	you would have broadcast(ed)
	he (she, it) would have broadcast(ed)	they would have broadcast(ed)

IMPERATIVE MOOD
broadcast

SUBJUNCTIVE MOOD

Pres.	if I broadcast	if we broadcast
	if you broadcast	if you broadcast
	if he (she, it) broadcast	if they broadcast
Past	if I broadcast(ed)	if we broadcast(ed)
	if you broadcast(ed)	if you broadcast(ed)
	if he (she, it) broadcast(ed)	if they broadcast(ed)
Fut.	if I should broadcast	if we should broadcast
	if you should broadcast	if you should broadcast
	if he (she, it) should broadcast	if they should broadcast

(passive voice)

Infinitive: to be broadcast(ed)
Perfect Infinitive: to have been broadcast(ed)

Present Participle: being broadcast(ed)
Past Participle: been broadcast(ed)

INDICATIVE MOOD

Pres. I am broadcast(ed)
you are broadcast(ed)
he (she, it) is broadcast(ed)

we are broadcast(ed)
you are broadcast(ed)
they are broadcast(ed)

Pres.
Prog. I am being broadcast(ed)
you are being broadcast(ed)
he (she, it) is being broadcast(ed)

we are being broadcast(ed)
you are being broadcast(ed)
they are being broadcast(ed)

Pres.
Int. I do get broadcast(ed)
you do get broadcast(ed)
he (she, it) does get broadcast(ed)

we do get broadcast(ed)
you do get broadcast(ed)
they do get broadcast(ed)

Fut. I shall be broadcast(ed)
you will be broadcast(ed)
he (she, it) will be broadcast(ed)

we shall be broadcast(ed)
you will be broadcast(ed)
they will be broadcast(ed)

Cond. I would be broadcast(ed)
you would be broadcast(ed)
he (she, it) would be broadcast(ed)

we would be broadcast(ed)
you would be broadcast(ed)
they would be broadcast(ed)

Past I was broadcast(ed)
you were broadcast(ed)
he (she, it) was broadcast(ed)

we were broadcast(ed)
you were broadcast(ed)
they were broadcast(ed)

Past
Prog. I was being broadcast(ed)
you were being broadcast(ed)
he (she, it) was being broadcast(ed)

we were being broadcast(ed)
you were being broadcast(ed)
they were being broadcast(ed)

Past
Int. I did get broadcast(ed)
you did get broadcast(ed)
he (she, it) did get broadcast(ed)

we did get broadcast(ed)
you did get broadcast(ed)
they did get broadcast(ed)

Pres.
Perf. I have been broadcast(ed)
you have been broadcast(ed)
he (she, it) has been broadcast(ed)

we have been broadcast(ed)
you have been broadcast(ed)
they have been broadcast(ed)

Past
Perf. I had been broadcast(ed)
you had been broadcast(ed)
he (she, it) had been broadcast(ed)

we had been broadcast(ed)
you had been broadcast(ed)
they had been broadcast(ed)

Fut.
Perf. I shall have been broadcast(ed)
you will have been broadcast(ed)
he (she, it) will have been broadcast(ed)

we shall have been broadcast(ed)
you will have been broadcast(ed)
they will have been broadcast(ed)

Cond.
Perf. I would have been broadcast(ed)
you would have been broadcast(ed)
he (she, it) would have been broadcast(ed)

we would have been broadcast(ed)
you would have been broadcast(ed)
they would have been broadcast(ed)

IMPERATIVE MOOD
be broadcast

SUBJUNCTIVE MOOD

Pres. if I be broadcast(ed)
if you be broadcast(ed)
if he (she, it) be broadcast(ed)

if we be broadcast(ed)
if you be broadcast(ed)
if they be broadcast(ed)

Past if I were broadcast(ed)
if you were broadcast(ed)
If he (she, it) were broadcast(ed)

if we were broadcast(ed)
if you were broadcast(ed)
if they were broadcast(ed)

Fut. if I should be broadcast(ed)
if you should be broadcast(ed)
if he (she, it) should be broadcast(ed)

if we should be broadcast(ed)
if you should be broadcast(ed)
if they should be broadcast(ed)

155

to build (active voice)   *Principal Parts:* build, building, built, built

Infinitive: to build   *Present Participle:* building
Perfect Infinitive: to have built   *Past Participle:* built

INDICATIVE MOOD

Pres.	I build	we build
	you build	you build
	he (she, it) builds	they build
Pres.	I am building	we are building
Prog.	you are building	you are building
	he (she, it) is building	they are building
Pres.	I do build	we do build
Int.	you do build	you do build
	he (she, it) does build	they do build
Fut.	I shall build	we shall build
	you will build	you will build
	he (she, it) will build	they will build
Cond.	I would build	we would build
	you would build	you would build
	he (she, it) would build	they would build
Past	I built	we built
	you built	you built
	he (she, it) built	they built
Past	I was building	we were building
Prog.	you were building	you were building
	he (she, it) was building	they were building
Past	I did build	we did build
Int.	you did build	you did build
	he (she, it) did build	they did build
Pres.	I have built	we have built
Perf.	you have built	you have built
	he (she, it) has built	they have built
Past	I had built	we had built
Perf.	you had built	you had built
	he (she, it) had built	they had built
Fut.	I shall have built	we shall have built
Perf.	you will have built	you shall have built
	he (she, it) will have built	they will have built
Cond.	I would have built	we would have built
Perf.	you would have built	you would have built
	he (she, it) would have built	they would have built

IMPERATIVE MOOD
build

SUBJUNCTIVE MOOD

Pres.	if I build	if we build
	if you build	if you build
	if he (she, it) build	if they build
Past	if I built	if we built
	if you built	if you built
	if he (she, it) built	if they built
Fut.	if I should build	if we should build
	if you should build	if you should build
	if he (she, it) should build	if they should build

156

Infinitive: to be built   *Present Participle:* being built
Perfect Infinitive: to have been built   *Past Participle:* been built

INDICATIVE MOOD

Pres. I am built	we are built
you are built	you are built
he (she, it) is built	they are built
Pres. I am being built	we are being built
Prog. you are being built	you are being built
he (she, it) is being built	they are being built
Pres. I do get built	we do get built
Int. you do get built	you do get built
he (she, it) does get built	they do get built
Fut. I shall be built	we shall be built
you will be built	you will be built
he (she, it) will be built	they will be built
Cond. I would be built	we would be built
you would be built	you would be built
he (she, it) would be built	they would be built
Past I was built	we were built
you were built	you were built
he (she, it) was built	they were built
Past I was being built	we were being built
Prog. you were being built	you were being built
he (she, it) was being built	they were being built
Past I did get built	we did get built
Int. you did get built	you did get built
he (she, it) did get built	they did get built
Pres. I have been built	we have been built
Perf. you have been built	you have been built
he (she, it) has been built	they have been built
Past I had been built	we had been built
Perf. you had been built	you had been built
he (she, it) had been built	they had been built
Fut. I shall have been built	we shall have been built
Perf. you will have been built	you will have been built
he (she, it) will have been built	they will have been built
Cond. I would have been built	we would have been built
Perf. you would have been built	you would have been built
he (she, it) would have been built	they would have been built

IMPERATIVE MOOD
be built

SUBJUNCTIVE MOOD

Pres. if I be built	if we be built
if you be built	if you be built
if he (she, it) be built	if they be built
Past if I were built	if we were built
if you were built	if you were built
if he (she, it) were built	if they were built
Fut. if I should be built	if we should be built
if you should be built	if you should be built
if he (she, it) should be built	if they should be built

to burst (active voice)   *Principal Parts:* burst, bursting, burst, burst

Infinitive: to burst   *Present Participle:* bursting
Perfect Infinitive: to have burst   *Past Participle:* burst

INDICATIVE MOOD

Pres.	I burst	we burst
	you burst	you burst
	he (she, it) bursts	they burst
Pres.	I am bursting	we are bursting
Prog.	you are bursting	you are bursting
	he (she, it) is bursting	they are bursting
Pres.	I do burst	we do burst
Int.	you do burst	you do burst
	he (she, it) does burst	they do burst
Fut.	I shall burst	we shall burst
	you will burst	you will burst
	he (she, it) will burst	they will burst
Cond.	I would burst	we would burst
	you would burst	you would burst
	he (she, it) would burst	they would burst
Past	I burst	we burst
	you burst	you burst
	he (she, it) burst	they burst
Past	I was bursting	we were bursting
Prog.	you were bursting	you were bursting
	he (she, it) was bursting	they were bursting
Past	I did burst	we did burst
Int.	you did burst	you did burst
	he (she, it) did burst	they did burst
Pres.	I have burst	we have burst
Perf.	you have burst	you have burst
	he (she, it) has burst	they have burst
Past	I had burst	we had burst
Perf.	you had burst	you had burst
	he (she, it) had burst	they had burst
Fut.	I shall have burst	we shall have burst
Perf.	you will have burst	you will have burst
	he (she, it) will have burst	they will have burst
Cond.	I would have burst	we would have burst
Perf.	you would have burst	you would have burst
	he (she, it) would have burst	they would have burst

IMPERATIVE MOOD
burst

SUBJUNCTIVE MOOD

Pres.	if I burst	if we burst
	if you burst	if you burst
	if he (she, it) burst	if they burst
Past	if I burst	if we burst
	if you burst	if you burst
	if he (she, it) burst	if they burst
Fut.	if I should burst	if we should burst
	if you should burst	if you should burst
	if he (she, it) should burst	if they should burst

Infinitive: to be burst
Perfect Infinitive: to have been burst

Present Participle: being burst
Past Participle: been burst

INDICATIVE MOOD

Pres.	I am burst	we are burst
	you are burst	you are burst
	he (she, it) is burst	they are burst
Pres.	I am being burst	we are being burst
Prog.	you are being burst	you are being burst
	he (she, it) is being burst	they are being burst
Pres.	I do get burst	we do get burst
Int.	you do get burst	you do get burst
	he (she, it) does get burst	they do get burst
Fut.	I shall be burst	we shall be burst
	you will be burst	you will be burst
	he (she, it) will be burst	they will be burst
Cond.	I would be burst	we would be burst
	you would be burst	you would be burst
	he (she, it) would be burst	they would be burst
Past	I was burst	we were burst
	you were burst	you were burst
	he (she, it) was burst	they were burst
Past	I was being burst	we were being burst
Prog.	you were being burst	you were being burst
	he (she, it) was being burst	they were being burst
Past	I did get burst	we did get burst
Int.	you did get burst	you did get burst
	he (she, it) did get burst	they did get burst
Pres.	I have been burst	we have been burst
Perf.	you have been burst	you have been burst
	he (she, it) has been burst	they have been burst
Past	I had been burst	we had been burst
Perf.	you had been burst	you had been burst
	he (she, it) had been burst	they had been burst
Fut.	I shall have been burst	we shall have been burst
Perf.	you will have been burst	you will have been burst
	he (she, it) will have been burst	they will have been burst
Cond.	I would have been burst	we would have been burst
Perf.	you would have been burst	you would have been burst
	he (she, it) would have been burst	they would have been burst

IMPERATIVE MOOD
be burst

SUBJUNCTIVE MOOD

Pres.	if I be burst	if we be burst
	if you be burst	if you be burst
	if he (she, it) be burst	if they be burst
Past	if I were burst	if we were burst
	if you were burst	if you were burst
	if he (she, it) were burst	if they were burst
Fut.	if I should be burst	if we should be burst
	if you should be burst	if you should be burst
	if he (she, it) should be burst	if they should be burst

Infinitive: to buy   *Present Participle:* buying
Perfect Infinitive: to have bought   *Past Participle:* bought

INDICATIVE MOOD

Pres.	I buy	we buy
	you buy	you buy
	he (she, it) buys	they buy
Pres.	I am buying	we are buying
Prog.	you are buying	you are buying
	he (she, it) is buying	they are buying
Pres.	I do buy	we do buy
Int.	you do buy	you do buy
	he (she, it) does buy	they do buy
Fut.	I shall buy	we shall buy
	you will buy	you will buy
	he (she, it) will buy	they will buy
Cond.	I would buy	we would buy
	you would buy	you would buy
	he (she, it) would buy	they would buy
Past	I bought	we bought
	you bought	you bought
	he (she, it) bought	they bought
Past	I was buying	we were buying
Prog.	you were buying	you were buying
	he (she, it) was buying	they were buying
Past	I did buy	we did buy
Int.	you did buy	you did buy
	he (she, it) did buy	they did buy
Pres.	I have bought	we have bought
Perf.	you have bought	you have bought
	he (she, it) has bought	they have bought
Past	I had bought	we had bought
Perf.	you had bought	you had bought
	he (she, it) had bought	they had bought
Fut.	I shall have bought	we shall have bought
Perf.	you will have bought	you will have bought
	he (she, it) will have bought	they will have bought
Cond.	I would have bought	we would have bought
Perf.	you would have bought	you would have bought
	he (she, it) would have bought	they would have bought

IMPERATIVE MOOD
buy

SUBJUNCTIVE MOOD

Pres.	if I buy	if we buy
	if you buy	if you buy
	if he (she, it) buy	if they buy
Past	if I bought	if we bought
	if you bought	if you bought
	if he (she, it) bought	if they bought
Fut.	if I should buy	if we should buy
	if you should buy	if you should buy
	if he (she, it) should buy	if they should buy

Infinitive: to be bought   *Present Participle:* being bought
Perfect Infinitive: to have been bought   *Past Participle:* been bought

INDICATIVE MOOD

Pres. I am bought
you are bought
he (she, it) is bought

we are bought
you are bought
they are bought

Pres. I am being bought
Prog. you are being bought
he (she, it) is being bought

we are being bought
you are being bought
they are being bought

Pres. I do get bought
Int. you do get bought
he (she, it) does get bought

we do get bought
you do get bought
they do get bought

Fut. I shall be bought
you will be bought
he (she, it) will be bought

we shall be bought
you will be bought
they will be bought

Cond. I would be bought
you would be bought
he (she, it) would be bought

we would be bought
you would be bought
they would be bought

Past I was bought
you were bought
he (she, it) was bought

we were bought
you were bought
they were bought

Past I was being bought
Prog. you were being bought
he (she, it) was being bought

we were being bought
you were being bought
they were being bought

Past I did get bought
Int. you did get bought
he (she, it) did get bought

we did get bought
you did get bought
they did get bought

Pres. I have been bought
Perf. you have been bought
he (she, it) has been bought

we have been bought
you have been bought
they have been bought

Past I had been bought
Perf. you had been bought
he (she, it) had been bought

we had been bought
you had been bought
they had been bought

Fut. I shall have been bought
Perf. you will have been bought
he (she, it) will have been bought

we shall have been bought
you will have been bought
they will have been bought

Cond. I would have been bought
Perf. you would have been bought
he (she, it) would have been bought

we would have been bought
you would have been bought
they would have been bought

IMPERATIVE MOOD
be bought

SUBJUNCTIVE MOOD

Pres. if I be bought
if you be bought
if he (she, it) be bought

if we be bought
if you be bought
if they be bought

Past if I were bought
if you were bought
if he (she, it) were bought

if we were bought
if you were bought
if they were bought

Fut. if I should be bought
if you should be bought
if he (she, it) should be bought

if we should be bought
if you should be bought
if they should be bought

Infinitive: to cast
Perfect Infinitive: to have cast

Present Participle: casting
Past Participle: cast

INDICATIVE MOOD

Pres. I cast
you cast
he (she, it) casts

we cast
you cast
they cast

Pres.
Prog. I am casting
you are casting
he (she, it) is casting

we are casting
you are casting
they are casting

Pres.
Int. I do cast
you do cast
he (she, it) does cast

we do cast
you do cast
they do cast

Fut. I shall cast
you will cast
he (she, it) will cast

we shall cast
you will cast
they will cast

Cond. I would cast
you would cast
he (she, it) would cast

we would cast
you would cast
they would cast

Past I cast
you cast
he (she, it) cast

we cast
you cast
they cast

Past
Prog. I was casting
you were casting
he (she, it) was casting

we were casting
you were casting
they were casting

Past
Int. I did cast
you did cast
he (she, it) did cast

we did cast
you did cast
they did cast

Pres.
Perf. I have cast
you have cast
he (she, it) has cast

we have cast
you have cast
they have cast

Past
Perf. I had cast
you had cast
he (she, it) had cast

we had cast
you had cast
they had cast

Fut.
Perf. I shall have cast
you will have cast
he (she, it) will have cast

we shall have cast
you will have cast
they will have cast

Cond.
Perf. I would have cast
you would have cast
he (she, it) would have cast

we would have cast
you would have cast
they would have cast

IMPERATIVE MOOD
cast

SUBJUNCTIVE MOOD

Pres. if I cast
if you cast
if he (she, it) cast

if we cast
if you cast
if they cast

Past if I cast
if you cast
if he (she, it) cast

if we cast
if you cast
if they cast

Fut. if I should cast
if you should cast
if he (she, it) should cast

if we should cast
if you should cast
if they should cast

Infinitive: to be cast
Perfect Infinitive: to háve been cast

Present Participle: being cast
Past Participle: been cast

INDICATIVE MOOD

Pres.	I am cast	we are cast
	you are cast	you are cast
	he (she, it) is cast	they are cast
Pres.	I am being cast	we are being cast
Prog.	you are being cast	you are being cast
	he (she, it) is being cast	they are being cast
Pres.	I do get cast	we do get cast
Int.	you do get cast	you do get cast
	he (she, it) does get cast	they do get cast
Fut.	I shall be cast	we shall be cast
	you will be cast	you will be cast
	he (she, it) will be cast	they will be cast
Cond.	I would be cast	we would be cast
	you would be cast	you would be cast
	he (she, it) would be cast	they would be cast
Past	I was cast	we were cast
	you were cast	you were cast
	he (she, it) was cast	they were cast
Past	I was being cast	we were being cast
Prog.	you were being cast	you were being cast
	he (she, it) was being cast	they were being cast
Past	I did get cast	we did get cast
Int.	you did get cast	you did get cast
	he (she, it) did get cast	they did get cast
Pres.	I have been cast	we have been cast
Perf.	you have been cast	you have been cast
	he (she, it) has been cast	they have been cast
Past	I had been cast	we had been cast
Perf.	you had been cast	you had been cast
	he (she, it) had been cast	they had been cast
Fut.	I shall have been cast	we shall have been cast
Perf.	you will have been cast	you will have been cast
	he (she, it) will have been cast	they will have been cast
Cond.	I would have been cast	we would have been cast
Perf.	you would have been cast	you would have been cast
	he (she, it) would have been cast	they would have been cast

IMPERATIVE MOOD
be cast

SUBJUNCTIVE MOOD

Pres.	if I be cast	if we be cast
	if you be cast	if you be cast
	if he (she, it) be cast	if they be cast
Past	if I were cast	if we were cast
	if you were cast	if you were cast
	if he (she, it) were cast	if they were cast
Fut.	if I should be cast	if we should be cast
	if you should be cast	if you should be cast
	if he (she, it) should be cast	if they should be cast

to catch (active voice)   *Principal Parts:* catch, catching, caught, caught

---

Infinitive: to catch   *Present Participle:* catching
Perfect Infinitive: to have caught   *Past Participle:* caught

INDICATIVE MOOD

Pres.	I catch	we catch
	you catch	you catch
	he (she, it) catches	they catch
Pres.	I am catching	we are catching
Prog.	you are catching	you are catching
	he (she, it) is catching	they are catching
Pres.	I do catch	we do catch
Int.	you do catch	you do catch
	he (she, it) does catch	they do catch
Fut.	I shall catch	we shall catch
	you will catch	you will catch
	he (she, it) will catch	they will catch
Cond.	I would catch	we would catch
	you would catch	you would catch
	he (she, it) would catch	they would catch
Past.	I caught	we caught
	you caught	you caught
	he (she, it) caught	they caught
Past	I was catching	we were catching
Prog.	you were catching	you were catching
	he (she, it was catching	they were catching
Past	I did catch	we did catch
Int.	you did catch	you did catch
	he (she, it) did catch	they did catch
Pres.	I have caught	we have caught
Perf.	you have caught	you have caught
	he (she, it) has caught	they have caught
Past	I had caught	we had caught
Perf.	you had caught	you had caught
	he (she, it) had caught	they had caught
Fut.	I shall have caught	we shall have caught
Perf.	you will have caught	you will have caught
	he (she, it) will have caught	they will have caught
Cond.	I would have caught	we would have caught
Perf.	you would have caught	you would have caught
	he (she, it) would have caught	they would have caught

IMPERATIVE MOOD
catch

SUBJUNCTIVE MOOD

Pres.	if I catch	if we catch
	if you catch	if you catch
	if he (she, it) catch	if they catch
Past	if I caught	if we caught
	if you caught	if you caught
	if he (she, it) caught	if they caught
Fut.	if I should catch	if we should catch
	if you should catch	if you should catch
	if he (she, it) should catch	if they should catch

Infinitive: to be caught   *Present Participle:* being caught
Perfect Infinitive: to have been caught   *Past Participle:* been caught

INDICATIVE MOOD

Pres. I am caught
you are caught
he (she, it) is caught

we are caught
you are caught
they are caught

Pres. Prog. I am being caught
you are being caught
he (she, it) is being caught

we are being caught
you are being caught
they are being caught

Pres. Int. I do get caught
you do get caught
he (she, it) does get caught

we do get caught
you do get caught
they do get caught

Fut. I shall be caught
you will be caught
he (she, it) will be caught

we shall be caught
you will be caught
they will be caught

Cond. I would be caught
you would be caught
he (she, it) would be caught

we would be caught
you would be caught
they would be caught

Past I was caught
you were caught
he (she, it) was caught

we were caught
you were caught
they were caught

Past Prog. I was being caught
you were being caught
he (she, it) was being caught

we were being caught
you were being caught
they were being caught

Past Int. I did get caught
you did get caught
he (she, it) did get caught

we did get caught
you did get caught
they did get caught

Pres. Perf. I have been caught
you have been caught
he (she, it) has been caught

we have been caught
you have been caught
they have been caught

Past Perf. I had been caught
you had been caught
he (she, it) had been caught

we had been caught
you had been caught
they had been caught

Fut. Perf. I shall have been caught
you will have been caught
he (she, it) will have been caught

we shall have been caught
you will have been caught
they will have been caught

Cond. Perf. I would have been caught
you would have been caught
he (she, it) would have been caught

we would have been caught
you would have been caught
they would have been caught

IMPERATIVE MOOD
be caught

SUBJUNCTIVE MOOD

Pres. if I be caught
if you be caught
if he (she, it) be caught

if we be caught
if you be caught
if they be caught

Past if I were caught
if you were caught
if he (she, it) were caught

if we were caught
if you were caught
if they were caught

Fut. if I should be caught
if you should be caught
if he (she, it) should be caught

if we should be caught
if you should be caught
if they should be caught

to choose (active voice) *Principal Parts:* choose, choosing, chose, chosen

---

Infinitive: to choose
Perfect Infinitive: to have chosen

Present Participle: choosing
Past Participle: chosen

INDICATIVE MOOD

Pres.	I choose	we choose
	you choose	you choose
	he (she, it) chooses	they choose
Pres.	I am choosing	we are choosing
Prog.	you are choosing	you are choosing
	he (she, it) is choosing	they are choosing
Pres.	I do choose	we do choose
Int.	you do choose	you do choose
	he (she, it) does choose	they do choose
Fut.	I shall choose	we shall choose
	you will choose	you will choose
	he (she, it) will choose	they will choose
Cond.	I would choose	we would choose
	you would choose	you would choose
	he (she, it) would choose	they would choose
Past	I chose	we chose
	you chose	you chose
	he (she, it) chose	they chose
Past	I was choosing	we were choosing
Prog.	you were choosing	you were choosing
	he (she, it) was choosing	they were choosing
Past	I did choose	we did choose
Int.	you did choose	you did choose
	he (she, it) did choose	they did choose
Pres.	I have chosen	we have chosen
Perf.	you have chosen	you have chosen
	he (she, it) has chosen	they have chosen
Past	I had chosen	we had chosen
Perf.	you had chosen	you had chosen
	he (she, it) had chosen	they had chosen
Fut.	I shall have chosen	we shall have chosen
Perf.	you will have chosen	you will have chosen
	he (she, it) will have chosen	they will have chosen
Cond.	I would have chosen	we would have chosen
Perf.	you would have chosen	you would have chosen
	he (she, it) would have chosen	they would have chosen

IMPERATIVE MOOD
choose

SUBJUNCTIVE MOOD

Pres.	if I choose	if we choose
	if you choose	if you choose
	if he (she, it) choose	if they choose
Past	if I chose	if we chose
	if you chose	if you chose
	if he (she, it) chose	if they chose
Fut.	if I should choose	if we should choose
	if you should choose	if you should choose
	if he (she, it) should choose	if they should choose

Infinitive: to be chosen
Perfect Infinitive: to have been chosen

Present Participle: being chosen
Past Participle: been chosen

INDICATIVE MOOD

Pres. I am chosen
you are chosen
he (she, it) is chosen

we are chosen
you are chosen
they are chosen

Pres.
Prog. I am being chosen
you are being chosen
he (she, it) is being chosen

we are being chosen
you are being chosen
they are being chosen

Pres.
Int. I do get chosen
you do get chosen
he (she, it) does get chosen

we do get chosen
you do get chosen
they do get chosen

Fut. I shall be chosen
you will be chosen
he (she, it) will be chosen

we shall be chosen
you will be chosen
they will be chosen

Cond. I would be chosen
you would be chosen
he (she, it) would be chosen

we would be chosen
you would be chosen
they would be chosen

Past I was chosen
you were chosen
he (she, it) was chosen

we were chosen
you were chosen
they were chosen

Past
Prog. I was being chosen
you were being chosen
he (she, it) was being chosen

we were being chosen
you were being chosen
they were being chosen

Past
Int. I did get chosen
you did get chosen
he (she, it) did get chosen

we did get chosen
you did get chosen
they did get chosen

Pres.
Perf. I have been chosen
you have been chosen
he (she, it) has been chosen

we have been chosen
you have been chosen
they have been chosen

Past
Perf. I had been chosen
you had been chosen
he (she, it) had been chosen

we had been chosen
you had been chosen
they had been chosen

Fut.
Perf. I shall have been chosen
you will have been chosen
he (she, it) will have been chosen

we shall have been chosen
you will have been chosen
they will have been chosen

Cond.
Perf. I would have been chosen
you would have been chosen
he (she, it) would have been chosen

we would have been chosen
you would have been chosen
they would have been chosen

IMPERATIVE MOOD
be chosen

SUBJUNCTIVE MOOD

Pres. if I be chosen
if you be chosen
if he (she, it) be chosen

if we be chosen
if you be chosen
if they be chosen

Past if I were chosen
if you were chosen
if he (she, it) were chosen

if we were chosen
if you were chosen
if they were chosen

Fut. if I should be chosen
if you should be chosen
if he (she, it) should be chosen

if we should be chosen
if you should be chosen
if they should be chosen

to cling (active voice only)   *Principal Parts:* cling, clinging, clung, clung

(intransitive verb)

Infinitive: to cling   *Present Participle:* clinging
Perfect Infinitive: to have clung   *Past Participle:* clung

INDICATIVE MOOD

Pres.	I cling	we cling
	you cling	you cling
	he (she, it) clings	they cling
Pres.	I am clinging	we are clinging
Prog.	you are clinging	you are clinging
	he (she, it) is clinging	they are clinging
Pres.	I do cling	we do cling
Int.	you do cling	you do cling
	he (she, it) does cling	they do cling
Fut.	I shall cling	we shall cling
	you will cling	you will cling
	he (she, it) will cling	they will cling
Cond.	I would cling	we would cling
	you would cling	you would cling
	he (she, it) would cling	they would cling
Past	I clung	we clung
	you clung	you clung
	he (she, it) clung	they clung
Past	I was clinging	we were clinging
Prog.	you were clinging	you were clinging
	he (she, it) was clinging	they were clinging
Past	I did cling	we did cling
Int.	you did cling	you did cling
	he (she, it) did cling	they did cling
Pres.	I have clung	we have clung
Perf.	you have clung	you have clung
	he (she, it) has clung	they have clung
Past	I had clung	we had clung
Perf.	you had clung	you had clung
	he (she, it) had clung	they had clung
Fut.	I shall have clung	we shall have clung
Perf.	you will have clung	you will have clung
	he (she, it) will have clung	they will have clung
Cond.	I would have clung	we would have clung
Perf.	you would have clung	you would have clung
	he (she, it) would have clung	they would have clung

IMPERATIVE MOOD
cling

SUBJUNCTIVE MOOD

Pres.	if I cling	if we cling
	if you cling	if you cling
	if he (she, it) cling	if they cling
Past	if I clung	if we clung
	if you clung	if you clung
	if he (she, it) clung	if they clung
Fut.	if I should cling	if we should cling
	if you should cling	if you should cling
	if he (she, it) should cling	if they should cling

to come (active verb only)   *Principal Parts:* come, coming, came, come

---

(intransitive verb)

Infinitive: to come   *Present Participle:* coming
Perfect Infinitive: to have come   *Past Participle:* come

INDICATIVE MOOD

Pres.	I come	we come
	you come	you come
	he (she, it) comes	they come
Pres.	I am coming	we are coming
Prog.	you are coming	you are coming
	he (she, it) is coming	they are coming
Pres.	I do come	we do come
Int.	you do come	you do come
	he (she, it) does come	they do come
Fut.	I shall come	we shall come
	you will come	you will come
	he (she, it) will come	they will come
Cond.	I would come	we would come
	you would come	you would come
	he (she, it) would come	they would come
Past	I came	we came
	you came	you came
	he (she, it) came	they came
Past	I was coming	we were coming
Prog.	you were coming	you were coming
	he (she, it) was coming	they were coming
Past	I did come	we did come
Int.	you did come	you did come
	he (she, it) did come	they did come
Pres.	I have come	we have come
Perf.	you have come	you have come
	he (she, it) has come	they have come
Past	I had come	we had come
Perf.	you had come	you had come
	he (she, it) had come	they had come
Fut.	I shall have come	we shall have come
Perf	you will have come	you will have come
	he (she, it) will have come	they will have come
Cond.	I would have come	we would have come
Perf.	you would have come	you would have come
	he (she, it) would have come	they would have come

IMPERATIVE MOOD
come

SUBJUNCTIVE MOOD

Pres.	if I come	if we come
	if you come	if you come
	if he (she, it) come	if they come
Past	if I came	if we came
	if you came	if you came
	if he (she, it) came	if they came
Fut.	if I should come	if we should come
	if you should come	if you should come
	if he (she, it) should come	if they should come

to creep (active verb only) *Principal Parts:* creep, creeping, crept, crept

(intransitive verb)

Infinitive: to creep *Present Participle:* creeping
Perfect Infinitive: to have crept *Past Participle:* crept

INDICATIVE MOOD

Pres.	I creep	we creep
	you creep	you creep
	he (she, it) creeps	they creep
Pres.	I am creeping	we are creeping
Prog.	you are creeping	you are creeping
	he (she, it) is creeping	they are creeping
Pres.	I do creep	we do creep
Int.	you do creep	you do creep
	he (she, it) does creep	they do creep
Fut.	I shall creep	we shall creep
	you will creep	you will creep
	he (she, it) will creep	they will creep
Cond.	I would creep	we would creep
	you would creep	you would creep
	he (she, it) would creep	they would creep
Past	I crept	we crept
	you crept	you crept
	he (she, it) crept	they crept
Past	I was creeping	we were creeping
Prog.	you were creeping	you were creeping
	he (she, it) was creeping	they were creeping
Past	I did creep	we did creep
Int.	you did creep	you did creep
	he (she, it) did creep	they did creep
Pres.	I have crept	we have crept
Perf.	you have crept	you have crept
	he (she, it) has crept	they have crept
Past	I had crept	we had crept
Perf.	you had crept	you had crept
	he (she, it) had crept	they had crept
Fut.	I shall have crept	we shall have crept
Perf.	you will have crept	you will have crept
	he (she, it) will have crept	they will have crept
Cond.	I would have crept	we would have crept
Perf.	you would have crept	you would have crept
	he (she, it) would have crept	they would have crept

IMPERATIVE MOOD
creep

SUBJUNCTIVE MOOD

Pres.	if I creep	if we creep
	if you creep	if you creep
	if he (she, it) creep	if they creep
Past	if I crept	if we crept
	if you crept	if you crept
	if he (she, it) crept	if they crept
Fut.	if I should creep	if we should creep
	if you should creep	if you should creep
	if he (she, it) should creep	if they should creep

To creep is an intransitive verb.

It does not take an object.

It describes action, but the action is self-contained.

Like other intransitive verbs, it may be followed by adverbs, adverbial phrases and clauses describing the how, why, when, and where of the action:

HOW: The baby crept *quietly.* (adverb)

WHY: The baby crept *because it could not walk.* (adverbial clause)

WHEN: The baby will creep *soon.* (adverb)

WHERE: The baby crept *around the room.* (adverbial phrase)

to cut (active voice) Principal Parts: cut, cutting, cut, cut

Infinitive: to cut *Present Participle:* cutting
Perfect Infinitive: to have cut *Past Participle:* cut

INDICATIVE MOOD

Pres.	I cut	we cut	
	you cut	you cut	
	he (she, it) cuts	they cut	
Pres.	I am cutting	we are cutting	
Prog.	you are cutting	you are cutting	
	he (she, it) is cutting	they are cutting	
Pres.	I do cut	we do cut	
Int.	you do cut	you do cut	
	he (she, it) does cut	they do cut	
Fut.	I shall cut	we shall cut	
	you will cut	you will cut	
	he (she, it) will cut	they will cut	
Cond.	I would cut	we would cut	
	you would cut	you would cut	
	he (she, it) would cut	they would cut	
Past	I cut	we cut	
	you cut	you cut	
	he (she, it) cut	they cut	
Past	I was cutting	we were cutting	
Prog.	you were cutting	you were cutting	
	he (she, it) was cutting	they were cutting	
Past	I did cut	we did cut	
Int.	you did cut	you did cut	
	he (she, it) did cut	they did cut	
Pres.	I have cut	we have cut	
Perf.	you have cut	you have cut	
	he (she, it) has cut	they have cut	
Past	I had cut	we had cut	
Perf.	you had cut	you had cut	
	he (she, it) had cut	they had cut	
Fut.	I shall have cut	we shall have cut	
Perf.	you will have cut	you will have cut	
	he (she, it) will have cut	they will have cut	
Cond.	I would have cut	we would have cut	
Perf.	you would have cut	you would have cut	
	he (she, it) would have cut	they would have cut	

IMPERATIVE MOOD
cut

SUBJUNCTIVE MOOD

Pres.	if I cut	if we cut	
	if you cut	if you cut	
	if he (she, it) cut	if they cut	
Past	if I cut	if we cut	
	if you cut	if you cut	
	if he (she, it) cut	if they cut	
Fut.	if I should cut	if we should cut	
	if you should cut	if you should cut	
	if he (she, it) should cut	if they should cut	

Infinitive: to be cut *Present Participle:* being cut
Perfect Infinitive: to have been cut *Past Participle:* been cut

INDICATIVE MOOD

Pres.	I am cut	we are cut
	you are cut	you are cut
	he (she, it) is cut	they are cut
Pres.	I am being cut	we are being cut
Prog.	you are being cut	you are being cut
	he (she, it) is being cut	they are being cut
Pres.	I do get cut	we do get cut
Int.	you do get cut	you do get cut
	he (she, it) does get cut	they do get cut
Fut.	I shall be cut	we shall be cut
	you will be cut	you will be cut
	he (she, it) will be cut	they will be cut
Cond.	I would be cut	we would be cut
	you would be cut	you would be cut
	he (she, it) would be cut	they would be cut
Past	I was cut	we were cut
	you were cut	you were cut
	he (she, it) was cut	they were cut
Past	I was being cut	we were being cut
Prog.	you were being cut	you were being cut
	he (she, it) was being cut	they were being cut
Past	I did get cut	we did get cut
Int.	you did get cut	you did get cut
	he (she, it) did get cut	they did get cut
Pres.	I have been cut	we have been cut
Perf.	you have been cut	you have been cut
	he (she, it) has been cut	they have been cut
Past	I had been cut	we had been cut
Perf.	you had been cut	you had been cut
	he (she, it) had been cut	they had been cut
Fut.	I shall have been cut	we shall have been cut
Perf.	you will have been cut	you will have been cut
	he (she, it) will have been cut	they will have been cut
Cond.	I would have been cut	we would have been cut
Perf.	you would have been cut	you would have been cut
	he (she, it) would have been cut	they would have been cut

IMPERATIVE MOOD
be cut

SUBJUNCTIVE MOOD

Pres.	if I be cut	if we be cut
	if you be cut	if you be cut
	if he (she, it) be cut	if they be cut
Past	if I were cut	if we were cut
	if you were cut	if you were cut
	if he (she, it) were cut	if they were cut
Fut.	if I should be cut	if we should be cut
	if you should be cut	if you should be cut
	if he (she, it) should be cut	if they should be cut

173

Infinitive: to deal   *Present Participle:* dealing
Perfect Infinitive: to have dealt   *Past Participle:* dealt

INDICATIVE MOOD

Pres. I deal   we deal
you deal   you deal
he (she, it) deals   they deal

Pres. I am dealing   we are dealing
Prog. you are dealing   you are dealing
he (she, it) is dealing   they are dealing

Pres. I do deal   we do deal
Int. you do deal   you do deal
he (she, it) does deal   they do deal

Fut. I shall deal   we shall deal
you will deal   you will deal
he (she, it) will deal   they will deal

Cond. I would deal   we would deal
you would deal   you would deal
he (she, it) would deal   they would deal

Past I dealt   we dealt
you dealt   you dealt
he (she, it) dealt   they dealt

Past I was dealing   we were dealing
Prog. you were dealing   you were dealing
he (she, it) was dealing   they were dealing

Past I did deal   we did deal
Int. you did deal   you did deal
he (she, it) did deal   they did deal

Pres. I have dealt   we have dealt
Perf. you have dealt   you have dealt
he (she, it) has dealt   they have dealt

Past I had dealt   we had dealt
Perf. you had dealt   you had dealt
he (she, it) had dealt   they had dealt

Fut. I shall have dealt   we shall have dealt
Perf. you will have dealt   you will have dealt
he (she, it) will have dealt   they will have dealt

Cond. I would have dealt   we would have dealt
Perf. you would have dealt   you would have dealt
he (she, it) would have dealt   they would have dealt

IMPERATIVE MOOD
deal

SUBJUNCTIVE MOOD

Pres. if I deal   if we deal
if you deal   if you deal
if he (she, it) deal   if they deal

Past if I dealt   if we dealt
if you dealt   if you dealt
if he (she, it) dealt   if they dealt

Fut. if I should deal   if we should deal
if you should deal   if you should deal
if he (she, it) should deal   if they should deal

Infinitive: to be dealt   *Present Participle:* being dealt
Perfect Infinitive: to have been dealt   *Past Participle:* been dealt

INDICATIVE MOOD

Pres.   I am dealt   we are dealt
       you are dealt   you are dealt
       he (she, it) is dealt   they are dealt

Pres.   I am being dealt   we are being dealt
Prog.   you are being dealt   you are being dealt
       he (she, it) is being dealt   they are being dealt

Pres.   I do get dealt   we do get dealt
Int.   you do get dealt   you do get dealt
       he (she, it) does get dealt   they do get dealt

Fut.   I shall be dealt   we shall be dealt
       you will be dealt   you will be dealt
       he (she, it) will be dealt   they will be dealt

Cond.   I would be dealt   we would be dealt
       you would be dealt   you would be dealt
       he (she, it) would be dealt   they would be dealt

Past   I was dealt   we were dealt
       you were dealt   you were dealt
       he (she, it) was dealt   they were dealt

Past   I was being dealt   we were being dealt
Prog.   you were being dealt   you were being dealt
       he (she, it) was being dealt   they were being dealt

Past   I did get dealt   we did get dealt
Int.   you did get dealt   you did get dealt
       he (she, it) did get dealt   they did get dealt

Pres.   I have been dealt   we have been dealt
Perf.   you have been dealt   you have been dealt
       he (she, it) has been dealt   they have been dealt

Past   I had been dealt   we had been dealt
Perf.   you had been dealt   you had been dealt
       he (she, it) had been dealt   they had been dealt

Fut.   I shall have been dealt   we shall have been dealt
Perf.   you will have been dealt   you will have been dealt
       he (she, it) will have been dealt   they will have been dealt

Cond.   I would have been dealt   we would have been dealt
Perf.   you would have been dealt   you would have been dealt
       he (she, it) would have been dealt   they would have been dealt

IMPERATIVE MOOD
be dealt

SUBJUNCTIVE MOOD

Pres.   if I be dealt   if we be dealt
       if you be dealt   if you be dealt
       if he (she, it) be dealt   if they be dealt

Past   if I were dealt   if we were dealt
       if you were dealt   if you were dealt
       if he (she, it) were dealt   if they were dealt

Fut.   if I should be dealt   if we should be dealt
       if you should be dealt   if you should be dealt
       if he (she, it) should be dealt   if they should be dealt

to dive (active verb only) *Principal Parts:* dive, diving, dived, dived

(intransitive verb)

Infinitive: to dive
Perfect Infinitive: to have dived

Present Participle: diving
Past Participle: dived

INDICATIVE MOOD

Pres.	I dive	we dive
	you dive	you dive
	he (she, it) dives	they dive
Pres. Prog.	I am diving	we are diving
	you are diving	you are diving
	he (she, it) is diving	they are diving
Pres. Int.	I do dive	we do dive
	you do dive	you do dive
	he (she, it) does dive	they do dive
Fut.	I shall dive	we shall dive
	you will dive	you will dive
	he (she, it) will dive	they will dive
Cond.	I would dive	we would dive
	you would dive	you would dive
	he (she, it) would dive	they would dive
Past	I dived	we dived
	you dived	you dived
	he (she, it) dived	they dived
Past Prog.	I was diving	we were diving
	you were diving	you were diving
	he (she, it) was diving	they were diving
Past Int.	I did dive	we did dive
	you did dive	you did dive
	he (she, it) did dive	they did dive
Pres. Perf.	I have dived	we have dived
	you have dived	you have dived
	he (she, it) has dived	they have dived
Past Perf.	I had dived	we had dived
	you had dived	you had dived
	he (she, it) had dived	they had dived
Fut. Perf.	I shall have dived	we shall have dived
	you will have dived	you will have dived
	he (she, it) will have dived	they will have dived
Cond. Perf.	I would have dived	we would have dived
	you would have dived	you would have dived
	he (she, it) would have dived	they would have dived

IMPERATIVE MOOD
dive

SUBJUNCTIVE MOOD

Pres.	if I dive	if we dive
	if you dive	if you dive
	if he (she, it) dive	if they dive
Past	if I dived	if we dived
	if you dived	if you dived
	if he (she, it) dived	if they dived
Fut.	if I should dive	if we should dive
	if you should dive	if you should dive
	if he (she, it) should dive	if they should dive

176

To dive is an intransitive verb.

It does not take an object.

It describes action, but the action is self-contained.

Like other intransitive verbs, it may be followed by adverbs, adverbial phrases and clauses describing the how, why, when, and where of the action:

HOW: She dived *beautifully*. (adverb)

WHY: The submarine dived *because an enemy ship was in sight*. (adverbial clause)

WHEN: The boys dived *until late in the afternoon*. (adverbial phrases)

WHERE: I dived *into the pool*. (adverbial phrase)

Infinitive: to do　　　　　　　*Present Participle:* doing
Perfect Infinitive: to have done　*Past Participle:* done

INDICATIVE MOOD

Pres.	I do	we do
	you do	you do
	he (she, it) does	they do

Prog.	I am doing	we are doing
Pres.	you are doing	you are doing
	he (she, it) is doing	they are doing

Pres.	I do do	we do do
Int.	you do do	you do do
	he (she, it) does do	they do do

Fut.	I shall do	we shall do
	you will do	you will do
	he (she, it) will do	they will do

Cond.	I would do	we would do
	you would do	you would do
	he (she, it) would do	they would do

Past	I did	we did
	you did	you did
	he (she, it) did	they did

Past	I was doing	we were doing
Prog.	you were doing	you were doing
	he (she, it) was doing	they were doing

Past	I did do	we did do
Int.	you did do	you did do
	he (she, it) did do	they did do

Pres.	I have done	we have done
Perf.	you have done	you have done
	he (she, it) has done	they have done

Past	I had done	we had done
Perf.	you had done	you had done
	he (she, it) had done	they had done

Fut.	I shall have done	we shall have done
Perf.	you will have done	you will have done
	he (she, it) will have done	they will have done

Cond.	I would have done	we would have done
Perf.	you would have done	you would have done
	he (she, it) would have done	they would have done

IMPERATIVE MOOD
do

SUBJUNCTIVE MOOD

Pres.	if I do	if we do
	if you do	if you do
	if he (she, it) do	if they do

Past	if I did	if we did
	if you did	if you did
	if he (she, it) did	if they did

Fut.	if I should do	if we should do
	if you should do	if you should do
	if he (she, it) should do	if they should do

(passive voice)

Infinitive: to be done   *Present Participle:* being done
Perfect Infinitive: to have been done   *Past Participle:* been done

INDICATIVE MOOD

Pres.	I am done	we are done
	you are done	you are done
	he (she, it) is done	they are done
Pres.	I am being done	we are being done
Prog.	you are being done	you are being done
	he (she, it) is being done	they are being done
Pres.	I do get done	we do get done
Int.	you do get done	you do get done
	he (she, it) does get done	they do get done
Fut.	I shall be done	we shall be done
	you will be done	you will be done
	he (she, it) will be done	they will be done
Cond.	I would be done	we would be done
	you would be done	you would be done
	he (she, it) would be done	they would be done
Past	I was done	we were done
	you were done	you were done
	he (she, it) was done	they were done
Past	I was being done	we were being done
Prog.	you were being done	you were being done
	he (she, it) was being done	they were being done
Past	I did get done	we did get done
Int.	you did get done	you did get done
	he (she, it) did get done	they did get done
Pres.	I have been done	we have been done
Perf.	you have been done	you have been done
	he (she, it) has been done	they have been done
Past	I had been done	we had been done
Perf.	you had been done	you had been done
	he (she, it) had been done	they had been done
Fut.	I shall have been done	we shall have been done
Perf.	you will have been done	you will have been done
	he (she, it) will have been done	they will have been done
Cond.	I would have been done	we would have been done
Perf.	you would have been done	you would have been done
	he (she, it) would have been done	they would have been done

IMPERATIVE MOOD
be done

SUBJUNCTIVE MOOD

Pres.	if I be done	if we be done
	if you be done	if you be done
	if he (she, it) be done	if they be done
Past	if I were done	if we were done
	if you were done	if you were done
	if he (she, it) were done	if they were done
Fut.	if I should be done	if we should be done
	if you should be done	if you should be done
	if he (she, it) should be done	if they should be done

Infinitive: to draw　　　　　　*Present Participle:* drawing
Perfect Infinitive: to have drawn　*Past Participle:* drawn

INDICATIVE MOOD

Pres. I draw	we draw
you draw	you draw
he (she, it) draws	they draw
Pres. I am drawing	we are drawing
Prog. you are drawing	you are drawing
he (she, it) is drawing	they are drawing
Pres. I do draw	we do draw
Int. you do draw	you do draw
he (she, it) does draw	they do draw
Fut. I shall draw	we shall draw
you will draw	you will draw
he (she, it) will draw	they will draw
Cond. I would draw	we would draw
you would draw	you would draw
he (she, it) would draw	they would draw
Past I drew	we drew
you drew	you drew
he (she, it) drew	they drew
Past I was drawing	we were drawing
Prog. you were drawing	you were drawing
he (she, it) was drawing	they were drawing
Past I did draw	we did draw
Int. you did draw	you did draw
he (she, it) did draw	they did draw
Pres. I have drawn	we have drawn
Perf. you have drawn	you have drawn
he (she, it) has drawn	they have drawn
Past I had drawn	we had drawn
Perf. you had drawn	you had drawn
he (she, it) had drawn	they had drawn
Fut. I shall have drawn	we shall have drawn
Perf. you will have drawn	you will have drawn
he (she, it) will have drawn	they will have drawn
Cond. I would have drawn	we would have drawn
Perf. you would have drawn	you would have drawn
he (she, it) would have drawn	they would have drawn

IMPERATIVE MOOD
draw

SUBJUNCTIVE MOOD

Pres. if I draw	if we draw
if you draw	if you draw
if he (she, it) draw	if they draw
Past if I drew	if we drew
if you drew	if you drew
if he (she, it) drew	if they drew
Fut. if I should draw	if we should draw
if you should draw	if you should draw
if he (she, it) should draw	if they should draw

Infinitive: to be drawn   *Present Participle:* being drawn
Perfect Infinitive: to have been drawn   *Past Participle:* been drawn

INDICATIVE MOOD

Pres. I am drawn	we are drawn
you are drawn	you are drawn
he (she, it) is drawn	they are drawn
Pres. I am being drawn	we are being drawn
Prog. you are being drawn	you are being drawn
he (she, it) is being drawn	they are being drawn
Pres. I do get drawn	we do get drawn
Int. you do get drawn	you do get drawn
he (she, it) does get drawn	they do get drawn
Fut. I shall be drawn	we shall be drawn
you will be drawn	you will be drawn
he (she, it) will be drawn	they will be drawn
Cond. I would be drawn	we would be drawn
you would be drawn	you would be drawn
he (she, it) would be drawn	they would be drawn
Past I was drawn	we were drawn
you were drawn	you were drawn
he (she, it) was drawn	they were drawn
Past I was being drawn	we were being drawn
Prog. you were being drawn	you were being drawn
he (she, it) was being drawn	they were being drawn
Past I did get drawn	we did get drawn
Int. you did get drawn	you did get drawn
he (she, it) did get drawn	they did get drawn
Pres. I have been drawn	we have been drawn
Perf. you have been drawn	you have been drawn
he (she, it) has been drawn	they have been drawn
Past I had been drawn	we had been drawn
Perf. you had been drawn	you had been drawn
he (she, it) had been drawn	they had been drawn
Fut. I shall have been drawn	we shall have been drawn
Perf. you will have been drawn	you will have been drawn
he (she, it) will have been drawn	they will have been drawn
Cond. I would have been drawn	we would have been drawn
Perf. you would have been drawn	you would have been drawn
he (she, it) would have been drawn	they would have been drawn

IMPERATIVE MOOD
be drawn

SUBJUNCTIVE MOOD

Pres. if I be drawn	if we be drawn
if you be drawn	if you be drawn
if he (she, it) be drawn	if they be drawn
Past if I were drawn	if we were drawn
if you were drawn	if you were drawn
if he (she, it) were drawn	if they were drawn
Fut. if I should be drawn	if we should be drawn
if you should be drawn	if you should be drawn
if he (she, it) should be drawn	if they should be drawn

to drink (active voice)   *Principal Parts:* drink, drinking, drank, drunk

---

Infinitive: to drink
Perfect Infinitive: to have drunk

Present Participle: drinking
Past Participle: drunk

INDICATIVE MOOD

Pres. I drink
you drink
he (she, it) drinks

we drink
you drink
they drink

Pres.
Prog. I am drinking
you are drinking
he (she, it) is drinking

we are drinking
you are drinking
they are drinking

Pres.
Int. I do drink
you do drink
he (she, it) does drink

we do drink
you do drink
they do drink

Fut. I shall drink
you will drink
he (she, it) will drink

we shall drink
you will drink
they will drink

Cond. I would drink
you would drink
he (she, it) would drink

we would drink
you would drink
they would drink

Past I drank
you drank
he (she, it) drank

we drank
you drank
they drank

Past
Prog. I was drinking
you were drinking
he (she, it) was drinking

we were drinking
you were drinking
they were drinking

Past
Int. I did drink
you did drink
he (she, it) did drink

we did drink
you did drink
they did drink

Pres.
Perf. I have drunk
you have drunk
he (she, it) has drunk

we have drunk
you have drunk
they have drunk

Past.
Perf. I had drunk
you had drunk
he (she, it) had drunk

we had drunk
you had drunk
they had drunk

Fut.
Perf. I shall have drunk
you will have drunk
he (she, it) will have drunk

we shall have drunk
you will have drunk
they will have drunk

Cond.
Perf. I would have drunk
you would have drunk
he (she, it) would have drunk

we would have drunk
you would have drunk
they would have drunk

IMPERATIVE MOOD
drink

SUBJUNCTIVE MOOD

Pres. if I drink
if you drink
if he (she, it) drink

if we drink
if you drink
if they drink

Past if I drank
if you drank
if he (she, it) drank

if we drank
if you drank
if they drank

Fut. if I should drink
if you should drink
if he (she, it) should drink

if we should drink
if you should drink
if they should drink

Infinitive: to be drunk
Perfect Infinitive: to have been drunk

Present Participle: being drunk
Past Participle: been drunk

INDICATIVE MOOD

Pres.	I am drunk	we are drunk
	you are drunk	you are drunk
	he (she, it) is drunk	they are drunk
Pres.	I am being drunk	we are being drunk
Prog.	you are being drunk	you are being drunk
	he (she, it) is being drunk	they are being drunk
Pres.	I do get drunk	we do get drunk
Int.	you do get drunk	you do get drunk
	he (she, it) does get drunk	they do get drunk
Fut.	I shall be drunk	we shall be drunk
	you will be drunk	you will be drunk
	he (she, it) will be drunk	they will be drunk
Cond.	I would be drunk	we would be drunk
	you would be drunk	you would be drunk
	he (she, it) would be drunk	they would be drunk
Past	I was drunk	we were drunk
	you were drunk	you were drunk
	he (she, it) was drunk	they were drunk
Past	I was being drunk	we were being drunk
Prog.	you were being drunk	you were being drunk
	he (she, it) was being drunk	they were being drunk
Past	I did get drunk	we did get drunk
Int.	you did get drunk	you did get drunk
	he (she, it) did get drunk	they did get drunk
Pres.	I have been drunk	we have been drunk
Perf.	you have been drunk	you have been drunk
	he (she, it) has been drunk	they have been drunk
Past	I had been drunk	we had been drunk
Perf.	you had been drunk	you had been drunk
	he (she, it) had been drunk	they had been drunk
Fut.	I shall have been drunk	we shall have been drunk
Perf.	you will have been drunk	you will have been drunk
	he (she, it) will have been drunk	they will have been drunk
Cond.	I would have been drunk	we would have been drunk
Perf.	you would have been drunk	you would have been drunk
	he (she, it) would have been drunk	they would have been drunk

IMPERATIVE MOOD
be drunk

SUBJUNCTIVE MOOD

Pres.	if I be drunk	if we be drunk
	if you be drunk	if you be drunk
	if he (she, it) be drunk	if they be drunk
Past	if I were drunk	if we were drunk
	if you were drunk	if you were drunk
	if he (she, it) were drunk	if they were drunk
Fut.	if I should be drunk	if we should be drunk
	if you should be drunk	if you should be drunk
	if he (she, it) should be drunk	if they should be drunk

to drive (active voice)   *Principal Parts:* drive, driving, drove, driven

Infinitive: to drive
Perfect Infinitive: to have driven

Present Participle: driving
Past Participle: driven

INDICATIVE MOOD

Pres. I drive
you drive
he (she, it) drives

we drive
you drive
they drive

Pres. Prog. I am driving
you are driving
he (she, it) is driving

we are driving
you are driving
they are driving

Pres. Int. I do drive
you do drive
he (she, it) does drive

we do drive
you do drive
they do drive

Fut. I shall drive
you will drive
he (she, it) will drive

we shall drive
you will drive
they will drive

Cond. I would drive
you would drive
he (she, it) would drive

we would drive
you would drive
they would drive

Past I drove
you drove
he (she, it) drove

we drove
you drove
they drove

Past Prog. I was driving
you were driving
he (she, it) was driving

we were driving
you were driving
they were driving

Past Int. I did drive
you did drive
he (she, it) did drive

we did drive
you did drive
they did drive

Pres. Perf. I have driven
you have driven
he (she, it) has driven

we have driven
you have driven
they have driven

Past Perf. I had driven
you had driven
he (she, it) had driven

we had driven
you had driven
they had driven

Fut. Perf. I shall have driven
you will have driven
he (she, it) will have driven

we shall have driven
you will have driven
they will have driven

Cond. Perf. I would have driven
you would have driven
he (she, it) would have driven

we would have driven
you would have driven
they would have driven

IMPERATIVE MOOD
drive

SUBJUNCTIVE MOOD

Pres. if I drive
if you drive
if he (she, it) drive

if we drive
if you drive
if they drive

Past if I drove
if you drove
if he (she, it) drove

if we drove
if you drove
if they drove

Fut. if I should drive
if you should drive
if he (she, it) should drive

if we should drive
if you should drive
if they should drive

Infinitive: to be driven *Present Participle:* being driven
Perfect Infinitive: to have been driven *Past Participle:* been driven

INDICATIVE MOOD

Pres.	I am driven	we are driven
	you are driven	you are driven
	he (she, it) is driven	they are driven
Pres.	I am being driven	we are being driven
Prog.	you are being driven	you are being driven
	he (she, it) is being driven	they are being driven
Pres.	I do get driven	we do get driven
Int.	you do get driven	you do get driven
	he (she, it) does get driven	they do get driven
Fut.	I shall be driven	we shall be driven
	you will be driven	you will be driven
	he (she, it) will be driven	they will be driven
Cond.	I would be driven	we would be driven
	you would be driven	you would be driven
	he (she, it) would be driven	they would be driven
Past	I was driven	we were driven
	you were driven	you were driven
	he (she, it) was driven	they were driven
Past	I was being driven	we were being driven
Prog.	you were being driven	you were being driven
	he (she, it) was being driven	they were being driven
Past	I did get driven	we did get driven
Int.	you did get driven	you did get driven
	he (she, it) did get driven	they did get driven
Pres.	I have been driven	we have been driven
Perf.	you have been driven	you have been driven
	he (she, it) has been driven	they have been driven
Past	I had been driven	we had been driven
Perf.	you had been driven	you had been driven
	he (she, it) had been driven	they had been driven
Fut.	I shall have been driven	we shall have been driven
Perf.	you will have been driven	you will have been driven
	he (she, it) will have been driven	they will have been driven
Cond.	I would have been driven	we would have been driven
Perf.	you would have been driven	you would have been driven
	he (she, it) would have been driven	they would have been driven

IMPERATIVE MOOD
be driven

SUBJUNCTIVE MOOD

Pres.	if I be driven	if we be driven
	if you be driven	if you be driven
	if he (she, it) be driven	if they be driven
Past	if I were driven	if we were driven
	if you were driven	if you were driven
	if he (she, it) were driven	if they were driven
Fut.	if I should be driven	if we should be driven
	if you should be driven	if you should be driven
	if he (she, it) should be driven	if they should be driven

to eat (active voice)   *Principal Parts:* eat, eating, ate, eaten

---

Infinitive: to eat   *Present Participle:* eating
Perfect Infinitive: to have eaten   *Past Participle:* eaten

INDICATIVE MOOD

Pres. I eat	we eat
you eat	you eat
he (she, it) eats	they eat
Pres. I am eating	we are eating
Prog. you are eating	you are eating
he (she, it) is eating	they are eating
Pres. I do eat	we do eat
Int. you do eat	you do eat
he (she, it) does eat	they do eat
Fut. I shall eat	we shall eat
you will eat	you will eat
he (she, it) will eat	they will eat
Cond. I would eat	we would eat
you would eat	you would eat
he (she, it) would eat	they would eat
Past I ate	we ate
you ate	you ate
he (she, it) ate	they ate
Past I was eating	we were eating
Prog. you were eating	you were eating
he (she, it) was eating	they were eating
Past I did eat	we did eat
Int. you did eat	you did eat
he (she, it) did eat	they did eat
Pres. I have eaten	we have eaten
Perf. you have eaten	you have eaten
he (she, it) has eaten	they have eaten
Past I had eaten	we had eaten
Perf. you had eaten	you had eaten
he (she, it) had eaten	they had eaten
Fut. I shall have eaten	we shall have eaten
Perf. you will have eaten	you will have eaten
he (she, it) will have eaten	they will have eaten
Cond. I would have eaten	we would have eaten
Perf. you would have eaten	you would have eaten
he (she, it) would have eaten	they would have eaten

IMPERATIVE MOOD
eat

SUBJUNCTIVE MOOD

Pres. if I eat	if we eat
if you eat	if you eat
if he (she, it) eat	if they eat
Past if I ate	if we ate
if you ate	if you ate
if he (she, it) ate	if they ate
Fut. if I should eat	if we should eat
if you should eat	if you should eat
if he (she, it) should eat	if they should eat

186

Infinitive: to be eaten
Perfect Infinitive: to have been eaten

Present Participle: being eaten
Past Participle: been eaten

INDICATIVE MOOD

Pres.
I am eaten
you are eaten
he (she, it) is eaten

we are eaten
you are eaten
they are eaten

Pres. Prog.
I am being eaten
you are being eaten
he (she, it) is being eaten

we are being eaten
you are being eaten
they are being eaten

Pres. Int.
I do get eaten
you do get eaten
he (she, it) does get eaten

we do get eaten
you do get eaten
they do get eaten

Fut.
I shall be eaten
you will be eaten
he (she, it) will be eaten

we shall be eaten
you will be eaten
they will be eaten

Cond.
I would be eaten
you would be eaten
he (she, it) would be eaten

we would be eaten
you would be eaten
they would be eaten

Past
I was eaten
you were eaten
he (she, it) was eaten

we were eaten
you were eaten
they were eaten

Past Prog.
I was being eaten
you were being eaten
he (she, it) was being eaten

we were being eaten
you were being eaten
they were being eaten

Past Int.
I did get eaten
you did get eaten
he (she, it) did get eaten

we did get eaten
you did get eaten
they did get eaten

Pres. Perf.
I have been eaten
you have been eaten
he (she, it) has been eaten

we have been eaten
you have been eaten
they have been eaten

Past Perf.
I had been eaten
you had been eaten
he (she, it) had been eaten

we had been eaten
you had been eaten
they had been eaten

Fut. Perf.
I shall have been eaten
you will have been eaten
he (she, it) will have been eaten

we shall have been eaten
you will have been eaten
they will have been eaten

Cond. Perf.
I would have been eaten
you would have been eaten
he (she, it) would have been eaten

we would have been eaten
you would have been eaten
they would have been eaten

IMPERATIVE MOOD
be eaten

SUBJUNCTIVE MOOD

Pres.
if I be eaten
if you be eaten
if he (she, it) be eaten

if we be eaten
if you be eaten
if they be eaten

Past
if I were eaten
if you were eaten
if he (she, it) were eaten

if we were eaten
if you were eaten
if they were eaten

Fut.
if I should be eaten
if you should be eaten
if he (she, it) should be eaten

if we should be eaten
if you should be eaten
if they should be eaten

to fall (active verb only)   *Principal Parts:* fall, falling, fell, fallen

---

(intransitive verb)

Infinitive: to fall   *Present Participle:* falling
Perfect Infinitive: to have fallen   *Past Participle:* fallen

INDICATIVE MOOD

Pres.	I fall	we fall
	you fall	you fall
	he (she, it) falls	they fall
Pres.	I am falling	we are falling
Prog.	you are falling	you are falling
	he (she, it) is falling	they are falling
Pres.	I do fall	we do fall
Int.	you do fall	you do fall
	he (she, it) does fall	they do fall
Fut.	I shall fall	we shall fall
	you will fall	you will fall
	he (she, it) will fall	they will fall
Cond.	I would fall	we would fall
	you would fall	you would fall
	he (she, it) would fall	they would fall
Past	I fell	we fell
	you fell	you fell
	he (she, it) fell	they fell
Past	I was falling	we were falling
Prog.	you were falling	you were falling
	he (she, it) was falling	they were falling
Past	I did fall	we did fall
Int.	you did fall	you did fall
	he (she, it) did fall	they did fall
Pres.	I have fallen	we have fallen
Perf.	you have fallen	you have fallen
	he (she, it) has fallen	they have fallen
Past	I had fallen	we had fallen
Perf.	you had fallen	you had fallen
	he (she, it) had fallen	they had fallen
Fut.	I shall have fallen	we shall have fallen
Perf.	you will have fallen	you will have fallen
	he (she, it) will have fallen	they will have fallen
Cond.	I would have fallen	we would have fallen
Perf.	you would have fallen	you would have fallen
	he (she, it) would have fallen	they would have fallen

IMPERATIVE MOOD
fall

SUBJUNCTIVE MOOD

Pres.	if I fall	if we fall
	if you fall	if you fall
	if he (she, it) fall	if they fall
Past	if I fell	if we fell
	if you fell	if you fell
	if he (she, it) fell	if they fell
Fut.	if I should fall	if we should fall
	if you should fall	if you should fall
	if he (she, it) should fall	if they should fall

To fall is an intransitive verb.

It does not take an object.

It describes action, but the action is self-contained.

Like other intransitive verbs, it may be followed by adverbs, adverbial phrases and clauses describing the how, why, when, and where of the action:

HOW: The rain fell *slowly*. (adverb)

WHY: He fell *because he could not keep his balance*. (adverbial clause)

WHEN: Leaves fall *in the autumn*. (adverbial phrase)

WHERE: He fell *off the ladder*. (adverbial phrase)

1

to feed (active voice)   *Principal Parts:* feed, feeding, fed, fed

Infinitive: to feed   *Present Participle:* feeding
Perfect Infinitive: to have fed   *Past Participle:* fed

INDICATIVE MOOD

Pres.	I feed	we feed
	you feed	you feed
	he (she, it) feeds	they feed
Pres.	I am feeding	we are feeding
Prog.	you are feeding	you are feeding
	he (she, it) is feeding	they are feeding
Pres.	I do feed	we do feed
Int.	you do feed	you do feed
	he (she, it) does feed	they do feed
Fut.	I shall feed	we shall feed
	you will feed	you will feed
	he (she, it) will feed	they will feed
Cond.	I would feed	we would feed
	you would feed	you would feed
	he (she, it) would feed	they would feed
Past	I fed	we fed
	you fed	you fed
	he (she, it) fed	they fed
Past	I was feeding	we were feeding
Prog.	you were feeding	you were feeding
	he (she, it) was feeding	they were feeding
Past	I did feed	we did feed
Int.	you did feed	you did feed
	he (she, it) did feed	they did feed
Pres.	I have fed	we have fed
Perf.	you have fed	you have fed
	he (she, it) has fed	they have fed
Past	I had fed	we had fed
Perf.	you had fed	you had fed
	he (she, it) had fed	they had fed
Fut.	I shall have fed	we shall have fed
Perf.	you will have fed	you will have fed
	he (she, it) will have fed	they will have fed
Cond.	I would have fed	we would have fed
Perf.	you would have fed	you would have fed
	he (she, it) would have fed	they would have fed

IMPERATIVE MOOD
feed

SUBJUNCTIVE MOOD

Pres.	if I feed	if we feed
	if you feed	if you feed
	if he (she, it) feed	if they feed
Past	if I fed	if we fed
	if you fed	if you fed
	if he (she, it) fed	if they fed
Fut.	if I should feed	if we should feed
	if you should feed	if you should feed
	if he (she, it) should feed	if they should feed

Infinitive: to be fed   *Present Participle:* being fed
Perfect Infinitive: to have been fed   *Past Participle:* been fed

INDICATIVE MOOD

Pres.	I am fed	we are fed
	you are fed	you are fed
	he (she, it) is fed	they are fed
Pres.	I am being fed	we are being fed
Prog.	you are being fed	you are being fed
	he (she, it) is being fed	they are being fed
Pres.	I do get fed	we do get fed
Int.	you do get fed	you do get fed
	he (she, it) does get fed	they do get fed
Fut.	I shall be fed	we shall be fed
	you will be fed	you will be fed
	he (she, it) will be fed	they will be fed
Cond.	I would be fed	we would be fed
	you would be fed	you would be fed
	he (she, it) would be fed	they would be fed
Past	I was fed	we were fed
	you were fed	you were fed
	he (she, it) was fed	they were fed
Past	I was being fed	we were being fed
Prog.	you were being fed	you were being fed
	he (she, it) was being fed	they were being fed
Past	I did get fed	we did get fed
Int.	you did get fed	you did get fed
	he (she, it) did get fed	they did get fed
Pres.	I have been fed	we have been fed
Perf.	you have been fed	you have been fed
	he (she, it) has been fed	they have been fed
Past	I had been fed	we had been fed
Perf.	you had been fed	you had been fed
	he (she, it) had been fed	they had been fed
Fut.	I shall have been fed	we shall have been fed
Perf.	you will have been fed	you will have been fed
	he (she, it) will have been fed	they will have been fed
Cond.	I would have been fed	we would have been fed
Perf.	you would have been fed	you would have been fed
	he (she, it) would have been fed	they would have been fed

IMPERATIVE MOOD
be fed

SUBJUNCTIVE MOOD

Pres.	if I be fed	if we be fed
	if you be fed	if you be fed
	if he (she, it) be fed	if they be fed
Past	if I were fed	if we were fed
	if you were fed	if you were fed
	if he (she, it) were fed	if they were fed
Fut.	if I should be fed	if we should be fed
	if you should be fed	if you should be fed
	if he (she, it) should be fed	if they should be fed

Infinitive: to fight   *Present Participle:* fighting
Perfect Infinitive: to have fought   *Past Participle:* fought

INDICATIVE MOOD

Pres. I fight	we fight
you fight	you fight
he (she, it) fights	they fight
Pres. I am fighting	we are fighting
Prog. you are fighting	you are fighting
he (she, it) is fighting	they are fighting
Pres. I do fight	we do fight
Int. you do fight	you do fight
he (she, it) does fight	they do fight
Fut. I shall fight	we shall fight
you will fight	you will fight
he (she, it) will fight	they will fight
Cond. I would fight	we would fight
you would fight	you would fight
he (she, it) would fight	they would fight
Past I fought	we fought
you fought	you fought
he (she, it) fought	they fought
Past I was fighting	we were fighting
Prog. you were fighting	you were fighting
he (she, it) was fighting	they were fighting
Past I did fight	we did fight
Int. you did fight	you did fight
he (she, it) did fight	they did fight
Pres. I have fought	we have fought
Perf. you have fought	you have fought
he (she, it) has fought	they have fought
Past I had fought	we had fought
Perf.. you had fought	you had fought
he (she, it) had fought	they had fought
Fut. I shall have fought	we shall have fought
Perf. you will have fought	you will have fought
he (she, it) will have fought	they will have fought
Cond. I would have fought	we would have fought
Perf. you would have fought	you would have fought
he (she, it) would have fought	they would have fought

IMPERATIVE MOOD
fight

SUBJUNCTIVE MOOD

Pres. if I fight	if we fight
if you fight	if you fight
if he (she, it) fight	if they fight
Past if I fought	if we fought
if you fought	if you fought
if he (she, it) fought	if they fought
Fut. if I should fight	if we should fight
if you should fight	if you should fight
if he (she, it) should fight	if they should fight

192

Infinitive: to be fought   *Present Participle:* being fought
Perfect Infinitive: to have been fought   *Past Participle:* been fought

INDICATIVE MOOD

Pres.	I am fought	we are fought
	you are fought	you are fought
	he (she, it) is fought	they are fought
Pres.	I am being fought	we are being fought
Prog.	you are being fought	you are being fought
	he (she, it) is being fought	they are being fought
Pres.	I do get fought	we do get fought
Int.	you do get fought	you do get fought
	he (she, it) does get fought	they do get fought
Fut.	I shall be fought	we shall be fought
	you will be fought	you will be fought
	he (she, it) will be fought	they will be fought
Cond.	I would be fought	we would be fought
	you would be fought	you would be fought
	he (she, it) would be fought	they would be fought
Past	I was fought	we were fought
	you were fought	you were fought
	he (she, it) was fought	they were fought
Past	I was being fought	we were being fought
Prog.	you were being fought	you were being fought
	he (she, it) was being fought	they were being fought
Past	I did get fought	we did get fought
Int.	you did get fought	you did get fought
	he (she, it) did get fought	they did get fought
Pres.	I have been fought	we have been fought
Perf.	you have been fought	you have been fought
	he (she, it) has been fought	they have been fought
Past	I had been fought	we had been fought
Perf.	you had been fought	you had been fought
	he (she, it) had been fought	they had been fought
Fut.	I shall have been fought	we shall have been fought
Perf.	you will have been fought	you will have been fought
	he (she, it) will have been fought	they will have been fought
Cond.	I would have been fought	we would have been fought
Perf.	you would have been fought	you would have been fought
	he (she, it) would have been fought	they would have been fought

IMPERATIVE MOOD
be fought

SUBJUNCTIVE MOOD

Pres.	if I be fought	if we be fought
	if you be fought	if you be fought
	if he (she, it) be fought	if they be fought
Past	if I were fought	if we were fought
	if you were fought	if you were fought
	if he (she, it) were fought	if they were fought
Fut.	if I should be fought	if we should be fought
	if you should be fought	if you should be fought
	if he (she, it) should be fought	if they should be fought

Infinitive: to find
Perfect Infinitive: to have found

Present Participle: finding
Past Participle: found

INDICATIVE MOOD

Pres.	I find	we find
	you find	you find
	he (she, it) finds	they find
Pres.	I am finding	we are finding
Prog.	you are finding	you are finding·
	he (she, it) is finding	they are finding
Pres.	I do find	we do find
Int.	you do find	you do find
	he (she, it) does find	they do find
Fut.	I shall find	we shall find
	you will find	you will find
	he (she, it) will find	they will find
Cond.	I would find	we would find
	you would find	you would find
	he (she, it) would find	they would find
Past	I found	we found
	you found	you found
	he (she, it) found	they found
Past	I was finding	we were finding
Prog.	you were finding	you were finding
	he (she, it) was finding	they were finding
Past	I did find	we did find
Int.	you did find	you did find
	he (she, it) did find	they did find
Pres.	I have found	we have found
Perf.	you have found	you have found
	he (she, it) has found	they have found
Past	I had found	we had found
Perf.	you had found	you had found
	he (she, it) had found	they had found
Fut.	I shall have found	we shall have found
Perf.	you will have found	you will have found
	he (she, it) will have found	they will have found
Cond.	I would have found	we would have found
Perf.	you would have found	you would have found
	he (she, it) would have found	they would have found

IMPERATIVE MOOD
find

SUBJUNCTIVE MOOD

Pres.	if I find	if we find
	if you find	if you find
	if he (she, it) find	if they find
Past	if I found	if we found
	if you found	if you found
	if he (she, it) found	if they found
Fut.	if I should find	if we should find
	if you should find	if you should find
	if he (she, it) should find	if they should find

Infinitive: to be found   *Present Participle:* being found
Perfect Infinitive: to have been found   *Past Participle:* been found

INDICATIVE MOOD

Pres.	I am found	we are found
	you are found	you are found
	he (she, it) is found	they are found
Pres.	I am being found	we are being found
Prog	you are being found	you are being found
	he (she, it) is being found	they are being found
Pres.	I do get found	we do get found
Int.	you do get found	you do get found
	he (she, it) does get found	they do get found
Fut.	I shall be found	we shall be found
	you will be found	you will be found
	he (she, it) will be found	they will be found
Cond.	I would be found	we would be found
	you would be found	you would be found
	he (she, it) would be found	they would be found
Past	I was found	we were found
	you were found	you were found
	he (she, it) was found	they were found
Past	I was being found	we were being found
Prog.	you were being found	you were being found
	he (she, it) was being found	they were being found
Past	I did get found	we did get found
Int.	you did get found	you did get found
	he (she, it) did get found	they did get found
Pres.	I have been found	we have been found
Perf.	you have been found	you have been found
	he (she, it) has been found	they have been found
Past	I had been found	we had been found
Perf.	you had been found	you had been found
	he (she, it) had been found	they had been found
Fut.	I shall have been found	we shall have been found
Perf.	you will have been found	you will have been found
	he (she, it) will have been found	they will have been found
Cond.	I would have been found	we would have been found
Perf.	you would have been found	you would have been found
	he (she, it) would have been found	they would have been found

IMPERATIVE MOOD
be found

SUBJUNCTIVE MOOD

Pres.	if I be found	if we be found
	if you be found	if you be found
	if he (she, it) be found	if they be found
Past	if I were found	if we were found
	if you were found	if you were found
	if he (she, it) were found	if they were found
Fut.	if I should be found	if we should be found
	if you should be found	if you should be found
	if he (she, it) should be found	if they should be found

to flee (active voice only)   *Principal Parts:* flee, fleeing, fled, fled

(intransitive verb)

Infinitive: to flee   *Present Participle:* fleeing
Perfect Infinitive: to have fled   *Past Participle:* fled

INDICATIVE MOOD

Pres.	I flee	we flee
	you flee	you flee
	he (she, it) flees	they flee

Pres.	I am fleeing	we are fleeing
Prog.	you are fleeing	you are fleeing
	he (she, it) is fleeing	they are fleeing

Pres.	I do flee	we do flee
Int.	you do flee	you do flee
	he (she, it) does flee	they do flee

Fut.	I shall flee	we shall flee
	you will flee	you will flee
	he (she, it) will flee	they will flee

Cond.	I would flee	we would flee
	you would flee	you would flee
	he (she, it) would flee	they would flee

Past	I fled	we fled
	you fled	you fled
	he (she, it) fled	they fled

Past	I was fleeing	we were fleeing
Prog.	you were fleeing	you were fleeing
	he (she, it) was fleeing	they were fleeing

Past	I did flee	we did flee
Int.	you did flee	you did flee
	he (she, it) did flee	they did flee

Pres.	I have fled	we have fled
Perf.	you have fled	you have fled
	he (she, it) has fled	they have fled

Past	I had fled	we had fled
Perf.	you had fled	you had fled
	he (she, it) had fled	they had fled

Fut.	I shall have fled	we shall have fled
Perf.	you will have fled	you will have fled
	he (she, it) will have fled	they will have fled

Cond.	I would have fled	we would have fled
Perf.	you would have fled	you would have fled
	he (she, it) would have fled	they would have fled

IMPERATIVE MOOD
flee

SUBJUNCTIVE MOOD

Pres.	if I flee	it we flee
	if you flee	if you flee
	if he (she, it) flee	if they flee

Past	if I fled	if we fled
	if you fled	if you fled
	if he (she, it) fled	if they fled

Fut.	if I should flee	if we should flee
	if you should flee	if you should flee
	if he (she, it) should flee	if they should flee

To flee **is an intransitive verb.**

It does not take an object.

It describes action, but the action is self-contained.

Like other intransitive verbs, it may be followed by adverbs, adverbial phrases and clauses describing the how, why, when, and where of the action:

HOW: The thieves fled *quickly.* (adverb)

WHY: He fled *because he was wanted for murder.* (adverbial clause)

WHEN: The army will flee *when it meets the enemy.* (adverbial clause)

WHERE: He fled *into the forest.* (adverbial phrase)

to fling (active voice)　　　*Principal Parts:* fling, flinging, flung, flung

---

Infinitive: to fling　　　　　　　　*Present Participle:* flinging
Perfect Infinitive: to have flung　　*Past Participle:* flung

INDICATIVE MOOD

Pres.	I fling	we fling
	you fling	you fling
	he (she, it) flings	they fling
Pres.	I am flinging	we are flinging
Prog.	you are flinging	you are flinging
	he (she, it) is flinging	they are flinging
Pres.	I do fling	we do fling
Int.	you do fling	you do fling
	he (she, it) does fling	they do fling
Fut.	I shall fling	we shall fling
	you will fling	you will fling
	he (she, it) will fling	they will fling
Cond.	I would fling	we would fling
	you would fling	you would fling
	he (she, it) would fling	they would fling
Past	I flung	we flung
	you flung	you flung
	he (she, it) flung	they flung
Past	I was flinging	we were flinging
Prog.	you were flinging	you were flinging
	he (she, it) was flinging	they were flinging
Past	I did fling	we did fling
Int.	you did fling	you did fling
	he (she, it) did fling	they did fling
Pres.	I have flung	we have flung
Perf.	you have flung	you have flung
	he (she, it) has flung	they have flung
Past	I had flung	we had flung
Perf.	you had flung	you had flung
	he (she, it) had flung	they had flung
Fut.	I shall have flung	we shall have flung
Perf.	you will have flung	you will have flung
	he (she, it) will have flung	they will have flung
Cond.	I would have flung	we would have flung
Perf.	you would have flung	you would have flung
	he (she, it) would have flung	they would have flung

IMPERATIVE MOOD
fling

SUBJUNCTIVE MOOD

Pres.	if I fling	if we fling
	if you fling	if you fling
	if he (she, it) fling	if they fling
Past	if I flung	if we flung
	if you flung	if you flung
	if he (she, it) flung	if they flung
Fut.	if I should fling	if we should fling
	if you should fling	if you should fling
	if he (she, it) should fling	if they should fling

Infinitive: to be flung
Perfect Infinitive: to have been flung

Present Participle: being flung
Past Participle been flung

INDICATIVE MOOD

Pres. I am flung you are flung he (she, it) is flung	we are flung you are flung they are flung
Pres. *Prog.* I am being flung you are being flung he (she, it) is being flung	we are being flung you are being flung they are being flung
Pres. *Int.* I do get flung you do get flung he (she, it) does get flung	we do get flung you do get flung they do get flung
Fut. I shall be flung you will be flung he (she, it) will be flung	we shall be flung you will be flung they will be flung
Cond. I would be flung you would be flung he (she, it) would be flung	we would be flung you would be flung they would be flung
Past I was flung you were flung he (she, it) was flung	we were flung you were flung they were flung
Past *Prog.* I was being flung you were being flung he (she, it) was being flung	we were being flung you were being flung they were being flung
Past *Int.* I did get flung you did get flung he (she, it) did get flung	we did get flung you did get flung they did get flung
Pres. *Perf.* I have been flung you have been flung he (she, it) has been flung	we have been flung you have been flung they have been flung
Past *Perf.* I had been flung you had been flung he (she, it) had been flung	we had been flung you had been flung they had been flung
Fut. *Perf.* I shall have been flung you will have been flung he (she, it) will have been flung	we shall have been flung you will have been flung they will have been flung
Cond. *Perf.* I would have been flung you would have been flung he (she, it) would have been flung	we would have been flung you would have been flung they would have been flung

IMPERATIVE MOOD
be flung

SUBJUNCTIVE MOOD

Pres. if I be flung if you be flung if he (she, it) be flung	if we be flung if you be flung if they be flung
Past if I were flung if you were flung if he (she, it) were flung	if we were flung if you were flung if they were flung
Fut. if I should be flung if you should be flung if he (she, it) should be flung	if we should be flung if you should be flung if they should be flung

to fly (active voice)   *Principal Parts:* fly, flying, flew, flown

---

Infinitive: to fly   *Present Participle:* flying
Perfect Infinitive: to have flown   *Past Participle:* flown

INDICATIVE MOOD

Pres.	I fly	we fly
	you fly	you fly
	he (she, it) flies	they fly
Pres.	I am flying	we are flying
Prog.	you are flying	you are flying
	he (she, it) is flying	they are flying
Pres.	I do fly	we do fly
Int.	you do fly	you do fly
	he (she, it) does fly	they do fly
Fut.	I shall fly	we shall fly
	you will fly	you will fly
	he (she, it) will fly	they will fly
Cond.	I would fly	we would fly
	you would fly	you would fly
	he (she, it) would fly	they would fly
Past	I flew	we flew
	you flew	you flew
	he (she, it) flew	they flew
Past	I was flying	we were flying
Prog.	you were flying	you were flying
	he (she, it) was flying	they were flying
Past	I did fly	we did fly
Int.	you did fly	you did fly
	he (she, it) did fly	they did fly
Pres.	I have flown	we have flown
Perf.	you have flown	you have flown
	he (she, it) has flown	they have flown
Past	I had flown	we had flown
Perf.	you had flown	you had flown
	he (she, it) had flown	they had flown
Fut.	I shall have flown	we shall have flown
Perf.	you will have flown	you will have flown
	he (she, it) will have flown	they will have flown
Cond.	I would have flown	we would have flown
Perf.	you would have flown	you would have flown
	he (she, it) would have flown	they would have flown

IMPERATIVE MOOD
fly

SUBJUNCTIVE MOOD

Pres.	if I fly	if we fly
	if you fly	if you fly
	if he (she, it) fly	if they fly
Past	if I flew	if we flew
	if you flew	if you flew
	if he (she, it) flew	if they flew
Fut.	if I should fly	if we should fly
	if you should fly	if you should fly
	if he (she, it) should fly	if they should fly

Infinitive: to be flown   *Present Participle:* being flown
Perfect Infinitive: to have been flown   *Past Participle:* been flown

INDICATIVE MOOD

Pres. I am flown
you are flown
he (she, it) is flown

we are flown
you are flown
they are flown

Pres. I am being flown .
Prog. you are being flown
he (she, it) is being flown

we are being flown
you are being flown
they are being flown

Pres. I do get flown
Int. you do get flown
he (she, it) does get flown

we do get flown
you do get flown
they do get flown

Fut. I shall be flown
you will be flown
he (she, it) will be flown

we shall be flown
you will be flown
they will be flown

Cond. I would be flown
you would be flown
he (she, it) would be flown

we would be flown
you would be flown
they would be flown

Past I was flown
you were flown
he (she, it) was flown

we were flown
you were flown
they were flown

Past I was being flown
Prog. you were being flown
he (she, it) was being flown

we were being flown
you were being flown
they were being flown

Past I did get flown
Int. you did get flown
he (she, it) did get flown

we did get flown
you did get flown
they did get flown

Pres. I have been flown
Perf. you have been flown
he (she, it) has been flown

we have been flown
you have been.flown
they have been flown

Past I had been flown
Perf. you had been flown
he (she, it) had been flown

we had been flown
you had been flown
they had been flown

Fut. I shall have been flown
Perf. you will have been flown
he (she, it) will have been flown

we shall have been flown
you will have been flown
they will have been flown

Cond. I would have been flown
Perf. you would have been flown
he (she, it) would have been flown

we would have been flown
you would have been flown
they would have been flown

IMPERATIVE MOOD
be flown

SUBJUNCTIVE MOOD

Pres. if I be flown
if you be flown
if he (she, it) be flown

if we be flown
if you be flown
if they be flown

Past if I were flown
if you were flown
if he (she, it) were flown

if we were flown
if you were flown
if they were flown

Fut. if I should be flown
if you should be flown
if he (she, it) should be flown

if we should be flown
if you should be flown
if they should be flown

to forbid (active voice)   *Principal Parts:* forbid, forbidding, forbade
(forbad), forbidden

Infinitive: to forbid   *Present Participle:* forbidding
Perfect Infinitive: to have forbidden   *Past Participle:* forbidden

INDICATIVE MOOD

Pres. I forbid
you forbid
he (she, it) forbids

we forbid
you forbid
they forbid

Pres. I am forbidding
Prog. you are forbidding
he (she, it) is forbidding

we are forbidding
you are forbidding
they are forbidding

Pres. I do forbid
Int. you do forbid
he (she, it) does forbid

we do forbid
you do forbid
they do forbid

Fut. I shall forbid
you will forbid
he (she, it) will forbid

we shall forbid
you will forbid
they will forbid

Cond. I would forbid
you would forbid
he (she, it) would forbid

we would forbid
you would forbid
they would forbid

Past I forbade, forbad
you forbade, forbad
he (she, it) forbade, forbad

we forbade, forbad
you forbade, forbad
they forbade, forbad

Past I was forbidding
Prog. you were forbidding
he (she, it) was forbidding

we were forbidding
you were forbidding
they were forbidding

Past I did forbid
Int. you did forbid
he (she, it) did forbid

we did forbid
you did forbid
they did forbid

Pres. I have forbidden
Perf. you have forbidden
he (she, it) has forbidden

we have forbidden
you have forbidden
they have forbidden

Past I had forbidden
Perf. you had forbidden
he (she, it) had forbidden

we had forbidden
you had forbidden
they had forbidden

Fut. I shall have forbidden
Perf. you will have forbidden
he (she, it) will have forbidden

we shall have forbidden
you will have forbidden
they will have forbidden

Cond. I would have forbidden
Perf. you would have forbidden
he (she, it) would have forbidden

we would have forbidden
you would have forbidden
they would have forbidden

IMPERATIVE MOOD
forbid

SUBJUNCTIVE MOOD

Pres. if I forbid
if you forbid
if he (she, it) forbid

if we forbid
if you forbid
if they forbid

Past if I forbade, forbad
if you forbade, forbad
if he (she, it) forbade, forbad

if we forbade, forbad
if you forbade, forbad
if they forbade, forbad

Fut. if I should forbid
if you should forbid
if he (she, it) should forbid

if we should forbid
if you should forbid
if they should forbid

(passive voice)

Infinitive: to be forbidden
Perfect Infinitive: to have been forbidden

Present Participle: being forbidden
Past Participle: been forbidden

INDICATIVE MOOD

Pres. I am forbidden
you are forbidden
he (she, it) is forbidden

we are forbidden
you are forbidden
they are forbidden

Pres. I am being forbidden
Prog. you are being forbidden
he (she, it) is being forbidden

we are being forbidden
you are being forbidden
they are being forbidden

Pres. I do get forbidden
Int. you do get forbidden
he (she, it) does get forbidden

we do get forbidden
you do get forbidden
they do get forbidden

Fut. I shall be forbidden
you will be forbidden
he (she, it) will be forbidden

we shall be forbidden
you will be forbidden
they will be forbidden

Cond. I would be forbidden
you would be forbidden
he (she, it) would be forbidden

we would be forbidden
you would be forbidden
they would be forbidden

Past I was forbidden
you were forbidden
he (she, it) was forbidden

we were forbidden
you were forbidden
they were forbidden

Past I was being forbidden
Prog. you were being forbidden
he (she, it) was being forbidden

we were being forbidden
you were being forbidden
they were being forbidden

Past I did get forbidden
Int. you did get forbidden
he (she, it) did get forbidden

we did get forbidden
you did get forbidden
they did get forbidden

Pres. I have been forbidden
Perf. you have been forbidden
he (she, it) has been forbidden

we have been forbidden
you have been forbidden
they have been forbidden

Past I had been forbidden
Perf. you had been forbidden
he (she, it) had been forbidden

we had been forbidden
you had been forbidden
they had been forbidden

Fut. I shall have been forbidden
Perf. you will have been forbidden
he (she, it) will have been forbidden

we shall have been forbidden
you will have been forbidden
they will have been forbidden

Cond I would have been forbidden
Perf. you would have been forbidden
he (she, it) would have been forbidden

we would have been forbidden
you would have been forbidden
they would have been forbidden

IMPERATIVE MOOD
be forbidden

SUBJUNCTIVE MOOD

Pres. if I be forbidden
if you be forbidden
if he (she, it) be forbidden

if we be forbidden
if you be forbidden
if they be forbidden

Past if I were forbidden
if you were forbidden
if he (she, it) were forbidden

if we were forbidden
if you were forbidden
if they were forbidden

Fut. if I should be forbidden
if you should be forbidden
if he (she, it) should be forbidden

if we should be forbidden
if you should be forbidden
if they should be forbidden

to forget (active voice) *Principal Parts:* forget, forgetting, forgot, forgotten
(forgot)

Infinitive: to forget
Perfect Infinitive: to have forgotten

Present Participle: forgetting
Past Participle: forgotten, forgot

INDICATIVE MOOD

Pres.	I forget you forget he (she, it) forgets	we forget you forget they forget
Pres. *Prog.*	I am forgetting you are forgetting he (she, it) is forgetting	we are forgetting you are forgetting they are forgetting
Pres. *Int.*	I do forget you do forget he (she, it) does forget	we do forget you do forget they do forget
Fut.	I shall forget you will forget he (she, it) will forget	we shall forget you will forget they will forget
Cond.	I would forget you would forget he (she, it) would forget	we would forget you would forget they would forget
Past	I forgot you forgot he (she, it) forgot	we forgot you forgot they forgot
Past *Prog.*	I was forgetting you were forgetting he (she, it) was forgetting	we were forgetting you were forgetting they were forgetting
Past *Int.*	I did forget you did forget he (she, it) did forget	we did forget you did forget they did forget
Pres. *Perf.*	I have forgotten, forgot you have forgotten, forgot he (she, it) has forgotten, forgot	we have forgotten, forgot you have forgotten, forgot they have forgotten, forgot
Past *Perf.*	I had forgotten, forgot you had forgotten, forgot he (she, it) had forgotten, forgot	we had forgotten, forgot you had forgotten, forgot they had forgotten, forgot
Fut. *Perf.*	I shall have forgotten, forgot you will have forgotten, forgot he (she, it) will have forgotten, forgot	we shall have forgotten, forgot you will have forgotten, forgot they will have forgotten, forgot
Cond. *Perf.*	I would have forgotten, forgot you would have forgotten, forgot he (she, it) would have forgotten, forgot	we would have forgotten, forgot you would have forgotten, forgot they would have forgotten, forgot

IMPERATIVE MOOD
forget

SUBJUNCTIVE MOOD

Pres.	if I forget	if we forget
	if you forget	if you forget
	if he (she, it) forget	if they forget
Past	if I forgot	if we forgot
	if you forgot	if you forgot
	if he (she, it) forgot	if they forgot
Fut.	if I should forget	if we should forget
	if you should forget	if you should forget
	if he (she, it) should forget	if they should forget

(passive voice)

Infinitive: to be forgotten
Perfect Infinitive: to have been forgotten

Present Participle: being forgotten
Past Participle: been forgotten

INDICATIVE MOOD

Pres. I am forgotten, forgot
you are forgotten, forgot
he (she, it) is forgotten, forgot

we are forgotten, forgot
you are forgotten, forgot
they are forgotten, forgot

Pres. Prog. I am being forgotten, forgot
you are being forgotten, forgot
he (she, it) is being forgotten, forgot

we are being forgotten, forgot
you are being forgotten, forgot
they are being forgotten, forgot

Pres. Int. I do get forgotten, forgot
you do get forgotten, forgot
he (she, it) does get forgotten, forgot

we do get forgotten, forgot
you do get forgotten, forgot
they do get forgotten, forgot

Fut. I shall be forgotten, forgot
you will be forgotten, forgot
he (she, it) will be forgotten, forgot

we shall be forgotten, forgot
you will be forgotten, forgot
they will be forgotten, forgot

Cond. I would be forgotten, forgot
you would be forgotten, forgot
he (she, it) would be forgotten, forgot

we would be forgotten, forgot
you would be forgotten, forgot
they would be forgotten, forgot

Past I was forgotten, forgot
you were forgotten, forgot
he (she, it) was forgotten, forgot

we were forgotten, forgot
you were forgotten, forgot
they were forgotten, forgot

Past Prog. I was being forgotten, forgot
you were being forgotten, forgot
he (she, it) was being forgotten, forgot

we were being forgotten, forgot
you were being forgotten, forgot
they were being forgotten, forgot

Past Int. I did get forgotten, forgot
you did get forgotten, forgot
he (she, it) did get forgotten, forgot

we did get forgotten, forgot
you did get forgotten, forgot
they did get forgotten, forgot

Pres. Perf. I have been forgotten, forgot
you have been forgotten, forgot
he (she, it) has been forgotten, forgot

we have been forgotten, forgot
you have been forgotten, forgot
they have been forgotten, forgot

Past Perf. I had been forgotten, forgot
you had been forgotten, forgot
he (she, it) had been forgotten, forgot

we had been forgotten, forgot
you had been forgotten, forgot
they had been forgotten, forgot

Fut. Perf. I shall have been forgotten, forgot
you will have been forgotten, forgot
he (she, it) will have been forgotten, forgot

we shall have been forgotten, forgot
you will have been forgotten, forgot
they will have been forgotten, forgot

Cond. Perf. I would have been forgotten, forgot
you would have been forgotten, forgot
he (she, it) would have been forgotten, forgot

we would have been forgotten, forgot
you would have been forgotten, forgot
they would have been forgotten, forgot

IMPERATIVE MOOD
be forgotten

SUBJUNCTIVE MOOD

Pres. if I be forgotten, forgot
if you be forgotten, forgot
if he (she, it) be forgotten, forgot

if we be forgotten, forgot
if you be forgotten, forgot
if they be forgotten, forgot

Past if I were forgotten, forgot
if you were forgotten, forgot
if he (she, it) were forgotten, forgot

if we were forgotten, forgot
if you were forgotten, forgot
if they were forgotten, forgot

Fut. if I should be forgotten, forgot
if you should be forgotten, forgot
if he (she, it) should be forgotten, forgot

if we should be forgotten, forgot
if you should be forgotten, forgot
if they should be forgotten, forgot

to forgive (active voice)   *Principal Parts:* forgive, forgiving, forgave, forgiven

---

Infinitive: to forgive
Perfect Infinitive: to have forgiven

Present Participle: forgiving
Past Participle: forgiven

INDICATIVE MOOD

Pres.	I forgive	we forgive
	you forgive	you forgive
	he (she, it) forgives	they forgive
Pres.	I am forgiving	we are forgiving
Prog.	you are forgiving	you are forgiving
	he (she, it) is forgiving	they are forgiving
Pres.	I do forgive	we do forgive
Int.	you do forgive	you do forgive
	he (she, it) does forgive	they do forgive
Fut.	I shall forgive	we shall forgive
	you will forgive	you will forgive
	he (she, it) will forgive	they will forgive
Cond.	I would forgive	we would forgive
	you would forgive	you would forgive
	he (she, it) would forgive	they would forgive
Past	I forgave	we forgave
	you forgave	you forgave
	he (she, it) forgave	they forgave
Past	I was forgiving	we were forgiving
Prog.	you were forgiving	you were forgiving
	he (she, it) was forgiving	they were forgiving
Past	I did forgive	we did forgive
Int.	you did forgive	you did forgive
	he (she, it) did forgive	they did forgive
Pres.	I have forgiven	we have forgiven
Perf.	you have forgiven	you have forgiven
	he (she, it) has forgiven	they have forgiven
Past	I had forgiven	we had forgiven
Perf.	you had forgiven	you had forgiven
	he (she, it) had forgiven	they had forgiven
Fut.	I shall have forgiven	we shall have forgiven
Perf.	you will have forgiven	you will have forgiven
	he (she, it) will have forgiven	they will have forgiven
Cond.	I would have forgiven	we would have forgiven
Perf.	you would have forgiven	you would have forgiven
	he (she, it) would have forgiven	they would have forgiven

IMPERATIVE MOOD
forgive

SUBJUNCTIVE MOOD

Pres.	if I forgive	if we forgive
	if you forgive	if you forgive
	if he (she, it) forgive	if they forgive
Past	if I forgave	if we forgave
	if you forgave	if you forgave
	if he (she, it) forgave	if they forgave
Fut.	if I should forgive	if we should forgive
	if you should forgive	if you should forgive
	if he (she, it) should forgive	if they should forgive

Infinitive: to be forgiven   *Present Participle:* being forgiven
Perfect Infinitive: to have been forgiven   *Past Participle:* been forgiven

INDICATIVE MOOD

Pres.	I am forgiven	we are forgiven
	you are forgiven	you are forgiven
	he (she, it) is forgiven	they are forgiven
Pres.	I am being forgiven	we are being forgiven
Prog.	you are being forgiven	you are being forgiven
	he (she, it) is being forgiven	they are being forgiven
Pres.	I do get forgiven	we do get forgiven
Int.	you do get forgiven	you do get forgiven
	he (she, it) does get forgiven	they do get forgiven
Fut.	I shall be forgiven	we shall be forgiven
	you will be forgiven	you will be forgiven
	he (she, it) will be forgiven	they will be forgiven
Cond.	I would be forgiven	we would be forgiven
	you would be forgiven	you would be forgiven
	he (she, it) would be forgiven	they would be forgiven
Past	I was forgiven	we were forgiven
	you were forgiven	you were forgiven
	he (she, it) was forgiven	they were forgiven
Past	I was being forgiven	we were being forgiven
Prog.	you were being forgiven	you were being forgiven
	he (she, it) was being forgiven	they were being forgiven
Past	I did get forgiven	we did get forgiven
Int.	you did get forgiven	you did get forgiven
	he (she, it) did get forgiven	they did get forgiven
Pres.	I have been forgiven	we have been forgiven
Perf.	you have been forgiven	you have been forgiven
	he (she, it) has been forgiven	they have been forgiven
Past	I had been forgiven	we had been forgiven
Perf.	you had been forgiven	you had been forgiven
	he (she, it) had been forgiven	they had been forgiven
Fut.	I shall have been forgiven	we shall have been forgiven
Perf.	you will have been forgiven	you will have been forgiven
	he (she, it) will have been forgiven	they will have been forgiven
Cond.	I would have been forgiven	we would have been forgiven
Perf.	you would have been forgiven	you would have been forgiven
	he (she, it) would have been forgiven	they would have been forgiven

IMPERATIVE MOOD
be forgiven

SUBJUNCTIVE MOOD

Pres.	if I be forgiven	if we be forgiven
	if you be forgiven	if you be forgiven
	if he (she, it) be forgiven	if they be forgiven
Past	if I were forgiven	if we were forgiven
	if you were forgiven	if you were forgiven
	if he (she, it) were forgiven	if they were forgiven
Fut.	if I should be forgiven	if we should be forgiven
	if you should be forgiven	if you should be forgiven
	if he (she, it) should be forgiven	if they should be forgiven

209

to forsake (active voice)

Principal Parts: forsake, forsaking, forsook, forsaken

Infinitive: to forsake
Perfect Infinitive: to have forsaken

Present Participle: forsaking
Past Participle: forsaken

INDICATIVE MOOD

Pres. I forsake you forsake he (she, it) forsakes	we forsake you forsake they forsake
Pres. I am forsaking *Prog.* you are forsaking he (she, it) is forsaking	we are forsaking you are forsaking they are forsaking
Pres. I do forsake *Int.* you do forsake he (she, it) does forsake	we do forsake you do forsake they do forsake
Fut. I shall forsake you will forsake he (she, it) will forsake	we shall forsake you will forsake they will forsake
Cond. I would forsake you would forsake he (she, it) would forsake	we would forsake you would forsake they would forsake
Past I forsook you forsook he (she, it) forsook	we forsook you forsook they forsook
Past I was forsaking *Prog.* you were forsaking he (she, it) was forsaking	we were forsaking you were forsaking they were forsaking
Past I did forsake *Int.* you did forsake he (she, it) did forsake	we did forsake you did forsake they did forsake
Pres. I have forsaken *Perf.* you have forsaken he (she, it) has forsaken	we have forsaken you have forsaken they have forsaken
Past I had forsaken *Perf.* you had forsaken he (she, it) had forsaken	we had forsaken you had forsaken they had forsaken
Fut. I shall have forsaken *Perf.* you will have forsaken he (she, it) will have forsaken	we shall have forsaken you will have forsaken they will have forsaken
Cond. I would have forsaken *Perf.* you would have forsaken he (she, it) would have forsaken	we would have forsaken you would have forsaken they would have forsaken

IMPERATIVE MOOD
forsake

SUBJUNCTIVE MOOD

Pres. if I forsake if you forsake if he (she, it) forsake	if we forsake if you forsake if they forsake
Past if I forsook if you forsook if he (she, it) forsook	if we forsook if you forsook if they forsook
Fut. if I should forsake if you should forsake if he (she, it) should forsake	if we should forsake if you should forsake if they should forsake

(passive voice)

Infinitive: to be forsaken
Perfect Infinitive: to have been forsaken

Present Participle: being forsaken
Past Participle: been forsaken

INDICATIVE MOOD

Pres. I am forsaken
you are forsaken
he (she, it) is forsaken

we are forsaken
you are forsaken
they are forsaken

Pres. Prog. I am being forsaken
you are being forsaken
he (she, it) is being forsaken

we are being forsaken
you are being forsaken
they are being forsaken

Pres. Int. I do get forsaken
you do get forsaken
he (she, it) does get forsaken

we do get forsaken
you do get forsaken
they do get forsaken

Fut. I shall be forsaken
you will be forsaken
he (she, it) will be forsaken

we shall be forsaken
you will be forsaken
they will be forsaken

Cond. I would be forsaken
you would be forsaken
he (she, it) would be forsaken

we would be forsaken
you would be forsaken
they would be forsaken

Past I was forsaken
you were forsaken
he (she, it) was forsaken

we were forsaken
you were forsaken
they were forsaken

Past Prog. I was being forsaken
you were being forsaken
he (she, it) was being forsaken

we were being forsaken
you were being forsaken
they were being forsaken

Past Int. I did get forsaken
you did get forsaken
he (she, it) did get forsaken

we did get forsaken
you did get forsaken
they did get forsaken

Pres. Perf. I have been forsaken
you have been forsaken
he (she, it) has been forsaken

we have been forsaken
you have been forsaken
they have been forsaken

Past Perf. I had been forsaken
you had been forsaken
he (she, it) had been forsaken

we had been forsaken
you had been forsaken
they had been forsaken

Fut. Perf. I shall have been forsaken
you will have been forsaken
he (she, it) will have been forsaken

we shall have been forsaken
you will have been forsaken
they will have been forsaken

Cond. Perf. I would have been forsaken
you would have been forsaken
he (she, it) would have been forsaken

we would have been forsaken
you would have been forsaken
they would have been forsaken

IMPERATIVE MOOD
be forsaken

SUBJUNCTIVE MOOD

Pres. if I be forsaken
if you be forsaken
if you were forsaken

if we be forsaken
if you be forsaken
if they be forsaken

Past if I were forsaken
if you were forsaken
if he (she, it) were forsaken

if we were forsaken
if you were forsaken
if they were forsaken

Fut. if I should be forsaken
if you should be forsaken
if he (she, it) should be forsaken

if we should be forsaken
if you should be forsaken
if they should be forsaken

to freeze (active voice)   *Principal Parts:* freeze, freezing, froze, frozen

---

Infinitive: to freeze   *Present Participle:* freezing
Perfect Infinitive: to have frozen   *Past Participle:* frozen

INDICATIVE MOOD

Pres. I freeze	we freeze
you freeze	you freeze
he (she, it) freezes	they freeze
Pres. I am freezing	we are freezing
Prog. you are freezing	you are freezing
he (she, it) is freezing	they are freezing
Pres. I do freeze	we do freeze
Int. you do freeze	you do freeze
he (she, it) does freeze	they do freeze
Fut. I shall freeze	we shall freeze
you will freeze	you will freeze
he (she, it) will freeze	they will freeze
Cond. I would freeze	we would freeze
you would freeze	you would freeze
he (she, it) would freeze	they would freeze
Past I froze	we froze
you froze	you froze
he (she, it) froze	they froze
Past I was freezing	we were freezing
Prog. you were freezing	you were freezing
he (she, it) was freezing	they were freezing
Past I did freeze	we did freeze
Int. you did freeze	you did freeze
he (she, it) did freeze	they did freeze
Pres. I have frozen	we have frozen
Perf. you have frozen	you have frozen
he (she, it) has frozen	they have frozen
Past I had frozen	we had frozen
Perf. you had frozen	you had frozen
he (she, it) had frozen	they had frozen
Fut. I shall have frozen	we shall have frozen
Perf. you will have frozen	you will have frozen
he (she, it) will have frozen	they will have frozen
Cond. I would have frozen	we would have frozen
Perf. you would have frozen	you would have frozen
he (she, it) would have frozen	they would have frozen

IMPERATIVE MOOD
freeze

SUBJUNCTIVE MOOD

Pres. if I freeze	if we freeze
if you freeze	if you freeze
if he (she, it) freeze	if they freeze
Past if I froze	if we froze
if you froze	if you froze
if he (she, it) froze	if they froze
Fut. if I should freeze	if we should freeze
if you should freeze	if you should freeze
if he (she, it) should freeze	if they should freeze

Infinitive: to be frozen   *Present Participle:* being frozen
Perfect Infinitive: to have been frozen   *Past Participle:* been frozen

INDICATIVE MOOD

Pres. I am frozen   we are frozen
you are frozen   you are frozen
he (she, it) is frozen   they are frozen

Pres. I am being frozen   we are being frozen
Prog. you are being frozen   you are being frozen
he (she, it) is being frozen   they are being frozen

Pres. I do get frozen   we do get frozen
Int. you do get frozen   you do get frozen
he (she, it) does get frozen   they do get frozen

Fut. I shall be frozen   we shall be frozen
you will be frozen   you will be frozen
he (she, it) will be frozen   they will be frozen

Cond. I would be frozen   we would be frozen
you would be frozen   you would be frozen
he (she, it) would be frozen   they would be frozen

Past I was frozen   we were frozen
you were frozen   you were frozen
he (she, it) was frozen   they were frozen

Past I was being frozen   we were being frozen
Prog. you were being frozen   you were being frozen
he (she, it) was being frozen   they were being frozen

Past I did get frozen   we did get frozen
Int. you did get frozen   you did get frozen
he (she, it) did get frozen   they did get frozen

Pres. I have been frozen   we have been frozen
Perf. you have been frozen   you have been frozen
he (she, it) has been frozen   they have been frozen

Past I had been frozen   we had been frozen
Perf. you had been frozen   you had been frozen
he (she, it) had been frozen   they had been frozen

Fut. I shall have been frozen   we shall have been frozen
Perf. you will have been frozen   you will have been frozen
he (she, it) will have been frozen   they will have been frozen

Cond. I would have been frozen   we would have been frozen
Perf. you would have been frozen   you would have been frozen
he (she, it) would have been frozen   they would have been frozen

IMPERATIVE MOOD
be frozen

SUBJUNCTIVE MOOD

Pres. if I be frozen   if we be frozen
if you be frozen   if you be frozen
if he (she, it) be frozen   if they be frozen

Past if I were frozen   if we were frozen
if you were frozen   if you were frozen
if he (she, it) were frozen   if they were frozen

Fut. if I should be frozen   if we should be frozen
if you should be frozen   if you should be frozen
if he (she, it) should be frozen   if they should be frozen

to get (active voice)   *Principal Parts:* get, getting, got, got (gotten)

Infinitive: to get   *Present Participle:* getting
Perfect Infinitive: to have got, gotten   *Past Participle:* got, gotten

INDICATIVE MOOD

Pres.	I get	we get
	you get	you get
	he (she, it) gets	they get
Pres.	I am getting	we are getting
Prog.	you are getting	you are getting
	he (she, it) is getting	they are getting
Pres.	I do get	we do get
Int.	you do get	you do get
	he (she, it) does get	they do get
Fut.	I shall get	we shall get
	you will get	you will get
	he (she, it) will get	they will get
Cond.	I would get	we would get
	you would get	you would get
	he (she, it) would get	they would get
Past	I got	we got
	you got	you got
	he (she, it) got	they got
Past	I was getting	we were getting
Prog.	you were getting	you were getting
	he (she, it) was getting	they were getting
Past	I did get	we did get
Int.	you did get	you did get
	he (she, it) did get	they did get
Pres.	I have got, gotten	we have got, gotten
Perf.	you have got, gotten	you have got, gotten
	he (she, it) has got, gotten	they have got, gotten
Past	I had got, gotten	we had got, gotten
Perf.	you had got, gotten	you had got, gotten
	he (she, it) had got, gotten	they had got, gotten
Fut.	I shall have got, gotten	we shall have got, gotten
Perf.	you will have got, gotten	you will have got, gotten
	he (she, it) will have got, gotten	they will have got, gotten
Cond.	I would have got, gotten	we would have got, gotten
Perf.	you would have got, gotten	you would have got, gotten
	he (she, it) would have got, gotten	they would have got, gotten

IMPERATIVE MOOD
get

SUBJUNCTIVE MOOD

Pres.	if I get	if we get
	if you get	if you get
	if he (she, it) get	if they get
Past	if I got	if we got
	if you got	if you got
	if he (she, it) got	if they got
Fut.	if I should get	if we should get
	if you should get	if you should get
	if he (she, it) should get	if they should get

Infinitive: to be gotten
Perfect Infinitive: to have been gotten

Present Participle: being gotten
Past Participle: been gotten

INDICATIVE MOOD

Pres.	I am gotten	we are gotten
	you are gotten	you are gotten
	he (she, it) is gotten	they are gotten
Pres.	I am being gotten	we are being gotten
Prog.	you are being gotten	you are being gotten
	he (she, it) is being gotten	they are being gotten
Pres.	I do get gotten	we do get gotten
Int.	you do get gotten	you do get gotten
	he (she, it) does get gotten	they do get gotten
Fut.	I shall be gotten	we shall be gotten
	you will be gotten	you will be gotten
	he (she, it) will be gotten	they will be gotten
Cond.	I would be gotten	we would be gotten
	you would be gotten	you would be gotten
	he (she, it) would be gotten	they would be gotten
Past	I was gotten	we were gotten
	you were gotten	you were gotten
	he (she, it) was gotten	they were gotten
Past	I was being gotten	we were being gotten
Prog.	you were being gotten	you were being gotten
	he (she, it) was being gotten	they were being gotten
Past	I did get gotten	we did get gotten
Int.	you did get gotten	you did get gotten
	he (she, it) did get gotten	they did get gotten
Pres.	I have been gotten	we have been gotten
Perf.	you have been gotten	you have been gotten
	he (she, it) has been gotten	they have been gotten
Past	I had been gotten	we had been gotten
Perf.	you had been gotten	you had been gotten
	he (she, it) had been gotten	they had been gotten
Fut.	I shall have been gotten	we shall have been gotten
Perf.	you will have been gotten	you will have been gotten
	he (she, it) will have been gotten	they will have been gotten
Cond.	I would have been gotten	we would have been gotten
Perf.	you would have been gotten	you would have been gotten
	he (she, it) would have been gotten	they would have been gotten

IMPERATIVE MOOD
be gotten

SUBJUNCTIVE MOOD

Pres.	if I be gotten	if we be gotten
	if you be gotten	if you be gotten
	if he (she, it) be gotten	if they be gotten
Past	if I were gotten	if we were gotten
	if you were gotten	if you were gotten
	if he (she, it) were gotten	if they were gotten
Fut.	if I should be gotten	if we should be gotten
	if you should be gotten	if you should be gotten
	if he (she, it) should be gotten	if they should be gotten

Infinitive: to give
Perfect Infinitive: to have given

Present Participle: giving
Past Participle: given

INDICATIVE MOOD

Pres. I give
you give
he (she, it) gives

we give
you give
they give

Pres.
Prog. I am giving
you are giving
he (she, it) is giving

we are giving
you are giving
they are giving

Pres.
Int. I do give
you do give
he (she, it) does give

we do give
you do give
they do give

Fut. I shall give
you will give
he (she, it) will give

we shall give
you will give
they will give

Cond. I would give
you would give
he (she, it) would give

we would give
you would give
they would give

Past I gave
you gave
he (she, it) gave

we gave
you gave
they gave

Past
Prog. I was giving
you were giving
he (she, it) was giving

we were giving
you were giving
they were giving

Past
Int. I did give
you did give
he (she, it) did give

we did give
you did give
they did give

Pres.
Perf. I have given
you have given
he (she, it) has given

we have given
you have given
they have given

Past
Perf. I had given
you had given
he (she, it) had given

we had given
you had given
they had given

Fut.
Perf. I shall have given
you will have given
he (she, it) will have given

we shall have given
you will have given
they will have given

Cond.
Perf. I would have given
you would have given
he (she, it) would have given

we would have given
you would have given
they would have given

IMPERATIVE MOOD
give

SUBJUNCTIVE MOOD

Pres. if I give
if you give
if he (she, it) give

if we give
if you give
if they give

Past if I gave
if you gave
if he (she, it) gave

if we gave
if you gave
if they gave

Fut. if I should give
if you should give
if he (she, it) should give

if we should give
if you should give
if they should give

Infinitive: to be given   *Present Participle:* being given
Perfect Infinitive: to have been given   *Past Participle:* been given

INDICATIVE MOOD

Pres. I am given
you are given
he (she, it) is given

we are given
you are given
they are given

Pres. I am being given
Prog. you are being given
he (she, it) is being given

we are being given
you are being given
they are being given

Pres. I do get given
Int. you do get given
he (she, it) does get given

we do get given
you do get given
they do get given

Fut. I shall be given
you will be given
he (she, it) will be given

we shall be given
you will be given
they will be given

Cond. I would be given
you would be given
he (she, it) would be given

we would be given
you would be given
they would be given

Past I was given
you were given
he (she, it) was given

we were given
you were given
they were given

Past I was being given
Prog. you were being given
he (she, it) was being given

we were being given
you were being given
they were being given

Past I did get given
Int. you did get given
he (she, it) did get given

we did get given
you did get given
they did get given

Pres. I have been given
Perf. you have been given
he (she, it) has been given

we have been given
you have been given
they have been given

Past I had been given
Perf. you had been given
he (she, it) had been given

we had been given
you had been given
they had been given

Fut. I shall have been given
Perf. you will have been given
he (she, it) will have been given

we shall have been given
you will have been given
they will have been given

Cond. I would have been given
Perf. you would have been given
he (she, it) would have been given

we would have been given
you would have been given
they would have been given

IMPERATIVE MOOD
be given

SUBJUNCTIVE MOOD

Pres. if I be given
if you be given
if he (she, it) be given

if we be given
if you be given
if they be given

Past if I were given
if you were given
if he (she, it) were given

if we were given
if you were given
if they were given

Fut. if I should be given
if you should be given
if he (she, it) should be given

if we should be given
if you should be given
if they should be given

to go (active voice only)   *Principal Parts:* go, going, went, gone

(intransitive verb)

Infinitive: to go   *Present Participle:* going
Perfect Infinitive: to have gone   *Past Participle:* gone

INDICATIVE MOOD

Pres. I go	we go
you go	you go
he (she, it) goes	they go
Pres. I am going	we are going
Prog. you are going	you are going
he (she, it) is going	they are going
Pres. I do go	we do go
Int. you do go	you do go
he (she, it) does go	they do go
Fut. I shall go	we shall go
you will go	you will go
he (she, it) will go	they will go
Cond. I would go	we would go
you would go	you would go
he (she, it) would go	they would go
Past I went	we went
you went	you went
he (she, it) went	they went
Past I was going	we were going
Prog. you were going	you were going
he (she, it) was going	they were going
Past I did go	we did go
Int. you did go	you did go
he (she, it) did go	they did go
Pres. I have gone	we have gone
Perf. you have gone	you have gone
he (she, it) has gone	they have gone
Past I had gone	we had gone
Perf. you had gone	you had gone
he (she, it) had gone	they had gone
Fut. I shall have gone	we shall have gone
Perf. you will have gone	you will have gone
he (she, it) will have gone	they will have gone
Cond. I would have gone	we would have gone
Perf. you would have gone	you would have gone
he (she, it) would have gone	they would have gone

IMPERATIVE MOOD
go

SUBJUNCTIVE MOOD

Pres. if I go	if we go
if you go	if you go
if he (she, it) go	if they go
Past if I went	if we went
if you went	if you went
if he (she, it) went	if they went
Fut. if I should go	if we should go
if you should go	if you should go
if he (she, it) should go	if they should go

To go is an intransitive verb.

It does not take an object.

It describes action, but the action is self-contained.

Like other intransitive verbs, it may be followed by adverbs, adverbial phrases and clauses describing the how, why, when, and where of the action:

HOW: They will go *slowly*. (adverb)

WHY: Mary went *to meet her mother*. (abverbial phrase)

WHEN: All the birds will have gone *when winter comes*. (adverbial clause)

WHERE: The evening sun goes *down*. (adverb)

to grow (active voice)   *Principal Parts:* grow, growing, grew, grown

Infinitive: to grow   *Present Participle:* growing
Perfect Infinitive: to have grown   *Past Participle:* grown

INDICATIVE MOOD

Pres.	I grow	we grow
	you grow	you grow
	he (she, it) grows	they grow
Pres.	I am growing	we are growing
Prog.	you are growing	you are growing
	he (she, it) is growing	they are growing
Pres.	I do grow	we do grow
Int.	you do grow	you do grow
	he (she, it) does grow	they do grow
Fut.	I shall grow	we shall grow
	you will grow	you will grow
	he (she, it) will grow	they will grow
Cond.	I would grow	we would grow
	you would grow	you would grow
	he (she, it) would grow	they would grow
Past	I grew	we grew
	you grew	you grew
	he (she, it) grew	they grew
Past	I was growing	we were growing
Prog.	you were growing	you were growing
	he (she, it) was growing	they were growing
Past	I did grow	we did grow
Int.	you did grow	you did grow
	he (she, it) did grow	they did grow
Pres.	I have grown	we have grown
Perf.	you have grown	you have grown
	he (she, it) has grown	they have grown
Past	I had grown	we had grown
Perf.	you had grown	you had grown
	he (she, it) had grown	they had grown
Fut.	I shall have grown	we shall have grown
Perf.	you will have grown	you will have grown
	he (she, it) will have grown	they will have grown
Cond.	I would have grown	we would have grown
Perf.	you would have grown	you would have grown
	he (she, it) would have grown	they would have grown

IMPERATIVE MOOD
grow

SUBJUNCTIVE MOOD

Pres.	if I grow	if we grow
	if you grow	if you grow
	if he (she, it) grow	if they grow
Past	if I grew	if we grew
	if you grew	if you grew
	if he (she, it) grew	if they grew
Fut.	if I should grow	if we should grow
	if you should grow	if you should grow
	if he (she, it) should grow	if they should grow

(passive voice)

Infinitive: to be grown   *Present Participle:* being grown
Perfect Infinitive: to have been grown   *Past Participle:* been grown

INDICATIVE MOOD

Pres.	I am grown	we are grown
	you are grown	you are grown
	he (she, it) is grown	they are grown
Pres.	I am being grown	we are being grown
Prog.	you are being grown	you are being grown
	he (she, it) is being grown	they are being grown
Pres.	I do get grown	we do get grown
Int.	you do get grown	you do get grown
	he (she, it) does get grown	they do get grown
Fut.	I shall be grown	we shall be grown
	you will be grown	you will be grown
	he (she, it) will be grown	they will be grown
Cond.	I would be grown	we would be grown
	you would be grown	you would be grown
	he (she, it) would be grown	they would be grown
Past	I was grown	we were grown
	you were grown	you were grown
	he (she, it) was grown	they were grown
Past	I was being grown	we were being grown
Prog.	you were being grown	you were being grown
	he (she, it) was being grown	they were being grown
Past	I did get grown	we did get grown
Int.	you did get grown	you did get grown
	he (she, it) did get grown	they did get grown
Pres.	I have been grown	we have been grown
Perf.	you have been grown	you have been grown
	he (she, it) has been grown	they have been grown
Past	I had been grown	we had been grown
Perf.	you had been grown	you had been grown
	he (she, it) had been grown	they had been grown
Fut.	I shall have been grown	we shall have been grown
Perf.	you will have been grown	you will have been grown
	he (she, it) will have been grown	they will have been grown
Cond.	I would have been grown	we would have been grown
Perf.	you would have been grown	you would have been grown
	he (she, it) would have been grown	they would have been grown

IMPERATIVE MOOD
be grown

SUBJUNCTIVE MOOD

Pres.	if I be grown	if we be grown
	if you be grown	if you be grown
	if he (she, it) be grown	if they be grown
Past	if I were grown	if we were grown
	if you were grown	if you were grown
	if he (she, it) were grown	if they were grown
Fut.	if I should be grown	if we should be grown
	if you should be grown	if you should be grown
	if he (she, it) should be grown	if they should be grown

to hang (active voice)   *Principal Parts:* hang, hanging, hanged, hanged
                                    (hung, hung: to fasten to an elevated point)

Infinitive: to hang   *Present Participle:* hanging
Perfect Infinitive: to have hanged (persons)   *Past Participle:* hanged, hung
          to have hung (things)

INDICATIVE MOOD

Pres.	I hang	we hang
	you hang	you hang
	he (she, it) hangs	they hang
Pres.	I am hanging	we are hanging
Prog.	you are hanging	you are hanging
	he (she, it) is hanging	they are hanging
Pres.	I do hang	we do hang
Int.	you do hang	you do hang
	he (she, it) does hang	they do hang
Fut.	I shall hang	we shall hang
	you will hang	you will hang
	he (she, it) will hang	they will hang
Cond.	I would hang	we would hang
	you would hang	you would hang
	he (she, it) would hang	they would hang
Past	I hung, hanged	we hung, hanged
	you hung, hanged	you hung, hanged
	he (she, it) hung, hanged	they hung, hanged
Past	I was hanging	we were hanging
Prog.	you were hanging	you were hanging
	he (she, it) was hanging	they were hanging
Past.	I did hang	we did hang
Int.	you did hang	you did hang
	he (she, it) did hang	they did hang
Pres.	I have hanged, hung	we have hanged, hung
Perf.	you have hanged, hung	you have hanged, hung
	he (she, it) has hanged, hung	they have hanged, hung
Past	I had hanged, hung	we had hanged, hung
Perf.	you had hanged, hung	you had hanged, hung
	he (she, it) had hanged, hung	they had hanged, hung
Fut.	I shall have hanged, hung	we shall have hanged, hung
Perf.	you will have hanged, hung	you will have hanged, hung
	he (she, it) will have hanged, hung	they will have hanged, hung
Cond.	I would have hanged, hung	we would have hanged, hung
Perf.	you would have hanged, hung	you would have hanged, hung
	he (she, it) would have hanged, hung	they would have hanged, hung

(active voice, continued)

IMPERATIVE MOOD

hang

SUBJUNCTIVE MOOD

Pres.	if I hang if you hang if he (she, it) hang	if we hang if you hang if they hang
Past	if I hanged, hung if you hanged, hung if he (she, it) hanged, hung	if we hanged, hung if you hanged, hung if they hanged, hung
Fut.	if I should hang if you should hang if he (she, it) should hang	if we should hang if you should hang if they should hang

to hang (passive voice)

Infinitive: to be hanged (persons),
to be hung (things)
Perfect Infinitive: to have been hanged,
to have been hung

Present Participle: to be hanged, to
be hung
Past Participle: been hanged, been
hung

INDICATIVE MOOD

Pres. I am hanged
you are hanged
he (she) is hanged; it is hung

we are hanged
they are hanged
they are hanged, hung

Pres. I am being hanged
Prog. you are being hanged
he (she) is being hanged; it is being
hung

we are being hanged
you are being hanged
they are being hanged, hung

Pres. I do get hanged
Int. you do get hanged
he (she) does get hanged; it does get
hung

we do get hanged
you do get hanged
they do get hanged, hung

Fut. I shall be hanged
you will be hanged
he (she) will be hanged; it will be hung

we shall be hanged
you will be hanged
they will be hanged, hung

Cond. I would be hanged
you would be hanged
he (she) would be hanged; it would be
hung

we would be hanged
you would be hanged
they would be hanged, hung

Past I was hanged
you were hanged
he (she) was hanged; it was hung

we were hanged
you were hanged
they were hanged, hung

Past I was being hanged
Prog. you were being hanged
he (she) was being hanged; it was being
hung

we were being hanged
you were being hanged
they were being hanged, hung

Past I did get hanged
Int. you did get hanged
he (she) did get hanged; it did get hung

we did get hanged
you did get hanged
they did get hanged, hung

Pres. I have been hanged
Perf. you have been hanged
he (she) has been hanged; it has been
hung

we have been hanged
you have been hanged
they have been hung

Past I had been hanged
Perf. you had been hanged
he (she) had been hanged; it had been
hung

we had been hanged
you had been hanged
they had been hanged, hung

Fut.	I shall have been hanged		we shall have been hanged
Perf.	you will have been hanged		you will have been hanged
	he (she) will have been hanged; it will have been hung		they will have been hanged, hung

Cond.	I would have been hanged		we would have been hanged
Perf.	you would have been hanged		you would have been hanged
	he (she) would have been hanged; it would have been hung		they would have been hanged, hung

IMPERATIVE MOOD
be hanged
SUBJUNCTIVE MOOD

Pres.	if I be hanged		if we be hanged
	if you be hanged		if you be hanged
	if he (she) be hanged; if it be hung		if they be hanged, hung

Past	if I were hanged		if we were hanged
	if you were hanged		if you were hanged
	if he (she) were hanged; if it were hung		if they were hanged, hung

Fut.	if I should be hanged		if we should be hanged
	if you should be hanged		if you should be hanged
	if he (she) should be hanged; if it should be hung		if they should be hanged, hung

to have (active voice)   *Principal Parts:* have, having, had, had

---

Infinitive: to have   *Present Participle:* having
Perfect Infinitive: to have had   *Past Participle:* had

INDICATIVE MOOD

Pres. I have	we have
you have	you have
he (she, it) has	they have
Pres. I am having	we are having
Prog. you are having	you are having
he (she, it) is having	they are having
Pres. I do have	we do have
Int. you do have	you do have
he (she, it) does have	they do have
Fut. I shall have	we shall have
you will have	you will have
he (she, it) will have	they will have
Cond. I would have	we would have
you would have	you would have
he (she, it) would have	they would have
Past I had	we had
you had	you had
he (she, it) had	they had
Past I was having	we were having
Prog. you were having	you were having
he (she, it) was having	they were having
Past I did have	we did have
Int. you did have	you did have
he (she, it) did have	they did have
Pres. I have had	we have had
Perf. you have had	you have had
he (she, it) has had	they have had
Past I had had	we had had
Perf. you had had	you had had
he (she, it) had had	they had had
Fut. I shall have had	we shall have had
Perf. you will have had	you will have had
he (she, it) will have had	they will have had
Cond. I would have had	we would have had
Perf. you would have had	you would have had
he (she, it) would have had	they would have had

IMPERATIVE MOOD
have

SUBJUNCTIVE MOOD

Pres. if I have	if we have
if you have	if you have
if he (she, it) have	if they have
Past if I had	if we had
if you had	if you had
if he (she, it) had	if they had
Fut. if I should have	if we should have
if you should have	if you should have
if he (she, it) should have	if they would have

(passive voice)

Infinitive: to be had
Perfect Infinitive: to have been had

Present Participle: being had
Past Participle: been had

INDICATIVE MOOD

Pres. I am had
you are had
he (she, it) is had

we are had
you are had
they are had

Pres.
Prog. I am being had
you are being had
he (she, it) is being had

we are being had
you are being had
they are being had

Pres.
Int. I do get had
you do get had
he (she, it) does get had

we do get had
you do get had
they do get had

Fut. I shall be had
you will be had
he (she, it) will be had

we shall be had
you will be had
they will be had

Cond. I would be had
you would be had
he (she, it) would be had

we would be had
you would be had
they would be had

Past I was had
you were had
he (she, it) was had

we were had
you were had
they were had

Past
Prog. I was being had
you were being had
he (she, it) was being had

we were being had
you were being had
they were being had

Past
Int. I did get had
you did get had
he (she, it) did get had

we did get had
you did get had
they did get had

Pres.
Perf. I have been had
you have been had
he (she, it) has been had

we have been had
you have been had
they have been had

Past
Perf. I had been had
you had been had
he (she, it) had been had

we had been had
you had been had
they had been had

Fut.
Perf. I shall have been had
you will have been had
he (she, it) will have been had

we shall have been had
you will have been had
they will have been had

Cond.
Perf. I would have been had
you would have been had
he (she, it) would have been had

we would have been had
you would have been had
they would have been had

IMPERATIVE MOOD
be had

SUBJUNCTIVE MOOD

Pres. if I be had
if you be had
if he (she, it) be had

if we be had
if you be had
if they be had

Past if I were had
if you were had
if he (she, it) were had

if we were had
if you were had
if they were had

Fut. if I should be had
if you should be had
if he (she, it) should be had

if we should be had
if you should be had
if they should be had

to hear (active voice)   *Principal Parts:* hear, hearing, heard, heard

Infinitive: to hear   *Present Participle:* hearing
Perfect Infinitive: to have heard   *Past Participle:* heard

INDICATIVE MOOD

Pres.	I hear	we hear	
	you hear	you hear	
	he (she, it) hears	they hear	
Pres.	I am hearing	we are hearing	
Prog.	you are hearing	you are hearing	
	he (she, it) is hearing	they are hearing	
Pres.	I do hear	we do hear	
Int.	you do hear	you do hear	
	he (she, it) does hear	they do hear	
Fut.	I shall hear	we shall hear	
	you will hear	you will hear	
	he (she, it) will hear	they will hear	
Cond.	I would hear	we would hear	
	you would hear	you would hear	
	he (she, it) would hear	they would hear	
Past	I heard	we heard	
	you heard	you heard	
	he (she, it) heard	they heard	
Past	I was hearing	we were hearing	
Prog.	you were hearing	you were hearing	
	he (she, it) was hearing	they were hearing	
Past	I did hear	we did hear	
Int.	you did hear	you did hear	
	he (she, it) did hear	they did hear	
Pres.	I have heard	we have heard	
Perf.	you have heard	you have heard	
	he (she, it) has heard	they have heard	
Past	I had heard	we had heard	
Perf.	you had heard	you had heard	
	he (she, it) had heard	they had heard	
Fut.	I shall have heard	we shall have heard	
Perf.	you will have heard	you will have heard	
	he (she, it) will have heard	they will have heard	
Cond.	I would have heard	we would have heard	
Perf.	you would have heard	you would have heard	
	he (she, it) would have heard	they would have heard	

IMPERATIVE MOOD
hear

SUBJUNCTIVE MOOD

Pres.	if I hear	if we hear	
	if you hear	if you hear	
	if he (she, it) hear	if they hear	
Past	if I heard	if we heard	
	if you heard	if you heard	
	if he (she, it) heard	if they heard	
Fut.	if I should hear	if we should hear	
	if you should hear	if you should hear	
	if he (she, it) should hear	if they should hear	

Infinitive: to be heard *Present Participle:* being heard
Perfect Infinitive: to have been heard *Past Participle:* been heard

INDICATIVE MOOD

Pres.	I am heard	we are heard
	you are heard	you are heard
	he (she, it) is heard	they are heard
Pres.	I am being heard	we are being heard
Prog.	you are being heard	you are being heard
	he (she, it) is being heard	they are being heard
Pres.	I do get heard	we do get heard
Int.	you do get heard	you do get heard
	he (she, it) does get heard	they do get heard
Fut.	I shall be heard	we shall be heard
	you will be heard	you will be heard
	he (she, it) will be heard	they will be heard
Cond.	I would be heard	we would be heard
	you would be heard	you would be heard
	he (she, it) would be heard	they would be heard
Past	I was heard	we were heard
	you were heard	you were heard
	he (she, it) was heard	they were heard
Past	I was being heard	we were being heard
Prog.	you were being heard	you were being heard
	he (she, it) was being heard	they were being heard
Past	I did get heard	we did get heard
Int.	you did get heard	you did get heard
	he (she, it) did get heard	they did get heard
Pres.	I have been heard	we have been heard
Perf.	you have been heard	you have been heard
	he (she, it) has been heard	they have been heard
Past	I had been heard	we had been heard
Perf.	you had been heard	you had been heard
	he (she, it) had been heard	they had been heard
Fut.	I shall have been heard	we shall have been heard
Perf.	you will have been heard	you will have been heard
	he (she, it) will have been heard	they will have been heard
Cond.	I would have been heard	we would have been heard
Perf.	you would have been heard	you would have been heard
	he (she, it) would have been heard	they would have been heard

IMPERATIVE MOOD
be heard

SUBJUNCTIVE MOOD

Pres.	if I be heard	if we be heard
	if you be heard	if you be heard
	if he (she, it) be heard	if they be heard
Past	if I were heard	if we were heard
	if you were heard	if you were heard
	if he (she, it) were heard	if they were heard
Fut.	if I should be heard	if we should be heard
	if you should be heard	if you should be heard
	if he (she, it) should be heard	if they should be heard

Infinitive: to hit　　　　　　*Present Participle:* hitting
Perfect Infinitive: to have hit　　*Past Participle:* hit

INDICATIVE MOOD

Pres.	I hit	we hit
	you hit	you hit
	he (she, it) hits	they hit
Pres.	I am hitting	we are hitting
Prog.	you are hitting	you are hitting
	he (she, it) is hitting	they are hitting
Pres.	I do hit	we do hit
Int.	you do hit	you do hit
	he (she, it) does hit	they do hit
Fut.	I shall hit	we shall hit
	you will hit	you will hit
	he (she, it) will hit	they will hit
Cond.	I would hit	we would hit
	you would hit	you would hit
	he (she, it) would hit	they would hit
Past	I hit	we hit
	you hit	you hit
	he (she, it) hit	they hit
Past	I was hitting	we were hitting
Prog.	you were hitting	you were hitting
	he (she, it) was hitting	they were hitting
Past	I did hit	we did hit
Int.	you did hit	you did hit
	he (she, it) did hit	they did hit
Pres.	I have hit	we have hit
Perf.	you have hit	you have hit
	he (she, it) has hit	they have hit
Past	I had hit	we had hit
Perf.	you had hit	you had hit
	he (she, it) had hit	they had hit
Fut.	I shall have hit	we shall have hit
Perf.	you will have hit	you will have hit
	he (she, it) will have hit	they will have hit
Cond.	I would have hit	we would have hit
Perf.	you would have hit	you would have hit
	he (she, it) would have hit	they would have hit

IMPERATIVE MOOD
hit

SUBJUNCTIVE MOOD

Pres.	if I hit	if we hit
	if you hit	if you hit
	if he (she, it) hit	if they hit
Past	if I hit	if we hit
	if you hit	if you hit
	if he (she, it) hit	if they hit
Fut.	if I should hit	if we should hit
	if you should hit	if you should hit
	if he (she, it) should hit	if they should hit

Infinitive: to be hit   *Present Participle:* being hit
Perfect Infinitive: to have been hit   *Past Participle:* been hit

INDICATIVE MOOD

Pres. I am hit
you are hit
he (she, it) is hit

we are hit
you are hit
they are hit

Pres. I am being hit
Prog. you are being hit
he (she, it) is being hit

we are being hit
you are being hit
they are being hit

Pres. I do get hit
Int. you do get hit
he (she, it) does get hit

we do get hit
you do get hit
they do get hit

Fut. I shall be hit
you will be hit
he (she, it) will be hit

we shall be hit
you will be hit
they will be hit

Cond. I would be hit
you would be hit
he (she, it) would be hit

we would be hit
you would be hit
they would be hit

Past I was hit
you were hit
he (she, it) was hit

we were hit
you were hit
they were hit

Past I was being hit
Prog. you were being hit
he (she, it) was being hit

we were being hit
you were being hit
they were being hit

Past I did get hit
Int. you did get hit
he (she, it) did get hit

we did get hit
you did get hit
they did get hit

Pres. I have been hit
Perf. you have been hit
he (she, it) has been hit

we have been hit
you have been hit
they have been hit

Past I had been hit
Perf. you had been hit
he (she, it) had been hit

we had been hit
you had been hit
they had been hit

Fut. I shall have been hit
Perf. you will have been hit
he (she, it) will have been hit

we shall have been hit
you will have been hit
they will have been hit

Cond. I would have been hit
Perf. you would have been hit
he (she, it) would have been hit

we would have been hit
you would have been hit
they would have been hit

IMPERATIVE MOOD
be hit

SUBJUNCTIVE MOOD

Pres. if I be hit
if you be hit
if he (she, it) be hit

if we be hit
if you be hit
if they be hit

Past if I were hit
if you were hit
if he (she, it) were hit

if we were hit
if you were hit
if they were hit

Fut. if I should be hit
if you should be hit
if he (she, it) should be hit

if we should be hit
if you should be hit
if they should be hit

to hold (active voice)   *Principal Parts:* hold, holding, held, held

Infinitive: to hold   *Present Participle:* holding
Perfect Infinitive: to have held   *Past Participle:* held

INDICATIVE MOOD

Pres.   I hold   we hold
        you hold   you hold
        he (she, it) holds   they hold

Pres.   I am holding   we are holding
Prog.   you are holding   you are holding
        he (she, it) is holding   they are holding

Pres.   I do hold   we do hold
Int.   you do hold   you do hold
        he (she, it) does hold   they do hold

Fut.   I shall hold   we shall hold
        you will hold   you will hold
        he (she, it) will hold   they will hold

Cond.   I would hold   we would hold
        you would hold   you would hold
        he (she, it) would hold   they would hold

Past   I held   we held
        you held   you held
        he (she, it) held   they held

Past   I was holding   we were holding
Prog.   you were holding   you were holding
        he (she, it) was holding   they were holding

Past   I did hold   we did hold
Int.   you did hold   you did hold
        he (she, it) did hold   they did hold

Pres.   I have held   we have held
Perf.   you have held   you have held
        he (she, it) has held   they have held

Past   I had held   we had held
Perf.   you had held   you had held
        he (she, it) had held   they had held

Fut.   I shall have held   we shall have held
Perf.   you will have held   you will have held
        he (she, it) will have held   they will have held

Cond.   I would have held   we would have held
Perf.   you would have held   you would have held
        he (she, it) would have held   they would have held

IMPERATIVE MOOD
hold

SUBJUNCTIVE MOOD

Pres.   if I hold   if we hold
        if you hold   if you hold
        if he (she, it) hold   if they hold

Past   if I held   if we held
        if you held   if you held
        if he (she, it) held   if they held

Fut.   if I should hold   if we should hold
        if you should hold   if you should hold
        if he (she, it) should hold   if they should hold

Infinitive: to be held   *Present Participle:* being held
Perfect Infinitive: to have been held   *Past Participle:* been held

INDICATIVE MOOD

Pres.	I am held	we are held
	you are held	you are held
	he (she, it) is held	they are held
Pres.	I am being held	we are being held
Prog.	you are being held	you are being held
	he (she, it) is being held	they are being held
Pres.	I do get held	we do get held
Int.	you do get held	you do get held
	he (she, it) does get held	they do get held
Fut.	I shall be held	we shall be held
	you will be held	you will be held
	he (she, it) will be held	they will be held
Cond.	I would be held	we would be held
	you would be held	you would be held
	he (she, it) would be held	they would be held
Past	I was held	we were held
	you were held	you were held
	he (she, it) was held	they were held
Past	I was being held	we were being held
Prog.	you were being held	you were being held
	he (she, it) was being held	they were being held
Past	I did get held	we did get held
Int.	you did get held	you did get held
	he (she, it) did get held	they did get held
Pres.	I have been held	we have been held
Perf.	you have been held	you have been held
	he (she, it) has been held	they have been held
Past	I had been held	we had been held
Perf.	you had been held	you had been held
	he (she, it) had been held	they had been held
Fut.	I shall have been held	we shall have been held
Perf.	you will have been held	you will have been held
	he (she, it) will have been held	they will have been held
Cond.	I would have been held	we would have been held
Perf.	you would have been held	you would have been held
	he (she, it) would have been held	they would have been held

IMPERATIVE MOOD
be held

SUBJUNCTIVE MOOD

Pres.	if I be held	if we be held
	if you be held	if you be held
	if he (she, it) be held	if they be held
Past	if I were held	if we were held
	if you were held	if you were held
	if he (she, it) were held	if they were held
Fut.	if I should be held	if we should be held
	if you should be held	if you should be held
	if he (she, it) should be held	if they should be held

to hurt (active voice)   *Principal Parts:* hurt, hurting, hurt, hurt

---

Infinitive: to hurt
Perfect Infinitive: to have hurt

Present Participle: hurting
Past Participle: hurt

INDICATIVE MOOD

Pres.	I hurt	we hurt
	you hurt	you hurt
	he (she, it) hurts	they hurt
Pres.	I am hurting	we are hurting
Prog.	you are hurting	you are hurting
	he (she, it) is hurting	they are hurting
Pres.	I do hurt	we do hurt
Int.	you do hurt	you do hurt
	he (she, it) does hurt	they do hurt
Fut.	I shall hurt	we shall hurt
	you will hurt	you will hurt
	he (she, it) will hurt	they will hurt
Cond.	I would hurt	we would hurt
	you would hurt	you would hurt
	he (she, it) would hurt	they would hurt
Past	I hurt	we hurt
	you hurt	you hurt
	he (she, it) hurt	they hurt
Past	I was hurting	we were hurting
Prog.	you were hurting	you were hurting
	he (she, it) was hurting	they were hurting
Past	I did hurt	we did hurt
Int.	you did hurt	you did hurt
	he (she, it) did hurt	they did hurt
Pres.	I have hurt	we have hurt
Perf.	you have hurt	you have hurt
	he (she, it) has hurt	they have hurt
Past	I had hurt	we had hurt
Perf.	you had hurt	you had hurt
	he (she, it) had hurt	they had hurt
Fut.	I shall have hurt	we shall have hurt
Perf.	you will have hurt	you will have hurt
	he (she, it) will have hurt	they will have hurt
Cond.	I would have hurt	we would have hurt
Perf.	you would have hurt	you would have hurt
	he (she, it) would have hurt	they would have hurt

IMPERATIVE MOOD
hurt

SUBJUNCTIVE MOOD

Pres.	if I hurt	if we hurt
	if you hurt	if you hurt
	if he (she, it) hurt	if they hurt
Past	if I hurt	if we hurt
	if you hurt	if you hurt
	if he (she, it) hurt	if they hurt
Fut.	if I should hurt	if we should hurt
	if you should hurt	if you should hurt
	if he (she, it) should hurt	if they should hurt

Infinitive: to be hurt
Perfect Infinitive: to have been hurt

Present Participle: being hurt
Past Participle: been hurt

INDICATIVE MOOD

Pres.	I am hurt	we are hurt
	you are hurt	you are hurt
	he (she, it) is hurt	they are hurt
Pres.	I am being hurt	we are being hurt
Prog.	you are being hurt	you are being hurt
	he (she, it) is being hurt	they are being hurt
Pres.	I do get hurt	we do get hurt
Int.	you do get hurt	you do get hurt
	he (she, it) does get hurt	they do get hurt
Fut.	I shall be hurt	we shall be hurt
	you will be hurt	you will be hurt
	he (she, it) will be hurt	they will be hurt
Cond.	I would be hurt	we would be hurt
	you would be hurt	you would be hurt
	he (she, it) would be hurt	they would be hurt
Past	I was hurt	we were hurt
	you were hurt	you were hurt
	he (she, it) was hurt	they were hurt
Past	I was being hurt	we were being hurt
Prog.	you were being hurt	you were being hurt
	he (she, it) was being hurt	they were being hurt
Past	I did get hurt	we did get hurt
Int.	you did get hurt	you did get hurt
	he (she, it) did get hurt	they did get hurt
Pres.	I have been hurt	we have been hurt
Perf.	you have been hurt	you have been hurt
	he (she, it) has been hurt	they have been hurt
Past	I had been hurt	we had been hurt
Perf.	you had been hurt	you had been hurt
	he (she, it) had been hurt	they had been hurt
Fut.	I shall have been hurt	we shall have been hurt
Perf.	you will have been hurt	you will have been hurt
	he (she, it) will have been hurt	they will have been hurt
Cond.	I would have been hurt	we would have been hurt
Perf.	you would have been hurt	you would have been hurt
	he (she, it) would have been hurt	they would have been hurt

IMPERATIVE MOOD
be hurt

SUBJUNCTIVE MOOD

Pres.	if I be hurt	if we be hurt
	if you be hurt	if you be hurt
	if he (she, it) be hurt	if they be hurt
Past	if I were hurt	if we were hurt
	if you were hurt	if you were hurt
	if he (she, it) were hurt	if they were hurt
Fut.	if I should be hurt	if we should be hurt
	if you should be hurt	if you should be hurt
	if he (she, it) should be hurt	if they should be hurt

to kneel (active voice only)   *Principal Parts:*   kneel,   kneeling,   knelt
(kneeled), knelt

(intransitive verb)

Infinitive: to kneel   *Present Participle:* kneeling
Perfect Infinitive: to have knelt   *Past Participle:* knelt

INDICATIVE MOOD

Pres.	I kneel	we kneel
	you kneel	you kneel
	he (she, it) kneels	they kneel
Pres.	I am kneeling	we are kneeling
Prog.	you are kneeling	you are kneeling
	he (she, it) is kneeling	they are kneeling
Pres.	I do kneel	we do kneel
Int.	you do kneel	you do kneel
	he (she, it) does kneel	they do kneel
Fut.	I shall kneel	we shall kneel
	you will kneel	you will kneel
	he (she, it) will kneel	they will kneel
Cond.	I would kneel	we would kneel
	you would kneel	you would kneel
	he (she, it) would kneel	they would kneel
Past	I knelt, kneeled	we knelt, kneeled
	you knelt, kneeled	you knelt, kneeled
	he (she, it) knelt, kneeled	they knelt, kneeled
Past	I was kneeling	we were kneeling
Prog.	you were kneeling	you were kneeling
	he (she, it) was kneeling	they were kneeling
Past	I did kneel	we did kneel
Int.	you did kneel	you did kneel
	he (she, it) did kneel	they did kneel
Pres.	I have knelt	we have knelt
Perf.	you have knelt	you have knelt
	he (she, it) has knelt	they have knelt
Past	I had knelt	we had knelt
Perf.	you had knelt	you had knelt
	he (she, it) had knelt	they had knelt
Fut.	I shall have knelt	we shall have knelt
Perf.	you will have knelt	you will have knelt
	he (she, it) will have knelt	they will have knelt
Cond.	I would have knelt	we would have knelt
Perf.	you would have knelt	you would have knelt
	he (she, it) would have knelt	they would have knelt

IMPERATIVE MOOD
kneel

SUBJUNCTIVE MOOD

Pres.	if I kneel	if we kneel
	if you kneel	if you kneel
	if he (she, it) kneel	if they kneel
Past	if I knelt	if we knelt
	if you knelt	if you knelt
	if he (she, it) knelt	if they knelt
Fut.	if I should kneel	if we should kneel
	if you should kneel	if you should kneel
	if he (she, it) should kneel	if they should kneel

236

To kneel is an intransitive verb.

It does not take an object.

It describes action, but the action is self-contained.

Like other intransitive verbs, it may be followed by adverbs, adverbial phrases and clauses describing the how, why, when, and where of the action:

HOW: The congregation knelt *slowly*. (adverb)

WHY: The people will kneel *to pray*. (adverbial phrase)

WHEN: I *always* kneel *when I say my prayers*. (adverb and adverbial clause)

WHERE: The page knelt *in front of the king*. (adverbial phrase)

Infinitive: to know   *Present Participle:* knowing
Perfect Infinitive: to have known   *Past Participle:* known

INDICATIVE MOOD

Pres.	I know	we know
	you know	you know
	he (she, it) knows	they know
Pres.	I do know	we do know
Int.	you do know	you do know
	he (she, it) does know	they do know
Fut.	I shall know	we shall know
	you will know	you will know
	he (she, it) will know	they will know
Cond.	I would know	we would know
	you would know	you would know
	he (she, it) would know	they would know
Past	I knew	we knew
	you knew	you knew
	he (she, it) knew	they knew
Past	I did know	we did know
Int.	you did know	you did know
	he (she, it) did know	they did know
Pres.	I have known	we have known
Perf.	you have known	you have known
	he (she, it) has known	they have known
Past	I had known	we had known
Perf.	you had known	you had known
	he (she, it) had known	they had known
Fut.	I shall have known	we shall have known
Perf.	you will have known	you will have known
	he (she, it) will have known	they will have known
Cond.	I would have known	we would have known
Perf.	you would have known	you would have known
	he (she, it) would have known	they would have known

IMPERATIVE MOOD
know

SUBJUNCTIVE MOOD

Pres.	if I know	if we know
	if you know	if you know
	if he (she, it) know	if they know
Past	if I knew	if we knew
	if you knew	if you knew
	if he (she, it) knew	if they knew
Fut.	if I should know	if we should know
	if you should know	if you should know
	if he (she, it) should know	if they should know

(passive voice)

Infinitive: to be known
Perfect Infinitive: to have been known

Present Participle: being known
Past Participle: been known

INDICATIVE MOOD

Pres.	I am known	we are known
	you are known	you are known
	he (she, it) is known	they are known
Pres.	I am being known	we are being known
Prog.	you are being known	you are being known
	he (she, it) is being known	they are being known
Pres.	I do get known	we do get known
Int.	you do get known	you do get known
	he (she, it) does get known	they do get known
Fut.	I shall be known	we shall be known
	you will be known	you will be known
	he (she, it) will be known	they will be known
Cond.	I would be known	we would be known
	you would be known	you would be known
	he (she, it) would be known	they would be known
Past	I was known	we were known
	you were known	you were known
	he (she, it) was known	they were known
Past	I was being known	we were being known
Prog.	you were being known	you were being known
	he (she, it) was being known	they were being known
Past	I did get known	we did get known
Int.	you did get known	you did get known
	he (she, it) did get known	they did get known
Pres.	I have been known	we have been known
Perf.	you have been known	you have been known
	he (she, it) has been known	they have been known
Past	I had been known	we had been known
Perf.	you had been known	you had been known
	he (she, it) had been known	they had been known
Fut.	I shall have been known	we shall have been known
Perf.	you will have been known	you will have been known
	he (she, it) will have been known	they will have been known
Cond.	I would have been known	we would have been known
Perf.	you would have been known	you would have been known
	he (she, it) would have been known	they would have been known

IMPERATIVE MOOD
be known

SUBJUNCTIVE MOOD

Pres.	if I be known	if we be known
	if you be known	if you be known
	if he (she, it) be known	if they be known
Past	if I were known	if we were known
	if you were known	if you were known
	if he (she, it) were known	if they were known
Fut.	if I should be known	if we should be known
	if you should be known	if you should be known
	if he (she, it) should be known	if they should be known

to lay (active voice)   *Principal Parts:* lay, laying, laid, laid

Infinitive: to lay   *Present Participle:* laying
Perfect Infinitive: to have laid   *Past Participle:* laid

INDICATIVE MOOD

Pres. I lay
you lay
he (she, it) lays

we lay
you lay
they lay

Pres.
Prog. I am laying
you are laying
he (she, it) is laying

we are laying
you are laying
they are laying

Pres.
Int. I do lay
you do lay
he (she, it) does lay

we do lay
you do lay
they do lay

Fut. I shall lay
you will lay
he (she, it) will lay

we shall lay
you will lay
they will lay

Cond. I would lay
you would lay
he (she, it) would lay

we would lay
you would lay
they would lay

Past I laid
you laid
he (she, it) laid

we laid
you laid
they laid

Past
Prog. I was laying
you were laying
he (she, it) was laying

we were laying
you were laying
they were laying

Past
Int. I did lay
you did lay
he (she, it) did lay

we did lay
you did lay
they did lay

Pres.
Perf. I have laid
you have laid
he (she, it) has laid

we have laid
you have laid
they have laid

Past
Perf. I had laid
you had laid
he (she, it) had laid

we had laid
you had laid
they had laid

Fut.
Perf. I shall have laid
you will have laid
he (she, it) will have laid

we shall have laid
you will have laid
they will have laid

Cond. I would have laid
you would have laid
he (she, it) would have laid

we would have laid
you would have laid
they would have laid

IMPERATIVE MOOD
lay

SUBJUNCTIVE MOOD

Pres. if I lay
if you lay
if he (she, it) lay

if we lay
if you lay
if they lay

Past if I laid
if you laid
if he (she, it) laid

if we laid
if you laid
if they laid

Fut. if I should lay
if you should lay
if he (she, it) should lay

if we should lay
if you should lay
if they should lay

240

(passive voice)

Infinitive: to be laid   *Past Participle:* been laid
Perfect Infinitive: to have been laid   *Present Participle:* being laid

INDICATIVE MOOD

Pres.	I am laid	we are laid
	you are laid	you are laid
	he (she, it) is laid	they are laid
Pres.	I am being laid	we are being laid
Prog.	you are being laid	you are being laid
	he (she, it) is being laid	they are being laid
Pres.	I do get laid	we do get laid
Int.	you do get laid	you do get laid
	he (she, it) does get laid	they do get laid
Fut.	I shall be laid	we shall be laid
	you will be laid	you will be laid
	he (she, it) will be laid	they will be laid
Cond.	I would be laid	we would be laid
	you would be laid	you would be laid
	he (she, it) would be laid	they would be laid
Past	I was laid	we were laid
	you were laid	you were laid
	he (she, it) was laid	they were laid
Past	I was being laid	we were being laid
Prog.	you were being laid	you were being laid
	he (she, it) was being laid	they were being laid
Past	I did get laid	we did get laid
Int.	you did get laid	you did get laid
	he (she, it) did get laid	they did get laid
Pres.	I have been laid	we have been laid
Perf.	you have been laid	you have been laid
	he (she, it) has been laid	they have been laid
Past	I had been laid	we had been laid
Perf.	you had been laid	you had been laid
	he (she, it) had been laid	they had been laid
Fut.	I shall have been laid	we shall have been laid
Perf.	you will have been laid	you will have been laid
	he (she, it) will have been laid	they will have been laid
Cond.	I would have been laid	we would have been laid
Perf.	you would have been laid	you would have been laid
	he (she, it) would have been laid	they would have been laid

IMPERATIVE MOOD
be laid

SUBJUNCTIVE MOOD

Pres.	if I be laid	if we be laid
	if you be laid	if you be laid
	if he (she, it) be laid	if they be laid
Past	if I were laid	if we were laid
	if you were laid	if you were laid
	if he (she, it) were laid	if they were laid
Fut.	if I should be laid	if we should be laid
	if you should be laid	if you should be laid
	if he (she, it) should be laid	if they should be laid

Infinitive: to lead   *Present Participle:* leading
Perfect Infinitive: to have led   *Past Participle:* led

INDICATIVE MOOD

Pres.	I lead	we lead
	you lead	you lead
	he (she, it) leads	they lead
Pres.	I am leading	we are leading
Prog.	you are leading	you are leading
	he (she, it) is leading	they are leading
Pres.	I do lead	we do lead
Int.	you do lead	you do lead
	he (she, it) does lead	they do lead
Fut.	I shall lead	we shall lead
	you will lead	you will lead
	he (she, it) will lead	they will lead
Cond.	I would lead	we would lead
	you would lead	you would lead
	he (she, it) would lead	they would lead
Past	I led	we led
	you led	you led
	he (she, it) led	they led
Past	I was leading	we were leading
Prog.	you were leading	you were leading
	he (she, it) was leading	they were leading
Past	I did lead	we did lead
Int.	you did lead	you did lead
	he (she, it) did lead	they did lead
Pres.	I have led	we have led
Perf.	you have led	you have led
	he (she, it) has led	they have led
Past	I had led	we had led
Perf.	you had led	you had led
	he (she, it) had led	they had led
Fut.	I shall have led	we shall have led
Perf.	you will have led	you will have led
	he (she, it) will have led	they will have led
Cond.	I would have led	we would have led
Perf.	you would have led	you would have led
	he (she, it) would have led	they would have led

IMPERATIVE MOOD
lead

SUBJUNCTIVE MOOD

Pres.	if I lead	if we lead
	if you lead	if you lead
	if he (she, it) lead	if they lead
Past	if I led	if we led
	if you led	if you led
	if he (she, it) led	if they led
Fut.	if I should lead	if we should lead
	if you should lead	if you should lead
	if he (she, it) should lead	if they should lead

Infinitive: to be led
Perfect Infinitive: to have been led

Present Participle: being led
Past Participle: been led

INDICATIVE MOOD

Pres. I am led
you are led
he (she, it) is led

we are led
you are led
they are led

Pres. Prog. I am being led
you are being led
he (she, it) is being led

we are being led
you are being led
they are being led

Pres. Int. I do get led
you do get led
he (she, it) does get led

we do get led
you do get led
they do get led

Fut. I shall be led
you will be led
he (she, it) will be led

we shall be led
you will be led
they will be led

Cond. I would be led
you would be led
he (she, it) would be led

we would be led
you would be led
they would be led

Past I was led
you were led
he (she, it) was led

we were led
you were led
they were led

Past Prog. I was being led
you were being led
he (she, it) was being led

we were being led
you were being led
they were being led

Past Int. I did get led
you did get led
he (she, it) did get led

we did get led
you did get led
they did get led

Pres. Perf. I have been led
you have been led
he (she, it) has been led

we have been led
you have been led
they have been led

Past Perf. I had been led
you had been led
he (she, it) had been led

we had been led
you had been led
they had been led

Fut. Perf. I shall have been led
you will have been led
he (she, it) will have been led

we shall have been led
you will have been led
they will have been led

Cond. Perf. I would have been led
you would have been led
he (she, it) would have been led

we would have been led
you would have been led
they would have been led

IMPERATIVE MOOD
be led

SUBJUNCTIVE MOOD

Pres. if I be led
if you be led
if he (she, it) be led

if we be led
if you be led
if they be led

Past if I were led
if you were led
if he (she, it) were led

if we were led
if you were led
if they were led

Fut. if I should be led
if you should be led
if he (she, it) should be led

if we should be led
if you should be led
if they should be led

to leap (active voice only)   *Principal Parts:* leap, leaping, leaped (leapt), leaped (leapt)

(intransitive verb)

Infinitive: to leap   *Present Participle:* leaping
Perfect Infinitive: to have leaped (leapt)   *Past Participle:* leaped (leapt)

INDICATIVE MOOD

Pres.	I leap	we leap
	you leap	you leap
	he (she, it) leaps	they leap
Pres.	I am leaping	we are leaping
Prog.	you are leaping	you are leaping
	he (she, it) is leaping	they are leaping
Pres.	I do leap	we do leap
Int.	you do leap	you do leap
	he (she, it) does leap	they do leap
Fut.	I shall leap	we shall leap
	you will leap	you will leap
	he (she, it) will leap	they will leap
Cond.	I would leap	we would leap
	you would leap	you would leap
	he (she, it) would leap	they would leap
Past	I leaped, leapt	we leaped, leapt
	you leaped, leapt	you leaped, leapt
	he (she, it) leaped, leapt	they leaped, leapt
Past	I was leaping	we were leaping
Prog.	you were leaping	you were leaping
	he (she, it) was leaping	they were leaping
Past	I did leap	we did leap
Int.	you did leap	you did leap
	he (she, it) did leap	they did leap
Pres.	I have leaped, leapt	we have leaped, leapt
Perf.	you have leaped, leapt	you have leaped, leapt
	he (she, it) has leaped, leapt	they have leaped, leapt
Past	I had leaped, leapt	we had leaped, leapt
Perf.	you had leaped, leapt	you had leaped, leapt
	he (she, it) had leaped, leapt	they had leaped, leapt
Fut.	I shall have leaped, leapt	we shall have leaped, leapt
Perf.	you will have leaped, leapt	you will have leaped, leapt
	he (she, it) will have leaped, leapt	they will have leaped, leapt,
Cond.	I would have leaped, leapt	we would have leaped, leapt
Perf.	you would have leaped, leapt	you would have leaped, leapt
	he (she, it) would have leaped, leapt	they would have leaped, leapt

IMPERATIVE MOOD
leap

SUBJUNCTIVE MOOD

Pres.	if I leap	if we leap
	if you leap	if you leap
	if he (she, it) leap	if they leap
Past	if I leaped, leapt	if we leaped, leapt
	if you leaped, leapt	if you leaped, leapt
	if he (she, it) leaped, leapt	if they leaped, leapt
Fut.	if I should leap	if we should leap
	if you should leap	if you should leap
	if he (she, it) should leap	if they should leap

To leap is an intransitive verb.

It does not take an object.

It describes action, but the action is self-contained.

Like other intransitive verbs, it may be followed by adverbs, adverbial phrases and clauses describing the how, when, and where of the action:

HOW: The dancers leapt *vigorously*. (adverb)

WHY: They leapt *for joy*. (adverbial phrase)

WHEN: The fish will be leaping *as soon as the ice leaves the lake*. (adverbial clause)

WHERE: I shall leap *into my bed*. (adverbial phrase)

Infinitive: to leave   *Present Participle:* leaving
Perfect Infinitive: to have left   *Past Participle:* left

INDICATIVE MOOD

Pres. I leave   we leave
you leave   you leave
he (she, it) leaves   they leave

Pres. I am leaving   we are leaving
Prog. you are leaving   you are leaving
he (she, it) is leaving   they are leaving

Pres. I do leave   we do leave
Int. you do leave   you do leave
he (she, it) does leave   they do leave

Fut. I shall leave   we shall leave
you will leave   you will leave
he (she, it) will leave   they will leave

Cond. I would leave   we would leave
you would leave   you would leave
he (she, it) would leave   they would leave

Past I left   we left
you left   you left
he (she, it) left   they left

Past I was leaving   we were leaving
Prog. you were leaving   you were leaving
he (she, it) was leaving   they were leaving

Past I did leave   we did leave
Int. you did leave   you did leave
he (she, it) did leave   they did leave

Pres. I have left   we have left
Perf. you have left   you have left
he (she, it) has left   they have left

Past I had left   we had left
Perf. you had left   you had left
he (she, it) had left   they had left

Fut. I shall have left   we shall have left
Perf. you will have left   you will have left
he (she, it) will have left   they will have left

Cond. I would have left   we would have left
Perf. you would have left   you would have left
he (she, it) would have left   they would have left

IMPERATIVE MOOD
leave

SUBJUNCTIVE MOOD

Pres. if I leave   if we leave
if you leave   if you leave
if he (she, it) leave   if they leave

Past if I left   if we left
if you left   if you left
if he (she, it) left   if they left

Fut. if I should leave   if we should leave
if you should leave   if you should leave
if he (she, it) should leave   if they should leave

(passive voice)

Infinitive: to be left

Perfect Infinitive: to have been left

Present Participle: being left

Past Participle: been left

INDICATIVE MOOD

Pres.	I am left you are left he (she, it) is left	we are left you are left they are left
Pres. Prog.	I am being left you are being left he (she, it) is being left	we are being left you are being left they are being left
Pres. Int.	I do get left you do get left he (she, it) does get left	we do get left you do get left they do get left
Fut.	I shall be left you will be left he (she, it) will be left	we shall be left you will be left they will be left
Cond.	I would be left you would be left he (she, it) would be left	we would be left you would be left they would be left
Past	I was left you were left he (she, it) was left	we were left you were left they were left
Past Prog.	I was being left you were being left he (she, it) was being left	we were being left you were being left they were being left
Past Int.	I did get left you did get left he (she, it) did get left	we did get left you did get left they did get left
Pres. Perf.	I have been left you have been left he (she, it) has been left	we have been left you have been left they have been left
Past Perf.	I had been left you had been left he (she, it) had been left	we had been left you had been left they had been left
Fut. Perf.	I shall have been left you will have been left he (she, it) will have been left	we shall have been left you will have been left they will have been left
Cond. Perf.	I would have been left you would have been left he (she, it) would have been left	we would have been left you would have been left they would have been left

IMPERATIVE MOOD
be left

SUBJUNCTIVE MOOD

Pres.	if I be left if you be left if he (she, it) be left	if we be left if you be left if they be left
Past	if I were left if you were left if he (she, it) were left	if we were left if you were left if they were left
Fut.	if I should be left if you should be left if he (she, it) should be left	if we should be left if you should be left if they should be left

to lend (active voice)   *Principal Parts: lend, lending, lent, lent*

Infinitive: to lend   *Present Participle:* lending
Perfect Infinitive: to have lent   *Past Participle:* lent

INDICATIVE MOOD

Pres.	I lend	we lend
	you lend	you lend
	he (she, it) lends	they lend
Pres.	I am lending	we are lending
Prog.	you are lending	you are lending
	he (she, it) is lending	they are lending
Pres.	I do lend	we do lend
Int.	you do lend	you do lend
	he (she, it) does lend	they do lend
Fut.	I shall lend	we shall lend
	you will lend	you will lend
	he (she, it) will lend	they will lend
Cond.	I would lend	we would lend
	you would lend	you would lend
	he (she, it) would lend	they would lend
Past	I lent	we lent
	you lent	you lent
	he (she, it) lent	they lent
Past	I was lending	we were lending
Prog.	you were lending	you were lending
	he (she, it) was lending	they were lending
Past	I did lend	we did lend
Int.	you did lend	you did lend
	he (she, it) did lend	they did lend
Pres.	I have lent	we have lent
Perf.	you have lent	you have lent
	he (she, it) has lent	they have lent
Past	I had lent	we had lent
Perf.	you had lent	you had lent
	he (she, it) had lent	they had lent
Fut.	I shall have lent	we shall have lent
Perf.	you will have lent	you will have lent
	he (she, it) will have lent	they will have lent
Cond.	I would have lent	we would have lent
Perf.	you would have lent	you would have lent
	he (she, it) would have lent	they would have lent

IMPERATIVE MOOD
lend

SUBJUNCTIVE MOOD

Pres.	if I lend	if we lend
	if you lend	if you lend
	if he (she, it) lend	if they lend
Past	if I lent	if we lent
	if you lent	if you lent
	if he (she, it) lent	if they lent
Fut.	if I should lend	if we should lend
	if you should lend	if you should lend
	if he (she, it) should lend	if they should lend

(passive voice)

Infinitive: to be lent   *Present Participle:* being lent
Perfect Infinitive: to have been lent   *Past Participle:* been lent

INDICATIVE MOOD

Pres.	I am lent you are lent he (she, it) is lent	we are lent you are lent they are lent	
Pres. Prog.	I am being lent you are being lent he (she, it) is being lent	we are being lent you are being lent they are being lent	
Pres. Int.	I do get lent you do get lent he (she, it) does get lent	we do get lent you do get lent they do get lent	
Fut.	I shall be lent you will be lent he (she, it) will be lent	we shall be lent you will be lent they will be lent	
Cond.	I would be lent you would be lent he (she, it) would be lent	we would be lent you would be lent they would be lent	
Past	I was lent you were lent he (she, it) was lent	we were lent you were lent they were lent	
Past Prog.	I was being lent you were being lent he (she, it) was being lent	we were being lent you were being lent they were being lent	
Past Int.	I did get lent you did get lent he (she, it) did get lent	we did get lent you did get lent they did get lent	
Pres. Perf.	I have been lent you have been lent he (she, it) has been lent	we have been lent you have been lent they have been lent	
Past Perf.	I had been lent you had been lent he (she, it) had been lent	we had been lent you had been lent they had been lent	
Fut. Perf.	I shall have been lent you will have been lent he (she, it) will have been lent	we shall have been lent you will have been lent they will have been lent	
Cond. Perf.	I would have been lent you would have been lent he (she, it) would have been lent	we would have been lent you would have been lent they would have been lent	

IMPERATIVE MOOD
be lent

SUBJUNCTIVE MOOD

Pres.	if I be lent if you be lent if he (she, it) be lent	if we be lent if you be lent if they be lent
Past	if I were lent if you were lent if he (she, it) were lent	if we were lent if you were lent if they were lent
Fut.	if I should be lent if you should be lent if he (she, it) should be lent	if we should be lent if you should be lent if they should be lent

249

to let (active voice)   *Principal Parts:* let, letting, let, let

Infinitive: to let
Perfect Infinitive: to have let

Present Participle: letting
Past Participle: let

INDICATIVE MOOD

Pres.	I let	we let
	you let	you let
	he (she, it) lets	they let
Pres.	I am letting	we are letting
Prog.	you are letting	you are letting
	he (she, it) is letting	they are letting
Pres.	I do let	we do let
Int.	you do let	you do let
	he (she, it) does let	they do let
Fut.	I shall let	we shall let
	you will let	you will let
	he (she, it) will let	they will let
Cond.	I would let	we would let
	you would let	you would let
	he (she, it) would let	they would let
Past	I let	we let
	you let	you let
	he (she, it) lets	they let
Past	I was letting	we were letting
Prog.	you were letting	you were letting
	he (she, it) was letting	they were letting
Past	I did let	we did let
Int.	you did let	you did let
	he (she, it) did let	they did let
Pres.	I have let	we have let
Perf.	you have let	you have let
	he (she, it) has let	they have let
Past	I had let	we had let
Perf.	you had let	you had let
	he (she, it) had let	they had let
Fut.	I shall have let	we shall have let
Perf.	you will have let	you will have let
	he (she, it) will have let	they will have let
Cond.	I would have let	we would have let
Perf.	you would have let	you would have let
	he (she, it) would have let	they would have let

IMPERATIVE MOOD
let

SUBJUNCTIVE MOOD

Pres.	if I let	if we let
	if you let	if you let
	if he (she, it) let	if they let
Past	if I let	if we let
	if you let	if you let
	if he (she, it) let	if they let
Fut.	if I should let	if we should let
	if you should let	if you should let
	if he (she, it) should let	if they should let

(passive voice)

Infinitive: to be let   *Present Participle:* being let
Perfect Infinitive: to have been let   *Past Participle:* been let

INDICATIVE MOOD

Pres. I am let   we are let
         you are let   you are let
         he (she, it) is let   they are let

Pres. I am being let   we are being let
Prog. you are being let   you are being let
         he (she, it) is being let   they are being let

Pres. I do get let   we do get let
Int.   you do get let   you do get let
         he (she, it) does get let   they do get let

Fut.   I shall be let   we shall be let
         you will be let   you will be let
         he (she, it) will be let   they will be let

Cond. I would be let   we would be let
         you would be let   you would be let
         he (she, it) would be let   they would be let

Past   I was let   we were let
         you were let   you were let
         he (she, it) was let   they were let

Past   I was being let   we are being let
Prog. you were being let   you were being let
         he (she, it) was being let they were being let

Past   I did get let   we did get let
Int.   you did get let   you did get let
         he (she, it) did get let   they did get let

Pres. I have been let   we have been let
Perf. you have been let   you have been let
         he (she, it) has been let   they have been let

Past   I had been let   we had been let
Perf. you had been let   you had been let
         he (she, it) had been let   they had been let

Fut.   I shall have been let   we shall have been let
Perf. you will have been let   you will have been let
         he (she, it) will have been let they will have been let

Cond. I would have been let   we would have been let
Perf. you would have been let   you would have been let
         he (she, it) would have been let they would have been let

IMPERATIVE MOOD
be let

SUBJUNCTIVE MOOD

Pres. if I be let   if we be let
         if you be let   if you be let
         if he (she, it) be let   if they be let

Past   if I were let   if we were let
         if you were let   if you were let
         if he (she, it) were let   if they were let

Fut.   if I should be let   if we should be let
         if you should be let   if you should be let
         if he (she, it) should be let if they should be let

to lie (active voice only)

(intransitive verb)

Infinitive: to lie
Perfect Infinitive: to have lain

Present Participle: lying
Past Participle: lain

INDICATIVE MOOD

Pres.	I lie	we lie
	you lie	you lie
	he (she, it) lies	they lie

Pres. Prog.	I am lying	we are lying
	you are lying	you are lying
	he (she, it) is lying	they are lying

Pres. Int.	I do lie	we do lie
	you do lie	you do lie
	he (she, it) does lie	they do lie

Fut.	I shall lie	we shall lie
	you will lie	you will lie
	he (she, it) will lie	they will lie

Cond.	I would lie	we would lie
	you would lie	you would lie
	he (she, it) would lie	they would lie

Past	I lay	we lay
	you lay	you lay
	he (she, it) lay	they lay

Past Prog.	I was lying	we were lying
	you were lying	you were lying
	he (she, it) was lying	they were lying

Past Int.	I did lay	we did lay
	you did lay	you did lay
	he (she, it) did lay	they did lay

Pres. Perf.	I have lain	we have lain
	you have lain	you have lain
	he (she, it) has lain	they have lain

Past Perf.	I had lain	we had lain
	you had lain	you had lain
	he (she, it) had lain	they had lain

Fut. Perf.	I shall have lain	we shall have lain
	you will have lain	you will have lain
	he (she, it) will have lain	they will have lain

Cond. Perf.	I would have lain	we would have lain
	you would have lain	you would have lain
	he (she, it) would have lain	they would have lain

IMPERATIVE MOOD
lay

SUBJUNCTIVE MOOD

Pres.	if I lie	if we lie
	if you lie	if you lie
	if he (she, it) lie	if they lie

Past	if I lay	if we lay
	if you lay	if you lay
	if he (she, it) lay	if they lay

Fut.	if I should lie	if we should lie
	if you should lie	if you should lie
	if he (she, it) should lie	if they should lie

To lie is an intransitive verb.

It does not take an object.
It describes action, but the action is self-contained.
Like other intransitive verbs, it may be followed by adverbs, adverbial phrases and clauses describing the how, why, when, and where of the action:

HOW: The body lay *in a strange position.* (adverbial phrase)
WHY: She will lie down *to take a nap.* (adverbial phrase)
WHEN: The books have lain untouched *ever since I bought them.* (adverbial clause)
WHERE: It seemed best to lie *low.* (adverb)

NOTE:
Do not confuse this verb with *to lay,* which means *to put, to place:*
I *put* my books on the table.
I *laid* my books on the table

Infinitive: to lose   *Present Participle:* losing
Perfect Infinitive: to have lost   *Past Participle:* lost

INDICATIVE MOOD

Pres.	I lose	we lose
	you lose	you lose
	he (she, it) loses	they lose
Pres.	I am losing	we are losing
Prog.	you are losing	you are losing
	he (she, it) is losing	they are losing
Pres.	I do lose	we do lose
Int.	you do lose	you do lose
	he (she, it) does lose	they do lose
Fut.	I shall lose	we shall lose
	you will lose	you will lose
	he (she, it) will lose	they will lose
Cond.	I would lose	we would lose
	you would lose	you would lose
	he (she, it) would lose	they would lose
Past	I lost	we lost
	you lost	you lost
	he (she, it) lost	they lost
Past	I was losing	we were losing
Prog.	you were losing	you were losing
	he (she, it) was losing	they were losing
Past	I did lose	we did lose
Int.	you did lose	you did lose
	he (she, it) did lose	they did lose
Pres.	I have lost	we have lost
Perf.	you have lost	you have lost
	he (she, it) has lost	they have lost
Past	I had lost	we had lost
Perf.	you had lost	you had lost
	he (she, it) had lost	they had lost
Fut.	I shall have lost	we shall have lost
Perf.	you will have lost	you will have lost
	he (she, it) will have lost	they will have lost
Cond.	I would have lost	we would have lost
Perf.	you would have lost	you would have lost
	he (she, it) would have lost	they would have lost

IMPERATIVE MOOD
lose

SUBJUNCTIVE MOOD

Pres.	if I lose	if we lose
	if you lose	if you lose
	if he (she, it) lose	if they lose
Past	if I lost	if we lost
	if you lost	if you lost
	if he (she, it) lost	if they lost
Fut.	if I should lose	if we should lose
	if you should lose	if you should lose
	if he (she, it) should lose	if they should lose

(passive voice)

Infinitive: to be lost   *Present Participle:* being lost
Perfect Infinitive: to have been lost   *Past Participle:* been lost

INDICATIVE MOOD

Pres. I am lost	we are lost
you are lost	you are lost
he (she, it) is lost	they are lost
Pres. I am being lost	we are being lost
Prog. you are being lost	you are being lost
he (she, it) is being lost	they are being lost
Pres. I do get lost	we do get lost
Int. you do get lost	you do get lost
he (she, it) does get lost	they do get lost
Fut. I shall be lost	we shall be lost
you will be lost	you will be lost
he (she, it) will be lost	they will be lost
Cond. I would be lost	we would be lost
you would be lost	you would be lost
he (she, it) would be lost	they would be lost
Past I was lost	we were lost
you were lost	you were lost
he (she, it) was lost	they were lost
Past I was being lost	we were being lost
Prog. you were being lost	you were being lost
he (she, it) was being lost	they were being lost
Past I did get lost	we did get lost
Int. you did get lost	you did get lost
he (she, it) did get lost	they did get lost
Pres. I have been lost	we have been lost
Perf. you have been lost	you have been lost
he (she, it) has been lost	they have been lost
Past I had been lost	we had been lost
Perf. you had been lost	you had been lost
he (she, it) had been lost	they had been lost
Fut. I shall have been lost	we shall have been lost
Perf. you will have been lost	you will have been lost
he (she, it) will have been lost	they will have been lost
Cond. I would have been lost	we would have been lost
Perf. you would have been lost	you would have been lost
he (she, it) would have been lost	they would have been lost

IMPERATIVE MOOD
be lost

SUBJUNCTIVE MOOD

Pres. if I be lost	if we be lost
if you be lost	if you be lost
if he (she, it) be lost	if they be lost
Past if I were lost	if we were lost
if you were lost	if you were lost
if he (she, it) were lost	if they were lost
Fut. if I should be lost	if we should be lost
if you should be lost	if you should be lost
if he (she, it) should be lost	if they should be lost

Infinitive: to make
Perfect Infinitive: to have made

Present Participle: making
Past Participle: made

INDICATIVE MOOD

Pres.	I make	we make
	you make	you make
	he (she, it) makes	they make

Pres. Prog.	I am making	we are making
	you are making	you are making
	he (she, it) is making	they are making

Pres. Int.	I do make	we do make
	you do make	you do make
	he (she, it) does make	they do make

Fut.	I shall make	we shall make
	you will make	you will make
	he (she, it) will make	they will make

Cond.	I would make	we would make
	you would make	you would make
	he (she, it) would make	they would make

Past	I made	we made
	you made	you made
	he (she, it) made	they made

Past Prog.	I was making	we were making
	you were making	you were making
	he (she, it) was making	they were making

Past Int.	I did make	we did make
	you did make	you did make
	he (she, it) did make	they did make

Pres. Perf.	I have made	we have made
	you have made	you have made
	he (she, it) has made	they have made

Past Perf.	I had made	we had made
	you had made	you had made
	he (she, it) had made	they had made

Fut. Perf.	I shall have made	we shall have made
	you will have made	you will have made
	he (she, it) will have made	they will have made

Cond. Perf.	I would have made	we would have made
	you would have made	you would have made
	he (she, it) would have made	they would have made

IMPERATIVE MOOD
make

SUBJUNCTIVE MOOD

Pres.	if I make	if we make
	if you make	if you make
	if he (she, it) make	if they make

Past	if I made	if we made
	if you made	if you made
	if he (she, it) made	if they made

Fut.	if I should make	if we should make
	if you should make	if you should make
	if he (she, it) should make	if they should make

(passive voice)

Infinitive: to be made   *Present Participle:* being made
Perfect Infinitive: to have been made   *Past Participle:* been made

INDICATIVE MOOD

Pres. I am made
you are made
he (she, it) is made

we are made
you are made
they are made

Pres.
Prog. I am being made
you are being made
he (she, it) is being made

we are being made
you are being made
they are being made

Pres.
Int. I do get made
you do get made
he (she, it) does get made

we do get made
you do get made
they do get made

Fut. I shall be made
you will be made
he (she, it) will be made

we shall be made
you will be made
they will be made

Cond. I would be made
you would be made
he (she, it) would be made

we would be made
you would be made
they would be made

Past I was made
you were made
he (she, it) was made

we were made
you were made
they were made

Past
Prog. I was being made
you were being made
he (she, it) was being made

we were being made
you were being made
they were being made

Past
Int. I did get made
you did get made
he (she, it) did get made

we did get made
you did get made
they did get made

Pres.
Perf. I have been made
you have been made
he (she, it) has been made

we have been made
you have been made
they have been made

Past
Perf. I had been made
you had been made
he (she, it) had been made

we had been made
you had been made
they had been made

Fut.
Perf. I shall have been made
you will have been made
he (she, it) will have been made

we shall have been made
you will have been made
they will have been made

Cond.
Perf. I would have been made
you would have been made
he (she, it) would have been made

we would have been made
you would have been made
they would have been made

IMPERATIVE MOOD
be made

SUBJUNCTIVE MOOD

Pres. if I be made
if you be made
if he (she, it) be made

if we be made
if you be made
if they be made

Past if I were made
if you were made
if he (she, it) were made

if we were made
if you were made
if they were made

Fut. if I should be made
if you should be made
if he (she, it) should be made

if we should be made
if you should be made
if they should be made

to meet (active voice)　　　*Principal Parts:* meet, meeting, met, met

Infinitive: to meet　　　　　　　*Present Participle:* meeting
Perfect Infinitive: to have met　　*Past Participle:* met

INDICATIVE MOOD

Pres.	I meet	we meet
	you meet	you meet
	he (she, it) meets	they meet
Pres.	I am meeting	we are meeting
Prog.	you are meeting	you are meeting
	he (she, it) is meeting	they are meeting
Pres.	I do meet	we do meet
Int.	you do meet	you do meet
	he (she, it) does meet	they do meet
Fut.	I shall meet	we shall meet
	you will meet	you will meet
	he (she, it) will meet	they will meet
Cond.	I would meet	we would meet
	you would meet	you would meet
	he (she, it) would meet	they would meet
Past	I met	we met
	you met	you met
	he (she, it) met	they met
Past	I was meeting	we were meeting
Prog.	you were meeting	you were meeting
	he (she, it) was meeting	they were meeting
Past	I did meet	we did meet
Int.	you did meet	you did meet
	he (she, it) did meet	they did meet
Pres.	I have met	we have met
Perf.	you have met	you have met
	he (she, it) has met	they have met
Past	I had met	we had met
Perf.	you had met	you had met
	he (she, it) had met	they had met
Fut.	I shall have met	we shall have met
Perf.	you will have met	you will have met
	he (she, it) will have met	they will have met
Cond.	I would have met	we would have met
Perf.	you would have met	you would have met
	he (she, it) would have met	they would have met

IMPERATIVE MOOD
meet

SUBJUNCTIVE MOOD

Pres.	if I meet	if we meet
	if you meet	if you meet
	if he (she, it) meet	if they meet
Past	if I met	if we met
	if you met	if you met
	if he (she, it) met	if they met
Fut.	if I should meet	if we should meet
	if you should meet	if you should meet
	if he (she, it) should meet	if they should meet

(passive voice)

Infinitive: to be met   *Present Participle:* being met
Perfect Infinitive: to have been met   *Past Participle:* been met

INDICATIVE MOOD

Pres.	I am met	we are met
	you are met	you are met
	he (she, it) is met	they are met
Pres.	I am being met	we are being met
Prog.	you are being met	you are being met
	he (she, it) is being met	they are being met
Pres.	I do get met	we do get met
Int.	you do get met	you do get met
	he (she, it) does get met	they do get met
Fut.	I shall be met	we shall be met
	you will be met	you will be met
	he (she, it) will be met	they will be met
Cond.	I would be met	we would be met
	you would be met	you would be met
	he (she, it) would be met	they would be met
Past	I was met	we were met
	you were met	you were met
	he (she, it) was met	they were met
Past	I was being met	we were being met
Prog.	you were being met	you were being met
	he (she, it) was being met	they were being met
Past	I did get met	we did get met
Int.	you did get met	you did get met
	he (she, it) did get met	they did get met
Pres.	I have been met	we have been met
Perf.	you have been met	you have been met
	he (she, it) has been met	they have been met
Past	I had been met	we had been met
Perf.	you had been met	you had been met
	he (she, it) had been met	they had been met
Fut.	I shall have been met	we shall have been met
Perf.	you will have been met	you will have been met
	he (she, it) will have been met	they will have been met
Cond.	I would have been met	we would have been met
Perf.	you would have been met	you would have been met
	he (she, it) would have been met	they would have been met

IMPERATIVE MOOD
be met

SUBJUNCTIVE MOOD

Pres.	if I be met	if we be met
	if you be met	if you be met
	if he (she, it) be met	if they be met
Past	if I were met	if we were met
	if you were met	if you were met
	if he (she, it) were met	if they were met
Fut.	if I should be met	if we should be met
	if you should be met	if you should be met
	if he (she, it) should be met	if they should be met

to pay (active voice)   *Principal Parts:* pay, paying, paid, paid

---

Infinitive: to pay   *Present Participle:* paying
Perfect Infinitive: to have paid   *Past Participle:* paid

INDICATIVE MOOD

Pres.	I pay	we pay
	you pay	you pay
	he (she, it) pays	they pay
Pres.	I am paying	we are paying
Prog.	you are paying	you are paying
	he (she, it) is paying	they are paying
Pres.	I do pay	we do pay
Int.	you do pay	you do pay
	he (she, it) does pay	they do pay
Fut.	I shall pay	we shall pay
	you will pay	you will pay
	he (she, it) will pay	they will pay
Cond.	I would pay	we would pay
	you would pay	you would pay
	he (she, it) would pay	they would pay
Past	I paid	we paid
	you paid	you paid
	he (she, it) paid	they paid
Past	I was paying	we were paying
Prog.	you were paying	you were paying
	he (she, it) was paying	they were paying
Past	I did pay	we did pay
Int.	you did pay	you did pay
	he (she, it) did pay	they did pay
Pres.	I have paid	we have paid
Perf.	you have paid	you have paid
	he (she, it) has paid	they have paid
Past	I had paid	we had paid
Perf.	you had paid	you had paid
	he (she, it) had paid	they had paid
Fut.	I shall have paid	we shall have paid
Perf.	you will have paid	you will have paid
	he (she, it) will have paid	they will have paid
Cond.	I would have paid	we would have paid
Perf.	you would have paid	you would have paid
	he (she, it) would have paid	they would have paid

IMPERATIVE MOOD
pay

SUBJUNCTIVE MOOD

Pres.	if I pay	if we pay
	if you pay	if you pay
	if he (she, it) pay	if they pay
Past	if I paid	if we paid
	if you paid	if you paid
	if he (she, it) paid	if they paid
Fut.	if I should pay	if we should pay
	if you should pay	if you should pay
	if he (she, it) should pay	if they should pay

(passive voice)

Infinitive: to be paid   *Present Participle:* being paid
Perfect Infinitive: to have been paid   *Past Participle:* been paid

INDICATIVE MOOD

Pres. I am paid	we are paid
you are paid	you are paid
he (she, it) is paid	they are paid
Pres. I am being paid	we are being paid
Prog. you are being paid	you are being paid
he (she, it) is being paid	they are being paid
Pres. I do get paid	we do get paid
Int. you do get paid	you do get paid
he (she, it) does get paid	they do get paid
Fut. I shall be paid	we shall be paid
you will be paid	you will be paid
he (she, it) will be paid	they will be paid
Cond. I would be paid	we would be paid
you would be paid	you would be paid
he (she, it) would be paid	they would be paid
Past I was paid	we were paid
you were paid	you were paid
he (she, it) was paid	they were paid
Past I was being paid	we were being paid
Prog. you were being paid	you were being paid
he (she, it) was being paid	they were being paid
Past I did get paid	we did get paid
Int. you did get paid	you did get paid
he (she, it) did get paid	they did get paid
Pres. I have been paid	we have been paid
Perf. you have been paid	you have been paid
he (she, it) has been paid	they have been paid
Past I had been paid	we had been paid
Perf. you had been paid	you had been paid
he (she, it) had been paid	they had been paid
Fut. I shall have been paid	we shall have been paid
Perf. you will have been paid	you will have been paid
he (she, it) will have been paid	they will have been paid
Cond. I would have been paid	we would have been paid
Perf. you would have been paid	you would have been paid
he (she, it) would have been paid	they would have been paid

IMPERATIVE MOOD
be paid

SUBJUNCTIVE MOOD

Pres. if I be paid	if we be paid
if you be paid	if you be paid
if he (she, it) be paid	if they be paid
Past if I were paid	if we were paid
if you were paid	if you were paid
if he (she, it) were paid	if they were paid
Fut. if I should be paid	if we should be paid
if you should be paid	if you should be paid
if he (she, it) should be paid	if they should be paid

to put (active voice)   *Principal Parts:* put, putting, put, put

---

Infinitive: to put   *Present Participle:* putting
Perfect Infinitive: to have put   *Past Participle:* put

INDICATIVE MOOD

Pres.	I put	we put
	you put	you put
	he (she, it) puts	they put
Pres.	I am putting	we are putting
Prog.	you are putting	you are putting
	he (she, it) is putting	they are putting
Pres.	I do put	we do put
Int.	you do put	you do put
	he (she, it) does put	they do put
Fut.	I shall put	we shall put
	you will put	you will put
	he (she, it) will put	they will put
Cond.	I would put	we would put
	you would put	you would put
	he (she, it) would put	they would put
Past	I put	we put
	you put	you put
	he (she, it) put	they put
Past	I was putting	we were putting
Prog.	you were putting	you were putting
	he (she, it) was putting	they were putting
Past	I did put	we did put
Int.	you did put	you did put
	he (she, it) did put	they did put
Pres.	I have put	we have put
Perf.	you have put	you have put
	he (she, it) has put	they have put
Past	I had put	we had put
Perf.	you had put	you had put
	he (she, it) had put	they had put
Fut.	I shall have put	we shall have put
Perf.	you will have put	you will have put
	he (she, it) will have put	they will have put
Cond.	I would have put	we would have put
Perf.	you would have put	you would have put
	he (she, it) would have put	they would have put

IMPERATIVE MOOD
put

SUBJUNCTIVE MOOD

Pres.	if I put	if we put
	if you put	if you put
	if he (she, it) put	if they put
Past	if I put	if we put
	if you put	if you put
	if he (she, it) put	if they put
Fut.	if I should put	if we should put
	if you should put	if you should put
	if he (she, it) should put	if they should put

Infinitive: to be put   *Present Participle:* being put
Perfect Infinitive: to have been put   *Past Participle:* been put

INDICATIVE MOOD

Pres.   I am put
you are put
he (she, it) is put

we are put
you are put
they are put

Pres.
Prog.   I am being put
you are being put
he (she, it) is being put

we are being put
you are being put
they are being put

Pres.
Int.   I do get put
you do get put
he (she, it) does get put

we do get put
you do get put
they do get put

Fut.   I shall be put
you will be put
he (she, it) will be put

we shall be put
you will be put
they will be put

Cond.   I would be put
you would be put
he (she, it) would be put

we would be put
you would be put
they would be put

Past   I was put
you were put
he (she, it) was put

we were put
you were put
they were put

Past
Prog.   I was being put
you were being put
he (she, it) was being put

we were being put
you were being put
they were being put

Past
Int.   I did get put
you did get put
he (she, it) did get put

we did get put
you did get put
they did get put

Pres.
Perf.   I have been put
you have been put
he (she, it) has been put

we have been put
you have been put
they have been put

Past
Perf.   I had been put
you had been put
he (she, it) had been put

we had been put
you had been put
they had been put

Fut.
Perf.   I shall have been put
you will have been put
he (she, it) will have been put

we shall have been put
you will have been put
they will have been put

Cond.
Perf.   I would have been put
you would have been put
he (she, it) would have been put

we would have been put
you would have been put
they would have been put

IMPERATIVE MOOD
be put

SUBJUNCTIVE MOOD

Pres.   if I be put
if you be put
if he (she, it) be put

if we be put
if you be put
if they be put

Past   if I were put
if you were put
if he (she, it) were put

if we were put
if you were put
if they were put

Fut.   if I should be put
if you should be put
if he (she, it) should be put

if we should be put
if you should be put
if they should be put

263

to read (active voice)

Infinitive: to read
Perfect Infinitive: to have read

Present Participle: reading
Past Participle: read

INDICATIVE MOOD

Pres.
I read
you read
he (she, it) reads

we read
you read
they read

Pres. Prog.
I am reading
you are reading
he (she, it) is reading

we are reading
you are reading
they are reading

Pres. Int.
I do read
you do read
he (she, it) does read

we do read
you do read
they do read

Fut.
I shall read
you will read
he (she, it) will read

we shall read
you will read
they will read

Cond.
I would read
you would read
he (she, it) would read

we would read
you would read
they would read

Past
I read
you read
he (she, it) read

we read
you read
they read

Past Prog.
I was reading
you were reading
he (she, it) was reading

we were reading
you were reading
they were reading

Past Int.
I did read
you did read
he (she, it) did read

we did read
you did read
they did read

Pres. Perf.
I have read
you have read
he (she, it) has read

we have read
you have read
they have read

Past Perf.
I had read
you had read
he (she, it) had read

we had read
you had read
they had read

Fut. Perf.
I shall have read
you will have read
he (she, it) will have read

we shall have read
you will have read
they will have read

Cond. Perf.
I would have read
you would have read
he (she, it) would have read

we would have read
you would have read
they would have read

IMPERATIVE MOOD
read

SUBJUNCTIVE MOOD

Pres.
if I read
if you read
if he (she, it) read

if we read
if you read
if they read

Past
if I read
if you read
if he (she, it) read

if we read
if you read
if they read

Fut.
if I should read
if you should read
if he (she, it) should read

if we should read
if you should read
if they should read

Infinitive: to be read   *Present Participle:* being read
Perfect Infinitive: to have been read   *Past Participle:* been read

INDICATIVE MOOD

Pres.	I am read	we are read
	you are read	you are read
	he (she, it) is read	they are read
Pres.	I am being read	we are being read
Prog.	you are being read	you are being read
	he (she, it) is being read	they are being read
Pres.	I do get read	we do get read
Int.	you do get read	you do get read
	he (she, it) does get read	they do get read
Fut.	I shall be read	we shall be read
	you will be read	you will be read
	he (she, it) will be read	they will be read
Cond.	I would be read	we would be read
	you would be read	you would be read
	he (she, it) would be read	they would be read
Past	I was read	we were read
	you were read	you were read
	he (she, it) was read	they were read
Past	I was being read	we were being read
Prog.	you were being read	you were being read
	he (she, it) was being read	they were being read
Past	I did get read	we did get read
Int.	you did get read	you did get read
	he (she, it) did get read	they did get read
Pres.	I have been read	we have been read
Perf.	you have been read	you have been read
	he (she, it) has been read	they have been read
Past	I had been read	we had been read
Perf.	you had been read	you had been read
	he (she, it) had been read	they had been read
Fut.	I shall have been read	we shall have been read
Perf.	you will have been read	you will have been read
	he (she, it) will have been read	they will have been read
Cond.	I would have been read	we would have been read
Perf.	you would have been read	you would have been read
	he (she, it) would have been read	they would have been read

IMPERATIVE MOOD
be read

SUBJUNCTIVE MOOD

Pres.	if I be read	if we be read
	if you be read	if you be read
	if he (she, it) be read	if they be read
Past	if I were read	if we were read
	if you were read	if you were read
	if he (she, it) were read	if they were read
Fut.	if I should be read	if we should be read
	if you should be read	if you should be read
	if he (she, it) should be read	if they should be read

to ride (active voice)   *Principal Parts:* ride, riding, rode, ridden

---

Infinitive: to ride   *Present Participle:* riding
Perfect Infinitive: to have ridden   *Past Participle:* ridden

INDICATIVE MOOD

Pres. I ride   we ride
you ride   you ride
he (she, it) rides   they ride

Pres. I am riding   we are riding
Prog. you are riding   you are riding
he (she, it) is riding   they are riding

Pres. I do ride   we do ride
Int. you do ride   you do ride
he (she, it) does ride   they do ride

Fut. I shall ride   we shall ride
you will ride   you will ride
he (she, it) will ride   they will ride

Cond. I would ride   we would ride
you would ride   you would ride
he (she, it) would ride   they would ride

Past I rode   we rode
you rode   you rode
he (she, it) rode   they rode

Past I was riding   we were riding
Prog. you were riding   you were riding
he (she, it) was riding   they were riding

Past I did ride   we did ride
Int. you did ride   you did ride
he (she, it) did ride   they did ride

Pres. I have ridden   we have ridden
Perf. you have ridden   you have ridden
he (she, it) has ridden   they have ridden

Past I had ridden   we had ridden
Perf. you had ridden   you had ridden
he (she, it) had ridden   they had ridden

Fut. I shall have ridden   we shall have ridden
Perf. you will have ridden   you will have ridden
he (she, it) will have ridden   they will have ridden

Cond. I would have ridden   we would have ridden
Perf. you would have ridden   you would have ridden
he (she, it) would have ridden   they would have ridden

IMPERATIVE MOOD
ride

SUBJUNCTIVE MOOD

Pres. if I ride   if we ride
if you ride   if you ride
if he (she, it) ride   if they ride

Past if I rode   if we rode
if you rode   if you rode
if he (she, it) rode   if they rode

Fut. if I should ride   if we should ride
if you should ride   if you should ride
if he (she, it) should ride   if they should ride

Infinitive: to be ridden   *Present Participle:* being ridden
Perfect Infinitive: to have been ridden   *Past Participle:* been ridden

INDICATIVE MOOD

Pres. I am ridden   we are ridden
you are ridden   you are ridden
he (she, it) is ridden   they are ridden

Pres. I am being ridden   we are being ridden
Prog. you are being ridden   you are being ridden
he (she, it) is being ridden   they are being ridden

Pres. I do get ridden   we do get ridden
Int. you do get ridden   you do get ridden
he (she, it) does get ridden   they do get ridden

Fut. I shall be ridden   we shall be ridden
you will be ridden   you will be ridden
he (she, it) will be ridden   they will be ridden

Cond. I would be ridden   we would be ridden
you would be ridden   you would be ridden
he (she, it) would be ridden   they would be ridden

Past I was ridden   we were ridden
you were ridden   you were ridden
he (she, it) was ridden   they were ridden

Past I was being ridden   we were being ridden
Prog. you were being ridden   you were being ridden
he (she, it) was being ridden   they were being ridden

Past I did get ridden   we did get ridden
Int. you did get ridden   you did get ridden
he (she, it) did get ridden   they did get ridden

Pres. I have been ridden   we have been ridden
Perf. you have been ridden   you have been ridden
he (she, it) has been ridden   they have been ridden

Past I had been ridden   we had been ridden
Perf. you had been ridden   you had been ridden
he (she, it) had been ridden   they had been ridden

Fut. I shall have been ridden   we shall have been ridden
Perf. you will have been ridden   you will have been ridden
he (she, it) will have been ridden they will have been ridden

Cond. I would have been ridden   we would have been ridden
Perf. you would have been ridden   you would have been ridden
he (she, it) would have been ridden they would have been ridden

IMPERATIVE MOOD
be ridden

SUBJUNCTIVE MOOD

Pres. if I be ridden   if we be ridden
if you be ridden   if you be ridden
if he (she, it) be ridden   if they be ridden

Past if I were ridden   if we were ridden
if you were ridden   if you were ridden
if he (she, it) were ridden   if they were ridden

Fut. if I should be ridden   if we should be ridden
if you should be ridden   if you should be ridden
if he (she, it) should be ridden if they should be ridden

Infinitive: to ring
Perfect Infinitive: to have rung

Present Participle: ringing
Past Participle: rung

INDICATIVE MOOD

Pres.	I ring	we ring
	you ring	you ring
	he (she, it) rings	they ring
Pres. Prog.	I am ringing	we are ringing
	you are ringing	you are ringing
	he (she, it) is ringing	they are ringing
Pres. Int.	I do ring	we do ring
	you do ring	you do ring
	he (she, it) does ring	they do ring
Fut.	I shall ring	we shall ring
	you will ring	you will ring
	he (she, it) will ring	they will ring
Cond.	I would ring	we would ring
	you would ring	you would ring
	he (she, it) would ring	they would ring
Past	I rang	we rang
	you rang	you rang
	he (she, it) rang	they rang
Past Prog.	I was ringing	we were ringing
	you were ringing	you were ringing
	he (she, it) was ringing	they were ringing
Past Int.	I did ring	we did ring
	you did ring	you did ring
	he (she, it) did ring	they did ring
Pres. Perf.	I have rung	we have rung
	you have rung	you have rung
	he (she, it) has rung	they have rung
Past Perf.	I had rung	we had rung
	you had rung	you had rung
	he (she, it) had rung	they had rung
Fut. Perf.	I shall have rung	we shall have rung
	you will have rung	you will have rung
	he (she, it) will have rung	they will have rung
Cond. Perf.	I would have rung	we would have rung
	you would have rung	you would have rung
	he (she, it) would have rung	they would have rung

IMPERATIVE MOOD
ring

SUBJUNCTIVE MOOD

Pres.	if I ring	if we ring
	if you ring	if you ring
	if he (she, it) ring	if they ring
Past	if I rang	if we rang
	if you rang	if you rang
	if he (she, it) rang	if they rang
Fut.	if I should ring	if we should ring
	if you should ring	if you should ring
	if he (she, it) should ring	if they should ring

Infinitive: to be rung   *Present Participle:* being rung
Perfect Infinitive: to have been rung   *Past Participle:* been rung

INDICATIVE MOOD

Pres.   I am rung / we are rung
you are rung / you are rung
he (she, it) is rung / they are rung

Pres. I am being rung / we are being rung
Prog. you are being rung / you are being rung
he (she, it) is being rung / they are being rung

Pres. I do get rung / we do get rung
Int. you do get rung / you do get rung
he (she, it) does get rung / they do get rung

Fut. I shall be rung / we shall be rung
you will be rung / you will be rung
he (she, it) will be rung / they will be rung

Cond. I would be rung / we would be rung
you would be rung / you would be rung
he (she, it) would be rung / they would be rung

Past I was rung / we were rung
you were rung / you were rung
he (she, it) was rung / they were rung

Past I was being rung / we were being rung
Prog. you were being rung / you were being rung
he (she, it) was being rung / they were being rung

Past I did get rung / we did get rung
Int. you did get rung / you did get rung
he (she, it) did get rung / they did get rung

Pres. I have been rung / we have been rung
Perf. you have been rung / you have been rung
he (she, it) has been rung / they have been rung

Past I had been rung / we had been rung
Perf. you had been rung / you had been rung
he (she, it) had been rung / they had been rung

Fut. I shall have been rung / we shall have been rung
Perf. you will have been rung / you will have been rung
he (she, it) will have been rung / they will have been rung

Cond. I would have been rung / we would have been rung
Perf. you would have been rung / you would have been rung
he (she, it) would have been rung / they would have been rung

IMPERATIVE MOOD
be rung

SUBJUNCTIVE MOOD

Pres. if I be rung / if we be rung
if you be rung / if you be rung
if he (she, it) be rung / if they be rung

Past if I were rung / if we were rung
if you were rung / if you were rung
if he (she, it) were rung / if they were rung

Fut. if I should be rung / if we should be rung
if you should be rung / if you should be rung
if he (she, it) should be rung / if they should be rung

269

to rise (active voice only)
also: to arise

Principal Parts: rise, rising, rose, risen

(intransitive verb)

Infinitive: to rise
Perfect Infinitive: to have risen

Present Participle: rising
Past Participle: risen

INDICATIVE MOOD

Pres.	I rise	we rise
	you rise	you rise
	he (she, it) rises	they rise
Pres.	I am rising	we are rising
Prog.	you are rising	you are rising
	he (she, it) is rising	they are rising
Pres.	I do rise	we do rise
Int.	you do rise	you do rise
	he (she, it) does rise	they do rise
Fut.	I shall rise	we shall rise
	you will rise	you will rise
	he (she, it) will rise	they will rise
Cond.	I would rise	we would rise
	you would rise	you would rise
	he (she, it) would rise	they would rise
Past	I rose	we rose
	you rose	you rose
	he (she, it) rose	they rose
Past	I was rising	we were rising
Prog.	you were rising	you were rising
	he (she, it) was rising	they were rising
Past	I did rise	we did rise
Int.	you did rise	you did rise
	he (she, it) did rise	they did rise
Pres.	I have risen	we have risen
Perf.	you have risen	you have risen
	he (she, it) has risen	they have risen
Past	I had risen	we had risen
Perf.	you had risen	you had risen
	he (she, it) had risen	they had risen
Fut.	I shall have risen	we shall have risen
Perf.	you will have risen	you will have risen
	he (she, it) will have risen	they will have risen
Cond.	I would have risen	we would have risen
Perf.	you would have risen	you would have risen
	he (she, it) would have risen	they would have risen

IMPERATIVE MOOD
rise

SUBJUNCTIVE MOOD

Pres.	if I rise	if we rise
	if you rise	if you rise
	if he (she, it) rise	if they rise
Past	if I rose	if we rose
	if you rose	if you rose
	if he (she, it) rose	if they rose
Fut.	if I should rise	if we should rise
	if you should rise	if you should rise
	if he (she, it) should rise	if they should rise

***To rise* is an intransitive verb.**

It does not take an object.

It describes action, but the action is self-contained.

Like other intransitive verbs, it may be followed by adverbs, adverbial phrases and clauses describing the how, why, when, and where of the action.

HOW: The sun rose *brilliantly*. (adverb)

WHY: He rose *to address the audience*. (adverbial phrase)

WHEN: I always rise *when the alarm rings*. (adverbial clause)

WHERE: The moon has risen *above the horizon*. (adverbial phrase)

to run (active voice)

Infinitive: to run
Perfect Infinitive: to have run

Present Participle: running
Past Participle: run

INDICATIVE MOOD

Pres. I run
you run
he (she, it) runs

we run
you run
they run

Pres. Prog. I am running
you are running
he (she, it) is running

we are running
you are running
they are running

Pres. Int. I do run
you do run
he (she, it) does run

we do run
you do run
they do run

Fut. I shall run
you will run
he (she, it) will run

we shall run
you will run
they will run

Cond. I would run
you would run
he (she, it) would run

we would run
you would run
they would run

Past I ran
you ran
he (she, it) ran

we ran
you ran
they ran

Past Prog. I was running
you were running
he (she, it) was running

we were running
you were running
they were running

Past Int. I did run
you did run
he (she, it) did run

we did run
you did run
they did run

Pres. Perf. I have run
you have run
he (she, it) has run

we have run
you have run
they have run

Past Perf. I had run
you had run
he (she, it) had run

we had run
you had run
they had run

Fut. Perf. I shall have run
you will have run
he (she, it) will have run

we shall have run
you will have run
they will have run

Cond. Perf. I would have run
you would have run
he (she, it) would have run

we would have run
you would have run
they would have run

IMPERATIVE MOOD
run

SUBJUNCTIVE MOOD

Pres. if I run
if you run
if he (she, it) run

if we run
if you run
if they run

Past if I ran
if you ran
if he (she, it) ran

if we ran
if you ran
if they ran

Fut. if I should run
if you should run
if he (she, it) should run

if we should run
if you should run
if they should run

(passive voice)

Infinitive: to be run
Perfect Infinitive: to have been run

Present Participle: being run
Past Participle: been run

INDICATIVE MOOD

Pres.	I am run	we are run
	you are run	you are run
	he (she, it) is run	they are run
Pres.	I am being run	we are being run
Prog.	you are being run	you are being run
	he (she, it) is being run	they are being run
Pres.	I do get run	we do get run
Int.	you do get run	you do get run
	he (she, it) does get run	they do get run
Fut.	I shall be run	we shall be run
	you will be run	you will be run
	he (she, it) will be run	they will be run
Cond.	I would be run	we would be run
	you would be run	you would be run
	he (she, it) would be run	they would be run
Past	I was run	we were run
	you were run	you were run
	he (she, it) was run	they were run
Past	I was being run	we were being run
Prog.	you were being run	you were being run
	he (she, it) was being run	they were being run
Past	I did get run	we did get run
Int.	you did get run	you did get run
	he (she, it) did get run	they did get run
Pres.	I have been run	we have been run
Perf.	you have been run	you have been run
	he (she, it) has been run	they have been run
Past	I had been run	we had been run
Perf.	you had been run	you had been run
	he (she, it) had been run	they had been run
Fut.	I shall have been run	we shall have been run
Perf.	you will have been run	you will have been run
	he (she, it) will have been run	they will have been run
Cond.	I would have been run	we would have been run
Perf.	you would have been run	you would have been run
	he (she, it) would have been run	they would have been run

IMPERATIVE MOOD
be run

SUBJUNCTIVE MOOD

Pres.	if I be run	if we be run
	if you be run	if you be run
	if he (she, it) be run	if they be run
Past	if I were run	if we were run
	if you were run	if you were run
	if he (she, it) were run	if they were run
Fut.	if I should be run	if we should be run
	if you should be run	if you should be run
	if he (she, it) should be run	if they should be run

to say (active voice)   *Principal Parts:* say, saying, said, said

---

Infinitive: to say   *Present Participle:* saying
Perfect Infinitive: to have said   *Past Participle:* said

INDICATIVE MOOD

Pres.	I say	we say
	you say	you say
	he (she, it) says	they say
Pres.	I am saying	we are saying
Prog.	you are saying	you are saying
	he (she, it) is saying	they are saying
Pres.	I do say	we do say
Int.	you do say	you do say
	he (she, it) does say	they do say
Fut.	I shall say	we shall say
	you will say	you will say
	he (she, it) will say	they will say
Cond.	I would say	we would say
	you would say	you would say
	he (she, it) would say	they would say
Past	I said	we said
	you said	you said
	he (she, it) said	they said
Past	I was saying	we were saying
Prog.	you were saying	you were saying
	he (she, it) was saying	they were saying
Past	I did say	we did say
Int.	you did say	you did say
	he (she, it) did say	they did say
Pres.	I have said	we have said
Perf.	you have said	you have said
	he (she, it) has said	they have said
Past	I had said	we had said
Perf.	you had said	you had said
	he (she, it) had said	they had said
Fut.	I shall have said	we shall have said
Perf.	you will have said	you will have said
	he (she, it) will have said	they will have said
Cond.	I would have said	we would have said
Perf.	you would have said	you would have said
	he (she, it) would have said	they would have said

IMPERATIVE MOOD
say

SUBJUNCTIVE MOOD

Pres.	if I say	if we say
	if you say	if you say
	if he (she, it) say	if they say
Past	if I said	if we said
	if you said	if you said
	if he (she, it) said	if they said
Fut.	if I should say	if we should say
	if you should say	if you should say
	if he (she, it) should say	if they should say

274

(passive voice)

Infinitive: to be said   *Present Participle:* being said
Perfect Infinitive: to have been said   *Past Participle:* been said

INDICATIVE MOOD

Pres. I am said
you are said
he (she, it) is said

we are said
you are said
they are said

Pres. I am being said
Prog. you are being said
he (she, it) is being said

we are being said
you are being said
they are being said

Pres. I do get said
Int. you do get said
he (she, it) does get said

we do get said
you do get said
they do get said

Fut. I shall be said
you will be said
he (she, it) will be said

we shall be said
you will be said
they will be said

Cond. I would be said
you would be said
he (she, it) would be said

we would be said
you would be said
they would be said

Past I was said
you were said
he (she, it) was said

we were said
you were said
they were said

Past I was being said
Prog. you were being said
he (she, it) was being said

we were being said
you were being said
they were being said

Past I did get said
Int. you did get said
he (she, it) did get said

we did get said
you did get said
they did get said

Pres. I have been said
Perf. you have been said
he (she, it) has been said

we have been said
you have been said
they have been said

Past I had been said
Perf. you had been said
he (she, it) had been said

we had been said
you had been said
they had been said

Fut. I shall have been said
Perf. you will have been said
he (she, it) will have been said

we shall have been said
you will have been said
they will have been said

Cond. I would have been said
Perf. you would have been said
he (she, it) would have been said

we would have been said
you would have been said
they would have been said

IMPERATIVE MOOD
be said

SUBJUNCTIVE MOOD

Pres. if I be said
if you be said
if he (she, it) be said

if we be said
if you be said
if they be said

Past if I were said
if you were said
if he (she, it) were said

if we were said
if you were said
if they were said

Fut. if I should be said
if you should be said
if he (she, it) should be said

if we should be said
if you should be said
if they should be said

to see (active voice)   *Principal Parts:* see, seeing, saw, seen

Infinitive: to see   *Present Participle:* seeing
Perfect Infinitive: to have seen   *Past Participle:* seen

INDICATIVE MOOD

Pres.   I see   we see
         you see   you see
         he (she, it) sees   they see

Pres.   I am seeing   we are seeing
Prog.   you are seeing   you are seeing
         he (she, it) is seeing   they are seeing

Pres.   I do see   we do see
Int.   you do see   you do see
         he (she, it) does see   they do see

Fut.   I shall see   we shall see
         you will see   you will see
         he (she, it) will see   they will see

Cond.   I would see   we would see
         you would see   you would see
         he (she, it) would see   they would see

Past   I saw   we saw
         you saw   you saw
         he (she, it) saw   they saw

Past   I was seeing   we were seeing
Prog.   you were seeing   you were seeing
         he (she, it) was seeing   they were seeing

Past   I did see   we did see
Int.   you did see   you did see
         he (she, it) did see   they did see

Pres.   I have seen   we have seen
Perf.   you have seen   you have seen
         he (she, it) has seen   they have seen

Past   I had seen   we had seen
Perf.   you had seen   you had seen
         he (she, it) had seen   they had seen

Fut.   I shall have seen   we shall have seen
Perf.   you will have seen   you will have seen
         he (she, it) will have seen   they will have seen

Cond.   I would have seen   we would have seen
Perf.   you would have seen   you would have seen
         he (she, it) would have seen   they would have seen

IMPERATIVE MOOD
see

SUBJUNCTIVE MOOD

Pres.   if I see   if we see
         if you see   if you see
         if he (she, it) see   if they see

Past   if I saw   if we saw
         if you saw   if you saw
         if he (she, it) saw   if they saw

Fut.   if I should see   if we should see
         if you should see   if you should see
         if he (she, it) should see   if they should see

(passive voice)

Infinitive: to be seen   *Present Participle:* being seen
Perfect Infinitive: to have been seen   *Past Participle:* been seen

INDICATIVE MOOD

Pres. I am seen	we are seen
you are seen	you are seen
he (she, it) is seen	they are seen
Pres. I am being seen	we are being seen
Prog. you are being seen	you are being seen
he (she, it) is being seen	they are being seen
Pres. I do get seen	we do get seen
Int. you do get seen	you do get seen
he (she, it) does get seen	they do get seen
Fut. I shall be seen	we shall be seen
you will be seen	you will be seen
he (she, it) will be seen	they will be seen
Cond. I would be seen	we would be seen
you would be seen	you would be seen
he (she, it) would be seen	they would be seen
Past I was seen	we were seen
you were seen	you were seen
he (she, it) was seen	they were seen
Past I was being seen	we were being seen
Prog. you were being seen	you were being seen
he (she, it) was being seen	they were being seen
Past I did get seen	we did get seen
Int. you did get seen	you did get seen
he (she, it) did get seen	they did get seen
Pres. I have been seen	we have been seen
Perf. you have been seen	you have been seen
he (she, it) has been seen	they have been seen
Past I had been seen	we had been seen
Perf. you had been seen	you had been seen
he (she, it) had been seen	they had been seen
Fut. I shall have been seen	we shall have been seen
Perf. you will have been seen	you will have been seen
he (she, it) will have been seen	they will have been seen
Cond. I would have been seen	we would have been seen
Perf. you would have been seen	you would have been seen
he (she, it) would have been seen	they would have been seen

IMPERATIVE MOOD
be seen

SUBJUNCTIVE MOOD

Pres. if I be seen	if we be seen
if you be seen	if you be seen
if he (she, it) be seen	if they be seen
Past if I were seen	if we were seen
if you were seen	if you were seen
if he (she, it) were seen	if they were seen
Fut. if I should be seen	if we should be seen
if you should be seen	if you should be seen
if he (she, it) should be seen	if they should be seen

to seek (active voice)   *Principal Parts:* seek, seeking, sought, sought

Infinitive: to seek   *Present Participle:* seeking
Perfect Infinitive: to have sought   *Past Participle:* sought

INDICATIVE MOOD

Pres. I seek	we seek
you seek	you seek
he (she, it) seeks	they seek
Pres. I am seeking	we are seeking
Prog. you are seeking	you are seeking
he (she, it) is seeking	they are seeking
Pres. I do seek	we do seek
Int. you do seek	you do seek
he (she, it) does seek	they do seek
Fut. I shall seek	we shall seek
you will seek	you will seek
he (she, it) will seek	they will seek
Cond. I would seek	we would seek
you would seek	you would seek
he (she, it) would seek	they would seek
Past I sought	we sought
you sought	you sought
he (she, it) sought	they sought
Past I was seeking	we were seeking
Prog. you were seeking	you were seeking
he (she, it) was seeking	they were seeking
Past I did seek	we did seek
Int. you did seek	you did seek
he (she, it) did seek	they did seek
Pres. I have sought	we have sought
Perf. you have sought	you have sought
he (she, it) has sought	they have sought
Past I had sought	we had sought
Perf. you had sought	you had sought
he (she, it) had sought	they had sought
Fut. I shall have sought	we shall have sought
Perf. you will have sought	you will have sought
he (she, it) will have sought	they will have sought
Cond. I would have sought	we would have sought
Perf. you would have sought	you would have sought
he (she, it) would have sought	they would have sought

IMPERATIVE MOOD
seek

SUBJUNCTIVE MOOD

Pres. if I seek	if we seek
if you seek	if you seek
if he (she, it) seek	if they seek
Past if I sought	if we sought
if you sought	if you sought
if he (she, it) sought	if they sought
Fut. if I should seek	if we should seek
if you should seek	if you should seek
if he (she, it) should seek	if they should seek

(passive voice)

Infinitive: to be sought   *Present Participle:* being sought
Perfect Infinitive: to have been sought   *Past Participle:* been sought

INDICATIVE MOOD

Pres.   I am sought
you are sought
he (she, it) is sought

we are sought
you are sought
they are sought

Pres.   I am being sought
Prog.   you are being sought
he (she, it) is being sought

we are being sought
you are being sought
they are being sought

Pres.   I do get sought
Int.   you do get sought
he (she, it) does get sought

we do get sought
you do get sought
they do get sought

Fut.   I shall be sought
you will be sought
he (she, it) will be sought

we shall be sought
you will be sought
they will be sought

Cond.   I would be sought
you would be sought
he (she, it) would be sought

we would be sought
you would be sought
they would be sought

Past   I was sought
you were sought
he (she, it) was sought

we were sought
you were sought
they were sought

Past   I was being sought
Prog.   you were being sought
he (she, it) was being sought

we were being sought
you were being sought
they were being sought

Past   I did get sought
Int.   you did get sought
he (she, it) did get sought

we did get sought
you did get sought
they did get sought

Pres.   I have been sought
Perf.   you have been sought
he (she, it) has been sought

we have been sought
you have been sought
they have been sought

Past   I had been sought
Perf.   you had been sought
he (she, it) had been sought

we had been sought
you had been sought
they had been sought

Fut.   I shall have been sought
Perf.   you will have been sought
he (she, it) will have been sought

we shall have been sought
you will have been sought
they will have been sought

Cond.   I would have been sought
Perf.   you would have been sought
he (she, it) would have been sought

we would have been sought
you would have been sought
they would have been sought

IMPERATIVE MOOD
be sought

SUBJUNCTIVE MOOD

Pres.   if I be sought
if you be sought
if he (she, it) be sought

if we be sought
if you be sought
if they be sought

Past   if I were sought
if you were sought
if he (she, it) were sought

if we were sought
if you were sought
if they were sought

Fut.   if I should be sought
if you should be sought
if he (she, it) should be sought

if we should be sought
if you should be sought
if they should be sought

to sell (active voice)   *Principal Parts:* sell, selling, sold, sold

Infinitive: to sell
Perfect Infinitive: to have sold

Present Participle: selling
Past Participle: sold

INDICATIVE MOOD

Pres. I sell
you sell
he (she, it) sells

we sell
you sell
they sell

Pres. I am selling
Prog. you are selling
he (she, it) is selling

we are selling
you are selling
they are selling

Pres. I do sell
Int. you do sell
he (she, it) does sell

we do sell
you do sell
they do sell

Fut. I shall sell
you will sell
he (she, it) will sell

we shall sell
you will sell
they will sell

Cond. I would sell
you would sell
he (she, it) would sell

we would sell
you would sell
they would sell

Past I sold
you sold
he (she, it) sold

we sold
you sold
they sold

Past I was selling
Prog. you were selling
he (she, it) was selling

we were selling
you were selling
they were selling

Past I did sell
Int. you did sell
he (she, it) did sell

we did sell
you did sell
they did sell

Pres. I have sold
Perf. you have sold
he (she, it) has sold

we have sold
you have sold
they have sold

Past I had sold
Perf. you had sold
he (she, it) had sold

we had sold
you had sold
they had sold

Fut. I shall have sold
Perf. you will have sold
he (she, it) will have sold

we shall have sold
you will have sold
they will have sold

Cond. I would have sold
Perf. you would have sold
he (she, it) would have sold

we would have sold
you would have sold
they would have sold

IMPERATIVE MOOD
sell

SUBJUNCTIVE MOOD

Pres. if I sell
if you sell
if he (she, it) sell

if we sell
if you sell
if they sell

Past if I sold
if you sold
if he (she, it) sold

if we sold
if you sold
if they sold

Fut. if I should sell
if you should sell
if he (she, it) should sell

if we should sell
if you should sell
if they should sell

Infinitive: to be sold   *Present Participle:* being sold
Perfect Infinitive: to have been sold   *Past Participle:* been sold

INDICATIVE MOOD

Pres. I am sold
you are sold
he (she, it) is sold

we are sold
you are sold
they are sold

Pres. I am being sold
Prog. you are being sold
he (she, it) is being sold

we are being sold
you are being sold
they are being sold

Pres. I do get sold
Int. you do get sold
he (she, it) does get sold

we do get sold
you do get sold
they do get sold

Fut. I shall be sold
you will be sold
he (she, it) will be sold

we shall be sold
you will be sold
they will be sold

Cond. I would be sold
you would be sold
he (she, it) would be sold

we would be sold
you would be sold
they would be sold

Past I was sold
you were sold
he (she, it) was sold

we were sold
you were sold
they were sold

Past I was being sold
Prog. you were being sold
he (she, it) was being sold

we were being sold
you were being sold
they were being sold

Past I did get sold
Int. you did get sold
he (she, it) did get sold

we did get sold
you did get sold
they did get sold

Pres. I have been sold
Perf. you have been sold
he (she, it) has been sold

we have been sold
you have been sold
they have been sold

Past I had been sold
Perf. you had been sold
he (she, it) had been sold

we had been sold
you had been sold
they had been sold

Fut. I shall have been sold
Perf. you will have been sold
he (she, it) will have been sold

we shall have been sold
you will have been sold
they will have been sold

Cond. I would have been sold
Perf. you would have been sold
he (she, it) would have been sold

we would have been sold
you would have been sold
they would have been sold

IMPERATIVE MOOD
be sold

SUBJUNCTIVE MOOD

Pres. if I be sold
if you be sold
if he (she, it) be sold

if we be sold
if you be sold
if they be sold

Past if I were sold
if you were sold
if he (she, it) were sold

if we were sold
if you were sold
if they were sold

Fut. if I should be sold
if you should be sold
if he (she, it) should be sold

if we should be sold
if you should be sold
if they should be sold

to send (active voice)   *Principal Parts:* send, sending, sent, sent

Infinitive: to send   *Present Participle:* sending
Perfect Infinitive: to have sent   *Past Participle:* sent

INDICATIVE MOOD

Pres. I send   we send
        you send   you send
        he (she, it) sends   they send

Pres. I am sending   we are sending
Prog. you are sending   you are sending
        he (she, it) is sending   they are sending

Pres. I do send   we do send
Int. you do send   you do send
        he (she, it) does send   they do send

Fut. I shall send   we shall send
        you will send   you will send
        he (she, it) will send   they will send

Cond. I would send   we would send
        you would send   you would send
        he (she, it) would send   they would send

Past I sent   we sent
        you sent   you sent
        he (she, it) sent   they sent

Past I was sending   we were sending
Prog. you were sending   you were sending
        he (she, it) was sending   they were sending

Past I did send   we did send
Int. you did send   you did send
        he (she, it) did send   they did send

Pres. I have sent   we have sent
Perf. you have sent   you have sent
        he (she, it) has sent   they have sent

Past I had sent   we had sent
Perf. you had sent   you had sent
        he (she, it) had sent   they had sent

Fut. I shall have sent   we shall have sent
Perf. you will have sent   you will have sent
        he (she, it) will have sent   they will have sent

Cond. I would have sent   we would have sent
Perf. you would have sent   you would have sent
        he (she, it) would have sent   they would have sent

IMPERATIVE MOOD
send

SUBJUNCTIVE MOOD

Pres. if I send   if we send
        if you send   if you send
        if he (she, it) send   if they send

Past if I sent   if we sent
        if you sent   if you sent
        if he (she, it) sent   if they sent

Fut. if I should send   if we should send
        if you should send   if you should send
        if he (she, it) should send   if they should send

(passive voice)

Infinitive: to be sent   *Present Participle:* being sent
Perfect Infinitive: to have been sent   *Past Participle:* been sent

INDICATIVE MOOD

Pres.	I am sent	we are sent
	you are sent	you are sent
	he (she, it) is sent	they are sent
Pres.	I am being sent	we are being sent
Prog.	you are being sent	you are being sent
	he (she, it) is being sent	they are being sent
Pres.	I do get sent	we do get sent
Int.	you do get sent	you do get sent
	he (she, it) does get sent	they do get sent
Fut.	I shall be sent	we shall be sent
	you will be sent	you will be sent
	he (she, it) will be sent	they will be sent
Cond.	I would be sent	we would be sent
	you would be sent	you would be sent
	he (she, it) would be sent	they would be sent
Past	I was sent	we were sent
	you were sent	you were sent
	he (she, it) was sent	they were sent
Past	I was being sent	we were being sent
Prog.	you were being sent	you were being sent
	he (she, it) was being sent	they were being sent
Past	I did get sent	we did get sent
Int.	you did get sent	you did get sent
	he (she, it) did get sent	they did get sent
Pres.	I have been sent	we have been sent
Perf.	you have been sent	you have been sent
	he (she, it) has been sent	they have been sent
Past	I had been sent	we had been sent
Perf.	you had been sent	you had been sent
	he (she, it) had been sent	they had been sent
Fut.	I shall have been sent	we shall have been sent
Perf.	you will have been sent	you will have been sent
	he (she, it) will have been sent	they will have been sent
Cond.	I would have been sent	we would have been sent
Perf.	you would have been sent	you would have been sent
	he (she, it) would have been sent	they would have been sent

IMPERATIVE MOOD
be sent

SUBJUNCTIVE MOOD

Pres.	if I be sent	if we be sent
	if you be sent	if you be sent
	if he (she, it) be sent	if they be sent
Past	if I were sent	if we were sent
	if you were sent	if you were sent
	if he (she, it) were sent	if they were sent
Fut.	if I should be sent	if we should be sent
	if you should be sent	if you should be sent
	if he (she, it) should be sent	if they should be sent

to set (active voice)   *Principal Parts:* set, setting, set, set

Infinitive: to set   *Present Participle:* setting
Perfect Infinitive: to have set   *Past Participle:* set

INDICATIVE MOOD

Pres. I set	we set
you set	you set
he (she, it) sets	they set
Pres. I am setting	we are setting
Prog. you are setting	you are setting
he (she, it) is setting	they are setting
Pres. I do set	we do set
Int. you do set	you do set
he (she, it) does set	they do set
Fut. I shall set	we shall set
you will set	you will set
he (she, it) will set	they will set
Cond. I would set	we would set
you would set	you would set
he (she, it) would set	they would set
Past I set	we set
you set	you set
he (she, it) set	they set
Past I was setting	we were setting
Prog. you were setting	you were setting
he (she, it) was setting	they were setting
Past I did set	we did set
Int. you did set	you did set
he (she, it) did set	they did set
Pres. I have set	we have set
Perf. you have set	you have set
he (she, it) has set	they have set
Past I had set	we had set
Perf. you had set	you had set
he (she, it) had set	they had set
Fut. I shall have set	we shall have set
Perf. you will have set	you will have set
he (she, it) will have set	they will have set
Cond. I would have set	we would have set
Perf. you would have set	you would have set
he (she, it) would have set	they would have set

IMPERATIVE MOOD
set

SUBJUNCTIVE MOOD

Pres. if I set	if we set
if you set	if you set
if he (she, it) set	if they set
Past if I set	if we set
if you set	if you set
if he (she, it) set	if they set
Fut. if I should set	if we should set
if you should set	if you should set
if he (she, it) should set	if they should set

Infinitive: to be set   *Present Participle:* being set
Perfect Infinitive: to have been set   *Past Participle:* been set

INDICATIVE MOOD

Pres.   I am set   we are set
      you are set   you are set
      he (she, it) is set   they are set

Pres.   I am being set   we are being set
Prog.   you are being set   you are being set
      he (she, it) is being set   they are being set

Pres.   I do get set   we do get set
Int.   you do get set   you do get set
      he (she, it) does get set   they do get set

Fut.   I shall be set   we shall be set
      you will be set   you will be set
      he (she, it) will be set   they will be set

Cond.   I would be set   we would be set
      you would be set   you would be set
      he (she, it) would be set   they would be set

Past   I was set   we were set
      you were set   you were set
      he (she, it) was set   they were set

Past   I was being set   we were being set
Prog.   you were being set   you were being set
      he (she, it) was being set   they were being set

Past   I did get set   we did get set
Int.   you did get set   you did get set
      he (she, it) did get set   they did get set

Pres.   I have been set   we have been set
Perf.   you have been set   you have been set
      he (she, it) has been set   they have been set

Past   I had been set   we had been set
Perf.   you had been set   you had been set
      he (she, it) had been set   they had been set

Fut.   I shall have been set   we shall have been set
Perf.   you will have been set   you will have been set
      he (she, it) will have been set   they will have been set

Cond.   I would have been set   we would have been set
Perf.   you would have been set   you would have been set
      he (she, it) would have been set   they would have been set

IMPERATIVE MOOD
be set

SUBJUNCTIVE MOOD

Pres.   if I be set   if we be set
      if you be set   if you be set
      if he (she, it) be set   if they be set

Past   if I were set   if we were set
      if you were set   if you were set
      if he (she, it) were set   if they were set

Fut.   if I should be set   if we should be set
      if you should be set   if you should be set
      if he (she, it) should be set   if they should be set

to shake (active voice)　　*Principal Parts:* shake, shaking, shook, shaken

---

Infinitive: to shake　　　　　　　*Present Participle:* shaking
Perfect Infinitive: to have shaken　　*Past Participle:* shaken

INDICATIVE MOOD

Pres.	I shake	we shake
	you shake	you shake
	he (she, it) shakes	they shake
Pres.	I am shaking	we are shaking
Prog.	you are shaking	you are shaking
	he (she, it) is shaking	they are shaking
Pres.	I do shake	we do shake
Int.	you do shake	you do shake
	he (she, it) does shake	they do shake
Fut.	I shall shake	we shall shake
	you will shake	you will shake
	he (she, it) will shake	they will shake
Cond.	I would shake	we would shake
	you would shake	you would shake
	he (she, it) would shake	they would shake
Past	I shook	we shook
	you shook	you shook
	he (she, it) shook	they shook
Past	I was shaking	we were shaking
Prog.	you were shaking	you were shaking
	he (she, it) was shaking	they were shaking
Past	I did shake	we did shake
Int.	you did shake	you did shake
	he (she, it) did shake	they did shake
Pres.	I have shaken	we have shaken
Perf.	you have shaken	you have shaken
	he (she, it) has shaken	they have shaken
Past	I had shaken	we had shaken
Perf.	you had shaken	you had shaken
	he (she, it) had shaken	they had shaken
Fut.	I shall have shaken	we shall have shaken
Perf.	you will have shaken	you will have shaken
	he (she, it) will have shaken	they will have shaken
Cond.	I would have shaken	we would have shaken
Perf.	you would have shaken	you would have shaken
	he (she, it) would have shaken	they would have shaken

IMPERATIVE MOOD
shake

SUBJUNCTIVE MOOD

Pres.	if I shake	if we shake
	if you shake	if you shake
	if he (she, it) shake	if they shake
Past	if I shook	if we shook
	if you shook	if you shook
	if he (she, it) shook	if they shook
Fut.	if I should shake	if we should shake
	if you should shake	if you should shake
	if he (she, it) should shake	if they should shake

(passive voice)

Infinitive: to be shaken   *Present Participle:* being shaken
Perfect Infinitive: to have been shaken   *Past Participle:* been shaken

INDICATIVE MOOD

Pres. I am shaken   we are shaken
you are shaken   you are shaken
he (she, it) is shaken   they are shaken

Pres. I am being shaken   we are being shaken
Prog. you are being shaken   you are being shaken
he (she, it) is being shaken   they are being shaken

Pres. I do get shaken   we do get shaken
Int. you do get shaken   you do get shaken
he (she, it) does get shaken   they do get shaken

Fut. I shall be shaken   we shall be shaken
you will be shaken   you will be shaken
he (she, it) will be shaken   they will be shaken

Cond. I would be shaken   we would be shaken
you would be shaken   you would be shaken
he (she, it) would be shaken   they would be shaken

Past I was shaken   we were shaken
you were shaken   you were shaken
he (she, it) was shaken   they were shaken

Past I was being shaken   we were being shaken
Prog. you were being shaken   you were being shaken
he (she, it) was being shaken   they were being shaken

Past I did get shaken   we did get shaken
Int. you did get shaken   you did get shaken
he (she, it) did get shaken   they did get shaken

Pres. I have been shaken   we have been shaken
Perf. you have been shaken   you have been shaken
he (she, it) has been shaken   they have been shaken

Past I had been shaken   we had been shaken
Perf. you had been shaken   you had been shaken
he (she, it) had been shaken   they had been shaken

Fut. I shall have been shaken   we shall have been shaken
Perf. you will have been shaken   you will have been shaken
he (she, it) will have been shaken   they will have been shaken

Cond. I would have been shaken   we would have been shaken
Perf. you would have been shaken   you would have been shaken
he (she, it) would have been shaken   they would have been shaken

IMPERATIVE MOOD
be shaken

SUBJUNCTIVE MOOD

Pres. if I be shaken   if we be shaken
if you be shaken   if you be shaken
if he (she, it) be shaken   if they be shaken

Past if I were shaken   if we were shaken
if you were shaken   if you were shaken
if he (she, it) were shaken   if they were shaken

Fut. if I should be shaken   if we should be shaken
if you should be shaken   if you should be shaken
if he (she, it) should be shaken   if they should be shaken

to shine (active voice)

Infinitive: to shine
Perfect Infinitive: to have shone

Present Participle: shining
Past Participle: shone

INDICATIVE MOOD

Pres.	I shine	we shine
	you shine	you shine
	he (she, it) shines	they shine
Pres.	I am shining	we are shining
Prog.	you are shining	you are shining
	he (she, it) is shining	they are shining
Pres.	I do shine	we do shine
Int.	you do shine	you do shine
	he (she, it) does shine	they do shine
Fut.	I shall shine	we shall shine
	you will shine	you will shine
	he (she, it) will shine	they will shine
Cond.	I would shine	we would shine
	you would shine	you would shine
	he (she, it) would shine	they would shine
Past	I shone	we shone
	you shone	you shone
	he (she, it) shone	they shone
Past	I was shining	we were shining
Prog.	you were shining	you were shining
	he (she, it) was shining	they were shining
Past	I did shine	we did shine
Int.	you did shine	you did shine
	he (she, it) did shine	they did shine
Pres.	I have shone	we have shone
Perf.	you have shone	you have shone
	he (she, it) has shone	they have shone
Past	I had shone	we had shone
Perf.	you had shone	you had shone
	he (she, it) had shone	they had shone
Fut.	I shall have shone	we shall have shone
Perf.	you will have shone	you will have shone
	he (she, it) will have shone	they will have shone
Cond.	I would have shone	we would have shone
Perf.	you would have shone	you would have shone
	he (she, it) would have shone	they would have shone

IMPERATIVE MOOD
shine

SUBJUNCTIVE MOOD

Pres.	if I shine	if we shine
	if you shine	if you shine
	if he (she, it) shine	if they shine
Past	if I shone	if we shone
	if you shone	if you shone
	if he (she, it) shone	if they shone
Fut.	if I should shine	if we should shine
	if you should shine	if you should shine
	if he (she, it) should shine	if they should shine

Infinitive: to be shone
Perfect Infinitive: to have been shone

Present Participle: being shone
Past Participle: been shone

INDICATIVE MOOD

Pres. I am shone
you are shone
he (she, it) is shone

we are shone
you are shone
they are shone

Pres.
Prog. I am being shone
you are being shone
he (she, it) is being shone

we are being shone
you are being shone
they are being shone

Pres.
Int. I do get shone
you do get shone
he (she, it) does get shone

we do get shone
you do get shone
they do get shone

Fut. I shall be shone
you will be shone
he (she, it) will be shone

we shall be shone
you will be shone
they will be shone

Cond. I would be shone
you would be shone
he (she, it) would be shone

we would be shone
you would be shone
they would be shone

Past I was shone
you were shone
he (she, it) was shone

we were shone
you were shone
they were shone

Past
Prog. I was being shone
you were being shone
he (she, it) was being shone

we were being shone
you were being shone
they were being shone

Past
Int. I did get shone
you did get shone
he (she, it) did get shone

we did get shone
you did get shone
they did get shone

Pres.
Perf. I have been shone
you have been shone
he (she, it) has been shone

we have been shone
you have been shone
they have been shone

Past
Perf. I had been shone
you had been shone
he (she, it) had been shone

we had been shone
you had been shone
they had been shone

Fut.
Perf. I shall have been shone
you will have been shone
he (she, it) will have been shone

we shall have been shone
you will have been shone
they will have been shone

Cond.
Perf. I would have been shone
you would have been shone
he (she, it) would have been shone

we would have been shone
you would have been shone
they would have been shone

IMPERATIVE MOOD
be shone

SUBJUNCTIVE MOOD

Pres. if I be shone
if you be shone
if he (she, it) be shone

if we be shone
if you be shone
if they be shone

Past if I were shone
if you were shone
if he (she, it) were shone

if we were shone
if you were shone
if they were shone

Fut. if I should be shone
if you should be shone
if he (she, it) should be shone

if we should be shone
if you should be shone
if they should be shone

to shoot (active voice) Principal Parts: shoot, shooting, shot, shot

Infinitive: to shoot
Perfect Infinitive: to have shot

Present Participle: shooting
Past Participle: shot

INDICATIVE MOOD

Pres.	I shoot	we shoot
	you shoot	you shoot
	he (she, it) shoots	they shoot
Pres. Prog.	I am shooting	we are shooting
	you are shooting	you are shooting
	he (she, it) is shooting	they are shooting
Pres. Int.	I do shoot	we do shoot
	you do shoot	you do shoot
	he (she, it) does shoot	they do shoot
Fut.	I shall shoot	we shall shoot
	you will shoot	you will shoot
	he (she, it) will shoot	they will shoot
Cond.	I would shoot	we would shoot
	you would shoot	you would shoot
	he (she, it) would shoot	they would shoot
Past	I shot	we shot
	you shot	you shot
	he (she, it) shot	they shot
Past Prog.	I was shooting	we were shooting
	you were shooting	you were shooting
	he (she, it) was shooting	they were shooting
Past Int.	I did shoot	we did shoot
	you did shoot	you did shoot
	he (she, it) did shoot	they did shoot
Pres. Perf.	I have shot	we have shot
	you have shot	you have shot
	he (she, it) has shot	they have shot
Past Perf.	I had shot	we had shot
	you had shot	you had shot
	he (she, it) had shot	they had shot
Fut. Perf.	I shall have shot	we shall have shot
	you will have shot	you will have shot
	he (she, it) will have shot	they will have shot
Cond. Perf.	I would have shot	we would have shot
	you would have shot	you would have shot
	he (she, it) would have shot	they would have shot

IMPERATIVE MOOD
shoot

SUBJUNCTIVE MOOD

Pres.	if I shoot	if we shoot
	if you shoot	if you shoot
	if he (she, it) shoot	if they shoot
Past	if I shot	if we shot
	if you shot	if you shot
	if he (she, it) shot	if they shot
Fut.	if I should shoot	if we should shoot
	if you should shoot	if you should shoot
	if he (she, it) should shoot	if they should shoot

(passive voice)

Infinitive: to be shot
Perfect Infinitive: to have been shot

Present Participle: being shot
Past Participle: been shot

INDICATIVE MOOD

Pres.	I am shot	we are shot
	you are shot	you are shot
	he (she, it) is shot	they are shot
Pres. Prog.	I am being shot	we are being shot
	you are being shot	you are being shot
	he (she, it) is being shot	they are being shot
Pres. Int.	I do get shot	we do get shot
	you do get shot	you do get shot
	he (she, it) does get shot	they do get shot
Fut.	I shall be shot	we shall be shot
	you will be shot	you will be shot
	he (she, it) will be shot	they will be shot
Cond.	I would be shot	we would be shot
	you would be shot	you would be shot
	he (she, it) would be shot	they would be shot
Past	I was shot	we were shot
	you were shot	you were shot
	he (she, it) was shot	they were shot
Past Prog.	I was being shot	we were being shot
	you were being shot	you were being shot
	he (she, it) was being shot	they were being shot
Past Int.	I did get shot	we did get shot
	you did get shot	you did get shot
	he (she, it) did get shot	they did get shot
Pres. Perf.	I have been shot	we have been shot
	you have been shot	you have been shot
	he (she, it) has been shot	they have been shot
Past Perf.	I had been shot	we had been shot
	you had been shot	you had been shot
	he (she, it) had been shot	they had been shot
Fut. Perf.	I shall have been shot	we shall have been shot
	you will have been shot	you will have been shot
	he (she, it) will have been shot	they will have been shot
Cond. Perf.	I would have been shot	we would have been shot
	you would have been shot	you would have been shot
	he (she, it) would have been shot	they would have been shot

IMPERATIVE MOOD
be shot

SUBJUNCTIVE MOOD

Pres.	if I be shot	if we be shot
	if you be shot	if you be shot
	if he (she, it) be shot	if they be shot
Past	if I were shot	if we were shot
	if you were shot	if you were shot
	if he (she, it) were shot	if they were shot
Fut.	if I should be shot	if we should be shot
	if you should be shot	if you should be shot
	if he (she, it) should be shot	if they should be shot

to shrink (active voice) *Principal Parts:* shrink, shrinking, shrank (shrunk), shrunk (shrunken)

Infinitive: to shrink
Perfect Infinitive: to have shrunk, shrunken

Present Participle: shrinking
Past Participle: shrunk, shrunken

INDICATIVE MOOD

Pres. I shrink you shrink he (she, it) shrinks	we shrink you shrink they shrink
Pres. I am shrinking **Prog.** you are shrinking he (she, it) is shrinking	we are shrinking you are shrinking they are shrinking
Pres. I do shrink **Int.** you do shrink he (she, it) does shrink	we do shrink you do shrink they do shrink
Fut. I shall shrink you will shrink he (she, it) will shrink	we shall shrink you will shrink they will shrink
Cond. I would shrink you would shrink he (she, it) would shrink	we would shrink you would shrink they would shrink
Past I shrank, shrunk you shrank, shrunk he (she, it) shrank, shrunk	we shrank, shrunk you shrank, shrunk they shrank, shrunk
Past I was shrinking **Prog.** you were shrinking he (she, it) was shrinking	we were shrinking you were shrinking they were shrinking
Past I did shrink **Int.** you did shrink he (she, it) did shrink	we did shrink you did shrink they did shrink
Pres. I have shrunk, shrunken **Perf.** you have shrunk, shrunken he (she, it) has shrunk, shrunken	we have shrunk, shrunken you have shrunk, shrunken they have shrunk, shrunken
Past I had shrunk, shrunken **Perf.** you had shrunk, shrunken he (she, it) had shrunk, shrunken	we had shrunk, shrunken you had shrunk, shrunken they had shrunk, shrunken
Fut. I shall have shrunk, shrunken **Perf.** you will have shrunk, shrunken he (she, it) will have shrunk, shrunken	we shall have shrunk, shrunken you will have shrunk, shrunken they will have shrunk, shrunken
Cond. I would have shrunk, shrunken **Perf.** you would have shrunk, shrunken he (she, it) would have shrunk, shrunken	we would have shrunk, shrunken you would have shrunk, shrunken they would have shrunk, shrunken

IMPERATIVE MOOD
shrink

SUBJUNCTIVE MOOD

Pres. if I shrink if you shrink if he (she, it) shrink	if we shrink if you shrink if they shrink
Past if I shrank if you shrank if he (she, it) shrank	if we shrank if you shrank if they shrank
Fut. if I should shrink if you should shrink if he (she, it) should shrink	if we should shrink if you should shrink if they should shrink

Infinitive: to be shrunk, shrunken
Perfect Infinitive: to have been shrunk, shrunken
Present Participle: being shrunk, shrunken
Past Participle: been shrunk, shrunken

INDICATIVE MOOD

Pres. I am shrunk, shrunken
you are shrunk, shrunken
he (she, it) is shrunk, shrunken

we are shrunk, shrunken
you are shrunk, shrunken
they are shrunk, shrunken

Pres. I am being shrunk, shrunken
Prog. you are being shrunk, shrunken
he (she, it) is being shrunk, shrunken

we are being shrunk, shrunken
you are being shrunk, shrunken
they are being shrunk, shrunken

Pres. I do get shrunk, shrunken
Int. you do get shrunk, shrunken
he (she, it) does get shrunk, shrunken

we do get shrunk, shrunken
you do get shrunk, shrunken
they do get shrunk, shrunken

Fut. I shall be shrunk, shrunken
you will be shrunk, shrunken
he (she, it) will be shrunk, shrunken

we shall be shrunk, shrunken
you will be shrunk, shrunken
they will be shrunk, shrunken

Cond. I would be shrunk, shrunken
you would be shrunk, shrunken
he (she, it) would be shrunk, shrunken

we would be shrunk, shrunken
you would be shrunk, shrunken
they would be shrunk, shrunken

Past I was shrunk, shrunken
you were shrunk, shrunken
he (she, it) was shrunk, shrunken

we were shrunk, shrunken
you were shrunk, shrunken
they were shrunk, shrunken

Past I was being shrunk
Prog. you were being shrunk
he (she, it) was being shrunk

we were being shrunk
you were being shrunk
they were being shrunk

Past I did get shrunk, shrunken
Int. you did get shrunk, shrunken
he (she, it) did get shrunk, shrunken

we did get shrunk, shrunken
you did get shrunk, shrunken
they did get shrunk, shrunken

Pres. I have been shrunk, shrunken
Perf. you have been shrunk, shrunken
he (she, it) has been shrunk, shrunken

we have been shrunk, shrunken
you have been shrunk, shrunken
they have been shrunk, shrunken

Past I had been shrunk, shrunken
Perf. you had been shrunk, shrunken
he (she, it) had been shrunk, shrunken

we had been shrunk, shrunken
you had been shrunk, shrunken
they had been shrunk, shrunken

Fut. I shall have been shrunk, shrunken
Perf.

you will have been shrunk, shrunken
he (she, it) will have been shrunk, shrunken

we shall have been shrunk, shrunken
you will have been shrunk, shrunken
they will have been shrunk, shrunken

Cond. I would have been shrunk, shrunken
Perf.

you would have been shrunk, shrunken

he (she, it) would have been shrunk, shrunken

we would have been shrunk, shrunken
you would have been shrunk, shrunken
they would have been shrunk, shrunken

293

(passive voice, continued)

IMPERATIVE MOOD
be shrunk

SUBJUNCTIVE MOOD

Pres. if I be shrunk, shrunken
if you be shrunk, shrunken
if he (she, it) be shrunk, shrunken

if we be shrunk, shrunken
if you be shrunk, shrunken
if they be shrunk, shrunken

Past if I were shrunk, shrunken
if you were shrunk, shrunken
if he (she, it) were shrunk, shrunken

if we were shrunk, shrunken
if you were shrunk, shrunken
if they were shrunk, shrunken

Fut. if I should be shrunk, shrunken
if you should be shrunk, shrunken
if he (she, it) should be shrunk, shrunken

if we should be shrunk, shrunken
if you should be shrunk, shrunken
if they should be shrunk, shrunken

***To shrink* as a Transitive and Intransitive Verb.**

The verb *to shrink,* meaning to diminish in size, like a woolen sweater after being washed in hot water, is both a transitive and intransitive verb. As a transitive verb it describes the action of someone causing something to shrink: a person *shrinks* a sweater by putting it into hot water. As a result (passive voice) the sweater is shrunken by the person.

But *to shrink* is also an intransitive verb in the sense that the shrinking can be thought of as a self-contained action: "The sweater *is shrinking* in the hot water" or "My capital *is shrinking* every day because stock market prices are falling."

The verb also has a figurative meaning *to draw back,* implying *becoming smaller* or *attempting to become inconspicuous* as in the face of danger or embarrassment: "He *shrank* from a confrontation with his angry father."

to sing (active voice)   *Principal Parts:* sing, singing, sang, sung

---

Infinitive: to sing   *Present Participle:* singing
Perfect Infinitive: to have sung   *Past Participle:* sung

INDICATIVE MOOD

Pres.	I sing	we sing
	you sing	you sing
	he (she, it) sings	they sing
Pres.	I am singing	we are singing
Prog.	you are singing	you are singing
	he (she, it) is singing	they are singing
Pres.	I do sing	we do sing
Int.	you do sing	you do sing
	he (she, it) does sing	they do sing
Fut.	I shall sing	we shall sing
	you will sing	you will sing
	he (she, it) will sing	they will sing
Cond.	I would sing	we would sing
	you would sing	you would sing
	he (she, it) would sing	they would sing
Past	I sang	we sang
	you sang	you sang
	he (she, it) sang	they sang
Past	I was singing	we were singing
Prog.	you were singing	you were singing
	he (she, it) was singing	they were singing
Past	I did sing	we did sing
Int.	you did sing	you did sing
	he (she, it) did sing	they did sing
Pres.	I have sung	we have sung
Perf.	you have sung	you have sung
	he (she, it) has sung	they have sung
Past	I had sung	we had sung
Perf.	you had sung	you had sung
	he (she, it) had sung	they had sung
Fut.	I shall have sung	we shall have sung
Perf.	you will have sung	you will have sung
	he (she, it) will have sung	they will have sung
Cond.	I would have sung	we would have sung
Perf.	you would have sung	you would have sung
	he (she, it) would have sung	they would have sung

IMPERATIVE MOOD
sing

SUBJUNCTIVE MOOD

Pres.	if I sing	if we sing
	if you sing	if you sing
	if he (she, it) sing	if they sing
Past	if I sang	if we sang
	if you sang	if you sang
	if he (she, it) sang	if they sang
Fut.	if I should sing	if we should sing
	if you should sing	if you should sing
	if he (she, it) should sing	if they should sing

(passive voice)

Infinitive: to be sung
Perfect Infinitive: to have been sung

Present Participle: being sung
Past Participle: been sung

INDICATIVE MOOD

Pres.
I am sung
you are sung
he (she, it) is sung

we are sung
you are sung
they are sung

Pres. Prog.
I am being sung
you are being sung
he (she, it) is being sung

we are being sung
you are being sung
they are being sung

Pres. Int.
I do get sung
you do get sung
he (she, it) does get sung

we do get sung
you do get sung
they do get sung

Fut.
I shall be sung
you will be sung
he (she, it) will be sung

we shall be sung
you will be sung
they will be sung

Cond.
I would be sung
you would be sung
he (she, it) would be sung

we would be sung
you would be sung
they would be sung

Past
I was sung
you were sung
he (she, it) was sung

we were sung
you were sung
they were sung

Past Prog.
I was being sung
you were being sung
he (she, it) was being sung

we were being sung
you were being sung
they were being sung

Past Int.
I did get sung
you did get sung
he (she, it) did get sung

we did get sung
you did get sung
they did get sung

Pres. Perf.
I have been sung
you have been sung
he (she, it) has been sung

we have been sung
you have been sung
they have been sung

Past Perf.
I had been sung
you had been sung
he (she, it) had been sung

we had been sung
you had been sung
they had been sung

Fut. Perf.
I shall have been sung
you will have been sung
he (she, it) will have been sung

we shall have been sung
you will have been sung
they will have been sung

Cond. Perf.
I would have been sung
you would have been sung
he (she, it) would have been sung

we would have been sung
you would have been sung
they would have been sung

IMPERATIVE MOOD
be sung

SUBJUNCTIVE MOOD

Pres.
if I be sung
if you be sung
if he (she, it) be sung

if we be sung
if you be sung
if they be sung

Past
if I were sung
if you were sung
if he (she, it) were sung

if we were sung
if you were sung
if they were sung

Fut.
if I should be sung
if you should be sung
if he (she, it) should be sung

if we should be sung
if you should be sung
if they should be sung

to sink (active voice)   *Principal Parts:* sink, sinking, sank, sunk

---

Infinitive: to sink   *Present Participle:* sinking
Perfect Infinitive: to have sunk   *Past Participle:* sunk

INDICATIVE MOOD

Pres.	I sink	we sink
	you sink	you sink
	he (she, it) sinks	they sink
Pres.	I am sinking	we are sinking
Prog.	you are sinking	you are sinking
	he (she, it) is sinking	they are sinking
Pres.	I do sink	we do sink
Int.	you do sink	you do sink
	he (she, it) does sink	they do sink
Fut.	I shall sink	we shall sink
	you will sink	you will sink
	he (she, it) will sink	they will sink
Cond.	I would sink	we would sink
	you would sink	you would sink
	he (she, it) would sink	they would sink
Past	I sank	we sank
	you sank	you sank
	he (she, it) sank	they sank
Past	I was sinking	we were sinking
Prog.	you were sinking	you were sinking
	he (she, it) was sinking	they were sinking
Past	I did sink	we did sink
Int.	you did sink	you did sink
	he (she, it) did sink	they did sink
Pres.	I have sunk	we have sunk
Perf.	you have sunk	you have sunk
	he (she, it) has sunk	they have sunk
Past	I had sunk	we had sunk
Perf.	you had sunk	you had sunk
	he (she, it) had sunk	they had sunk
Fut.	I shall have sunk	we shall have sunk
Perf.	you will have sunk	you will have sunk
	he (she, it) will have sunk	they will have sunk
Cond.	I would have sunk	we would have sunk
Perf.	you would have sunk	you would have sunk
	he (she, it) would have sunk	they would have sunk

IMPERATIVE MOOD
sink

SUBJUNCTIVE MOOD

Pres.	if I sink	if we sink
	if you sink	if you sink
	if he (she, it) sink	if they sink
Past	if I sank	if we sank
	if you sank	if you sank
	if he (she, it) sank	if they sank
Fut.	if I should sink	if we should sink
	if you should sink	if you should sink
	if he (she, it) should sink	if they should sink

(passive voice)

Infinitive: to be sunk
Perfect Infinitive: to have been sunk

Present Participle: being sunk
Past Participle: been sunk

INDICATIVE MOOD

Pres.	I am sunk you are sunk he (she, it) is sunk	we are sunk you are sunk they are sunk
Pres. *Prog.*	I am being sunk you are being sunk he (she, it) is being sunk	we are being sunk you are being sunk they are being sunk
Pres. *Int.*	I do get sunk you do get sunk he (she, it) does get sunk	we do get sunk you do get sunk they do get sunk
Fut.	I shall be sunk you will be sunk he (she, it) will be sunk	we shall be sunk you will be sunk they will be sunk
Cond.	I would be sunk you would be sunk he (she, it) would be sunk	we would be sunk you would be sunk they would be sunk
Past	I was sunk you were sunk he (she, it) was sunk	we were sunk you were sunk they were sunk
Past *Prog.*	I was being sunk you were being sunk he (she, it) was being sunk	we were being sunk you were being sunk they were being sunk
Past *Int.*	I did get sunk you did get sunk he (she, it) did get sunk	we did get sunk you did get sunk they did get sunk
Pres. *Perf.*	I have been sunk you have been sunk he (she, it) has been sunk	we have been sunk you have been sunk they have been sunk
Past *Perf.*	I had been sunk you had been sunk he (she, it) had been sunk	we had been sunk you had been sunk they had been sunk
Fut. *Perf.*	I shall have been sunk you will have been sunk he (she, it) will have been sunk	we shall have been sunk you will have been sunk they will have been sunk
Cond. *Perf.*	I would have been sunk you would have been sunk he (she, it) would have been sunk	we would have been sunk you would have been sunk they would have been sunk

IMPERATIVE MOOD
be sunk

SUBJUNCTIVE MOOD

Pres.	if I be sunk if you be sunk if he (she, it) be sunk	if we be sunk if you be sunk if they be sunk
Past	if I were sunk if you were sunk if he (she, it) were sunk	if we were sunk if you were sunk if they were sunk
Fut.	if I should be sunk if you should be sunk if he (she, it) should be sunk	if we should be sunk if you should be sunk if they should be sunk

to sit (active voice only)   *Principal Parts:* sit, sitting, sat, sat

(intransitive verb)

Infinitive: to sit   *Present Participle:* sitting
Perfect Infinitive: to have sat   *Past Participle:* sat

INDICATIVE MOOD

Pres.	I sit	we sit
	you sit	you sit
	he (she, it) sits	they sit
Pres.	I am sitting	we are sitting
Prog.	you are sitting	you are sitting
	he (she, it) is sitting	they are sitting
Pres.	I do sit	we do sit
Int.	you do sit	you do sit
	he (she, it) does sit	they do sit
Fut.	I shall sit	we shall sit
	you will sit	you will sit
	he (she, it) will sit	they will sit
Cond.	I would sit	we would sit
	you would sit	you would sit
	he (she, it) would sit	they would sit
Past	I sat	we sat
	you sat	you sat
	he (she, it) sat	they sat
Past	I was sitting	we were sitting
Prog.	you were sitting	you were sitting
	he (she, it) was sitting	they were sitting
Past	I did sit	we did sit
Int.	you did sit	you did sit
	he (she, it) did sit	they did sit
Pres.	I have sat	we have sat
Perf.	you have sat	you have sat
	he (she, it) has sat	they have sat
Past	I had sat	we had sat
Perf.	you had sat	you had sat
	he (she, it) had sat	they had sat
Fut.	I shall have sat	we shall have sat
Perf.	you will have sat	you will have sat
	he (she, it) will have sat	they will have sat
Cond.	I would have sat	we would have sat
Perf.	you would have sat	you would have sat
	he (she, it) would have sat	they would have sat

IMPERATIVE MOOD
sit

SUBJUNCTIVE MOOD

Pres.	if I sit	if we sit
	if you sit	if you sit
	if he (she, it) sit	if they sit
Past	if I sat	if we sat
	if you sat	if you sat
	if he (she, it) sat	if they sat
Fut.	if I should sit	if we should sit
	if you should sit	if you should sit
	if he (she, it) should sit	if they should sit

To sit **is an intransitive verb.**

It does not take an object.
It describes action, but the action is self-contained.
Like other intransitive verbs, it may be followed by adverbs, adverbial phrases and clauses describing the how, why, when, and where of the action:
HOW: John, sit *straight!* (adverb)
WHY: They were sitting *because they were tired.* (adverbial clause)
WHEN: I expect to be sitting *all day.* (adverbial phrase)
WHERE: The baby sat *on a high chair.* (adverbial phrase)
NOTE: Do not confuse this verb with *to set,* which means *to put, to place:*
I *put* my books on the table.
I *set* my books on the table.

to slay (active voice)   *Principal Parts:* slay, slaying, slew, slain

---

Infinitive: to slay
Perfect Infinitive: to have slain

Present Participle: slaying
Past Participle: slain

INDICATIVE MOOD

Pres. I slay	we slay
you slay	you slay
he (she, it) slays	they slay
Pres. I am slaying	we are slaying
Prog. you are slaying	you are slaying
he (she, it) is slaying	they are slaying
Pres. I do slay	we do slay
Int. you do slay	you do slay
he (she, it) does slay	they do slay
Fut. I shall slay	we shall slay
you will slay	you will slay
he (she, it) will slay	they will slay
Cond. I would slay	we would slay
you would slay	you would slay
he (she, it) would slay	they would slay
Past I slew	we slew
you slew	you slew
he (she, it) slew	they slew
Past I was slaying	we were slaying
Prog. you were slaying	you were slaying
he (she, it) was slaying	they were slaying
Past I did slay	we did slay
Int. you did slay	you did slay
he (she, it) did slay	they did slay
Pres. I have slain	we have slain
Perf. you have slain	you have slain
he (she, it) has slain	they have slain
Past I had slain	we had slain
Perf. you had slain	you had slain
he (she, it) had slain	they had slain
Fut. I shall have slain	we shall have slain
Perf. you will have slain	you will have slain
he (she, it) will have slain	they will have slain
Cond. I would have slain	we would have slain
Perf. you would have slain	you would have slain
he (she, it) would have slain	they would have slain

IMPERATIVE MOOD
slay

SUBJUNCTIVE MOOD

Pres. if I slay	if we slay
if you slay	if you slay
if he (she, it) slay	if they slay
Past if I slew	if we slew
if you slew	if you slew
if he (she, it) slew	if they slew
Fut. if I should slay	if we should slay
if you should slay	if you should slay
if he (she, it) should slay	if they should slay

Infinitive: to be slain   *Present Participle:* being slain
Perfect Infinitive: to have been slain   *Past Participle:* been slain

INDICATIVE MOOD

Pres. I am slain
you are slain
he (she, it) is slain

we are slain
you are slain
they are slain

Pres. I am being slain
Prog. you are being slain
he (she, it) is being slain

we are being slain
you are being slain
they are being slain

Pres. I do get slain
Int. you do get slain
he (she, it) does get slain

we do get slain
you do get slain
they do get slain

Fut. I shall be slain
you will be slain
he (she, it) will be slain

we shall be slain
you will be slain
they will be slain

Cond. I would be slain
you would be slain
he (she, it) would be slain

we would be slain
you would be slain
they would be slain

Past I was slain
you were slain
he (she, it) was slain

we were slain
you were slain
they were slain

Past I was being slain
Prog. you were being slain
he (she, it) was being slain

we were being slain
you were being slain
they were being slain

Past I did get slain
Int. you did get slain
he (she, it) did get slain

we did get slain
you did get slain
they did get slain

Pres. I have been slain
Perf. you have been slain
he (she, it) has been slain

we have been slain
you have been slain
they have been slain

Past I had been slain
Perf. you had been slain
he (she, it) had been slain

we had been slain
you had been slain
they had been slain

Fut. I shall have been slain
Perf. you will have been slain
he (she, it) will have been slain

we shall have been slain
you will have been slain
they will have been slain

Cond. I would have been slain
Perf. you would have been slain
he (she, it) would have been slain

we would have been slain
you would have been slain
they would have been slain

IMPERATIVE MOOD
be slain

SUBJUNCTIVE MOOD

Pres. if I be slain
if you be slain
if he (she, it) be slain

if we be slain
if you be slain
if they be slain

Past if I were slain
if you were slain
if he (she, it) were slain

if we were slain
if you were slain
if they were slain

Fut. if I should be slain
if you should be slain
if he (she, it) should be slain

if we should be slain
if you should be slain
if they should be slain

to sleep (active voice only)   *Principal Parts:* sleep, sleeping, slept, slept

(intransitive verb)

Infinitive: to sleep   *Present Participle:* sleeping
Perfect Infinitive: to have slept   *Past Participle:* slept

INDICATIVE MOOD

Pres.	I sleep	we sleep
	you sleep	you sleep
	he (she, it) sleeps	they sleep
Pres.	I am sleeping	we are sleeping
Prog.	you are sleeping	you are sleeping
	he (she, it) is sleeping	they are sleeping
Pres.	I do sleep	we do sleep
Int.	you do sleep	you do sleep
	he (she, it) does sleep	they do sleep
Fut.	I shall sleep	we shall sleep
	you will sleep	you will sleep
	he (she, it) will sleep	they will sleep
Cond.	I would sleep	we would sleep
	you would sleep	you would sleep
	he (she, it) would sleep	they would sleep
Past	I slept	we slept
	you slept	you slept
	he (she, it) slept	they slept
Past	I was sleeping	we were sleeping
Prog.	you were sleeping	you were sleeping
	he (she, it) was sleeping	they were sleeping
Past	I did sleep	we did sleep
Int.	you did sleep	you did sleep
	he (she, it) did sleep	they did sleep
Pres.	I have slept	we have slept
Perf.	you have slept	you have slept
	he (she, it) has slept	they have slept
Past	I had slept	we had slept
Perf.	you had slept	you had slept
	he (she, it) had slept	they had slept
Fut.	I shall have slept	we shall have slept
Perf.	you will have slept	you will have slept
	he (she, it) will have slept	they will have slept
Cond.	I would have slept	we would have slept
Perf.	you would have slept	you would have slept
	he (she, it) would have slept	they would have slept

IMPERATIVE MOOD
sleep

SUBJUNCTIVE MOOD

Pres.	if I sleep	if we sleep
	if you sleep	if you sleep
	if he (she, it) sleep	if they sleep
Past	if I slept	if we slept
	if you slept	if you slept
	if he (she, it) slept	if they slept
Fut.	if I should sleep	if we should sleep
	if you should sleep	if you should sleep
	if he (she, it) should sleep	if they should sleep

To *sleep* is an intransitive verb.

It does not take an object.

It describes action, but the action is self-contained.

Like other intransitive verbs, it may be followed by adverbs, adverbial phrases and clauses describing the how, why, when, and where of the action:

HOW: Sleep *well.* (adverb)

WHY: She was sleeping *because she was tired.* (adverbial clause)

WHEN: Most people sleep *at night.* (adverbial phrase)

WHERE: I always sleep *when I ride on a train.* (adverbial clause)

to slide (active voice)   *Principal Parts:* slide, sliding, slid, slid

---

Infinitive: to slide   *Present Participle:* sliding
Perfect Infinitive: to have slid   *Past Participle:* slid

INDICATIVE MOOD

Pres.	I slide	we slide
	you slide	you slide
	he (she, it) slides	they slide
Pres.	I am sliding	we are sliding
Prog.	you are sliding	you are sliding
	he (she, it) is sliding	they are sliding
Pres.	I do slide	we do slide
Int.	you do slide	you do slide
	he (she, it) does slide	they do slide
Fut.	I shall slide	we shall slide
	you will slide	you will slide
	he (she, it) will slide	they will slide
Cond.	I would slide	we would slide
	you would slide	you would slide
	he (she, it) would slide	they would slide
Past	I slid	we slid
	you slid	you slid
	he (she, it) slid	they slid
Past	I was sliding	we were sliding
Prog.	you were sliding	you were sliding
	he (she, it) was sliding	they were sliding
Past	I did slide	we did slide
Int.	you did slide	you did slide
	he (she, it) did slide	they did slide
Pres.	I have slid	we have slid
Perf.	you have slid	you have slid
	he (she, it) has slid	they have slid
Past	I had slid	we had slid
Perf.	you had slid	you had slid
	he (she, it) had slid	they had slid
Fut.	I shall have slid	we shall have slid
Perf.	you will have slid	you will have slid
	he (she, it) will have slid	they will have slid
Cond.	I would have slid	we would have slid
Perf.	you would have slid	you would have slid
	he (she, it) would have slid	they would have slid

IMPERATIVE MOOD
slide

SUBJUNCTIVE MOOD

Pres.	if I slide	if we slide
	if you slide	if you slide
	if he (she, it) slide	if they slide
Past	if I slid	if we slid
	if you slid	if you slid
	if he (she, it) slid	if they slid
Fut.	if I should slide	if we should slide
	if you should slide	if you should slide
	if he (she, it) should slide	if they should slide

Infinitive: to be slid
Perfect Infinitive: to have been slid

Present Participle: being slid
Past Participle: been slid

INDICATIVE MOOD

Pres.	I am slid	we are slid
	you are slid	you are slid
	he (she, it) is slid	they are slid
Pres.	I am being slid	we are being slid
Prog.	you are being slid	you are being slid
	he (she, it) is being slid	they are being slid
Pres.	I do get slid	we do get slid
Int.	you do get slid	you do get slid
	he (she, it) does get slid	they do get slid
Fut.	I shall be slid	we shall be slid
	you will be slid	you will be slid
	he (she, it) will be slid	they will be slid
Cond.	I would be slid	we would be slid
	you would be slid	you would be slid
	he (she, it) would be slid	they would be slid
Past	I was slid	we were slid
	you were slid	you were slid
	he (she, it) was slid	they were slid
Past	I was being slid	we were being slid
Prog.	you were being slid	you were being slid
	he (she, it) was being slid	they were being slid
Past	I did get slid	we did get slid
Int.	you did get slid	you did get slid
	he (she, it) did get slid	they did get slid
Pres.	I have been slid	we have been slid
Perf.	you have been slid	you have been slid
	he (she, it) has been slid	they have been slid
Past	I had been slid	we had been slid
Perf.	you had been slid	you had been slid
	he (she, it) had been slid	they had been slid
Fut.	I shall have been slid	we shall have been slid
Perf.	you will have been slid	you will have been slid
	he (she, it) will have been slid	they will have been slid
Cond.	I would have been slid	we would have been slid
Perf.	you would have been slid	you would have been slid
	he (she, it) would have been slid	they would have been slid

IMPERATIVE MOOD
be slid

SUBJUNCTIVE MOOD

Pres.	if I be slid	if we be slid
	if you be slid	if you be slid
	if he (she, it) be slid	if they be slid
Past	if I were slid	if we were slid
	if you were slid	if you were slid
	if he (she, it) were slid	if they were slid
Fut.	if I should be slid	if we should be slid
	if you should be slid	if you should be slid
	if he (she, it) should be slid	if they should be slid

to speak (active voice)   *Principal Parts:* speak, speaking, spoke, spoken

---

Infinitive: to speak   *Present Participle:* speaking
Perfect Infinitive: to have spoken   *Past Participle:* spoken

INDICATIVE MOOD

Pres.	I speak	we speak
	you speak	you speak
	he (she, it) speaks	they speak
Pres.	I am speaking	we are speaking
Prog.	you are speaking	you are speaking
	he (she, it) is speaking	they are speaking
Pres.	I do speak	we do speak
Int.	you do speak	you do speak
	he (she, it) does speak	they do speak
Fut.	I shall speak	we shall speak
	you will speak	you will speak
	he (she, it) will speak	they will speak
Cond.	I would speak	we would speak
	you would speak	you would speak
	he (she, it) would speak	they would speak
Past	I spoke	we spoke
	you spoke	you spoke
	he (she, it) spoke	they spoke
Past	I was speaking	we were speaking
Prog.	you were speaking	you were speaking
	he (she, it) was speaking	they were speaking
Past	I did speak	we did speak
Int.	you did speak	you did speak
	he (she, it) did speak	they did speak
Pres.	I have spoken	we have spoken
Perf.	you have spoken	you have spoken
	he (she, it) has spoken	they have spoken
Past	I had spoken	we had spoken
Perf.	you had spoken	you had spoken
	he (she, it) had spoken	they had spoken
Fut.	I shall have spoken	we shall have spoken
Perf.	you will have spoken	you will have spoken
	he (she, it) will have spoken	they will have spoken
Cond.	I would have spoken	we would have spoken
Perf.	you would have spoken	you would have spoken
	he (she, it) would have spoken	they would have spoken

IMPERATIVE MOOD
speak

SUBJUNCTIVE MOOD

Pres.	if I speak	if we speak
	if you speak	if you speak
	if he (she, it) speak	if they speak
Past	if I spoke	if we spoke
	if you spoke	if you spoke
	if he (she, it) spoke	if they spoke
Fut.	if I should speak	if we should speak
	if you should speak	if you should speak
	if he (she, it) should speak	if they should speak

(passive voice)

Infinitive: to be spoken
Perfect Infinitive: to have been spoken

Present Participle: being spoken
Past Participle: been spoken

INDICATIVE MOOD

Pres. I am spoken
you are spoken
he (she, it) is spoken

we are spoken
you are spoken
they are spoken

Pres. I am being spoken
Prog. you are being spoken
he (she, it) is being spoken

we are being spoken
you are being spoken
they are being spoken

Pres. I do get spoken
Int. you do get spoken
he (she, it) does get spoken

we do get spoken
you do get spoken
they do get spoken

Fut. I shall be spoken
you will be spoken
he (she, it) will be spoken

we shall be spoken
you will be spoken
they will be spoken

Cond. I would be spoken
you would be spoken
he (she, it) would be spoken

we would be spoken
you would be spoken
they would be spoken

Past I was spoken
you were spoken
he (she, it) was spoken

we were spoken
you were spoken
they were spoken

Past I was being spoken
Prog. you were being spoken
he (she, it) was being spoken

we were being spoken
you were being spoken
they were being spoken

Past I did get spoken
Int. you did get spoken
he (she, it) did get spoken

we did get spoken
you did get spoken
they did get spoken

Pres. I have been spoken
Perf. you have been spoken
he (she, it) has been spoken

we have been spoken
you have been spoken
they have been spoken

Past I had been spoken
Perf. you had been spoken
he (she, it) had been spoken

we had been spoken
you had been spoken
they had been spoken

Fut. I shall have been spoken
Perf. you will have been spoken
he (she, it) will have been spoken

we shall have been spoken
you will have been spoken
they will have been spoken

Cond. I would have been spoken
Perf. you would have been spoken
he (she, it) would have been spoken

we would have been spoken
you would have been spoken
they would have been spoken

IMPERATIVE MOOD
be spoken

SUBJUNCTIVE MOOD

Pres. if I be spoken
if you be spoken
if he (she, it) be spoken

if we be spoken
if you be spoken
if they be spoken

Past if I were spoken
if you were spoken
if he (she, it) were spoken

if we were spoken
if you were spoken
if they were spoken

Fut. if I should be spoken
if you should be spoken
if he (she, it) should be spoken

if we should be spoken
if you should be spoken
if they should be spoken

to spend (active voice)   *Principal Parts:* spend, spending, spent, spent

---

Infinitive: to spend   *Present Participle:* spending
Perfect Infinitive: having spent   *Past Participle:* spent

INDICATIVE MOOD

Pres. I spend	we spend
you spend	you spend
he (she, it) spends	they spend
Pres. I am spending	we are spending
Prog. you are spending	you are spending
he (she, it) is spending	they are spending
Pres. I do spend	we do spend
Int. you do spend	you do spend
he (she, it) does spend	they do spend
Fut. I shall spend	we shall spend
you will spend	you will spend
he (she, it) will spend	they will spend
Cond. I would spend	we would spend
you would spend	you would spend
he (she, it) would spend	they would spend
Past I spent	we spent
you spent	you spent
he (she, it) spent	they spent
Past I was spending	we were spending
Prog. you were spending	you were spending
he (she, it) was spending	they were spending
Past I did spend	we did spend
Int. you did spend	you did spend
he (she, it) did spend	they did spend
Pres. I have spent	we have spent
Perf. you have spent	you have spent
he (she, it) has spent	they have spent
Past I had spent	we had spent
Perf. you had spent	you had spent
he (she, it) had spent	they had spent
Fut. I shall have spent	we shall have spent
Perf. you will have spent	you will have spent
he (she, it) will have spent	they will have spent
Cond. I would have spent	we would have spent
Perf. you would have spent	you would have spent
he (she, it) would have spent	they would have spent

IMPERATIVE MOOD
spend

SUBJUNCTIVE MOOD

Pres. if I spend	if we spend
if you spend	if you spend
if he (she, it) spend	if they spend
Past if I spent	if we spent
if you spent	if you spent
if he (she, it) spent	if they spent
Fut. if I should spend	if we should spend
if you should spend	if you should spend
if he (she, it) should spend	if they should spend

Infinitive: to be spent   *Present Participle:* being spent
Perfect Infinitive: to have been spent   *Past Participle:* been spent

INDICATIVE MOOD

Pres. I am spent you are spent he (she, it) is spent	we are spent you are spent they are spent
Pres. Prog. I am being spent you are being spent he (she, it) is being spent	we are being spent you are being spent they are being spent
Pres. Int. I do get spent you do get spent he (she, it) does get spent	we do get spent you do get spent they do get spent
Fut. I shall be spent you will be spent he (she, it) will be spent	we shall be spent you will be spent they will be spent
Cond. I would be spent you would be spent he (she, it) would be spent	we would be spent you would be spent they would be spent
Past I was spent you were spent he (she, it) was spent	we were spent you were spent they were spent
Past Prog. I was being spent you were being spent he (she, it) was being spent	we were being spent you were being spent they were being spent
Past Int. I did get spent you did get spent he (she, it) did get spent	we did get spent you did get spent they did get spent
Pres. Perf. I have been spent you have been spent he (she, it) has been spent	we have been spent you have been spent they have been spent
Past Perf. I had been spent you had been spent he (she, it) had been spent	we had been spent you had been spent they had been spent
Fut. Perf. I shall have been spent you will have been spent he (she, it) will have been spent	we shall have been spent you will have been spent they will have been spent
Cond. Perf. I would have been spent you would have been spent he (she, it) would have been spent	we would have been spent you would have been spent they would have been spent

IMPERATIVE MOOD
be spent

SUBJUNCTIVE MOOD

Pres. if I be spent if you be spent if he (she, it) be spent	if we be spent if you be spent if they be spent
Past if I were spent if you were spent if he (she, it) were spent	if we were spent if you were spent if they were spent
Fut. if I should be spent if you should be spent if he (she, it) should be spent	if we should be spent if you should be spent if they should be spent

to spin (active voice) *Principal Parts:* spin, spinning, spun, spun

Infinitive: to spin   *Present Participle:* spinning
Perfect Infinitive: to have spun   *Past Participle:* spun

INDICATIVE MOOD

Pres.	I spin	we spin
	you spin	you spin
	he (she, it) spins	they spin
Pres.	I am spinning	we are spinning
Prog.	you are spinning	you are spinning
	he (she, it) is spinning	they are spinning
Pres.	I do spin	we do spin
Int.	you do spin	you do spin
	he (she, it) does spin	they do spin
Fut.	I shall spin	we shall spin
	you will spin	you will spin
	he (she, it) will spin	they will spin
Cond.	I would spin	we would spin
	you would spin	you would spin
	he (she, it) would spin	they would spin
Past	I spun	we spun
	you spun	you spun
	he (she, it) spun	they spun
Past	I was spinning	we were spinning
Prog.	you were spinning	you were spinning
	he (she, it) was spinning	they were spinning
Past	I did spin	we did spin
Int.	you did spin	you did spin
	he (she, it) did spin	they did spin
Pres.	I have spun	we have spun
Perf.	you have spun	you have spun
	he (she, it) has spun	they have spun
Past	I had spun	we had spun
Perf.	you had spun	you had spun
	he (she, it) had spun	they had spun
Fut.	I shall have spun	we shall have spun
Perf.	you will have spun	you will have spun
	he (she, it) will have spun	they will have spun
Cond.	I would have spun	we would have spun
Perf.	you would have spun	you would have spun
	he (she, it) would have spun	they would have spun

IMPERATIVE MOOD
spin

SUBJUNCTIVE MOOD

Pres.	if I spin	if we spin
	if you spin	if you spin
	if he (she, it) spin	if they spin
Past	if I spun	if we spun
	if you spun	if you spun
	if he (she, it) spun	if they spun
Fut.	if I should spin	if we should spin
	if you should spin	if you should spin
	if he (she, it) should spin	if they should spin

Infinitive: to be spun
Perfect Infinitive: to have been spun

Present Participle: being spun
Past Participle: been spun

INDICATIVE MOOD

Pres.	I am spun you are spun he (she, it) is spun	we are spun you are spun they are spun
Pres. *Prog.*	I am being spun you are being spun he (she, it) is being spun	we are being spun you are being spun they are being spun
Pres. *Int.*	I do get spun you do get spun he (she, it) does get spun	we do get spun you do get spun they do get spun
Fut.	I shall be spun you will be spun he (she, it) will be spun	we shall be spun you will be spun they will be spun
Cond.	I would be spun you would be spun he (she, it) would be spun	we would be spun you would be spun they would be spun
Past	I was spun you were spun he (she, it) was spun	we were spun you were spun they were spun
Past *Prog.*	I was being spun you were being spun he (she, it) was being spun	we were being spun you were being spun they were being spun
Past *Int.*	I did get spun you did get spun he (she, it) did get spun	we did get spun you did get spun they did get spun
Pres. *Perf.*	I have been spun you have been spun he (she, it) has been spun	we have been spun you have been spun they have been spun
Past *Perf.*	I had been spun you had been spun ho (she, it) had been spun	we had been spun you had been spun they had been spun
Fut. *Perf.*	I shall have been spun you will have been spun he (she, it) will have been spun	we shall have been spun you will have been spun they will have been spun
Cond. *Perf.*	I would have been spun you would have been spun he (she, it) would have been spun	we would have been spun you would have been spun they would have been spun

IMPERATIVE MOOD
be spun

SUBJUNCTIVE MOOD

Pres.	if I be spun if you be spun if he (she, it) be spun	if we be spun if you be spun if they be spun
Past	if I were spun if you were spun if he (she, it) were spun	if we were spun if you were spun if they were spun
Fut.	if I should be spun if you should be spun if he (she, it) should be spun	if we should be spun if you should be spun if they should be spun

to spring (active voice)

Principal Parts: spring, springing, sprang (sprung), sprung

Infinitive: to spring
Perfect Infinitive: to have sprung

Present Participle: springing
Past Participle: sprung

INDICATIVE MOOD

Pres.	I spring	we spring
	you spring	you spring
	he (she, it) springs	they spring
Pres.	I am springing	we are springing
Prog.	you are springing	you are springing
	he (she, it) is springing	they are springing
Pres.	I do spring	we do spring
Int.	you do spring	you do spring
	he (she, it) does spring	they do spring
Fut.	I shall spring	we shall spring
	you will spring	you will spring
	he (she, it) will spring	they will spring
Cond.	I would spring	we would spring
	you would spring	you would spring
	he (she, it) would spring	they would spring
Past	I sprang, sprung	we sprang, sprung
	you sprang, sprung	you sprang, sprung
	he (she, it) sprang, sprung	they sprang, sprung
Past	I was springing	we were springing
Prog.	you were springing	you were springing
	he (she, it) was springing	they were springing
Past	I did spring	we did spring
Int.	you did spring	you did spring
	he (she, it) did spring	they did spring
Pres.	I have sprung	we have sprung
Perf.	you have sprung	you have sprung
	he (she, it) has sprung	they have sprung
Past	I had sprung	we had sprung
Perf.	you had sprung	you had sprung
	he (she, it) had sprung	they had sprung
Fut.	I shall have sprung	we shall have sprung
Perf.	you will have sprung	you will have sprung
	he (she, it) will have sprung	they will have sprung
Cond.	I would have sprung	we would have sprung
Perf.	you would have sprung	you would have sprung
	he (she, it) would have sprung	they would have sprung

IMPERATIVE MOOD
spring

SUBJUNCTIVE MOOD

Pres.	if I spring	if we spring
	if you spring	if you spring
	if he (she, it) spring	if they spring
Past	if I sprang, sprung	if we sprang, sprung
	if you sprang, sprung	if you sprang, sprung
	if he (she, it) sprang, sprung	if they sprang, sprung
Fut.	if I should spring	if we should spring
	if you should spring	if you should spring
	if he (she, it) should spring	if they should spring

(passive voice)

Infinitive: to be sprung *Present Participle:* being sprung
Perfect Infinitive: to have been sprung *Past Participle:* been sprung

INDICATIVE MOOD

Pres. I am sprung	we are sprung
you are sprung	you are sprung
he (she, it) is sprung	they are sprung
Pres. I am being sprung	we are being sprung
Prog. you are being sprung	you are being sprung
he (she, it) is being sprung	they are being sprung
Pres. I do get sprung	we do get sprung
Int. you do get sprung	you do get sprung
he (she, it) does get sprung	they do get sprung
Fut. I shall be sprung	we shall be sprung
you will be sprung	you will be sprung
he (she, it) will be sprung	they will be sprung
Cond. I would be sprung	we would be sprung
you would be sprung	you would be sprung
he (she, it) would be sprung	they would be sprung
Past I was sprung	we were sprung
you were sprung	you were sprung
he (she, it) was sprung	they were sprung
Past I was being sprung	we were being sprung
Prog. you were being sprung	you were being sprung
he (she, it) was being sprung	they were being sprung
Past I did get sprung	we did get sprung
Int. you did get sprung	you did get sprung
he (she, it) did get sprung	they did get sprung
Pres. I have been sprung	we have been sprung
Perf. you have been sprung	you have been sprung
he (she, it) has been sprung	they have been sprung
Past I had been sprung	we had been sprung
Perf. you had been sprung	you had been sprung
he she, it) had been sprung	they had been sprung
Fut. I shall have been sprung	we shall have been sprung
Perf. you will have been sprung	you will have been sprung
he (she, it) will have been sprung	they will have been sprung
Cond. I would have been sprung	we would have been sprung
Perf. you would have been sprung	you would have been sprung
he (she, it) would have been sprung	they would have been sprung

IMPERATIVE MOOD
be sprung

SUBJUNCTIVE MOOD

Pres. if I be sprung	if we be sprung
if you be sprung	if you be sprung
if he (she, it) be sprung	if they be sprung
Past if I were sprung	if we were sprung
if you were sprung	if you were sprung
if he (she, it) were sprung	if they were sprung
Fut. if I should be sprung	if we should be sprung
if you should be sprung	if you should be sprung
if he (she, it) should be sprung	if they should be sprung

315

to stand (active voice)

Infinitive: to stand
Perfect Infinitive: to have stood

Present Participle: standing
Past Participle: stood

INDICATIVE MOOD

Pres.	I stand	we stand
	you stand	you stand
	he (she, it) stands	they stand
Pres.	I am standing	we are standing
Prog.	you are standing	you are standing
	he (she, it) is standing	they are standing
Pres.	I do stand	we do stand
Int.	you do stand	you do stand
	he (she, it) does stand	they do stand
Fut.	I shall stand	we shall stand
	you will stand	you will stand
	he (she, it) will stand	they will stand
Cond.	I would stand	we would stand
	you would stand	you would stand
	he (she, it) would stand	they would stand
Past	I stood	we stood
	you stood	you stood
	he (she, it) stood	they stood
Past	I was standing	we were standing
Prog.	you were standing	you were standing
	he (she, it) was standing	they were standing
Past	I did stand	we did stand
Int.	you did stand	you did stand
	he (she, it) did stand	they did stand
Pres.	I have stood	we have stood
Perf.	you have stood	you have stood
	he (she, it) has stood	they have stood
Past	I had stood	we had stood
Perf.	you had stood	you had stood
	he (she, it) had stood	they had stood
Fut.	I shall have stood	we shall have stood
Perf.	you will have stood	you will have stood
	he (she, it) will have stood	they will have stood
Cond.	I would have stood	we would have stood
Perf.	you would have stood	you would have stood
	he (she, it) would have stood	they would have stood

IMPERATIVE MOOD
stand

SUBJUNCTIVE MOOD

Pres.	if I stand	if we stand
	if you stand	if you stand
	if he (she, it) stand	if they stand
Past	if I stood	if we stood
	if you stood	if you stood
	if he (she, it) stood	if they stood
Fut.	if I should stand	if we should stand
	if you should stand	if you should stand
	if he (she, it) should stand	if they should stand

Infinitive: to be stood
Perfect Infinitive: to have been stood

Present Participle: being stood
Past Participle: been stood

INDICATIVE MOOD

Pres. I am stood you are stood he (she, it) is stood	we are stood you are stood they are stood
Pres. I am being stood *Prog.* you are being stood he (she, it) is being stood	we are being stood you are being stood they are being stood
Pres. I do get stood *Int.* you do get stood he (she, it) does get stood	we do get stood you do get stood they do get stood
Fut. I shall be stood you will be stood he (she, it) will be stood	we shall be stood you will be stood they will be stood
Cond. I would be stood you would be stood he (she, it) would be stood	we would be stood you would be stood they would be stood
Past I was stood you were stood he (she, it) was stood	we were stood you were stood they were stood
Past I was being stood *Prog.* you were being stood he (she, it) was being stood	we were being stood you were being stood they were being stood
Past I did get stood *Int.* you did get stood he (she, it) did get stood	we did get stood you did get stood they did get stood
Pres. I have been stood *Perf.* you have been stood he (she, it) has been stood	we have been stood you have been stood they have been stood
Past I had been stood *Perf.* you had been stood he (she, it) had been stood	we had been stood you had been stood they had been stood
Fut. I shall have been stood *Perf.* you will have been stood he (she, it) will have been stood	we shall have been stood you will have been stood they will have been stood
Cond. I would have been stood *Perf.* you would have been stood he (she, it) would have been stood	we would have been stood you would have been stood they would have been stood

IMPERATIVE MOOD
be stood

SUBJUNCTIVE MOOD

Pres. if I be stood if you be stood if he (she, it) be stood	if we be stood if you be stood if they be stood
Past if I were stood if you were stood if he (she, it) were stood	if we were stood if you were stood if they were stood
Fut. if I should be stood if you should be stood if he (she, it) should be stood	if we should be stood if you should be stood if they should be stood

NOTE: The verb *to understand* follows the same form as for the verb *to stand.*

Infinitive: to steal
Perfect Infinitive: to have stolen

Present Participle: stealing
Past Participle: stolen

INDICATIVE MOOD

Pres. I steal	we steal
you steal	you steal
he (she, it) steals	they steal
Pres. I am stealing	we are stealing
Prog. you are stealing	you are stealing
he (she, it) is stealing	they are stealing
Pres. I do steal	we do steal
Int. you do steal	you do steal
he (she, it) does steal	they do steal
Fut. I shall steal	we shall steal
you will steal	you will steal
he (she, it) will steal	they will steal
Cond. I would steal	we would steal
you would steal	you would steal
he (she, it) would steal	they would steal
Past I stole	we stole
you stole	you stole
he (she, it) stole	they stole
Past I was stealing	we were stealing
Prog. you were stealing	you were stealing
he (she, it) was stealing	they were stealing
Past I did steal	we did steal
Int. you did steal	you did steal
he (she, it) did steal	they did steal
Pres. I have stolen	we have stolen
Perf. you have stolen	you have stolen
he (she, it) has stolen	they have stolen
Past I had stolen	we had stolen
Perf. you had stolen	you had stolen
he (she, it) had stolen	they had stolen
Fut. I shall have stolen	we shall have stolen
Perf. you will have stolen	you will have stolen
he (she, it) will have stolen	they will have stolen
Cond. I would have stolen	we would have stolen
Perf. you would have stolen	you would have stolen
he (she, it) would have stolen	they would have stolen

IMPERATIVE MOOD
steal

SUBJUNCTIVE MOOD

Pres. if I steal	if we steal
if you steal	if you steal
if he (she, it) steal	if they steal
Past if I stole	if we stole
if you stole	if you stole
if he (she, it) stole	if they stole
Fut. if I should steal	if we should steal
if you should steal	if you should steal
if he (she, it) should steal	if they should steal

Infinitive: to be stolen
Perfect Infinitive: to have been stolen

Present Participle: being stolen
Past Participle: been stolen

INDICATIVE MOOD

Pres.	I am stolen you are stolen he (she, it) is stolen	we are stolen you are stolen they are stolen
Pres. Prog.	I am being stolen you are being stolen he (she, it) is being stolen	we are being stolen you are being stolen they are being stolen
Pres. Int.	I do get stolen you do get stolen he (she, it) does get stolen	we do get stolen you do get stolen they do get stolen
Fut.	I shall be stolen you will be stolen he (she, it) will be stolen	we shall be stolen you will be stolen they will be stolen
Cond.	I would be stolen you would be stolen he (she, it) would be stolen	we would be stolen you would be stolen they would be stolen
Past	I was stolen you were stolen he (she, it) was stolen	we were stolen you were stolen they were stolen
Past Prog.	I was being stolen you were being stolen he (she, it) was being stolen	we were being stolen you were being stolen they were being stolen
Past Int.	I did get stolen you did get stolen he (she, it) did get stolen	we did get stolen you did get stolen they did get stolen
Pres. Perf.	I have been stolen you have been stolen he (she, it) has been stolen	we have been stolen you have been stolen they have been stolen
Past Perf.	I had been stolen you had been stolen he (she, it) had been stolen	we had been stolen you had been stolen they had been stolen
Fut. Perf.	I shall have been stolen you will have been stolen he (she, it) will have been stolen	we shall have been stolen you will have been stolen they will have been stolen
Cond. Perf.	I would have been stolen you would have been stolen he (she, it) would have been stolen	we would have been stolen you would have been stolen they would have been stolen

IMPERATIVE MOOD
be stolen

SUBJUNCTIVE MOOD

Pres.	if I be stolen if you be stolen if he (she, it) be stolen	if we be stolen if you be stolen if they be stolen
Past	if I were stolen if you were stolen if he (she, it) were stolen	if we were stolen if you were stolen if they were stolen
Fut.	if I should be stolen if you should be stolen if he (she, it) should be stolen	if we should be stolen if you should be stolen if they should be stolen

to stick (active voice)   *Principal Parts:* stick, sticking, stuck, stuck

---

Infinitive: to stick   *Present Participle:* sticking
Perfect Infinitive: to have stuck   *Past Participle:* stuck

INDICATIVE MOOD

Pres.   I stick

you stick

he (she, it) sticks

we stick

you stick

they stick

Pres.
Prog. I am sticking

you are sticking

he (she, it) is sticking

we are sticking

you are sticking

they are sticking

Pres.
Int. I do stick

you do stick

he (she, it) does stick

we do stick

you do stick

they do stick

Fut. I shall stick

you will stick

he (she, it) will stick

we shall stick

you will stick

they will stick

Cond. I would stick

you would stick

he (she, it) would stick

we would stick

you would stick

they would stick

Past I stuck

you stuck

he (she, it) stuck

we stuck

you stuck

they stuck

Past
Prog. I was sticking

you were sticking

he (she, it) was sticking

we were sticking

you were sticking

they were sticking

Past
Int. I did stick

you did stick

he (she, it) did stick

we did stick

you did stick

they did stick

Pres.
Perf. I have stuck

you have stuck

he (she, it) has stuck

we have stuck

you have stuck

they have stuck

Past
Perf. I had stuck

you had stuck

he (she, it) had stuck

we had stuck

you had stuck

they had stuck

Fut.
Perf. I shall have stuck

you will have stuck

he (she, it) will have stuck

we shall have stuck

you will have stuck

they will have stuck

Cond.
Perf. I would have stuck

you would have stuck

he (she, it) would have stuck

we would have stuck

you would have stuck

they would have stuck

IMPERATIVE MOOD
stick

SUBJUNCTIVE MOOD

Pres. if I stick

if you stick

if he (she, it) stick

if we stick

if you stick

if they stick

Past if I stuck

if you stuck

if he (she, it) stuck

if we stuck

if you stuck

if they stuck

Fut. if I should stick

if you should stick

if he (she, it) should stick

if we should stick

if you should stick

if they should stick

Infinitive: to be stuck   *Present Participle:* being stuck
Perfect Infinitive: to have been stuck   *Past Participle:* been stuck

INDICATIVE MOOD

Pres. I am stuck   we are stuck
you are stuck   you are stuck
he (she, it) is stuck   they are stuck

Pres. I am being stuck   we are being stuck
Prog. you are being stuck   you are being stuck
he (she, it) is being stuck   they are being stuck

Pres. I do get stuck   we do get stuck
Int.   you do get stuck   you do get stuck
he (she, it) does get stuck   they do get stuck

Fut.   I shall be stuck   we shall be stuck
you will be stuck   you will be stuck
he (she, it) will be stuck   they will be stuck

Cond. I would be stuck   we would be stuck
you would be stuck   you would be stuck
he (she, it) would be stuck   they would be stuck

Past   I was stuck   we were stuck
you were stuck   you were stuck
he (she, it) was stuck   they were stuck

Past   I was being stuck   we were being stuck
Prog. you were being stuck   you were being stuck
he (she, it) was being stuck   they were being stuck

Past   I did get stuck   we did get stuck
Int.   you did get stuck   you did get stuck
he (she, it) did get stuck   they did get stuck

Pres. I have been stuck   we have been stuck
Perf. you have been stuck   you have been stuck
he (she, it) has been stuck   they have been stuck

Past   I had been stuck   we had been stuck
Perf. you had been stuck   you had been stuck
he (she, it) had been stuck   they had been stuck

Fut.   I shall have been stuck   we shall have been stuck
Perf. you will have been stuck   you will have been stuck
he (she, it) will have been stuck   they will have been stuck

Cond. I would have been stuck   we would have been stuck
Perf. you would have been stuck   you would have been stuck
he (she, it) would have been stuck   they would have been stuck

IMPERATIVE MOOD
be stuck

SUBJUNCTIVE MOOD

Pres. if I be stuck   if we be stuck
if you be stuck   if you be stuck
if he (she, it) be stuck   if they be stuck

Past   if I were stuck   if we were stuck
if you were stuck   if you were stuck
if he (she, it) were stuck   if they were stuck

Fut.   if I should be stuck   if we should be stuck
if you should be stuck   if you should be stuck
if he (she, it) should be stuck   if they should be stuck

Infinitive: to sting
Perfect Infinitive: to have stung

Present Participle: stinging
Past Participle: stung

INDICATIVE MOOD

Pres.
I sting
you sting
he (she, it) stings

we sting
you sting
they sting

Pres. Prog.
I am stinging
you are stinging
he (she, it) is stinging

we are stinging
you are stinging
they are stinging

Pres. Int.
I do sting
you do sting
he (she, it) does sting

we do sting
you do sting
they do sting

Fut.
I shall sting
you will sting
he (she, it) will sting

we shall sting
you will sting
they will sting

Cond.
I would sting
you would sting
he (she, it) would sting

we would sting
you would sting
they would sting

Past
I stung
you stung
he (she, it) stung

we stung
you stung
they stung

Past Prog.
I was stinging
you were stinging
he (she, it) was stinging

we were stinging
you were stinging
they were stinging

Past Int.
I did sting
you did sting
he (she, it) did sting

we did sting
you did sting
they did sting

Pres. Perf.
I have stung
you have stung
he (she, it) has stung

we have stung
you have stung
they have stung

Past Perf.
I had stung
you had stung
he (she, it) had stung

we had stung
you had stung
they had stung

Fut. Perf.
I shall have stung
you will have stung
he (she, it) will have stung

we shall have stung
you will have stung
they will have stung

Cond. Perf.
I would have stung
you would have stung
he (she, it) would have stung

we would have stung
you would have stung
they would have stung

IMPERATIVE MOOD
sting

SUBJUNCTIVE MOOD

Pres.
if I sting
if you sting
if he (she, it) sting

if we sting
if you sting
if they sting

Past
if I stung
if you stung
if he (she, it) stung

if we stung
if you stung
if they stung

Fut.
if I should sting
if you should sting
if he (she, it) should sting

if we should sting
if you should sting
if they should sting

(passive voice)

Infinitive: to be stung
Perfect Infinitive: to have been stung

Present Participle: being stung
Past Participle: been stung

INDICATIVE MOOD

Pres. I am stung	we are stung
you are stung	you are stung
he (she, it) is stung	they are stung
Pres. I am being stung	we are being stung
Prog. you are being stung	you are being stung
he (she, it) is being stung	they are being stung
Pres. I do get stung	we do get stung
Int. you do get stung	you do get stung
he (she, it) does get stung	they do get stung
Fut. I shall be stung	we shall be stung
you will be stung	you will be stung
he (she, it) will be stung	they will be stung
Cond. I would be stung	we would be stung
you would be stung	you would be stung
he (she, it) would be stung	they would be stung
Past I was stung	we were stung
you were stung	you were stung
he (she, it) was stung	they were stung
Past I was being stung	we were being stung
Prog. you were being stung	you were being stung
he (she, it) was being stung	they were being stung
Past I did get stung	we did get stung
Int. you did get stung	you did get stung
he (she, it) did get stung	they did get stung
Pres. I have been stung	we have been stung
Perf. you have been stung	you have been stung
he (she, it) has been stung	they have been stung
Past I had been stung	we had been stung
Perf. you had been stung	you had been stung
he (she, it) had been stung	they had been stung
Fut. I shall have been stung	we shall have been stung
Perf. you will have been stung	you will have been stung
he (she, it) will have been stung	they will have been stung
Cond. I would have been stung	we would have been stung
Perf. you would have been stung	you would have been stung
he (she, it) would have been stung	they would have been stung

IMPERATIVE MOOD
be stung

SUBJUNCTIVE MOOD

Pres. if I be stung	if we be stung
if you be stung	if you be stung
if he (she, it) be stung	if they be stung
Past if I were stung	if we were stung
if you were stung	if you were stung
if he (she, it) were stung	if they were stung
Fut. if I should be stung	if we should be stung
if you should be stung	if you should be stung
if he (she, it) should be stung	if they should be stung

to stride (active voice only)   *Principal Parts:*   stride,   striding,   strode,
                                                              stridden
_____

(intransitive verb)

Infinitive: to stride   *Present Participle:* striding
Perfect Infinitive: to have stridden   *Past Participle:* stridden

INDICATIVE MOOD

Pres. I stride	we stride
you stride	you stride
he (she, it) strides	they stride
Pres. I am striding	we are striding
Prog. you are striding	you are striding
he (she, it) is striding	they are striding
Pres. I do stride	we do stride
Int. you do stride	you do stride
he (she, it) does stride	they do stride
Fut. I shall stride	we shall stride
you will stride	you will stride
he (she, it) will stride	they will stride
Cond. I would stride	we would stride
you would stride	you would stride
he (she, it) would stride	they would stride
Past I strode	we strode
you strode	you strode
he (she, it) strode	they strode
Past I was striding	we were striding
Prog. you were striding	you were striding
he (she, it) was striding	they were striding
Past I did stride	we did stride
Int. you did stride	you did stride
he (she, it) did stride	they did stride
Pres. I have stridden	we have stridden
Perf. you have stridden	you have stridden
he (she, it) has stridden	they have stridden
Past I had stridden	we had stridden
Perf. you had stridden	you had stridden
he (she, it) had stridden	they had stridden
Fut. I shall have stridden	we shall have stridden
Perf. you will have stridden	you will have stridden
he (she, it) will have stridden	they will have stridden
Cond. I would have stridden	we would have stridden
Perf. you would have stridden	you would have stridden
he (she, it) would have stridden	they would have stridden

IMPERATIVE MOOD
stride

SUBJUNCTIVE MOOD

Pres. if I stride	if we stride
if you stride	if you stride
if he (she, it) stride	if they stride
Past if I strode	if we strode
if you strode	if you strode
if he (she, it) strode	if they strode
Fut. if I should stride	if we should stride
if you should stride	if you should stride
if he (she, it) should stride	if they should stride

To stride is an intransitive verb.

It does not take an object.

It describes action, but the action is self-contained.

Like other intransitive verbs, it may be followed by adverbs, adverbial phrases and clauses describing the how, why, when, and where of the action:

HOW: The giant strode *mightily*. (adverb)

WHY: He was striding *to impress people with his vitality*. (adverbial phrase)

WHEN: Mephistopheles strode *when he left Arcadia to return to German soil*. (adverbial clause)

WHERE: I shall stride *into the room*. (adverbial phrase)

to strike (active voice)   *Principal Parts:* strike, striking, struck, struck (stricken)

Infinitive: to strike   *Present Participle:* striking
Perfect Infinitive: to have struck, stricken   *Past Participle:* struck, stricken

INDICATIVE MOOD

Pres.	I strike	we strike
	you strike	you strike
	he (she, it) strikes	they strike
Pres.	I am striking	we are striking
Prog.	you are striking	you are striking
	he (she, it) is striking	they are striking
Pres.	I do strike	we do strike
Int.	you do strike	you do strike
	he (she, it) does strike	they do strike
Fut.	I shall strike	we shall strike
	you will strike	you will strike
	he (she, it) will strike	they will strike
Cond.	I would strike	we would strike
	you would strike	you would strike
	he (she, it) would strike	they would strike
Past	I struck	we struck
	you struck	you struck
	he (she, it) struck	they struck
Past	I was striking	we were striking
Prog.	you were striking	you were striking
	he (she, it) was striking	they were striking
Past	I did strike	we did strike
Int.	you did strike	you did strike
	he (she, it) did strike	they did strike
Pres.	I have struck, stricken	we have struck, stricken
Perf.	you have struck, stricken	you have struck, stricken
	he (she, it) has struck, stricken	they have struck, stricken
Past	I had struck, stricken	we had struck, stricken
Perf.	you had struck, stricken	you had struck, stricken
	he (she, it) had struck, stricken	they had struck, stricken
Fut.	I shall have struck, stricken	we shall have struck, stricken
Perf.	you will have struck, stricken	you will have struck, stricken
	he (she, it) will have struck, stricken	they will have struck, stricken
Cond.	I would have struck, stricken	we would have struck, stricken
Perf.	you would have struck, stricken	you would have struck, stricken
	he (she, it) would have struck, stricken	they would have struck, stricken

IMPERATIVE MOOD
strike

SUBJUNCTIVE MOOD

Pres.	if I strike	if we strike
	if you strike	if you strike
	if he (she, it) strike	if they strike
Past	if I struck	if we struck
	if you struck	if you struck
	if he (she, it) struck	if they struck
Fut.	if I should strike	if we should strike
	if you should strike	if you should strike
	if he (she, it) should strike	if they should strike

326

(passive voice)

Infinitive: to be struck, stricken
Perfect Infinitive: to have been struck, stricken
Present Participle: being struck, stricken
Past Participle: been struck, stricken

INDICATIVE MOOD

Pres. I am struck, stricken
you are struck, stricken
he (she, it) is struck, stricken

we are struck, stricken
you are struck, stricken
they are struck, stricken

Pres. I am being struck, stricken
Prog. you are being struck, stricken
he (she, it) is being struck, stricken

we are being struck, stricken
you are being struck, stricken
they are being struck, stricken

Pres. I do get struck, stricken
Int. you do get struck, stricken
he (she, it) does get struck, stricken

we do get struck, stricken
you do get struck, stricken
they do get struck, stricken

Fut. I shall be struck, stricken
you will be struck, stricken
he (she, it) will be struck, stricken

we shall be struck, stricken
you will be struck, stricken
they will be struck, stricken

Cond. I would be struck, stricken
you would be struck, stricken
he (she, it) would be struck, stricken

we would be struck, stricken
you would be struck, stricken
they would be struck, stricken

Past I was struck, stricken
you were struck, stricken
he (she, it) was struck, stricken

we were struck, stricken
you were struck, stricken
they were struck, stricken

Past I was being struck, stricken
Prog. you were being struck, stricken
he (she, it) was being struck, stricken

we were being struck, stricken
you were being struck, stricken
they were being struck, stricken

Past I did get struck, stricken
Int. you did get struck, stricken
he (she, it) did get struck, stricken

we did get struck, stricken
you did get struck, stricken
they did get struck, stricken

Pres. I have been struck, stricken
Perf. you have been struck, stricken
he (she, it) has been struck, stricken

we have been struck, stricken
you have been struck, stricken
they have been struck, stricken

Past I had been struck, stricken
Perf. you had been struck, stricken
he (she, it) had been struck, stricken

we had been struck, stricken
you had been struck, stricken
they had been struck, stricken

Fut. I shall have been struck, stricken
Perf. you will have been struck, stricken
he (she, it) will have been struck, stricken

we shall have been struck, stricken
you will have been struck, stricken
they will have been struck, stricken

Cond. I would have been struck, stricken
Perf. you would have been struck, stricken
he (she, it) would have been struck, stricken

we would have been struck, stricken
you would have been struck, stricken
they would have been struck, stricken

(passive voice, continued)

IMPERATIVE MOOD
be struck, stricken

SUBJUNCTIVE MOOD

Pres. if I be struck, stricken
if you be struck, stricken
if he (she, it) be struck, stricken

if we be struck, stricken
if you be struck, stricken
if they be struck, stricken

Past if I were struck, stricken
if you were struck, stricken
if he (she, it) were struck, stricken

if we were struck, stricken
if you were struck, stricken
if they were struck, stricken

Fut. if I should be struck, stricken
if you should be struck, stricken
if he (she, it) should be struck, stricken

if we should be struck, stricken
if you should be struck, stricken
if they should be struck, stricken

to strive (active voice only) *Principal Parts:* strive, striving, strove, striven

(intransitive verb)

Infinitive: to strive	*Present Participle:* striving
Perfect Infinitive: to have striven	*Past Participle:* striven

INDICATIVE MOOD

Pres.	I strive	we strive
	you strive	you strive
	he (she, it) strives	they strive
Pres.	I am striving	we are striving
Prog.	you are striving	you are striving
	he (she, it) is striving	they are striving
Pres.	I do strive	we do strive
Int.	you do strive	you do strive
	he (she, it) does strive	they do strive
Fut.	I shall strive	we shall strive
	you will strive	you will strive
	he (she, it) will strive	they will strive
Cond.	I would strive	we would strive
	you would strive	you would strive
	he (she, it) would strive	they would strive
Past	I strove	we strove
	you strove	you strove
	he (she, it) strove	they strove
Past	I was striving	we were striving
Prog.	you were striving	you were striving
	he (she, it) was striving	they were striving
Past	I did strive	we did strive
Int.	you did strive	you did strive
	he (she, it) did strive	they did strive
Pres.	I have striven	we have striven
Perf.	you have striven	you have striven
	he (she, it) has striven	they have striven
Past	I had striven	we had striven
Perf.	you had striven	you had striven
	he (she, it) had striven	they had striven
Fut.	I shall have striven	we shall have striven
Perf.	you will have striven	you will have striven
	he (she, it) will have striven	they will have striven
Cond.	I would have striven	we would have striven
Perf.	you would have striven	you would have striven
	he (she, it) would have striven	they would have striven

IMPERATIVE MOOD
strive

SUBJUNCTIVE MOOD

Pres.	if I strive	if we strive
	if you strive	if you strive
	if he (she, it) strive	if they strive
Past	if I strove	if we strove
	if you strove	if you strove
	if he (she, it) strove	if they strove
Fut.	if I should strive	if we should strive
	if you should strive	if you should strive
	if he (she, it) should strive	if they should strive

to swear (active voice)   *Principal Parts:* swear, swearing, swore, sworn

---

Infinitive: to swear
Perfect Infinitive: to have sworn

Present Participle: swearing
Past Participle: sworn

INDICATIVE MOOD

Pres. I swear you swear he (she, it) swears	we swear you swear they swear
Pres. **Prog.** I am swearing you are swearing he (she, it) is swearing	we are swearing you are swearing they are swearing
Pres. **Int.** I do swear you do swear he (she, it) does swear	we do swear you do swear they do swear
Fut. I shall swear you will swear he (she, it) will swear	we shall swear you will swear they will swear
Cond. I would swear you would swear he (she, it) would swear	we would swear you would swear they would swear
Past I swore you swore he (she, it) swore	we swore you swore they swore
Past **Prog.** I was swearing you were swearing he (she, it) was swearing	we were swearing you were swearing they were swearing
Past **Int.** I did swear you did swear he (she, it) did swear	we did swear you did swear they did swear
Pres. **Perf.** I have sworn you have sworn he (she, it) has sworn	we have sworn you have sworn they have sworn
Past **Perf.** I had sworn you had sworn he (she, it) had sworn	we had sworn you had sworn they had sworn
Fut. **Perf.** I shall have sworn you will have sworn he (she, it) will have sworn	we shall have sworn you will have sworn they will have sworn
Cond. **Perf.** I would have sworn you would have sworn he (she, it) would have sworn	we would have sworn you would have sworn they would have sworn

IMPERATIVE MOOD
swear

SUBJUNCTIVE MOOD

Pres. if I swear if you swear if he (she, it) swear	if we swear if you swear if they swear
Past if I swore if you swore if he (she, it) swore	if we swore if you swore if they swore
Fut. if I should swear if you should swear if he (she, it) should swear	if we should swear if you should swear if they should swear

Infinitive: to be sworn
Perfect Infinitive: to have been sworn

Present Participle: being sworn
Past Participle: been sworn

INDICATIVE MOOD

Pres.	I am sworn	we are sworn
	you are sworn	you are sworn
	he (she, it) is sworn	they are sworn
Pres.	I am being sworn	we are being sworn
Prog.	you are being sworn	you are being sworn
	he (she, it) is being sworn	they are being sworn
Pres.	I do get sworn	we do get sworn
Int.	you do get sworn	you do get sworn
	he (she, it) does get sworn	they do get sworn
Fut.	I shall be sworn	we shall be sworn
	you will be sworn	you will be sworn
	he (she, it) will be sworn	they will be sworn
Cond.	I would be sworn	we would be sworn
	you would be sworn	you would be sworn
	he (she, it) would be sworn	they would be sworn
Past	I was sworn	we were sworn
	you were sworn	you were sworn
	he (she, it) was sworn	they were sworn
Past	I was being sworn	we were being sworn
Prog.	you were being sworn	you were being sworn
	he (she, it) was being sworn	they were being sworn
Past	I did get sworn	we did get sworn
Int.	you did get sworn	you did get sworn
	he (she, it) did get sworn	they did get sworn
Pres.	I have been sworn	we have been sworn
Perf.	you have been sworn	you have been sworn
	he (she, it) has been sworn	they have been sworn
Past	I had been sworn	we had been sworn
Perf.	you had been sworn	you had been sworn
	he (she, it) had been sworn	they had been sworn
Fut.	I shall have been sworn	we shall have been sworn
Perf.	you will have been sworn	you will have been sworn
	he (she, it) will have been sworn	they will have been sworn
Cond.	I would have been sworn	we would have been sworn
Perf.	you would have been sworn	you would have been sworn
	he (she, it) would have been sworn	they would have been sworn

IMPERATIVE MOOD
be sworn

SUBJUNCTIVE MOOD

Pres.	if I be sworn	if we be sworn
	if you be sworn	if you be sworn
	if he (she, it) be sworn	if they be sworn
Past	if I were sworn	if we were sworn
	if you were sworn	if you were sworn
	if he (she, it) were sworn	if they were sworn
Fut	if I should be sworn	if we should be sworn
	if you should be sworn	if you should be sworn
	if he (she, it) should be sworn	if they should be sworn

to sweat (active voice)*Principal Parts:* sweat, sweating, sweat (sweated), sweated

Infinitive: to sweat
Perfect Infinitive: to have sweated

Present Participle: sweating
Past Participle: sweated

INDICATIVE MOOD

Pres. I sweat you sweat he (she, it) sweats	we sweat you sweat they sweat
Pres. I am sweating **Prog.** you are sweating he (she, it) is sweating	we are sweating you are sweating they are sweating
Pres. I do sweat **Int.** you do sweat he (she, it) does sweat	we do sweat you do sweat they do sweat
Fut. I shall sweat you will sweat he (she, it) will sweat	we shall sweat you will sweat they will sweat
Cond. I would sweat you would sweat he (she, it) would sweat	we would sweat you would sweat they would sweat
Past I sweat, sweated you sweat, sweated he (she, it) sweat, sweated	we sweat, sweated you sweat, sweated they sweat, sweated
Past I was sweating **Prog.** you were sweating he (she, it) was sweating	we were sweating you were sweating they were sweating
Past I did sweat **Int.** you did sweat he (she, it) did sweat	we did sweat you did sweat they did sweat
Pres. I have sweated **Perf.** you have sweated he (she, it) has sweated	we have sweated you have sweated they have sweated
Past I had sweated **Perf.** you had sweated he (she, it) had sweated	we had sweated you had sweated they had sweated
Fut. I shall have sweated **Perf.** you will have sweated he (she, it) will have sweated	we shall have sweated you will have sweated they will have sweated
Cond. I would have sweated **Perf.** you would have sweated he (she, it) would have sweated	we would have sweated you would have sweated they would have sweated

IMPERATIVE MOOD
sweat

SUBJUNCTIVE MOOD

Pres. if I sweat if you sweat if he (she, it) sweat	if we sweat if you sweat if they sweat
Past if I sweat, sweated if you sweat, sweated if he (she, it) sweat, sweated	if we sweat, sweated if you sweat, sweated if they sweat, sweated
Fut. if I should sweat if you should sweat if he (she, it) should sweat	if we should sweat if you should sweat if they should sweat

Infinitive: to be sweated   *Present Participle:* being sweated
Perfect Infinitive: to have been sweated   *Past Participle:* been sweated

INDICATIVE MOOD

Pres.	I am sweated you are sweated he (she, it) is sweated	we are sweated you are sweated they are sweated
Pres. **Prog.**	I am being sweated you are being sweated he (she, it) is being sweated	we are being sweated you are being sweated they are being sweated
Pres. **Int.**	I do get sweated you do get sweated he (she, it) does get sweated	we do get sweated you do get sweated they do get sweated
Fut.	I shall be sweated you will be sweated he (she, it) will be sweated	we shall be sweated you will be sweated they will be sweated
Cond.	I would be sweated you would be sweated he (she, it) would be sweated	we would be sweated you would be sweated they would be sweated
Past	I was sweated you were sweated he (she, it) was sweated	we were sweated you were sweated they were sweated
Past **Prog.**	I was being sweated you were being sweated he (she, it) was being sweated	we were being sweated you were being sweated they were being sweated
Past **Int.**	I did get sweated you did get sweated he (she, it) did get sweated	we did get sweated you did get sweated they did get sweated
Pres. **Perf.**	I have been sweated you have been sweated he (she, it) has been sweated	we have been sweated you have been sweated they have been sweated
Past **Perf.**	I had been sweated you had been sweated he (she, it) had been sweated	we had been sweated you had been sweated they had been sweated
Fut. **Perf.**	I shall have been sweated you will have been sweated he (she, it) will have been sweated	we shall have been sweated you will have been sweated they will have been sweated
Cond. **Perf.**	I would have been sweated you would have been sweated he (she, it) would have been sweated	we would have been sweated you would have been sweated they would have been sweated

IMPERATIVE MOOD
be sweated

SUBJUNCTIVE MOOD

Pres.	if I be sweated if you be sweated if he (she, it) be sweated	if we be sweated if you be sweated if they be sweated
Past	if I were sweated if you were sweated if he (she, it) were sweated	if we were sweated if you were sweated if they were sweated
Fut.	if I should be sweated if you should be sweated if he (she, it) should be sweated	if we should be sweated if you should be sweated if they should be sweated

to sweep (active voice) *Principal Parts:* sweep, sweeping, swept, swept

---

Infinitive: to sweep
Perfect Infinitive: to have swept

Present Participle: sweeping
Past Participle: swept

INDICATIVE MOOD

Pres. I sweep
you sweep
he (she, it) sweeps

we sweep
you sweep
they sweep

Pres. Prog. I am sweeping
you are sweeping
he (she, it) is sweeping

we are sweeping
you are sweeping
they are sweeping

Pres. Int. I do sweep
you do sweep
he (she, it) does sweep

we do sweep
you do sweep
they do sweep

Fut. I shall sweep
you will sweep
he (she, it) will sweep

we shall sweep
you will sweep
they will sweep

Cond. I would sweep
you would sweep
he (she, it) would sweep

we would sweep
you would sweep
they would sweep

Past I swept
you swept
he (she, it) swept

we swept
you swept
they swept

Past Prog. I was sweeping
you were sweeping
he (she, it) was sweeping

we were sweeping
you were sweeping
they were sweeping

Past Int. I did sweep
you did sweep
he (she, it) did sweep

we did sweep
you did sweep
they did sweep

Pres. Perf. I have swept
you have swept
he (she, it) has swept

we have swept
you have swept
they have swept

Past Perf. I had swept
you had swept
he (she, it) had swept

we had swept
you had swept
they had swept

Fut. Perf. I shall have swept
you will have swept
he (she, it) will have swept

we shall have swept
you will have swept
they will have swept

Cond. Perf. I would have swept
you would have swept
he (she, it) would have swept

we would have swept
you would have swept
they would have swept

IMPERATIVE MOOD
sweep

SUBJUNCTIVE MOOD

Pres. if I sweep
if you sweep
if he (she, it) sweep

if we sweep
if you sweep
if they sweep

Past if I swept
if you swept
if he (she, it) swept

if we swept
if you swept
if they swept

Fut. if I should sweep
if you should sweep
if he (she, it) should sweep

if we should sweep
if you should sweep
if they should sweep

(passive voice)

Infinitive: to be swept
Perfect Infinitive: to have been swept

Present Participle: being swept
Past Participle: been swept

INDICATIVE MOOD

Pres.	I am swept	we are swept
	you are swept	you are swept
	he (she, it) is swept	they are swept
Pres.	I am being swept	we are being swept
Prog.	you are being swept	you are being swept
	he (she, it) is being swept	they are being swept
Pres.	I do get swept	we do get swept
Int.	you do get swept	you do get swept
	he (she, it) does get swept	they do get swept
Fut.	I shall be swept	we shall be swept
	you will be swept	you will be swept
	he (she, it) will be swept	they will be swept
Cond.	I would be swept	we would be swept
	you would be swept	you would be swept
	he (she, it) would be swept	they would be swept
Past	I was swept	we were swept
	you were swept	you were swept
	he (she, it) was swept	they were swept
Past	I was being swept	we were being swept
Prog.	you were being swept	you were being swept
	he (she, it) was being swept	they were being swept
Past	I did get swept	we did get swept
Int.	you did get swept	you did get swept
	he (she, it) did get swept	they did get swept
Pres.	I have been swept	we have been swept
Perf.	you have been swept	you have been swept
	he (she, it) has been swept	they have been swept
Past	I had been swept	we had been swept
Perf.	you had been swept	you had been swept
	he (she, it) had been swept	they had been swept
Fut.	I shall have been swept	we shall have been swept
Perf.	you will have been swept	you will have been swept
	he (she, it) will have been swept	they will have been swept
Cond.	I would have been swept	we would have been swept
Perf.	you would have been swept	you would have been swept
	he (she, it) would have been swept	they would have been swept

IMPERATIVE MOOD
be swept

SUBJUNCTIVE MOOD

Pres.	if I be swept	if we be swept
	if you be swept	if you be swept
	if he (she, it) be swept	if they be swept
Past	if I were swept	if we were swept
	if you were swept	if you were swept
	if he (she, it) were swept	if they were swept
Fut.	if I should be swept	if we should be swept
	if you should be swept	if you should be swept
	if he (she, it) should be swept	if they should be swept

to swim (active voice)

Principal Parts: swim, swimming, swam, swum

Infinitive: to swim
Perfect Infinitive: to have swum

Present Participle: swimming
Past Participle: swum

INDICATIVE MOOD

Pres.
I swim
you swim
he (she, it) swims

we swim
you swim
they swim

Pres. Prog.
I am swimming
you are swimming
he (she, it) is swimming

we are swimming
you are swimming
they are swimming

Pres. Int.
I do swim
you do swim
he (she, it) does swim

we do swim
you do swim
they do swim

Fut.
I shall swim
you will swim
he (she, it) will swim

we shall swim
you will swim
they will swim

Cond.
I would swim
you would swim
he (she, it) would swim

we would swim
you would swim
they would swim

Past
I swam
you swam
he (she, it) swam

we swam
you swam
they swam

Past Prog.
I was swimming
you were swimming
he (she, it) was swimming

we were swimming
you were swimming
they were swimming

Past Int.
I did swim
you did swim
he (she, it) did swim

we did swim
you did swim
they did swim

Pres. Perf.
I have swum
you have swum
he (she, it) has swum

we have swum
you have swum
they have swum

Past Perf.
I had swum
you had swum
he (she, it) had swum

we had swum
you had swum
they had swum

Fut. Perf.
I shall have swum
you will have swum
he (she, it) will have swum

we shall have swum
you will have swum
they will have swum

Cond. Perf.
I would have swum
you would have swum
he (she, it) would have swum

we would have swum
you would have swum
they would have swum

IMPERATIVE MOOD
swim

SUBJUNCTIVE MOOD

Pres.
if I swim
if you swim
if he (she, it) swim

if we swim
if you swim
if they swim

Past
if I swam
if you swam
if he (she, it) swam

if we swam
if you swam
if they swam

Fut.
if I should swim
if you should swim
if he (she, it) should swim

if we should swim
if you should swim
if they should swim

Infinitive: to be swum   *Present Participle:* being swum
Perfect Infinitive: to have been swum   *Past Participle:* been swum

INDICATIVE MOOD

Pres. I am swum
you are swum
he (she, it) is swum

we are swum
you are swum
they are swum

Pres.
Prog. I am being swum
you are being swum
he (she, it) is being swum

we are being swum
you are being swum
they are being swum

Pres.
Int. I do get swum
you do get swum
he (she, it) does get swum

we do get swum
you do get swum
they do get swum

Fut. I shall be swum
you will be swum
he (she, it) will be swum

we shall be swum
you will be swum
they will be swum

Cond. I would be swum
you would be swum
he (she, it) would be swum

we would be swum
you would be swum
they would be swum

Past I was swum
you were swum
he (she, it) was swum

we were swum
you were swum
they were swum

Past
Prog. I was being swum
you were being swum
he (she, it) was being swum

we were being swum
you were being swum
they were being swum

Past
Int. I did get swum
you did get swum
he (she, it) did get swum

we did get swum
you did get swum
they did get swum

Pres.
Perf. I have been swum
you have been swum
he (she, it) has been swum

we have been swum
you have been swum
they have been swum

Past
Perf. I had been swum
you had been swum
he (she, it) had been swum

we had been swum
you had been swum
they had been swum

Fut.
Perf. I shall have been swum
you will have been swum
he (she, it) will have been swum

we shall have been swum
you will have been swum
they will have been swum

Cond.
Perf. I would have been swum
you would have been swum
he (she, it) would have been swum

we would have been swum
you would have been swum
they would have been swum

IMPERATIVE MOOD
be swum

SUBJUNCTIVE MOOD

Pres. if I be swum
if you be swum
if he (she, it) be swum

if we be swum
if you be swum
if they be swum

Past if I were swum
if you were swum
if he (she, it) were swum

if we were swum
if you were swum
if they were swum

Fut. if I should be swum
if you should be swum
if he (she, it) should be swum

if we should be swum
if you should be swum
if they should be swum

to swing (active voice)   *Principal Parts:* swing, swinging, swung, swung

---

Infinitive: to swing   *Present Participle:* swinging
Perfect Infinitive: to have swung   *Past Participle:* swung

INDICATIVE MOOD

Pres.	I swing	we swing
	you swing	you swing
	he (she, it) swings	they swing
Pres.	I am swinging	we are swinging
Prog.	you are swinging	you are swinging
	he (she, it) is swinging	they are swinging
Pres.	I do swing	we do swing
Int.	you do swing	you do swing
	he (she, it) does swing	they do swing
Fut.	I shall swing	we shall swing
	you will swing	you will swing
	he (she, it) will swing	they will swing
Cond.	I would swing	we would swing
	you would swing	you would swing
	he (she, it) would swing	they would swing
Past	I swung	we swung
	you swung	you swung
	he (she, it) swung	they swung
Past	I was swinging	we were swinging
Prog.	you were swinging	you were swinging
	he (she, it) was swinging	they were swinging
Past	I did swing	we did swing
Int.	you did swing	you did swing
	he (she, it) did swing	they did swing
Pres.	I have swung	we have swung
Perf.	you have swung	you have swung
	he (she, it) has swung	they have swung
Past	I had swung	we had swung
Perf.	you had swung	you had swung
	he (she, it) had swung	they had swung
Fut.	I shall have swung	we shall have swung
Perf.	you will have swung	you will have swung
	he (she, it) will have swung	they will have swung
Cond.	I would have swung	we would have swung
Perf.	you would have swung	you would have swung
	he (she, it) would have swung	they would have swung

IMPERATIVE MOOD
swing

SUBJUNCTIVE MOOD

Pres.	if I swing	if we swing
	if you swing	if you swing
	if he (she, it) swing	if they swing
Past	if I swung	if we swung
	if you swung	if you swung
	if he (she, it) swung	if they swung
Fut.	if I should swing	if we should swing
	if you should swing	if you should swing
	if he (she, it) should swing	if they should swing

338

Infinitive: to be swung
Perfect Infinitive: to have been swung

Present Participle: being swung
Past Participle: been swung

INDICATIVE MOOD

Pres.
I am swung
you are swung
he (she, it) is swung

we are swung
you are swung
they are swung

Pres. Prog.
I am being swung
you are being swung
he (she, it) is being swung

we are being swung
you are being swung
they are being swung

Pres. Int.
I do get swung
you do get swung
he (she, it) does get swung

we do get swung
you do get swung
they do get swung

Fut.
I shall be swung
you will be swung
he (she, it) will be swung

we shall be swung
you will be swung.
they will be swung

Cond.
I would be swung
you would be swung
he (she, it) would be swung

we would be swung
you would be swung
they would be swung

Past
I was swung
you were swung
he (she, it) was swung

we were swung
you were swung
they were swung

Past Prog.
I was being swung
you were being swung
he (she, it) was being swung

we were being swung
you were being swung
they were being swung

Past Int.
I did get swung
you did get swung
he (she, it) did get swung

we did get swung
you did get swung
they did get swung

Pres. Perf.
I have been swung
you have been swung
he (she, it) has been swung

we have been swung
you have been swung
they have been swung

Past Perf.
I had been swung
you had been swung
he (she, it) had been swung

we had been swung
you had been swung
they had been swung

Fut. Perf.
I shall have been swung
you will have been swung
he (she, it) will have been swung

we shall have been swung
you will have been swung
they will have been swung

Cond. Perf.
I would have been swung
you would have been swung
he (she, it) would have been swung

we would have been swung
you would have been swung
they would have been swung

IMPERATIVE MOOD
be swung

SUBJUNCTIVE MOOD

Pres.
if I be swung
if you be swung
if he (she, it) be swung

if we be swung
if you be swung
if they be swung

Past
if I were swung
if you were swung
if he (she, it) were swung

if we were swung
if you were swung
if they were swung

Fut.
if I should be swung
if you should be swung
if he (she, it) should be swung

if we should be swung
if you should be swung
if they should be swung

to take (active voice)

Infinitive: to take
Perfect Infinitive: to have taken

Present Participle: taking
Past Participle: taken

INDICATIVE MOOD

Pres.	I take	we take
	you take	you take
	he (she, it) takes	they take
Pres.	I am taking	we are taking
Prog.	you are taking	you are taking
	he (she, it) is taking	they are taking
Pres.	I do take	we do take
Int.	you do take	you do take
	he (she, it) does take	they do take
Fut.	I shall take	we shall take
	you will take	you will take
	he (she, it) will take	they will take
Cond.	I would take	we would take
	you would take	you would take
	he (she, it) would take	they would take
Past	I took	we took
	you took	you took
	he (she, it) took	they took
Past	I was taking	we were taking
Prog.	you were taking	you were taking
	he (she, it) was taking	they were taking
Past	I did take	we did take
Int.	you did take	you did take
	he (she, it) did take	they did take
Pres.	I have taken	we have taken
Perf.	you have taken	you have taken
	he (she, it) has taken	they have taken
Past	I had taken	we had taken
Perf.	you had taken	you had taken
	he (she, it) had taken	they had taken
Fut.	I shall have taken	we shall have taken
Perf.	you will have taken	you will have taken
	he (she, it) will have taken	they will have taken
Cond.	I would have taken	we would have taken
Perf.	you would have taken	you would have taken
	he (she, it) would have taken	they would have taken

IMPERATIVE MOOD
take

SUBJUNCTIVE MOOD

Pres.	if I take	if we take
	if you take	if you take
	if he (she, it) take	if they take
Past	if I took	if we took
	if you took	if you took
	if he (she, it) took	if they took
Fut.	if I should take	if we should take
	if you should take	if you should take
	if he (she, it) should take	if they should take

(passive voice)

Infinitive: to be taken   *Present Participle:* being taken
Perfect Infinitive: to have been taken   *Past Participle:* been taken

INDICATIVE MOOD

Pres.	I am taken	we are taken
	you are taken	you are taken
	he (she, it) is taken	they are taken
Pres.	I am being taken	we are being taken
Prog.	you are being taken	you are being taken
	he (she, it) is being taken	they are being taken
Pres.	I do get taken	we do get taken
Int.	you do get taken	you do get taken
	he (she, it) does get taken	they do get taken
Fut.	I shall be taken	we shall be taken
	you will be taken	you will be taken
	he (she, it) will be taken	they will be taken
Cond.	I would be taken	we would be taken
	you would be taken	you would be taken
	he (she, it) would be taken	they would be taken
Past	I was taken	we were taken
	you were taken	you were taken
	he (she, it) was taken	they were taken
Past	I was being taken	we were being taken
Prog.	you were being taken	you were being taken
	he (she, it) was being taken	they were being taken
Past	I did get taken	we did get taken
Int.	you did get taken	you did get taken
	he (she, it) did get taken	they did get taken
Pres.	I have been taken	we have been taken
Perf.	you have been taken	you have been taken
	he (she, it) has been taken	they have been taken
Past	I had been taken	we had been taken
Perf.	you had been taken	you had been taken
	he (she, it) had been taken	they had been taken
Fut.	I shall have been taken	we shall have been taken
Perf.	you will have been taken	you will have been taken
	he (she, it) will have been taken	they will have been taken
Cond.	I would have been taken	we would have been taken
Perf.	you would have been taken	you would have been taken
	he (she, it) would have been taken	they would have been taken

IMPERATIVE MOOD
be taken

SUBJUNCTIVE MOOD

Pres.	if I be taken	if we be taken
	if you be taken	if you be taken
	if he (she, it) be taken	if they be taken
Past	if I were taken	if we were taken
	if you were taken	if you were taken
	if he (she, it) were taken	if they were taken
Fut.	if I should be taken	if we should be taken
	if you should be taken	if you should be taken
	if he (she, it) should be taken	if they should be taken

to teach (active voice)

Principal Parts: teach, teaching, taught, taught

Infinitive: to teach
Perfect Infinitive: to have taught

Present Participle: teaching
Past Participle: taught

INDICATIVE MOOD

Pres. I teach	we teach
you teach	you teach
he (she, it) teaches	they teach
Pres. I am teaching	we are teaching
Prog. you are teaching	you are teaching
he (she, it) is teaching	they are teaching
Pres. I do teach	we do teach
Int. you do teach	you do teach
he (she, it) does teach	they do teach
Fut. I shall teach	we shall teach
you will teach	you will teach
he (she, it) will teach	they will teach
Cond. I would teach	we would teach
you would teach	you would teach
he (she, it) would teach	they would teach
Past I taught	we taught
you taught	you taught
he (she, it) taught	they taught
Past I was teaching	we were teaching
Prog. you were teaching	you were teaching
he (she, it) was teaching	they were teaching
Past I did teach	we did teach
Int. you did teach	you did teach
he (she, it) did teach	they did teach
Pres. I have taught	we have taught
Perf. you have taught	you have taught
he (she, it) has taught	they have taught
Past I had taught	we had taught
Perf. you had taught	you had taught
he (she, it) had taught	they had taught
Fut. I shall have taught	we shall have taught
Perf. you will have taught	you will have taught
he (she, it) will have taught	they will have taught
Cond. I would have taught	we would have taught
Perf. you would have taught	you would have taught
he (she, it) would have taught	they would have taught

IMPERATIVE MOOD
teach

SUBJUNCTIVE MOOD

Pres. if I teach	if we teach
if you teach	if you teach
if he (she, it) teach	if they teach
Past if I taught	if we taught
if you taught	if you taught
if he (she, it) taught	if they taught
Fut. if I should teach	if we should teach
if you should teach	if you should teach
if he (she, it) should teach	if they should teach

Infinitive: to be taught
Perfect Infinitive: to have been taught

Present Participle: being taught
Past Participle: been taught

INDICATIVE MOOD

Pres.	I am taught	we are taught
	you are taught	you are taught
	he (she, it) is taught	they are taught
Pres.	I am being taught	we are being taught
Prog.	you are being taught	you are being taught
	he (she, it) is being taught	they are being taught
Pres.	I do get taught	we do get taught
Int.	you do get taught	you do get taught
	he (she, it) does get taught	they do get taught
Fut.	I shall be taught	we shall be taught
	you will be taught	you will be taught
	he (she, it) will be taught	they will be taught
Cond.	I would be taught	we would be taught
	you would be taught	you would be taught
	he (she, it) would be taught	they would be taught
Past	I was taught	we were taught
	you were taught	you were taught
	he (she, it) was taught	they were taught
Past	I was being taught	we were being taught
Prog.	you were being taught	you were being taught
	he (she, it) was being taught	they were being taught
Past	I did get taught	we did get taught
Int.	you did get taught	you did get taught
	he (she, it) did get taught	they did get taught
Pres.	I have been taught	we have been taught
Perf.	you have been taught	you have been taught
	he (she, it) has been taught	they have been taught
Past	I had been taught	we had been taught
Perf.	you had been taught	you had been taught
	he (she, it) had been taught	they had been taught
Fut.	I shall have been taught	we shall have been taught
Perf.	you will have been taught	you will have been taught
	he (she, it) will have been taught	they will have been taught
Cond.	I would have been taught	we would have been taught
Perf.	you would have been taught	you would have been taught
	he (she, it) would have been taught	they would have been taught

IMPERATIVE MOOD
be taught

SUBJUNCTIVE MOOD

Pres.	if I be taught	if we be taught
	if you be taught	if you be taught
	if he (she, it) be taught	if they be taught
Past	if I were taught	if we were taught
	if you were taught	if you were taught
	if he (she, it) were taught	if they were taught
Fut.	if I should be taught	if we should be taught
	if you should be taught	if you should be taught
	if he (she, it) should be taught	if they should be taught

343

to tear (active voice)   *Principal Parts:* **tear, tearing, tore, torn**

Infinitive: to tear   *Present Participle:* tearing
Perfect Infinitive: to have torn   *Past Participle:* torn

INDICATIVE MOOD

Pres. I tear	we tear
you tear	you tear
he (she, it) tears	they tear
Pres. I am tearing	we are tearing
Prog. you are tearing	you are tearing
he (she, it) is tearing	they are tearing
Pres. I do tear	we do tear
Int. you do tear	you do tear
he (she, it) does tear	they do tear
Fut. I shall tear	we shall tear
you will tear	you will tear
he (she, it) will tear	they will tear
Cond. I would tear	we would tear
you would tear	you would tear
he (she, it) would tear	they would tear
Past I tore	we tore
you tore	you tore
he (she, it) tore	they tore
Past I was tearing	we were tearing
Prog. you were tearing	you were tearing
he (she, it) was tearing	they were tearing
Past I did tear	we did tear
Int. you did tear	you did tear
he (she, it) did tear	they did tear
Pres. I have torn	we have torn
Perf. you have torn	you have torn
he (she, it) has torn	they have torn
Past I had torn	we had torn
Perf. you had torn	you had torn
he (she, it) had torn	they had torn
Fut. I shall have torn	we shall have torn
Perf. you will have torn	you will have torn
he (she, it) will have torn	they will have torn
Cond. I would have torn	we would have torn
Perf. you would have torn	you would have torn
he (she, it) would have torn	they would have torn

IMPERATIVE MOOD
tear

SUBJUNCTIVE MOOD

Pres. if I tear	if we tear
if you tear	if you tear
if he (she, it) tear	if they tear
Past if I tore	if we tore
if you tore	if you tore
if he (she, it) tore	if they tore
Fut. if I should tear	if we should tear
if you should tear	if you should tear
if he (she, it) should tear	if they should tear

(passive voice)

Infinitive: to be torn   *Present Participle:* being torn
Perfect Infinitive: to have been torn   *Past Participle:* been torn

INDICATIVE MOOD

Pres. I am torn	we are torn
you are torn	you are torn
he (she, it) is torn	they are torn
Pres. I am being torn	we are being torn
Prog. you are being torn	you are being torn
he (she, it) is being torn	they are being torn
Pres. I do get torn	we do get torn
Int. you do get torn	you do get torn
he (she, it) does get torn	they do get torn
Fut. I shall be torn	we shall be torn
you will be torn	you will be torn
he (she, it) will be torn	they will be torn
Cond. I would be torn	we would be torn
you would be torn	you would be torn
he (she, it) would be torn	they would be torn
Past I was torn	we were torn
you were torn	you were torn
he (she, it) was torn	they were torn
Past I was being torn	we were being torn
Prog. you were being torn	you were being torn
he (she, it) was being torn	they were being torn
Past I did get torn	we did get torn
Int. you did get torn	you did get torn
he (she, it) did get torn	they did get torn
Pres. I have been torn	we have been torn
Perf. you have been torn	you have been torn
he (she, it) has been torn	they have been torn
Past I had been torn	we had been torn
Perf. you had been torn	you had been torn
he (she, it) had been torn	they had been torn
Fut. I shall have been torn	we shall have been torn
Perf. you will have been torn	you will have been torn
he (she, it) will have been torn	they will have been torn
Cond. I would have been torn	we would have been torn
Perf. you would have been torn	you would have been torn
he (she, it) would have been torn	they would have been torn

IMPERATIVE MOOD
be torn

SUBJUNCTIVE MOOD

Pres. if I be torn	if we be torn
if you be torn	if you be torn
if he (she, it) be torn	if they be torn
Past if I were torn	if we were torn
if you were torn	if you were torn
if he (she, it) were torn	if they were torn
Fut. if I should be torn	if we should be torn
if you should be torn	if you should be torn
if he (she, it) should be torn	if they should be torn

to tell (active voice)   *Principal Parts:* tell, telling, told, told

Infinitive: to tell
Perfect Infinitive: to have told

Present Participle: telling
Past Participle: told

INDICATIVE MOOD

Pres.	I tell	we tell
	you tell	you tell
	he (she, it) tells	they tell
Pres.	I am telling	we are telling
Prog.	you are telling	you are telling
	he (she, it) is telling	they are telling
Pres.	I do tell	we do tell
Int.	you do tell	you do tell
	he (she, it) does tell	they do tell
Fut.	I shall tell	we shall tell
	you will tell	you will tell
	he (she, it) will tell	they will tell
Cond.	I would tell	we would tell
	you would tell	you would tell
	he (she, it) would tell	they would tell
Past	I told	we told
	you told	you told
	he (she, it) told	they told
Past	I was telling	we were telling
Prog.	you were telling	you were telling
	he (she, it) was telling	they were telling
Past	I did tell	we did tell
Int.	you did tell	you did tell
	he (she, it) did tell	they did tell
Pres.	I have told	we have told
Perf.	you have told	you have told
	he (she, it) has told	they have told
Past	I had told	we had told
Perf.	you had told	you had told
	he (she, it) had told	they had told
Fut.	I shall have told	we shall have told
Perf.	you will have told	you will have told
	he (she, it) will have told	they will have told
Cond.	I would have told	we would have told
Perf.	you would have told	you would have told
	he (she, it) would have told	they would have told

IMPERATIVE MOOD
tell

SUBJUNCTIVE MOOD

Pres.	if I tell	if we tell
	if you tell	if you tell
	if he (she, it) tell	if they tell
Past	if I told	if we told
	if you told	if you told
	if he (she, it) told	if they told
Fut.	if I should tell	if we should tell
	if you should tell	if you should tell
	if he (she, it) should tell	if they should tell

(passive voice)

Infinitive: to be told   *Present Participle:* being told
Perfect Infinitive: to have been told   *Past Participle:* been told

INDICATIVE MOOD

Pres. I am told
you are told
he (she, it) is told

we are told
you are told
they are told

Pres.
Prog. I am being told
you are being told
he (she, it) is being told

we are being told
you are being told
they are being told

Pres.
Int. I do get told
you do get told
he (she, it) does get told

we do get told
you do get told
they do get told

Fut. I shall be told
you will be told
he (she, it) will be told

we shall be told
you will be told
they will be told

Cond. I would be told
you would be told
he (she, it) would be told

we would be told
you would be told
they would be told

Past I was told
you were told
he (she, it) was told

we were told
you were told
they were told

Past
Prog. I was being told
you were being told
he (she, it) was being told

we were being told
you were being told
they were being told

Past
Int. I did get told
you did get told
he (she, it) did get told

we did get told
you did get told
they did get told

Pres.
Perf. I have been told
you have been told
he (she, it) has been told

we have been told
you have been told
they have been told

Past
Perf. I had been told
you had been told
he (she, it) had been told

we had been told
you had been told
they had been told

Fut.
Perf. I shall have been told
you will have been told
he (she, it) will have been told

we shall have been told
you will have been told
they will have been told

Cond.
Perf. I would have been told
you would have been told
he (she, it) would have been told

we would have been told
you would have been told
they would have been told

IMPERATIVE MOOD
be told

SUBJUNCTIVE MOOD

Pres. if I be told
if you be told
if he (she, it) be told

if we be told
if you be told
if they be told

Past if I were told
if you were told
if he (she, it) were told

if we were told
if you were told
if they were told

Fut. if I should be told
if you should be told
if he (she, it) should be told

if we should be told
if you should be told
if they should be told

to think (active voice) *Principal Parts:* think, thinking, thought, thought

---

Infinitive: to think *Present Participle:* thinking
Perfect Infinitive: to have thought *Past Participle:* thought

INDICATIVE MOOD

Pres.	I think	we think
	you think	you think
	he (she, it) thinks	they think
Pres.	I am thinking	we are thinking
Prog.	you are thinking	you are thinking
	he (she, it) is thinking	they are thinking
Pres.	I do think	we do think
Int.	you do think	you do think
	he (she, it) does think	they do think
Fut.	I shall think	we shall think
	you will think	you will think
	he (she, it) will think	they will think
Cond.	I would think	we would think
	you would think	you would think
	he (she. it) would think	they would think
Past	I thought	we thought
	you thought	you thought
	he (she, it) thought	they thought
Past	I was thinking	we were thinking
Prog.	you were thinking	you were thinking
	he (she, it) was thinking	they were thinking
Past	I did think	we did think
Int.	you did think	you did think
	he (she, it) did think	they did think
Pres.	I have thought	we have thought
Perf.	you have thought	you have thought
	he (she, it) has thought	they have thought
Past	I had thought	we had thought
Perf.	you had thought	you had thought
	he (she, it) had thought	they had thought
Fut.	I shall have thought	we shall have thought
Perf.	you will have thought	you will have thought
	he (she, it) will have thought	they will have thought
Cond.	I would have thought	we would have thought
Perf.	you would have thought	you would have thought
	he (she, it) would have thought	they would have thought

IMPERATIVE MOOD
think

SUBJUNCTIVE MOOD

Pres.	if I think	if we think
	if you think	if you think
	if he (she, it) think	if they think
Past	if I thought	if we thought
	if you thought	if you thought
	if he (she, it) thought	if they thought
Fut.	if I should think	if we should think
	if you should think	if you should think
	if he (she, it) should think	if they should think

(passive voice)

Infinitive: to be thought   *Present Participle:* being thought
Perfect Infinitive: to have been thought   *Past Participle:* been thought

INDICATIVE MOOD

Pres.	I am thought	we are thought
	you are thought	you are thought
	he (she, it) is thought	they are thought
Pres.	I am being thought	we are being thought
Prog.	you are being thought	you are being thought
	he (she, it) is being thought	they are being thought
Pres.	I do get thought	we do get thought
Int.	you do get thought	you do get thought
	he (she, it) does get thought	they do get thought
Fut.	I shall be thought	we shall be thought
	you will be thought	you will be thought
	he (she, it) will be thought	they will be thought
Cond.	I would be thought	we would be thought
	you would be thought	you would be thought
	he (she, it) would be thought	they would be thought
Past	I was thought	we were thought
	you were thought	you were thought
	he (she, it) was thought	they were thought
Past	I was being thought	we were being thought
Prog.	you were being thought	you were being thought
	he (she, it) was being thought	they were being thought
Past	I did get thought	we did get thought
Int.	you did get thought	you did get thought
	he (she, it) did get thought	they did get thought
Pres.	I have been thought	we have been thought
Perf.	you have been thought	you have been thought
	he (she, it) has been thought	they have been thought
Past	I had been thought	we had been thought
Perf.	you had been thought	you had been thought
	he (she, it) had been thought	they had been thought
Fut.	I shall have been thought	we shall have been thought
Perf.	you will have been thought	you will have been thought
	he (she, it) will have been thought	they will have been thought
Cond.	I would have been thought	we would have been thought
Perf.	you would have been thought	you would have been thought
	he (she, it) would have been thought	they would have been thought

IMPERATIVE MOOD
be thought

SUBJUNCTIVE MOOD

Pres.	if I be thought	if we be thought
	if you be thought	if you be thought
	if he (she, it) be thought	if they be thought
Past	if I were thought	if we were thought
	if you were thought	if you were thought
	if he (she, it) were thought	if they were thought
Fut.	if I should be thought	if we should be thought
	if you should be thought	if you should be thought
	if he (she, it) should be thought	if they should be thought

to thrive
(active voice only)

Principal Parts: thrive, thriving, throve (thrived), thrived (thriven)

(intransitive verb)

Infinitive: to thrive   *Present Participle:* thriving
Perfect Infinitive: to have thrived, thriven   *Past Participle:* thrived, thriven

INDICATIVE MOOD

Pres.	I thrive	we thrive
	you thrive	you thrive
	he (she, it) thrives	they thrive
Pres.	I am thriving	we are thriving
Prog.	you are thriving	you are thriving
	he (she, it) is thriving	they are thriving
Pres.	I do thrive	we do thrive
Int.	you do thrive	you do thrive
	he (she, it) does thrive	they do thrive
Fut.	I shall thrive	we shall thrive
	you will thrive	you will thrive
	he (she, it) will thrive	they will thrive
Cond	I would thrive	we would thrive
	you would thrive	you would thrive
	he (she, it) would thrive	they would thrive
Past	I throve, thrived	we throve, thrived
	you throve, thrived	you throve, thrived
	he (she, it) throve, thrived	they throve, thrived
Past	I was thriving	we were thriving
Prog.	you were thriving	you were thriving
	he (she, it) was thriving	they were thriving
Past	I did thrive	we did thrive
Int.	you did thrive	you did thrive
	he (she, it) did thrive	they did thrive
Pres.	I have thrived, thriven	we have thrived, thriven
Perf.	you have thrived, thriven	you have thrived, thriven
	he (she, it) has thrived, thriven	they have thrived, thriven
Past	I had thrived, thriven	we had thrived, thriven
Perf	you had thrived, thriven	you had thrived, thriven
	he (she, it) had thrived, thriven	they had thrived, thriven
Fut.	I shall have thrived, thriven	we shall have thrived, thriven
Perf.	you will have thrived, thriven	you will have thrived, thriven
	he (she, it) will have thrived, thriven	they will have thrived, thriven
Cond.	I would have thrived, thriven	we would have thrived, thriven
Perf.	you would have thrived, thriven	you would have thrived, thriven
	he (she, it) would have thrived, thriven	they would have thrived, thriven

IMPERATIVE MOOD
thrive

SUBJUNCTIVE MOOD

Pres.	if I thrive	if we thrive
	if you thrive	if you thrive
	if he (she, it) thrive	if they thrive
Past	if I throve, thrived	if we throve, thrived
	if you throve, thrived	if you throve, thrived
	if he (she, it) throve, thrived	if they throve, thrived
Fut.	if I should thrive	if we should thrive
	if you should thrive	if you should thrive
	if he (she, it) should thrive	if they should thrive

***To thrive* is an intransitive verb.**

It does not take an object.

It describes action, but the action is self-contained.

Like other intransitive verbs, it may be followed by adverbs, adverbial phrases and clauses describing the how, why, when, and where of the action:

HOW: The family has thriven *wonderfully.* (adverb)

WHY: The crops are thriving *because of the unusually warm weather.* (adverbial phrase)

WHEN: The animals will be thriving *when spring comes.* (adverbial clause)

WHERE: He was thriving *in his job at the bank.* (adverbial phrase)

to throw (active voice)   *Principal Parts:* throw, throwing, threw, thrown

---

Infinitive: to throw   *Present Participle:* throwing
Perfect Infinitive: to have thrown   *Past Participle:* thrown

INDICATIVE MOOD

Pres.	I throw	we throw
	you throw	you throw
	he (she, it) throws	they throw
Pres.	I am throwing	we are throwing
Prog.	you are throwing	you are throwing
	he (she, it) is throwing	they are throwing
Pres.	I do throw	we do throw
Int.	you do throw	you do throw
	he (she, it) does throw	they do throw
Fut.	I shall throw	we shall throw
	you will throw	you will throw
	he (she, it) will throw	they will throw
Cond.	I would throw	we would throw
	you would throw	you would throw
	he (she, it) would throw	they would throw
Past	I threw	we threw
	you threw	you threw
	he (she, it) threw	they threw
Past	I was throwing	we were throwing
Prog.	you were throwing	you were throwing
	he (she, it) was throwing	they were throwing
Past	I did throw	we did throw
Int.	you did throw	you did throw
	he (she, it) did throw	they did throw
Pres.	I have thrown	we have thrown
Perf.	you have thrown	you have thrown
	he (she, it) has thrown	they have thrown
Past	I had thrown	we had thrown
Perf.	you had thrown	you had thrown
	he (she, it) had thrown	they had thrown
Fut.	I shall have thrown	we shall have thrown
Perf.	you will have thrown	you will have thrown
	he (she, it) will have thrown	they will have thrown
Cond.	I would have thrown	we would have thrown
Perf.	you would have thrown	you would have thrown
	he (she, it) would have thrown	they would have thrown

IMPERATIVE MOOD
throw

SUBJUNCTIVE MOOD

Pres.	if I throw	if we throw
	if you throw	if you throw
	if he (she, it) throw	if they throw
Past	if I threw	if we threw
	if you threw	if you threw
	if he (she, it) threw	if they threw
Fut.	if I should throw	if we should throw
	if you should throw	if you should throw
	if he (she, it) should throw	if they should throw

(passive voice)

Infinitive: to be thrown   *Present Participle:* being thrown
Perfect Infinitive: to have been thrown   *Past Participle:* been thrown

INDICATIVE MOOD

Pres. I am thrown
you are thrown
he (she, it) is thrown

we are thrown
you are thrown
they are thrown

Pres. Prog. I am being thrown
you are being thrown
he (she, it) is being thrown

we are being thrown
you are being thrown
they are being thrown

Pres. Int. I do get thrown
you do get thrown
he (she, it) does get thrown

we do get thrown
you do get thrown
they do get thrown

Fut. I shall be thrown
you will be thrown
he (she, it) will be thrown

we shall be thrown
you will be thrown
they will be thrown

Cond. I would be thrown
you would be thrown
he (she, it) would be thrown

we would be thrown
you would be thrown
they would be thrown

Past I was thrown
you were thrown
he (she, it) was thrown

we were thrown
you were thrown
they were thrown

Past Prog. I was being thrown
you were being thrown
he (she, it) was being thrown

we were being thrown
you were being thrown
they were being thrown

Past Int. I did get thrown
you did get thrown
he (she, it) did get thrown

we did get thrown
you did get thrown
they did get thrown

Pres. Perf. I have been thrown
you have been thrown
he (she, it) has been thrown

we have been thrown
you have been thrown
they have been thrown

Past Perf. I had been thrown
you had been thrown
he (she, it) had been thrown

we had been thrown
you had been thrown
they had been thrown

Fut. Perf. I shall have been thrown
you will have been thrown
he (she, it) will have been thrown

we shall have been thrown
you will have been thrown
they will have been thrown

Cond. Perf. I would have been thrown
you would have been thrown
he (she, it) would have been thrown

we would have been thrown
you would have been thrown
they would have been thrown

IMPERATIVE MOOD
be thrown

SUBJUNCTIVE MOOD

Pres. if I be thrown
if you be thrown
if he (she, it) be thrown

if we be thrown
if you be thrown
if they be thrown

Past if I were thrown
if you were thrown
if he (she, it) were thrown

if we were thrown
if you were thrown
if they were thrown

Fut. if I should be thrown
if you should be thrown
if he (she, it) should be thrown

if we should be thrown
if you should be thrown
if they should be thrown

to wake (active voice)
(also: to awake)

Principal Parts: wake, waking, woke (waked),
waked (wakened)

Infinitive: to wake   *Present Participle:* waking
Perfect Infinitive: to have waked, wakened   *Past Participle:* wakened

INDICATIVE MOOD

Pres.	I wake	we wake
	you wake	you wake
	he (she, it) wakes	they wake
Pres.	I am waking	we are waking
Prog.	you are waking	you are waking
	he (she, it) is waking	they are waking
Pres.	I do wake	we do wake
Int.	you do wake	you do wake
	he (she, it) does wake	they do wake
Fut.	I shall wake	we shall wake
	you will wake	you will wake
	he (she, it) will wake	they will wake
Cond.	I would wake	we would wake
	you would wake	you would wake
	he (she, it) would wake	they would wake
Past	I woke	we woke
	you woke	you woke
	he (she, it) woke	they woke
Past	I was waking	we were waking
Prog.	you were waking	you were waking
	he (she, it) was waking	they were waking
Past	I did wake	we did wake
Int.	you did wake	you did wake
	he (she, it) did wake	they did wake
Pres.	I have waked, wakened	we have waked, wakened
Perf.	you have waked, wakened	you have waked, wakened
	he (she, it) has waked, wakened	they have waked, wakened
Past	I had waked, wakened	we had waked, wakened
Perf.	you had waked, wakened	you had waked, wakened
	he (she, it) had waked, wakened	they had waked, wakened
Fut.	I shall have waked, wakened	we shall have waked, wakened
Perf.	you will have waked, wakened	you will have waked, wakened
	he (she, it) will have waked, wakened	they will have waked, wakened
Cond.	I would have waked, wakened	we would have waked, wakened
Perf.	you would have waked, wakened	you would have waked, wakened
	he (she, it) would have waked, wakened	they would have waked, wakened

IMPERATIVE MOOD
wake

SUBJUNCTIVE MOOD

Pres.	if I wake	if we wake
	if you wake	if you wake
	if he (she, it) wake	if they wake
Past	if I woke	if we woke
	if you woke	if you woke
	if he (she, it) woke	if they woke
Fut.	if I should wake	if we should wake
	if you should wake	if you should wake
	if he (she, it) should wake	if they should wake

(passive voice)

Infinitive: to be waked, wakened
Perfect Infinitive: to have been waked, wakened

Present Participle: being waked, wakened
Past Participle: been waked, wakened

INDICATIVE MOOD

Pres. I am waked, wakened
you are waked, wakened
he (she, it) is waked, wakened

we are waked, wakened
you are waked, wakened
they are waked, wakened

Pres. I am being waked, wakened
Prog. you are being waked, wakened
he (she, it) is being waked, wakened

we are being waked, wakened
you are being waked, wakened
they are being waked, wakened

Pres. I do get waked, wakened
Int. you do get waked, wakened
he (she, it) does get waked, wakened

we do get waked, wakened
you do get waked, wakened
they do get waked, wakened

Fut. I shall be waked, wakened
you will be waked, wakened
he (she, it) will be waked, wakened

we shall be waked, wakened
you will be waked, wakened
they will be waked, wakened

Cond. I would be waked, wakened
you would be waked, wakened
he (she, it) would be waked, wakened

we would be waked, wakened
you would be waked, wakened
they would be waked, wakened

Past I was waked, wakened
you were waked, wakened
he (she, it) was waked, wakened

we were waked, wakened
you were waked, wakened
they were waked, wakened

Past I was being waked, wakened
Prog. you were being waked, wakened
he (she, it) was being waked, wakened

we were being waked, wakened
you were being waked, wakened
they were being waked, wakened

Past I did get waked, wakened
Int. you did get waked, wakened
he (she, it) did get waked, wakened

we did get waked, wakened
you did get waked, wakened
they did get waked, wakened

Pres. I have been waked, wakened
Perf. you have been waked, wakened
he (she, it) has been waked, wakened

we have been waked, wakened
you have been waked, wakened
they have been waked, wakened

Past I had been waked, wakened
Perf. you had been waked, wakened
he (she, it) had been waked, wakened

we had been waked, wakened
you had been waked, wakened
they had been waked, wakened

Fut. I shall have been waked, wakened
Perf. you will have been waked, wakened
he (she, it) will have been waked, wakened

we shall have been waked, wakened
you will have been waked, wakened
they will have been waked, wakened

Cond. I would have been waked, wakened
Perf. you would have been waked, wakened
he (she, it) would have been waked, wakened

we would have been waked, wakened
you would have been waked, wakened
they would have been waked, wakened

(passive voice, continued)

IMPERATIVE MOOD
be waked

SUBJUNCTIVE MOOD

Pres. if I be waked, wakened
if you be waked, wakened
if he (she, it) be waked, wakened

if we be waked, wakened
if you be waked, wakened
if they be waked, wakened

Past if I were waked, wakened
if you were waked, wakened
if he (she, it) were waked, wakened

if we were waked, wakened
if you were waked, wakened
if they were waked, wakened

Fut. if I should be waked, wakened
if you should be waked, wakened
if he (she, it) should be waked, wakened

if we should be waked, wakened
if you should be waked, wakened
if they should be waked, wakened

NOTE: The verb to *wake* is another form of the verb *to awake* (pp. 130-131). *To wake* is much more commonly used in English since *to awake* has a more formal connotation and poetic overtones: "I awake from dreams of thee." A similar usage pattern occurs in the verbs *to arise* and *to rise*.

Infinitive: to wear
Perfect Infinitive: to have worn

Present Participle: wearing
Past Participle: worn

INDICATIVE MOOD

Pres.
I wear
you wear
he (she, it) wears

we wear
you wear
they wear

Pres.
Prog.
I am wearing
you are wearing
he (she, it) is wearing

we are wearing
you are wearing
they are wearing

Pres.
Int.
I do wear
you do wear
he (she, it) does wear

we do wear
you do wear
they do wear

Fut.
I shall wear
you will wear
he (she, it) will wear

we shall wear
you will wear
they will wear

Cond.
I would wear
you would wear
he (she, it) would wear

we would wear
you would wear
they would wear

Past
I wore
you wore
he (she, it) wore

we wore
you wore
they wore

Past
Prog.
I was wearing
you were wearing
he (she, it) was wearing

we were wearing
you were wearing
they were wearing

Past
Int.
I did wear
you did wear
he (she, it) did wear

we did wear
you did wear
they did wear

Pres.
Perf.
I have worn
you have worn
he (she, it) has worn

we have worn
you have worn
they have worn

Past
Perf.
I had worn
you had worn
he (she, it) had worn

we had worn
you had worn
they had worn

Fut.
Perf.
I shall have worn
you will have worn
he (she, it) will have worn

we shall have worn
you will have worn
they will have worn

Cond.
Perf.
I would have worn
you would have worn
he (she, it) would have worn

we would have worn
you would have worn
they would have worn

IMPERATIVE MOOD
wear

SUBJUNCTIVE MOOD

Pres.
if I wear
if you wear
if he (she, it) wear

if we wear
if you wear
if they wear

Past
if I wore
if you wore
if he (she, it) wore

if we wore
if you wore
if they wore

Fut.
if I should wear
if you should wear
if he (she, it) should wear

if we should wear
if you should wear
if they should wear

Infinitive: to be worn
Perfect Infinitive: to have been worn

Present Participle: being worn
Past Participle: been worn

INDICATIVE MOOD

Pres.	I am worn	we are worn
	you are worn	you are worn
	he (she, it) is worn	they are worn
Pres.	I am being worn	we are being worn
Prog.	you are being worn	you are being worn
	he (she, it) is being worn	they are being worn
Pres.	I do get worn	we do get worn
Int.	you do get worn	you do get worn
	he (she, it) does get worn	they do get worr
Fut.	I shall be worn	we shall be worn
	you will be worn	you will be worn
	he (she, it) will be worn	they will be worn
Cond.	I would be worn	we would be worn
	you would be worn	you would be worn
	he (she, it) would be worn	they would be worn
Past	I was worn	we were worn
	you were worn	you were worn
	he (she, it) was worn	they were worn
Past	I was being worn	we were being worn
Prog.	you were being worn	you were being worn
	he (she, it) was being worn	they were being worn
Past	I did get worn	we did get worn
Int.	you did get worn	you did get worn
	he (she, it) did get worn	they did get worn
Pres.	I have been worn	we have been worn
Perf.	you have been worn	you have been worn
	he (she, it) has been worn	they have been worn
Past	I had been worn	we had been worn
Perf.	you had been worn	you had been worn
	he (she, it) had been worn	they had been worn
Fut.	I shall have been worn	we shall have been worn
Perf.	you will have been worn	you will have been worn
	he (she, it) will have been worn	they will have been worn
Cond.	I would have been worn	we would have been worn
Perf.	you would have been worn	you would have been worn
	he (she, it) would have been worn	they would have been worn

IMPERATIVE MOOD
be worn

SUBJUNCTIVE MOOD

Pres.	if I be worn	if we be worn
	if you be worn	if you be worn
	if he (she, it) be worn	if they be worn
Past	if I were worn	if we were worn
	if you were worn	if you were worn
	if he (she, it) were worn	if they were worn
Fut.	if I should be worn	if we should be worn
	if you should be worn	if you should be worn
	if he (she, it) should be worn	if they should be worn

to weave (active voice)   *Principal Parts:* weave, weaving, wove, woven

Infinitive: to weave   *Present Participle:* weaving
Perfect Infinitive: to have woven   *Past Participle:* woven

INDICATIVE MOOD

Pres.	I weave	we weave
	you weave	you weave
	he (she, it) weaves	they weave
Pres.	I am weaving	we are weaving
Prog.	you are weaving	you are weaving
	he (she, it) is weaving	they are weaving
Pres.	I do weave	we do weave
Int.	you do weave	you do weave
	he (she, it) does weave	they do weave
Fut.	I shall weave	we shall weave
	you will weave	you will weave
	he (she, it) will weave	they will weave
Cond.	I would weave	we would weave
	you would weave	you would weave
	he (she, it) would weave	they would weave
Past	I wove	we wove
	you wove	you wove
	he (she, it) wove	they wove
Past	I was weaving	we were weaving
Prog.	you were weaving	you were weaving
	he (she, it) was weaving	they were weaving
Past	I did weave	we did weave
Int.	you did weave	you did weave
	he (she, it) did weave	they did weave
Pres.	I have woven	we have woven
Perf.	you have woven	you have woven
	he (she, it) has woven	they have woven
Past	I had woven	we had woven
Perf.	you had woven	you had woven
	he (she, it) had woven	they had woven
Fut.	I shall have woven	we shall have woven
Perf.	you will have woven	you will have woven
	he (she, it) will have woven	they will have woven
Cond.	I would have woven	we would have woven
Perf.	you would have woven	you would have woven
	he (she, it) would have woven	they would have woven

IMPERATIVE MOOD
weave

SUBJUNCTIVE MOOD

Pres.	if I weave	if we weave
	if you weave	if you weave
	if he (she, it) weave	if they weave
Past	if I wove	if we wove
	if you wove	if you wove
	if he (she, it) wove	if they wove
Fut.	if I should weave	if we should weave
	if you should weave	if you should weave
	if he (she, it) should weave	if they should weave

(passive voice)

Infinitive: to be woven *Present Participle:* being woven
Perfect Infinitive: to have been woven *Past Participle:* been woven

INDICATIVE MOOD

Pres. I am woven
you are woven
he (she, it) is woven

we are woven
you are woven
they are woven

Pres. I am being woven
Prog. you are being woven
he (she, it) is being woven

we are being woven
you are being woven
they are being woven

Pres. I do get woven
Int. you do get woven
he (she, it) does get woven

we do get woven
you do get woven
they do get woven

Fut. I shall be woven
you will be woven
he (she, it) will be woven

we shall be woven
you will be woven
they will be woven

Cond. I would be woven
you would be woven
he (she, it) would be woven

we would be woven
you would be woven
they would be woven

Past I was woven
you were woven
he (she, it) was woven

we were woven
you were woven
they were woven

Past I was being woven
Prog. you were being woven
he (she, it) was being woven

we were being woven
you were being woven
they were being woven

Past I did get woven
Int. you did get woven
he (she, it) did get woven

we did get woven
you did get woven
they did get woven

Pres. I have been woven
Perf. you have been woven
he (she, it) has been woven

we have been woven
you have been woven
they have been woven

Past I had been woven
Perf. you had been woven
he (she, it) had been woven

we had been woven
you had been woven
they had been woven

Fut. I shall have been woven
Perf. you will have been woven
he (she, it) will have been woven

we shall have been woven
you will have been woven
they will have been woven

Cond. I would have been woven
Perf. you would have been woven
he (she, it) would have been woven

we would have been woven
you would have been woven
they would have been woven

IMPERATIVE MOOD
be woven

SUBJUNCTIVE MOOD

Pres. if I be woven
if you be woven
if he (she, it) be woven

if we be woven
if you be woven
if they be woven

Past if I were woven
if you were woven
if he (she, it) were woven

if we were woven
if you were woven
if they were woven

Fut. if I should be woven
if you should be woven
if he (she, it) should be woven

if we should be woven
if you should be woven
if they should be woven

Infinitive: to weep
Perfect Infinitive: to have wept

Present Participle: weeping
Past Participle: wept

INDICATIVE MOOD

Pres. I weep
you weep
he (she, it) weeps

we weep
you weep
they weep

Pres. Prog. I am weeping
you are weeping
he (she, it) is weeping

we are weeping
you are weeping
they are weeping

Pres. Int. I do weep
you do weep
he (she, it) does weep

we do weep
you do weep
they do weep

Fut. I shall weep
you will weep
he (she, it) will weep

we shall weep
you will weep
they will weep

Cond. I would weep
you would weep
he (she, it) would weep

we would weep
you would weep
they would weep

Past I wept
you wept
he (she, it) wept

we wept
you wept
they wept

Past Prog. I was weeping
you were weeping
he (she, it) was weeping

we were weeping
you were weeping
they were weeping

Past Int. I did weep
you did weep
he (she, it) did weep

we did weep
you did weep
they did weep

Pres. Perf. I have wept
you have wept
he (she, it) has wept

we have wept
you have wept
they have wept

Past Perf. I had wept
you had wept
he (she, it) had wept

we had wept
you had wept
they had wept

Fut. Perf. I shall have wept
you will have wept
he (she, it) will have wept

we shall have wept
you will have wept
they will have wept

Cond. Perf. I would have wept
you would have wept
he (she, it) would have wept

we would have wept
you would have wept
they would have wept

IMPERATIVE MOOD
weep

SUBJUNCTIVE MOOD

Pres. if I weep
if you weep
if he (she, it) weep

if we weep
if you weep
if they weep

Past if I wept
if you wept
if he (she, it) wept

if we wept
if you wept
if they wept

Fut. if I should weep
if you should weep
if he (she, it) should weep

if we should weep
if you should weep
if they should weep

(passive voice)

Infinitive: to be wept
Perfect Infinitive: to have been wept

Present Participle: being wept
Past Participle: been wept

INDICATIVE MOOD

Pres. I am wept
you are wept
he (she, it) is wept

we are wept
you are wept
they are wept

Pres. Prog. I am being wept
you are being wept
he (she, it) is being wept

we are being wept
you are being wept
they are being wept

Pres. Int. I do get wept
you do get wept
he (she, it) does get wept

we do get wept
you do get wept
they do get wept

Fut. I shall be wept
you will be wept
he (she, it) will be wept

we shall be wept
you will be wept
they will be wept

Cond. I would be wept
you would be wept
he (she, it) would be wept

we would be wept
you would be wept
they would be wept

Past I was wept
you were wept
he (she, it) was wept

we were wept
you were wept
they were wept

Past Prog. I was being wept
you were being wept
he (she, it) was being wept

we were being wept
you were being wept
they were being wept

Past Int. I did get wept
you did get wept
he (she, it) did get wept

we did get wept
you did get wept
they did get wept

Pres. Perf. I have been wept
you have been wept
he (she, it) has been wept

we have been wept
you have been wept
they have been wept

Past Perf. I had been wept
you had been wept
he (she, it) had been wept

we had been wept
you had been wept
they had been wept

Fut. Perf. I shall have been wept
you will have been wept
he (she, it) will have been wept

we shall have been wept
you will have been wept
they will have been wept

Cond. Perf. I would have been wept
you would have been wept
he (she, it) would have been wept

we would have been wept
you would have been wept
they would have been wept

IMPERATIVE MOOD
be wept

SUBJUNCTIVE MOOD

Pres. if I be wept
if you be wept
if he (she, it) be wept

if we be wept
if you be wept
if they be wept

Past if I were wept
if you were wept
if he (she, it) were wept

if we were wept
if you were wept
if they were wept

Fut. if I should be wept
if you should be wept
if he (she, it) should be wept

if we should be wept
if you should be wept
if they should be wept

Infinitive: to win
Perfect Infinitive: to have won

Present Participle: winning
Past Participle: won

INDICATIVE MOOD

Pres.	I win	we win
	you win	you win
	he (she, it) wins	they win
Pres. Prog.	I am winning	we are winning
	you are winning	you are winning
	he (she, it) is winning	they are winning
Pres. Int.	I do win	we do win
	you do win	you do win
	he (she, it) does win	they do win
Fut.	I shall win	we shall win
	you will win	you will win
	he (she, it) will win	they will win
Cond.	I would win	we would win
	you would win	you would win
	he (she, it) would win	they would win
Past	I won	we won
	you won	you won
	he (she, it) won	they won
Past Prog.	I was winning	we were winning
	you were winning	you were winning
	he (she, it) was winning	they were winning
Past Int.	I did win	we did win
	you did win	you did win
	he (she, it) did win	they did win
Pres. Perf.	I have won	we have won
	you have won	you have won
	he (she, it) has won	they have won
Past Perf.	I had won	we had won
	you had won	you had won
	he (she, it) had won	they had won
Fut. Perf.	I shall have won	we shall have won
	you will have won	you will have won
	he (she, it) will have won	they will have won
Cond. Perf.	I would have won	we would have won
	you would have won	you would have won
	he (she, it) would have won	they would have won

IMPERATIVE MOOD
win

SUBJUNCTIVE MOOD

Pres.	if I win	if we win
	if you win	if you win
	if he (she, it) win	if they win
Past	if I won	if we won
	if you won	if you won
	if he (she, it) won	if they won
Fut.	if I should win	if we should win
	if you should win	if you should win
	if he (she, it) should win	if they should win

Infinitive: to be won *Present Participle:* being won
Perfect Infinitive: to have been won *Past Participle:* been won

INDICATIVE MOOD

Pres.	I am won	we are won
	you are won	you are won
	he (she, it) is won	they are won
Pres.	I am being won	we are being won
Prog.	you are being won	you are being won
	he (she, it) is being won	they are being won
Pres.	I do get won	we do get won
Int.	you do get won	you do get won
	he (she, it) does get won	they do get won
Fut.	I shall be won	we shall be won
	you will be won	you will be won
	he (she, it) will be won	they will be won
Cond.	I would be won	we would be won
	you would be won	you would be won
	he (she, it) would be won	they would be won
Past	I was won	we were won
	you were won	you were won
	he (she, it) was won	they were won
Past	I was being won	we were being won
Prog.	you were being won	you were being won
	he (she, it) was being won	they were being won
Past	I did get won	we did get won
Int.	you did get won	you did get won
	he (she, it) did get won	they did get won
Pres.	I have been won	we have been won
Perf.	you have been won	you have been won
	he (she, it) has been won	they have been won
Past	I had been won	we had been won
Perf.	you had been won	you had been won
	he (she, it) had been won	they had been won
Fut.	I shall have been won	we shall have been won
Perf.	you will have been won	you will have been won
	he (she, it) will have been won	they will have been won
Cond.	I would have been won	we would have been won
Perf.	you would have been won	you would have been won
	he (she, it) would have been won	they would have been won

IMPERATIVE MOOD
be won

SUBJUNCTIVE MOOD

Pres.	if I be won	if we be won
	if you be won	if you be won
	if he (she, it) be won	if they be won
Past	if I were won	if we were won
	if you were won	if you were won
	if he (she, it) were won	if they were won
Fut.	if I should be won	if we should be won
	if you should be won	if you should be won
	if he (she, it) should be won	if they should be won

to wind (active voice)   *Principal Parts:* wind, winding, wound, wound

Infinitive: to wind   *Present Participle:* winding
Perfect Infinitive: to have wound   *Past Participle:* wound

INDICATIVE MOOD

Pres.	I wind	we wind
	you wind	you wind
	he (she, it) winds	they wind
Pres.	I am winding	we are winding
Prog.	you are winding	you are winding
	he (she, it) is winding	they are winding
Pres.	I do wind	we do wind
Int.	you do wind	you do wind
	he (she, it) does wind	they do wind
Fut.	I shall wind	we shall wind
	you will wind	you will wind
	he (she, it) will wind	they will wind
Cond.	I would wind	we would wind
	you would wind	you would wind
	he (she, it) would wind	they would wind
Past	I wound	we wound
	you wound	you wound
	he (she, it) wound	they wound
Past	I was winding	we were winding
Prog.	you were winding	you were winding
	he (she, it) was winding	they were winding
Past	I did wind	we did wind
Int.	you did wind	you did wind
	he (she, it) did wind	they did wind
Pres.	I have wound	we have wound
Perf.	you have wound	you have wound
	he (she, it) has wound	they have wound
Past	I had wound	we had wound
Perf.	you had wound	you had wound
	he (she, it) had wound	they had wound
Fut.	I shall have wound	we shall have wound
Perf.	you will have wound	you will have wound
	he (she, it) will have wound	they will have wound
Cond.	I would have wound	we would have wound
Perf.	you would have wound	you would have wound
	he (she, it) would have wound	they would have wound

IMPERATIVE MOOD
wind

SUBJUNCTIVE MOOD

Pres.	if I wind	if we wind
	if you wind	if you wind
	if he (she, it) wind	if they wind
Past	if I wound	if we wound
	if you wound	if you wound
	if he (she, it) wound	if they wound
Fut.	if I should wind	if we should wind
	if you should wind	if you should wind
	if he (she, it) should wind	if they should wind

Infinitive: to be wound
Perfect Infinitive: to have been wound

Present Participle: being wound
Past Participle: been wound

INDICATIVE MOOD

Pres.
I am wound
you are wound
he (she, it) is wound

we are wound
you are wound
they are wound

Pres.
Prog.
I am being wound
you are being wound
he (she, it) is being wound

we are being wound
you are being wound
they are being wound

Pres.
Int.
I do get wound
you do get wound
he (she, it) does get wound

we do get wound
you do get wound
they do get wound

Fut.
I shall be wound
you will be wound
he (she, it) will be wound

we shall be wound
you will be wound
they will be wound

Cond.
I would be wound
you would be wound
he (she, it) would be wound

we would be wound
you would be wound
they would be wound

Past
I was wound
you were wound
he (she, it) was wound

we were wound
you were wound
they were wound

Past
Prog.
I was being wound
you were being wound
he (she, it) was being wound

we were being wound
you were being wound
they were being wound

Past
Int.
I did get wound
you did get wound
he (she, it) did get wound

we did get wound
you did get wound
they did get wound

Pres.
Perf.
I have been wound
you have been wound
he (she, it) has been wound

we have been wound
you have been wound
they have been wound

Past
Perf.
I had been wound
you had been wound
he (she, it) had been wound

we had been wound
you had been wound
they had been wound

Fut.
Perf.
I shall have been wound
you will have been wound
he (she, it) will have been wound

we shall have been wound
you will have been wound
they will have been wound

Cond.
Perf.
I would have been wound
you would have been wound
he (she, it) would have been wound

we would have been wound
you would have been wound
they would have been wound

IMPERATIVE MOOD
be wound

SUBJUNCTIVE MOOD

Pres.
if I be wound
if you be wound
if he (she, it) be wound

if we be wound
if you be wound
if they be wound

Past
if I were wound
if you were wound
if he (she, it) were wound

if we were wound
if you were wound
if they were wound

Fut.
if I should be wound
if you should be wound
if he (she, it) should be wound

if we should be wound
if you should be wound
if they should be wound

367

to work (active voice)

Principal Parts: work, working, worked, worked

Infinitive: to work
Perfect Infinitive: to have worked

Present Participle: working
Past Participle: worked

INDICATIVE MOOD

Pres.	I work	we work
	you work	you work
	he (she, it) works	they work
Pres.	I am working	we are working
Prog.	you are working	you are working
	he (she, it) is working	they are working
Pres.	I do work	we do work
Int.	you do work	you do work
	he (she, it) does work	they do work
Fut.	I shall work	we shall work
	you will work	you will work
	he (she, it) will work	they will work
Cond.	I would work	we would work
	you would work	you would work
	he (she, it) would work	they would work
Past	I worked	we worked
	you worked	you worked
	he (she, it) worked	they worked
Past	I was working	we were working
Prog.	you were working	you were working
	he (she, it) was working	they were working
Past	I did work	we did work
Int.	you did work	you did work
	he (she, it) did work	they did work
Pres.	I have worked	we have worked
Perf.	you have worked	you have worked
	he (she, it) has worked	they have worked
Past	I had worked	we had worked
Perf.	you had worked	you had worked
	he (she, it) had worked	they had worked
Fut.	I shall have worked	we shall have worked
Perf.	you will have worked	you will have worked
	he (she, it) will have worked	they will have worked
Cond.	I would have worked	we would have worked
Perf.	you would have worked	you would have worked
	he (she, it) would have worked	they would have worked

IMPERATIVE MOOD
work

SUBJUNCTIVE MOOD

Pres.	if I work	if we work
	if you work	if you work
	if he (she, it) work	if they work
Past	if I worked	if we worked
	if you worked	if you worked
	if he (she, it) worked	if they worked
Fut.	if I should work	if we should work
	if you should work	if you should work
	if he (she, it) should work	if they should work

(passive voice)

Infinitive: to be worked   *Present Participle:* being worked
Perfect Infinitive: to have been worked   *Past Participle:* been worked

INDICATIVE MOOD

Pres.	I am worked	we are worked
	you are worked	you are worked
	he (she, it) is worked	they are worked
Pres.	I am being worked	we are being worked
Prog.	you are being worked	you are being worked
	he (she, it) is being worked	they are being worked
Pres.	I do get worked	we do get worked
Int.	you do get worked	you do get worked
	he (she, it) does get worked	they do get worked
Fut.	I shall be worked	we shall be worked
	you will be worked	you will be worked
	he (she, it) will be worked	they will be worked
Cond.	I would be worked	we would be worked
	you would be worked	you would be worked
	he (she, it) would be worked	they would be worked
Past	I was worked	we were worked
	you were worked	you were worked
	he (she, it) was worked	they were worked
Past	I was being worked	we were being worked
Prog.	you were being worked	you were being worked
	he (she, it) was being worked	they were being worked
Past	I did get worked	we did get worked
Int.	you did get worked	you did get worked
	he (she, it) did get worked	they did get worked
Pres.	I have been worked	we have been worked
Perf.	you have been worked	you have been worked
	he (she, it) has been worked	they have been worked
Past	I had been worked	we had been worked
Perf.	you had been worked	you had been worked
	he (she, it) had been worked	they had been worked
Fut.	I shall have been worked	we shall have been worked
Perf.	you will have been worked	you will have been worked
	he (she, it) will have been worked	they will have been worked
Cond.	I would have been worked	we would have been worked
Perf.	you would have been worked	you would have been worked
	he (she, it) would have been worked	they would have been worked

IMPERATIVE MOOD
be worked

SUBJUNCTIVE MOOD

Pres.	if I be worked	if we be worked
	if you be worked	if you be worked
	if he (she, it) be worked	if they be worked
Past	if I were worked	if we were worked
	if you were worked	if you were worked
	if he (she, it) were worked	if they were worked
Fut.	if I should be worked	if we should be worked
	if you should be worked	if you should be worked
	if he (she, it) should be worked	if they should be worked

to wring (active voice) *Principal Parts:* wring, wringing, wrung, wrung

Infinitive: to wring
Perfect Infinitive: to have wrung

Present Participle: wringing
Past Participle: wrung

INDICATIVE MOOD

Pres.
I wring
you wring
he (she, it) wrings

we wring
you wring
they wring

Pres. Prog.
I am wringing
you are wringing
he (she, it) is wringing

we are wringing
you are wringing
they are wringing

Pres. Int.
I do wring
you do wring
he (she, it) does wring

we do wring
you do wring
they do wring

Fut.
I shall wring
you will wring
he (she, it) will wring

we shall wring
you will wring
they will wring

Cond.
I would wring
you would wring
he (she, it) would wring

we would wring
you would wring
they would wring

Past
I wrung
you wrung
he (she, it) wrung

we wrung
you wrung
they wrung

Past Prog.
I was wringing
you were wringing
he (she, it) was wringing

we were wringing
you were wringing
they were wringing

Past Int.
I did wring
you did wring
he (she, it) did wring

we did wring
you did wring
they did wring

Pres. Perf.
I have wrung
you have wrung
he (she, it) has wrung

we have wrung
you have wrung
they have wrung

Past Perf.
I had wrung
you had wrung
he (she, it) had wrung

we had wrung
you had wrung
they had wrung

Fut. Perf.
I shall have wrung
you will have wrung
he (she, it) will have wrung

we shall have wrung
you will have wrung
they will have wrung

Cond. Perf.
I would have wrung
you would have wrung
he (she, it) would have wrung

we would have wrung
you would have wrung
they would have wrung

IMPERATIVE MOOD
wring

SUBJUNCTIVE MOOD

Pres.
if I wring
if you wring
if he (she, it) wring

if we wring
if you wring
if they wring

Past
if I wrung
if you wrung
if he (she, it) wrung

if we wrung
if you wrung
if they wrung

Fut.
if I should wring
if you should wring
if he (she, it) should wring

if we should wring
if you should wring
if they should wring

(passive voice)

Infinitive: to be wrung
Perfect Infinitive: to have been wrung

Present Participle: being wrung
Past Participle: been wrung

INDICATIVE MOOD

Pres. I am wrung you are wrung he (she, it) is wrung	we are wrung you are wrung they are wrung
Pres. I am being wrung *Prog.* you are being wrung he (she, it) is being wrung	we are being wrung you are being wrung they are being wrung
Pres. I do get wrung *Int.* you do get wrung he (she, it) does get wrung	we do get wrung you do get wrung they do get wrung
Fut. I shall be wrung you will be wrung he (she, it) will be wrung	we shall be wrung you will be wrung they will be wrung
Cond. I would be wrung you would be wrung he (she, it) would be wrung	we would be wrung you would be wrung they would be wrung
Past I was wrung you were wrung he (she, it) was wrung	we were wrung you were wrung they were wrung
Past I was being wrung *Prog.* you were being wrung he (she, it) was being wrung	we were being wrung you were being wrung they were being wrung
Past I did get wrung *Int.* you did get wrung he (she, it) did get wrung	we did get wrung you did get wrung they did get wrung
Pres. I have been wrung *Perf.* you have been wrung he (she, it) has been wrung	we have been wrung you have been wrung they have been wrung
Past I had been wrung *Perf.* you had been wrung he (she, it) had been wrung	we had been wrung you had been wrung they had been wrung
Fut. I shall have been wrung *Perf.* you will have been wrung he (she, it) will have been wrung	we shall have been wrung you will have been wrung they will have been wrung
Cond. I would have been wrung *Perf.* you would have been wrung he (she, it) would have been wrung	we would have been wrung you would have been wrung they would have been wrung

IMPERATIVE MOOD
be wrung

SUBJUNCTIVE MOOD

Pres. if I be wrung if you be wrung if he (she, it) be wrung	if we be wrung if you be wrung if they be wrung
Past if I were wrung if you were wrung if he (she, it) were wrung	if we were wrung if you were wrung if they were wrung
Fut. if I should be wrung if you should be wrung if he (she, it) should be wrung	if we should be wrung if you should be wrung if they should be wrung

Infinitive: to write   *Present Participle:* writing
Perfect Infinitive: to have written   *Past Participle:* written

INDICATIVE MOOD

Pres.	I write	we write
	you write	you write
	he (she, it) writes	they write
Pres.	I am writing	we are writing
Prog.	you are writing	you are writing
	he (she, it) is writing	they are writing
Pres.	I do write	we do write
Int.	you do write	you do write
	he (she, it) does write	they do write
Fut.	I shall write	we shall write
	you will write	you will write
	he (she, it) will write	they will write
Cond.	I would write	we would write
	you would write	you would write
	he (she, it) would write	they would write
Past	I wrote	we wrote
	you wrote	you wrote
	he (she, it) wrote	they wrote
Past	I was writing	we were writing
Prog.	you were writing	you were writing
	he (she, it) was writing	they were writing
Past	I did write	we did write
Int.	you did write	you did write
	he (she, it) did write	they did write
Pres.	I have written	we have written
Perf.	you have written	you have written
	he (she, it) has written	they have written
Past	I had written	we had written
Perf.	you had written	you had written
	he (she, it) had written	they had written
Fut.	I shall have written	we shall have written
Perf.	you will have written	you will have written
	he (she, it) will have written	they will have written
Cond.	I would have written	we would have written
Perf.	you would have written	you would have written
	he (she, it) would have written	they would have written

IMPERATIVE MOOD
write

SUBJUNCTIVE MOOD

Pres.	if I write	if we write
	if you write	if you write
	if he (she, it) write	if they write
Past	if I wrote	if we wrote
	if you wrote	if you wrote
	if he (she, it) wrote	if they wrote
Fut.	if I should write	if we should write
	if you should write	if they should write
	if he (she. it) should write	if you should write

(passive voice)

Infinitive: to be written   Present Participle: being written
Perfect Infinitive: to have been written   Past Participle: been written

INDICATIVE MOOD

Pres. I am written
    you are written
    he (she, it) is written

we are written
you are written
they are written

Pres. I am being written
Prog. you are being written
    he (she, it) is being written

we are being written
you are being written
they are being written

Pres. I do get written
Int. you do get written
    he (she, it) does get written

we do get written
you do get written
they do get written

Fut. I shall be written
    you will be written
    he (she, it) will be written

we shall be written
you will be written
they will be written

Cond. I would be written
    you would be written
    he (she, it) would be written

we would be written
you would be written
they would be written

Past I was written
    you were written
    he (she, it) was written

we were written
you were written
they were written

Past I was being written
Prog. you were being written
    he (she, it) was being written

we were being written
you were being written
they were being written

Past I did get written
Int. you did get written
    he (she, it) did get written

we did get written
you did get written
they did get written

Pres I have been written
Perf. you have been written
    he (she, it) has been written

we have been written
you have been written
they have been written

Past I had been written
Perf. you had been written
    he (she, it) had been written

we had been written
you had been written
they had been written

Fut. I shall have been written
Perf. you will have been written
    he (she, it) will have been written

we shall have been written
you will have been written
they will have been written

Cond. I would have been written
Perf. you would have been written
    he (she, it) would have been written

we would have been written
you would have been written
they would have been written

IMPERATIVE MOOD
be written

SUBJUNCTIVE MOOD

Pres. if I be written
    if you be written
    if he (she, it) be written

if we be written
if you be written
if they be written

Past if I were written
    if you were written
    if he (she, it) were written

if we were written
if you were written
if they were written

Fut. if I should be written
    if you should be written
    if he (she, it) should be written

if we should be written
if you should be written
if they should be written

■ Index

For conjugations of 120 irregular verbs in alphabetical order, see pages 129–373.

374

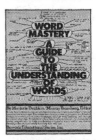